Glorify the Empire

Annika A. Culver

Glorify the Empire
Japanese Avant-Garde Propaganda in Manchukuo

UBCPress · Vancouver · Toronto

21 20 19 18 17 16 15 14 13   5 4 3 2 1

Printed in Canada on FSC-certified ancient-forest-free paper (100% post-consumer recycled) that is processed chlorine- and acid-free.

Library and Archives Canada Cataloguing in Publication

Culver, Annika A.,
Glorify the empire : Japanese avant-garde propaganda in Manchukuo / Annika A. Culver.

Includes bibliographical references and index.
Issued also in electronic formats.
ISBN 978-0-7748-2436-1

1. Propaganda, Japanese – China – Manchuria – History – 20th century. 2. Arts – Political aspects – China – Manchuria – History – 20th century. 3. Avant-garde (Aesthetics) – Political aspects – China – Manchuria – History – 20th century. 4. World War, 1939-1945 – China – Manchuria – Propaganda. 5. World War, 1939-1945 – China – Manchuria – Art and the war. 6. Artists – Japan – History – 20th century. 7. Propaganda in art. I. Title.

D810.P7J36 2013   940.54'88752   C2012-906975-2

Canadä

UBC Press gratefully acknowledges the financial support for our publishing program of the Government of Canada (through the Canada Book Fund), the Canada Council for the Arts, and the British Columbia Arts Council.

Financial support for the publication of this book has been provided by the Japan Foundation, the Association for Asian Studies, the Kajima Foundation for the Arts, and the University of North Carolina at Pembroke.

JAPANFOUNDATION

Printed and bound in Canada by Friesens
Set in Stone by Artegraphica Design Co. Ltd.
Copy editor: Joanne Richardson
Proofreader: Dianne Tiefensee
Indexer: Noeline Bridge
Cartographer: Eric Leinberger

UBC Press
The University of British Columbia
2029 West Mall
Vancouver, BC V6T 1Z2
www.ubcpress.ca

Contents

Figures

Acknowledgments

A constellation of support and encouragement from a large network of institutions, colleagues, friends, and family enabled the completion of this book. Most of the fieldwork and research for this study, along with the collection of primary and secondary materials in Japanese (and, to a lesser degree, in Chinese), were undertaken from mid-2004 to late 2005 in Tokyo and Kamakura, Japan, while working under a Fulbright USIIE Grant, and in northeast China (Dalian and Harbin) during winter 2000, summer 2001, and winter 2005. From September to October 2003, I spent six weeks in the Tokyo area, funded by a Kundstadter Travel Grant from the University of Chicago. I conducted additional research in Tokyo under an Association for Asian Studies (AAS) Northeast Asian Council (NEAC) Japanese Studies Grant in the summer of 2008. More recently, in spring 2010, under a Title VI Travel Grant, I collected sources at Duke University's Perkins and Bostock libraries; in summer 2010, under a Teaching and Learning Center Grant from the University of North Carolina at Pembroke (UNCP), I did the same at the University of Chicago's Regenstein Library.

For this study, I use information from contemporary writings, historical documents, personal interviews with Japanese scholars and museum curators, and the reminiscences of a limited number of Chinese commentators on "occupied northeast China." I also viewed paintings and drawings in the National Museum of Modern Art in Tokyo and the Museum of Modern Art in Kamakura and Hayama under the guidance of their curators. Most of my copies of contemporaneous pictorials and newspapers, as well as original writings on Manchukuo by Japanese intellectuals, were obtained at Waseda University in the Central and Tôyama libraries and, to some extent, at the University of Chicago and Duke University. I have also consulted librarians in, and used the collections of, the Dalian Municipal Library in China and the Museum of Modern Literature in Tokyo.

From mid-2004 to late 2005, a USIIE Fulbright Graduate Research Fellowship allowed me to serve as a visiting researcher affiliated with Waseda

University's political science and economics department, where I worked under the direction of art historian Tan'ô Yasunori and literary scholar Takahashi Seiori, who kindly invited me to attend his graduate seminar. My stay was also enriched by numerous conversations with historian Kobayashi Hideo about the *Mantetsu* research department and "right-wing" socialism. In 2003, Otani Shôgo first revealed to me the sublime images of Fukuzawa Ichirô and Ai Mitsu, which were under his curation at the National Museum of Modern Art in Tokyo. And, during several visits in 2004-5 and 2008, he inspired me to view art in its historical context. He also patiently answered my questions on Ai Mitsu, Fukuzawa Ichirô, and Shimizu Toshi during the book's editing. At the Museum of Modern Art in Kamakura and Hayama, Mizusawa Tsutomu granted me private viewings of Japanese avant-garde art that had been stored in the warehouse during the museum's reorganization in fall 2003. Since we first met in 1998 through Harvard University's US-Japan Forum, Isogawa Tomoyoshi, a Tokyo-based *Asahi Shimbun* journalist and editor, has shared with me his fascination for controversial issues in Sino-Japanese relations and modern Chinese history.

A 2005 trip to Dalian and Harbin during Chinese New Year permitted me to see these cities in their winter glory, while I retraced the vestiges of a Japanese colonial past. At the Dalian Municipal Library, Chen Yanjun helped me to search official Chinese historical records to find information regarding how the lives of Chinese coolies compared to the lives of the urban Japanese bourgeoisie. Visits to Harbin and to my husband's hometown in Tieli in 2000, 2001, and 2005 gave me glimpses into a complex history that continues to inform our present.

In 2008, a NEAC Japan Studies Grant from AAS permitted me to spend a productive July in Tokyo conducting research at the Waseda University Central Library. The librarians at the Museum of Modern Literature in Tokyo were especially helpful in finding wartime sources written by Kawabata Yasunari and Anzai Fuyue. Kishi Toshihiko also invited me to observe a conference at the Tokyo University of Foreign Cultures on the confluence of foreign cultures in Harbin, and sent me copies of recent work. In addition, Okubô Masao graciously welcomed me into the Manchukuo Literature Research Group. At a meeting in Shibuya, and in e-mail correspondence, Kim Jaeyong set me straight on the paucity of Korean representation in Manchukuo literature.

I also thank Kristina Troost, Japanese studies librarian at Duke University, for tirelessly procuring for me fifteen reprints of *Manshû gurafu;* a recent exhibition catalogue on Ai Mitsu's work; dozens of microfilm rolls of *Atorie, Chûô bijutsu,* and *Mizue;* along with original copies of *Kokka,* centring on art debates in Japan and the Empire. None of this would have been possible without her urging me to apply for a Title VI Library Research Grant, which enabled me to take several trips to Duke in spring 2010.

In the summer of 2010, UNCP's Teaching and Learning Center funded my return to Chicago to conduct research. Hibino Kaku, at the University of Chicago's Regenstein Library, helped me find rare sources such as *Senbu geppô* reprints and other obscure, Manchukuo-related materials. Discussions with Michael Raine on Japanese wartime film and propaganda prompted me to look for common images across media in Manchukuo. In the summer of 2009, a generous UNCP Summer Research Fellowship for junior faculty enabled me to work on a book proposal at my Chicago base, while course releases in spring of 2010 and 2011 allowed further research and writing. Additional grants from the Teaching and Learning Center at UNCP partially funded a subvention for this book and substantive editing of its introduction.

For their tireless help in obtaining reproductions of images and the permission to use them in this book, I would like to extend my appreciation to the publicity staff or curators of the following art museums: Ooki Yuko of the National Museum of Modern Art in Tokyo, Kawano Keiko of the Museum of Modern Art in Kamakura and Hayama, Fujisaki Aya of the Hiroshima Prefectural Museum of Modern Art, Hirukawa Yuko of the Tomioka City Museum/Fukuzawa Ichirô Memorial Gallery, and Endô Sôtarô of the Yokosuka Museum of Art. I also thank Yumani shobô for allowing me to reproduce images from their *Manshû gurafu* reprints. Okuizumi Eizaburô at the University of Chicago Regenstein Library and the reference librarians at Waseda University's Central Library kindly sent me scans of originals housed in their collections. A generous grant from the Kajima Foundation for the Arts funded reproduction costs for images.

I also thank Ronald Suleski, Norman Smith, Kari Shepherdson-Scott, and Victor Zatsepine, colleagues in our panel "Constructing a Multi-Ethnic Culture in Manchukuo," which was organized for the 2011 AAS/International Consortium of Asia Scholars (ICAS) Annual Meeting. They inspired me to think deeply about this project and future endeavours. As one of North America's leading scholars of occupied northeast China, Ron serves as our "unofficial" mentor and unceasingly encourages future generations of Manchukuo researchers. He also connects us with our Chinese, Japanese, and Korean counterparts. Numerous online conversations with Norman greatly enriched this study. His infectious enthusiasm for northeast China's people and culture consistently reminds me why I engage in this work.

I also thank Barak Kushner for his astute comments on my project and for prompting me to view propaganda in a multifaceted fashion. Daqing Yang provides inspiration by demonstrating the healing aspects that humanistic scholarship can bring to contentious topics in Sino-Japanese history.

Throughout my years as a graduate student at the University of Chicago, and during this project, Norma Field has consistently reminded me to view interwar period Japanese intellectuals as working in a complex political and socio-economic climate while being buffeted by multivalent forces. In North

Carolina, Gennifer Weisenfeld and Leo Ching at Duke University encouraged me to use interdisciplinary materials and to view cultural history "outside the box." Conversations about Mutô Tomio with Mark Driscoll of Chapel Hill highlighted the former's complexity and careerism in his alliance with the controversial Amakasu Masahiko.

I sincerely thank Emily Andrew, my editor at UBC Press, for her unflagging support and encouragement during this project, while Megan Brand guided the book toward completion. Lesley Erickson's judicious editing of the introduction reined in my prose, and an excellent copy editor enhanced the manuscript's precision. I am also deeply grateful to three anonymous reviewers for strengthening my study with their astute comments and critique.

In addition to generous book subventions from the Japan Foundation, the Kajima Foundation for the Arts, and the Association for Asian Studies, this book could never have been completed without the help and encouragement of numerous individuals in the United States, Canada, Japan, and China. I express my deepest gratitude to these individuals – including Mark Driscoll, Norma Field, Kishi Toshihiko, Kobayashi Hideo, Iino Masahito, Mizusawa Tsutomu, Otani Shôgo, Michael Raine, Norman Smith, Ron Suleski, Tan'ô Yasunori, Kristina Troost, Okuizumi Eizaburô,and Tsuruoka Yoshihisa – who generously gave me copies of important materials or pinpointed key sources. Any omissions in this list are my fault alone, and I will thank all of you personally when we meet again.

Last, but not least, Father Roger Kappel and the Trinity Episcopal Church congregation tended to my spiritual needs during research and writing in Lumberton, North Carolina.

Glorify the Empire

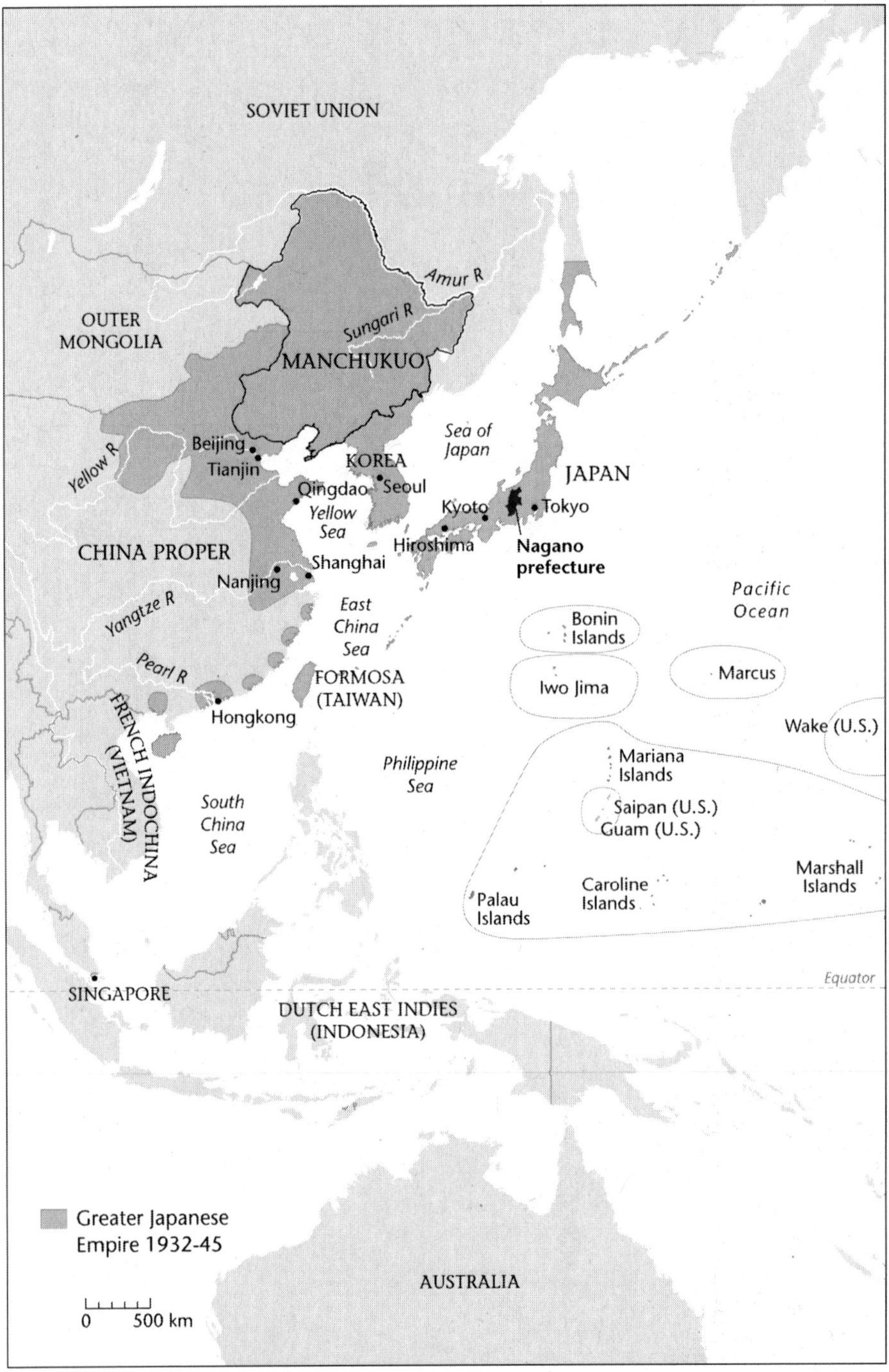

Greater Japanese Empire, 1880-1945. *Courtesy of Eric Leinberger.*

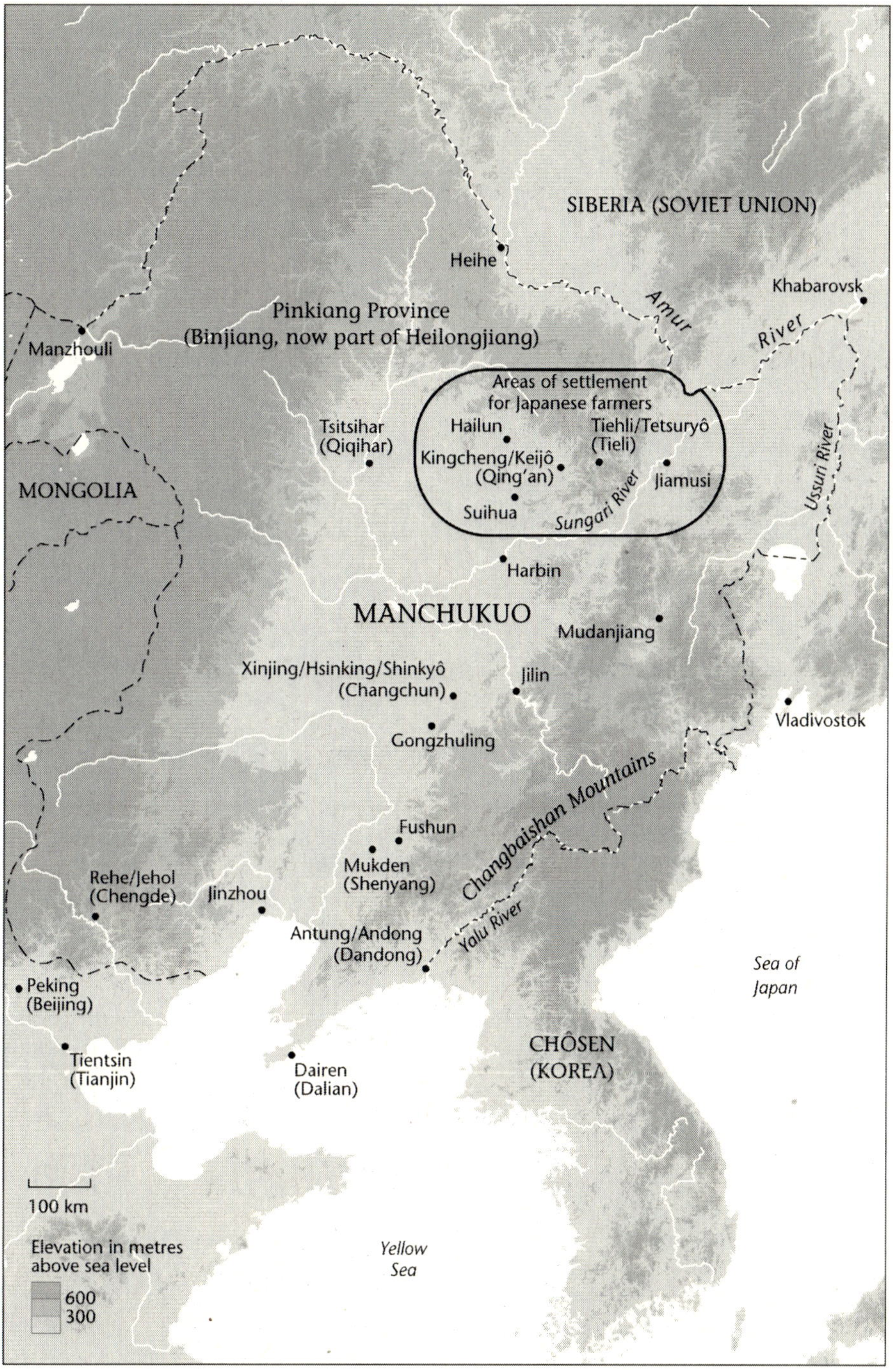

Manchukuo, 1932-45. *Courtesy of Eric Leinberger.*

Introduction: Propaganda in the Manchukuo Context, 1932-45

In late fall 1943, amidst the gathering gloom of wartime, Ai Mitsu's (1907-46) oil paints began to freeze as he attempted to depict Harbin's famed Russian-style Kitayskaya district. The harsh Manchurian climate felt out of place in the deceivingly bright exotic city, and he resisted the physical discomfort of the cold until his medium failed him. The Japanese painter then packed up his easel and painting materials and entered the well-appointed Hôtel Moderne, a venue that had lodged the Lytton Commission in late 1931. Manchukuo's continental climate, ultramodern cities, and vast sense of space all underlined its stark difference from Japan.[1] As he gazed at the frozen landscape through double-paned glass, Ai Mitsu's thoughts turned, with some trepidation, back to his island homeland and his imminent return. Not long afterwards, the Japanese government drafted the neurasthenic artist into the military. His last sojourn in Manchukuo would feel like a brief reprieve from his duties to the imperial state.

However, since the mid-1930s, Ai Mitsu's Manchurian connections had promoted not only his career but also the interests of the new state's Japanese handlers. In 1935, on the invitation of a brother-in-law who worked for the South Manchuria Railway Company (SMRC), he had come to Manchukuo and, on his return to Japan, reaffirmed his status as a cutting-edge oil painter. In a new nation obsessed with modernization, the modernity of his work and his membership in an important Tokyo-based avant-garde artists' group had helped bolster Manchukuo's emergent cultural scene. The Japanese-led government had overlooked Ai Mitsu's colleagues' earlier involvement with the Tsukiji Little Theatre and their flirtation with Marxism, along with their sympathy for the proletariat. Though often equivocal, Ai Mitsu's images of Manchuria piqued the interest of the Japanese public.

Ai Mitsu was only one of the many artists and writers with a history of left-wing sympathies or avant-garde style who flocked to Manchukuo during a period of crucial state formation under Imperial Japan. After 1932, the Manchukuo state attempted to couple traditional Asian values with a modern infrastructure and material culture by co-opting earlier intellectual discourses of Chinese nationalism – expressed in such Confucian-inspired slogans as *Ôdôrakudô* (Paradise of the Kingly Way) and *minzoku kyôwa* (ethnic/racial harmony). Attracted by Manchuria's exoticism, economic opportunities, and the publicity given to their endeavours, Japanese cultural producers snatched up invitations by SMRC, the Kantô Army, and various other Japanese-run commercial or governmental organizations, such as the *Kyôwakai* (Concordia Association). By enlisting visiting Japanese artists or observers, these organizations hoped, in images and written words, to evoke the state's ideals of a modern paradise and ethnic harmony. The visitors' observations, however, ranged from unabashedly positive to darkly equivocal. They also maintained some of the characteristics of the leftist literary and artistic movements of the 1920s and early 1930s, making them more avant-garde than modernist in character.

By accepting a tour to Manchukuo, formerly left-wing Japanese intellectuals were making a clear statement in favour of Imperial Japan and its endeavours. Literary scholar Kawamura Minato likens their journeys to *fumi-e,* the Tokugawa-era practice of treading on a Christian image to renounce one's allegiance to Christianity.[2] Indeed, 95 percent of all left-wing Japanese intellectuals *did* renounce their political ideals after the Manchurian Incident of 1931, which led to Japan's invasion of northeast China.[3] A Manchukuo tour was an important way for leftist artists and writers such as Yamada Seizaburô (1896-1970) to show their support for the imperial state. Yet, at least aesthetically and thematically, many of these sojourners' works remained the same as ever. Manchukuo was an important site for the convergence of both left- and right-wing ideologies, a place where the formation of the utopian state functioned as a collaborative project for media-makers of all stripes.[4] Indeed, fascism, in its original Italian inception, *was* a form of socialism – albeit a right-wing version – and this is what eventually prevailed in Manchukuo. Thus, the powerful imagery created by intellectuals who followed a socialist political philosophy could be used for various and diverging ends.

By the mid-1930s, a dissolving of the left/right political binary is evident in the efforts of Japanese cultural producers on both sides of the political spectrum. Through their cultural production, these people created an ideological framework for Manchukuo. In the Japanese context, Sheldon Garon argues that a shared commitment to modernization and modernity allowed seemingly politically disparate reformers to join forces with the state.[5] Joshua Fogel's translation of SMRC researcher Itô Takeo's (1895-1985) memoir also corroborates the occurrence of this in his organization, where elements of liberalism and Taishô intellectual trends remained alongside a Marxist analysis that was still used for its rational and "scientific" properties.[6] In Manchukuo, the science, modernity, and modernization of the West merged with Asian-inspired principles to form a compelling reason for Japanese and others to support the new nation. The writings of Japanese intellectuals invariably supported this rhetoric during a time when various actors increasingly began to view northeast China as valuable to the Japanese Empire. Moreover, by the late 1920s, Japan was headed toward a path that was to diverge from Taishô democracy and to embrace certain characteristics of the political experiments of 1930s fascist Italy and Germany. In fact, the Manchukuo state that emerged out of Kantô Army violence followed the fascist example even more closely than did Japan.

This study primarily investigates intellectuals who, in the Manchukuo context, either underwent a political conversion or at least expressed tacit support for Imperial Japan. I examine the cultural production and professional trajectories of writers, photographers, and artists who created modernist reflections of the new state, including Yamada Seizaburô, Fukuzawa Ichirô (1898-1994), Ai Mitsu, Fuchikami Hakuyô (1889-1960), Haruyama Yukio (1902-94), and Kawabata Yasunari (1899-1972).[7] These men were important in that they were Japan's leading representatives of cutting-edge literature, art, and photography during the 1930s and 1940s and had earlier expressed either a radical aesthetic (i.e., surrealism) or politics (i.e., proletarianism) in tandem with avant-garde forms of representation. The trip to Manchukuo, while overtly displaying their allegiance to Imperial Japan, also gave an important boost to these men's careers and even strengthened their role as "cultural authorities" back in Japan. Some, like Yamada, even suffered police persecution due to their left-wing orientation, and they saw the Manchukuo sojourn as a path toward rehabilitation after undergoing political conversion. Each of the intellectuals I discuss was inexorably drawn toward participating in the creation of what curator Takeba Jô calls a "reflected utopia."[8]

The representations of Manchukuo created by Japanese observers were distinctive in that they were usually made for a national, regional, or international audience, ostensibly justifying the modernity of the new state and its ideological aims. Like Walter Benjamin's concept of art in the age of mechanical reproduction, the works produced for the Manchukuo project functioned as agents of ideological mass mobilization – a key reason these works can be defined as "propaganda." Each of the individuals covered in this study participated in saturating Japan (and other places) with Manchukuo-themed literature, works of art, and photographs during the period of Imperial Japan's expansion on the continent, thus serving as unofficial propagandists. For this reason, I call their cultural production, which retained aspects of an earlier left-wing moment, "avant-garde propaganda." I investigate the nature of this "unofficial" propaganda in the Manchukuo context.

Regarding propaganda in Imperial Japan, Alan Tansman argues that, "to Japanese officialdom in the 1930s, propaganda meant the cultivation of cultural values and attitudes that would be held so deeply they would appear innate and not imposed."[9] For fascist Manchukuo's Japanese Confucian-inspired state framers, the popular assimilation of national ideals should, according to concrete principles inherent in nature *(li),* appear as a natural aspect of the rational ordering of a benevolent environment promoted by good governance. This idea was verifiable in observable phenomena in the natural world, thus rationalizing the superimposition of a largely Japanese political structure, supposedly based on *ren* (benevolence), on a Chinese populace. In Japanese eyes, such philosophies as *Ôdô* and *kyôwa,* already rejected by Republican Chinese reformers, had a quasi-scientific and, therefore, modern basis.

Thus, propaganda in the utopian state did not have to be forced on a materially and spiritually satisfied populace; rather, this populace actively participated in the state's ideological formation through mass culture organizations such as the Concordia Association, which imparted Confucian-inspired values.[10] Later (in Chapter 6), I examine the role of this organization and its connections to the Manchukuo Publicity and News Bureau, the new state's primary propaganda apparatus, both based in Shinkyô (contemporary Changchun, People's Republic of China [PRC]). I also investigate high-ranking Japanese bureaucrats' views of propaganda (or "official" propaganda) in relation to Manchukuo's culture during wartime and how the Concordia Association attempted to mollify social and political differences through the rhetoric of "culture." In Manchukuo, national propaganda chief Mutô Tomio (1904-98) and others believed that an effective way to realize the "cultivation of cultural values and attitudes" was to mobilize culture and the arts for propaganda purposes (see Chapters 4 and 6).

In clarifying categories of propaganda in Manchukuo, I refer to Barak Kushner, who, in his investigation of Imperial Japan's thought wars, recognizes two subsets of Japanese wartime propaganda, both "official" and "unofficial," which can also be applied to Manchukuo: "*Official propaganda* emanated from *government channels* and *related agencies. Unofficial propaganda* developed within *non-governmental institutions,* such as private companies that cut records, produced advertising, etc."[11] Here, I focus on elite Japanese intellectuals who were involved in making "unofficial propaganda," and I analyze the propagandistic significance of their works. Kushner notes that, in the Japanese wartime example, "Japan's propaganda comprised a mix of messages, from nativist to promotion of the modern, which were developed by an increasingly professional staff. The messages conveyed a sense not only of Japan's modernity, but also of its mission to bring culture and progress to the rest of Asia."[12] In the following chapters, I investigate how a Japanese-led culture and modernity became important themes in the propaganda that sustained the Manchukuo project.

I focus on how Japanese cultural producers of a formerly leftist or avant-garde orientation were attracted to Manchukuo for various reasons and eventually produced literary works, art, and photography that, for the most part, portrayed the region's development in a positive light. After 1932, government propaganda organizations like the Manchukuo Publicity and News Bureau worked closely with SMRC to promote a positive vision of the new state and its development by enlisting these intellectuals to create cultural propaganda. The heads of these organizations viewed the "avant-garde" as modern, or cutting edge, rather than, per the early 1920s definition of the term, as indicating a left-wing political orientation.[13] The works of these Japanese intellectuals, though falling under the general category of "arts," can be described as what Peter O'Connor terms "propaganda vehicles."[14] This is because they contributed to saturating Japan with positive media representations of Manchukuo – a Japan that, by the 1930s, was already obsessed with the new state. Following the 1937 eruption of the Second Sino-Japanese War, Manchukuo's prominence rose still further as it was put forward as an example of a peaceful, stable nation, unlike China proper, which was embroiled in a war with its more advanced imperialist neighbour. Moreover, after 1940, Manchukuo increasingly served as an ideological template for the territories in Southeast Asia subjected to Japanese military incursions. Of course, not all Japanese depictions of Manchukuo praised the nation, and some included unflattering critiques or avant-garde equivocation.

However, the individuals I discuss served as "unofficial propagandists" (Louise Young's term),[15] or "occasional propagandists" (O'Connor's term).[16] These people included "journalists and writers not specifically or consistently contracted to write for Japan – who found themselves drawn into official efforts to explain and justify Japan's position."[17] The latter category describes intellectuals much like Yamada, or the former avant-garde poet Haruyama, and also includes Fuchikami (in his brief employment as a temporary adviser for SMRC) and Kawabata (as a guest of the Kantô Army and *Manchuria Daily News*). At times, they were indeed official propagandists: consider Fuchikami's 1932 commissioned work for the Kantô Army and Mutô's 1939-43 role as head of the Manchukuo Publicity and News Bureau. Mutô also wrote plays and short stories and, thus, created "unofficial propaganda" that supported his role as official propagandist. In other words, instead of continuously serving as active propagandists on the state's behalf, these unofficial propagandists created works that functioned as "propaganda vehicles."[18]

By building on earlier assertions by Young, Jacqueline Atkins, and Kushner, I argue that any Manchukuo-themed works produced by a Japanese writer, artist, or photographer served as a *form* of propaganda – both because they increased awareness of the new state for general Japanese, regional, and international audiences and because of where they were published, displayed, or depicted. Often, they were presented through presses, exhibitions, or distribution networks connected to SMRC, the Concordia Association, or news organizations under the purview of the Manchukuo Publicity and News Bureau. If these intellectuals were hosted by the latter organizations, they were even more likely to mention the state and its patronage. Thus, their works contributed generally to saturating the mass media and art world with Manchukuo-related cultural production. In other words, through providing publicity, they indirectly supported state aims.

In her 1998 study, Louise Young notes how, in the Japan of the 1930s, "Mass culture industries flooded their marketplace with Manchurian-themed products, and in the process disseminated a specific package of information and a set interpretation of events on the continent."[19] In addition, Atkins's 2005 examination of war motif textiles in Japan, Britain, and the United States indicates that even fashion could support the propaganda aims of a government during wartime. Thus, it inspires a broadening of the definition of propaganda in the Manchukuo context.[20] Kushner's 2006 study of Japanese wartime propaganda similarly views it as a multifaceted category, including popular culture, performance, and the activities of cultural groups such as Japanese *manzai* (comic dialogue) troupes and the *pen-butai* (pen brigade) circulating in China during the war.[21] In wartime Japan and throughout its Empire, Kushner reveals how "plans called for propaganda that either sprang from society itself or was made to appear that way. Japanese on all levels of wartime society deemed reciprocity – alliances among the civilian, military and bureaucratic circles – to be the key to successful propaganda campaigns."[22]

Until recently, most Japanese and Chinese studies viewed "propaganda" as essentially a top-down phenomenon, whereby, in both Japan and occupied northeast China, the state issues a directive that is picked up by various organizations in charge of disseminating it to the public.[23] This approach, however, obscures a grassroots, entrepreneurial side to propaganda, like that envisioned by Young, Atkins, and Kushner, in which the state's ideas are continually reappropriated in a quasi-mercantile fashion by diverse groups such as itinerant drama troupes, sellers of themed foods, the fashion industry, and social clubs.

In contrast to earlier Japanese scholarship on propaganda, Kishi Toshihiko's 2010 study views SMRC promotional posters and advertisements, Concordia Association bills, and Manchukuo commemorative stamps/postcards as important artefacts supporting the aims of both Imperial Japan and the Manchukuo government.[24] This research stems from Kishi's analysis of hundreds of images of visual media related to Manchuria and Manchukuo, including posters, stored in a database that he once maintained.[25] His findings concur with those of Lincoln Cushing and Ann Thompkins, who, in their 2007 investigation of revolutionary art produced during China's 1966-76 Great Proletarian Cultural Revolution, argue that these mass-produced posters functioned as "commercial artworks" sold in government bookstores, shops, and local markets. Thus, they helped to assimilate the government's propaganda messages into ordinary life by serving as decorations for the home during festivals and other important occasions.[26] As Kishi notes, in the Manchukuo case, ordinary people came across SMRC advertisements in newspapers and magazines, viewed Concordia Association posters on city or village buildings, and sent each other depictions of the new state in the mail – all without realizing they were aiding in the diffusion of propaganda.[27] These two recent studies show how ideologically inspired visual media, by intruding into daily life through various patterns of public consumption, can support the propaganda aims of both left- and right-wing regimes.[28]

Manchukuo-themed literature, art, and photography of a fascist hue were assimilated into ordinary life through their consumption as cultural products. For example, Japanese consumer demand for Manchurian-themed paintings helped to generate support for Japan's development of Manchukuo by saturating the art market with certain depictions of the region. In this manner, images of Manchuria made their way into the middle-class Japanese family's Western-style drawing room, popularized in the early Shôwa period. As scholars like Kushner point out, this penetration into daily life is what differentiated Japanese propaganda from that of other countries.

The power of the literary, artistic, and photographic works produced by Japanese intellectuals arose from their ability to communicate symbols of Manchukuo that easily translated into an acceptance of the specific ideological paradigms that Japanese bureaucrats wished to cultivate. For Kushner, these symbols are indicative of the construction of a successful, greater Japanese Empire, emphasizing "physical strength, industrial capability, political stability, modern architecture, and advanced standards of hygiene."[29] I show how literature, art, and photography in the Manchukuo context propagated such recurring, and even contradictory, symbols as a "lazy" Chinese populace, superhuman Chinese coolies, productive urban worksites, "virgin" land, vast Manchurian plains, and well-organized Japanese *kaitakuchi* (rural development areas) – thereby reinforcing an ideology that necessitated further Japanese control of Manchukuo and its integration with domestic Japan *(naichi)*.

This also raises the question of how visual arts like painting or photography could serve as propaganda. By the mid-1930s, Manchurian-themed images in paintings and photographs abounded in Japan's official and avant-garde art worlds. The large canvases of the surrealist artist Fukuzawa and his cohort even decorated the walls of Japanese military and government offices. Depictions of empty plains with newly constructed buildings in Manchukuo's capital city Shinkyô highlighted the fact that development occurred amidst a naked, barren plane, or on "virgin land" – the term most commonly used. Imperialist powers like Japan often exploited such conceits as empty lands ripe for colonization, a view that negated the historical reality of Chinese and Korean resistance to an artificially promoted ethnic (or racial) harmony.

How might these symbols, produced by Japanese writers, artists, and photographers, have served Manchukuo's propaganda aims by fashioning a certain ideology? Alan Tansman, in his study of the aesthetics of Japanese fascism, argues that, "it is through the products of the imagination that ideology is most effectively diffused, even as these works absorb the ideological atmosphere in which they are created."[30] Whether in the proletarian context of late 1920s and early 1930s Japan, or in Manchukuo's fascist political climate after 1932, Japanese intellectuals (and the organizations hosting them) recognized the ideological power of cultural production (see Chapters 3, 4, and 5). In addition, if one accepts Tansman's argument that "culture is where fascism forms its ideological power" and that "Japanese fascism was fueled by a literary sensibility,"[31] then the importance of writers like Yamada (as a converted left-wing proponent of the proletarian arts) and Kawabata (as a modernist establishment writer supportive of Japanese literary expansion) to the cultural construction of Manchukuo becomes quite obvious (see Chapters 2 and 7).[32]

Yamada, as an earlier proponent of the proletarian literature and proletarian arts movements truly believed that the arts spurred concrete political change and could create a better society through social revolution. Chairman Mao's quote, "Revolutionary culture is a powerful revolutionary weapon for the broad masses of the people," exemplifies these earlier attitudes of the Japanese left, to which Yamada belonged prior to his political conversion following his mid-1930s imprisonment.[33] For example, the cover of the January 1928 edition of the proletarian arts magazine *Zen'ei* (*Avant-Garde* [subheaded *Antau-Gardo* in Esperanto]), which Yamada helped initiate, asks: "How should we struggle in 1928?" And, it contains an article by the critic Kurehara Korehito on the new stage of the proletarian literature and proletarian arts movements.[34] Dedicated to creating a revolutionary proletarian culture, this publication, edited by Yamada, aspired to bring the arts to a level that the nominally educated working class (and even children) could understand. It did this by including proletarian children's literature, woodblock prints, political cartoons, instructive songs, and theoretical essays made comprehensible by *rubi* (i.e., hiragana over Japanese characters) and symbols evoking the proletariat.[35] The arts thus served the masses by stimulating their consciousness of new social ideals. Their own participation in this endeavour would then lead to the construction of a flourishing proletarian culture.

In a Manchukuo where, by the late 1930s, the arts were increasingly used for propaganda purposes, Yamada's observations of Concordia Association national meetings, and his advocacy of rural development schemes for Japanese "pioneers," appeared little different from his earlier proletarian ideals lauding the self-determination of the working class and farmers. In the Manchukuo context, he helped to create what I term a "right-wing proletarianism" supportive of the new state, with the Concordia Association serving as a vehicle for propagating this message to the masses, along with cultural media like short stories serialized in newspapers. In many ways, Yamada's new role in Manchukuo maintained a surprising continuity with his earlier pursuits in Japan prior to his imprisonment.

However, exactly *why* did these intellectuals devote their talents to making propaganda on behalf of Manchukuo? Were they even aware that they were serving as propagandists for a fascist state and, after 1937, promoting the wartime aims of Imperial Japan?[36] In connection with explaining their varying levels of support for Manchukuo, I examine what attracted formerly leftist or avant-garde Japanese writers, photographers, and artists to Manchukuo between 1932 and 1945. In the following chapters, I analyze their myriad reasons for accepting invitations for tours or sojourns in the region. Kushner posits that shared conceptions of a powerful Japanese Empire "attracted well-known writers, politicians, educators, and businessmen to imperial propaganda."[37] In Manchukuo, a shared sense of participating in a process that was bringing imperial modernity to the region also motivated these individuals, with the result that their descriptions in various media attained a propaganda-like quality.

In what ways were these intellectuals collaborating with the state while furthering their own careers and political agendas? This question, which addresses personal motivations as well as political agendas, intersects with issues pertaining to the nature of propaganda in Manchukuo and to former leftists working in a fascist political context. Each of the intellectuals I examine is a progressive leader in his field, and each represents a case in which an individual chose to support a regime by making use of all the tools of mechanical reproduction available to propagate its message – printed materials (pictorials, journals, photo collections, posters), films, radio, and even art displayed in government venues in domestic Japan. These people clearly knew that the works they produced would end up in national, regional, and international venues. Here, promotion and opportunism overlapped with a desire to carry out political ideals that were impossible to achieve in the politically repressive environment of domestic Japan. Each chapter examines the reasons that led whichever cultural producer being studied to collaborate with the creation of a Japanese-led cultural enterprise in Manchukuo.

Various motives brought these individuals to Manchukuo: the ability to express similar political ideals in a different context after imprisonment for left-wing activism (Yamada, Chapter 2); curiosity about the new state while distancing oneself from the now dangerous taint of Marxism (Fukuzawa and his colleagues, Chapter 3); commercial prerogatives (Ai Mitsu, Chapter 4); jump-starting a flagging career (Fuchikami, Chapter 5); the desire to advance one's career while creating a new culture under corporatist ideals (Mutô, Chapter 6); and the opportunity to serve as a literary establishment leader for Manchukuo (Kawabata, Chapter 7). For these various reasons, each intellectual made a conscious choice either to travel to Manchukuo or to sojourn there: none was compelled to go or forced to depict the new state once he got there. However, they all believed that a multifaceted utopia was taking shape in a modernizing Manchukuo – a place where their personal aims could be realized and where, by virtue of their being Japanese, they held a privileged position. Therefore, one cannot conclusively apply a Marxist analysis of "false consciousness," the result of a hierarchical system of state-imposed propaganda wherein ideology filters downwards without being affected by the agency of those encountering it. Rather, these Japanese intellectuals consciously and conscientiously chose to depict messages and images that resonated with their own personal aims. This culminated in a form of cultural production that communicated a kind of "soft" propaganda.

In what follows, I argue that, by persuading the left-oriented avant-garde to create positive accounts of the state's progressive campaign to modernize Manchuria for a Japanese (and foreign) audience, the Japanese handlers of the Manchukuo experiment fought an ideological soft war of suasion in support of Japan's imperialist expansion in, and development of, Asia. Most importantly, the writings and images produced by these formerly left-wing intellectuals reflect the contradictions and selective omissions that characterize historical Japanese representations of the colonies in the interwar and wartime periods.

1

Laying the Groundwork for the Japanese Avant-Garde Propagandists

A number of developments laid the groundwork for the arrival of the Japanese avant-garde propagandists in the 1930s. When Japan emerged victorious from the Russo-Japanese War in 1905, many Japanese were pleased that they had trounced a great Western power but disappointed that, unlike after the First Sino-Japanese War, they had made few gains in territory or indemnities. Though Japan acquired the China Eastern Railway, many in the government and military desired greater control over Manchuria, which harboured valuable natural resources and would serve as a strategic counter to Russian power. The renamed railway soon became a key component in Japan's strategy of cultural imperialism, and, during the Manchukuo period, culture remained an important means for Japan to manage its interests in the region. From its inception in 1906, the South Manchuria Railway Company's foundational premises and organizational structure were thus concerned with fulfilling Imperial Japan's needs and linking Manchuria to the archipelago – including through invitations to cultural figures. I therefore examine the conglomerate's role as the foremost extender of invitations to Japanese observers and colonial settlers from 1907 to 1937. In 1907, concerned with Manchuria's economic and cultural development, SMRC moved its headquarters from Tokyo, Japan's imperial centre, to the cosmopolitan Chinese port city of Dairen (contemporary Dalian, PRC).

Following Japan's victory over Russia, garnering of administrative rights over the Liaodong Peninsula, and control over the China Eastern Railway, Manchuria became a topic of interest for Japanese who followed the Empire's developments. Beginning with its inception in Dairen, SMRC, wanting to promote a positive image of the area for domestic Japanese and international audiences, sponsored tours to Manchuria along associated rail lines. These junkets, described by prominent Japanese cultural figures like Natsume Sôseki (1867-1916), soon served as templates for future, often equivocal, depictions of the region, including those created by leftist intellectuals, or avant-garde artists. In order to provide a context for understanding the works of Japanese avant-garde propagandists in Manchukuo, I examine the impact of Sôseki's writings on successive Japanese observers as well as what "modernism" and "avant-garde" meant in interwar Japan.

After the 1931 Manchurian Incident, domestic Japan's increasingly fascist political climate affected cultural production and led to individuals' making difficult choices in order to retain their status as critical cultural producers. Nevertheless, the form of fascism espoused by the new state's Japanese handlers was so compelling that it attracted many former left-wing Japanese intellectuals with the promise of a developmental utopia that would safeguard the interests of both native workers and rural immigrants. After Manchukuo's controversial 1932 establishment, efforts by various organizations to enlist prominent Japanese to depict the new state only intensified, with, during wartime, the Kantô Army, the Concordia Association, and the Manchukuo Publicity and News Bureau and its associated media outfits increasingly serving as hosts. I first investigate SMRC's early history and the cultural extension of Japanese influence, along with the new state's contentious founding, the justifications for its existence, and its inherently fascistic character. This is crucial to understanding political conversion and, thus, why Japanese artists and writers chose to tour or sojourn in Manchukuo.

The South Manchuria Railway Company and Japanese Cultural Imperialism

To further Japan's aims, Taiwan's former colonial administrator Gotô Shimpei (1857-1929) and General Kodama Gentarô (1852-1906), chief of military staff in Manchuria, envisioned the development of the rail lines and the associated administrated areas garnered from Russia.[1] In November 1906, they founded SMRC in Tokyo, and new headquarters were built in Dairen, Manchuria, for the 1907 transfer of company operations overseas. This semi-public, semi-private enterprise, with its head office in Tokyo, would be funded by the Japanese government with the aid of Japanese investors: "The authorized amount of capital came to 200 million yen, with the government contributing half that amount; and only Japanese and Chinese could be shareholders."[2] SMRC hoped to showcase Asian ingenuity coupled with the latest Western technology, while it aided the imperial state in developing a region rich in valuable natural resources.

SMRC underwent three structural transformations prior to the Manchukuo period, revealing its intimate connections to the Japanese state.[3] Highlighting the conglomerate's importance to the Japanese government, the Japanese cabinet rested at the top of its hierarchy, under which served a president, vice-president, and board of directors. In April 1907, after SMRC's Manchurian genesis, the president, or *sôsai,* headed the operation. Under his control were the presidential office, research department, transportation department, mining department, regional department, Dairen Hospital,

Dairen Sankyô office, Dairen Yamato Hotel, Fushun Mine, and, finally, the Tokyo main office.[4]

Another change in organization occurred after the First World War, following the birth of the March 1919 Korean independence movement. Political unrest on the peninsula led to the Japanese government's desire to maintain stability and economic control over southeastern Manchuria. Japan now enjoyed overwhelming prosperity from a war to which it had contributed few troops, and government officials sought to extend its economic control over an area containing important resources (including coal, iron, and wood, along with the ability to harness them) for further domestic industrial growth. In July 1919, the president's title was changed to *shachô* and was situated at the top of a flow chart, presiding over the president's office and the general affairs department (including the East Asian Economic Research Bureau and Research Section), transportation department (including the port office), industrial development department (heading the Fushun Mines and Anshan Steelworks), commerce department, regional department (with regional office and central laboratory), technology department (heading the land and forestry section, construction section, and machinery section), accounting department, and the Tokyo main office.[5] Here, SMRC's growth as a partially state-sponsored conglomerate is clearly evident in the plethora of new departments, each of which indicates an area of concern to the Japanese government.

SMRC's last reorganization occurred a month before the Manchurian Incident in August 1931, with the president, now again referred to as *sôsai,* directing a hierarchy of departments, including general affairs, management, accounting, railway (with port office), regional (including the construction section, regional office, and hospital), commerce, technology bureau (with central laboratory), the Tokyo main office, the Fengtian office, the Harbin office, the Fushun Mine, and the Anshan Steelworks.[6] Each reorganization represented SMRC's further growth and the corresponding aggrandizement of its aims, which were united with those of its imperial overseers.

Due to its rapid expansion, SMRC hired a flood of middle-class Japanese professionals who soon became informal agents of Japanese imperialism by extending Japanese economic and cultural influence into the southeastern portion of Manchuria and the Liaodong Peninsula. Thus, the conglomerate's Dairen headquarters served as an important symbol of SMRC's civilizing mission. Japanese architects built this new white limestone building in the neoclassical style favoured by British imperialists. Japanese pictorials, newspaper photos, and company literature prominently featured its photograph in their accounts of the company's operations.[7]

The choice to locate SMRC in Dairen was a wise one. Neighbouring Lu Shun, or Port Arthur, had served the Russians well as a blue-water military port with easier sea access than Vladivostok. The adjoining city, known as

Dalny (Faraway) under the Russians and, in 1905, christened Dairen ("Great Linkage") by the Japanese, was the region's commercial port and primary access point to the China Eastern Railway. This rail network, now under SMRC's control, connected with Harbin in Manchuria's central hub and then joined lines headed west toward Chita, a terminus on the Trans-Siberian Railway that ran to Moscow and, from there, to other European cities. Well-protected by an adjacent naval port, commercial ships transporting Manchurian products (such as coal, iron, or soybeans) from Dairen could easily gain access to markets in China proper, Korea, and Japan by sea. These countries, in turn, sent their products to Manchuria by rail and sea. Thus, Dairen was at the centre of a profitable trade nexus, and Japanese investors in SMRC greatly benefited from an infrastructural base on the site of Qingniwa, a former Chinese fishing village that, after 1898, was developed by the Russians. Bruce A. Ellerman notes that, "just as maritime 'sea lines of communication' have played a vital role in supporting China's vibrant growth rates, the 'rivers of steel' running through Manchuria and into Central China were the 'land lines of communication' that held the promise of bringing modernization to many as-yet undeveloped rural areas of north-east China."[8] By controlling the means of transport and the types of goods sold in a prime location in the "Far East," SMRC could operate from a position of growing commercial and economic power. By the 1920s, Dairen was China's busiest port outside of Shanghai.[9]

However, the region's stability, and the success of Japanese economic and cultural aims, depended on the use of military force. According to Y. Tak Matsusaka: "The SMR's network, in effect, 'hardwired' the territory for war and occupation, reducing the southern part of the territory to a Japanese military protectorate."[10] Following the negotiations that ended the Russo-Japanese War, Japan was allowed to install a police force, consisting of soldiers, along certain portions of the railway track (usually, every hundred metres) and SMRC-administered areas to protect them from banditry. This division of troops was known as the Kwantung, or Kantô, Army, which periodically rotated with the First Division of the Japanese Imperial Army based in Tokyo. As the decades passed, the Kantô Army became a refuge for hot-headed military extremists and young fanatics who were often exiled to Manchuria as punishment for radical behaviour. This led to the Kantô Army's increasingly restive and independent-minded nature, and, by the late 1920s, certain individuals in the Japanese government and military establishment, like General Tanaka Gi'ichi (1864-1929), began to advocate a "forward policy" in China. For these men, Chiang Kai-Shek's (1887-1975) seemingly successful 1927 purge of Shanghai's communists and subsequent 1928 unification of China below the Great Wall were soon viewed as constituting threats to Japanese interests in Manchuria. On two occasions, the Kantô Army took upon itself the task of safeguarding these interests by staging a Chinese "terrorist attack" – one condemned by the Emperor in 1928,[11] and one tacitly condoned through belated imperial approval in 1931.[12] The latter led to the 18 September Manchurian Incident, which prompted the Kantô Army's 1931 invasion of the region and, by 1933, resulted in full Japanese control of Manchuria.

However, in the earliest stage of SMRC's development, a more peaceful agenda took hold. As the company's first president, Gotô utilized the expertise in colonial administration that he had gained during the 1895 incorporation of Taiwan into the Japanese Empire after Japan's victory in the First Sino-Japanese War. He soon applied a similar modernization agenda to Manchuria, advocating a policy of *bunsôteki bubi* ("the application of culture as military preparedness"), in part to avoid alienating Westerners and other foreign nations who also had business and missionary interests in the region.[13] According to Ramon H. Myers: "Under the guise of the SMR, then, Japan quietly and gradually expanded its influence in southern Manchuria while developing economic interdependency with the region."[14] However, due to growing Japanese interest in China, the rise of fascism in Japan, and an increasingly assertive Kantô Army, the nature of SMRC's activities would soon change. Nevertheless, "culture" remained an important means by which Japan controlled its interests in Manchuria, and Japanese cultural figures played a key role in this process.

"Imperial Eyes": Japanese Travellers in Manchuria, 1909-31

Since the late Meiji period (1868-1912), and moreso with Japan's imperial expansion, Japanese ventured abroad, avidly producing travel writing in the form of essays, published diaries, and travelogues. These writings were geared toward consumption in urban as well as rural areas, and stimulated the popular imagination.[15] Part of a long-standing domestic literary tradition of *kikô bungaku* (travel literature), these accounts created the desire to venture beyond armchair travel and to enter a world marked by constantly improving modes of transnational communications and transit that allowed the middle-class or elite traveller a comfortable, speedy voyage. The average Japanese tourist could now take a boat from Yokohama near Tokyo or Fukuoka in northern Kyûshû to Pusan, Korea, or Dairen, Manchuria, in a mere couple of days. From these ports, inland cities in Korea, Manchuria, and northern China could easily be reached by rail.

After SMRC was established in Dairen, its mission included showcasing the Japanese-led development of its administered areas to domestic Japanese, regional, and foreign audiences. The organization soon sponsored Japanese travellers who were esteemed for their cultural or religious achievements, and its corporate leaders expected them to write positive accounts of SMRC's development and the spread of Japanese cultural influence throughout the region. Through SMRC-organized tours, these famous tourists disseminated

Japanese culture while creating informal propaganda that favoured the corporation's (and Japanese government's) desire to expand the guiding role of Japanese civilization on the continent. Thus, their publicity, couched in the rhetoric of modernity and development, served the dual purpose of advertising SMRC's services and informing the general public of its broader political aims. Notably, in Japanese, the word *senden* means "advertisement," "publicity," and "public relations" as well as "exploitation" and "political propaganda."

The company's second president, Nakamura Zêko (1867-1927), worked hard to advertise SMRC's aspirations to the general public by enlisting high-profile Japanese intellectuals and literati, or *bunjin,* to produce positive accounts of Japanese-led development in Manchuria. These prominent cultural figures propagated the superiority of Japanese civilization and evoked the late Meiji-era philosophy of *risshin shusse* (self-reliance), which emphasizes the realization of personal success after attaining higher education and practising a strong work ethic. Nakamura soon set a precedent for subsequent SMRC tours for potential manufacturers of public opinion that featured planned whirlwind visits to cities, cultural sites, and industrial areas. These were organized by the presidential office, or *sôsai-shitsu,* situated at the pinnacle of the corporation's organizational structure and thus highlighting the importance of these promotional junkets. Locations featured on these tours usually included Dairen, Manchuria's commercial hub; Mukden (contemporary Shenyang, also known as Fengtian or Hôten), the region's industrial centre; Harbin, the area's Russian-influenced window to Europe; and Andong, a developing border town near neighbouring Korea.

One of SMRC's most famous early travellers was *Asahi Shimbun (Morning News)* journalist and writer Natsume Sôseki. In 1909, Nakamura, a former schoolmate of Sôseki's, invited the author to Manchuria as the guest of his corporation, hoping that he would serve as its mouthpiece.[16] Sôseki was chosen not only due to his personal connections to the company's president, who had known him during his youth at Tokyo Imperial University, but also because he was a respected member of Japan's literary establishment. Nakamura's invitation represents one of the company's early efforts to extend a Japanese cultural presence along the SMRC-administered railways as part of Japan's civilizing mission in East Asia. Not only was SMRC in charge of the railways in its administrative sphere, but it also expanded the Japanese colonial presence in Manchuria by opening up Japanese-language schools, hospitals, hotels, and clubs for its white-collar employees, while running profitable enterprises such as mining operations, ports of trade, and steelworks. As late as 1936, ads in the *Manchuria Daily News (Manshû nichi nichi shimbun)* and the English-language publication *Manchuria* touted the company as "carrying the light of civilization into Manchuria."[17] However, a rather curmudgeonly Sôseki never fully approved of these aims, revealing

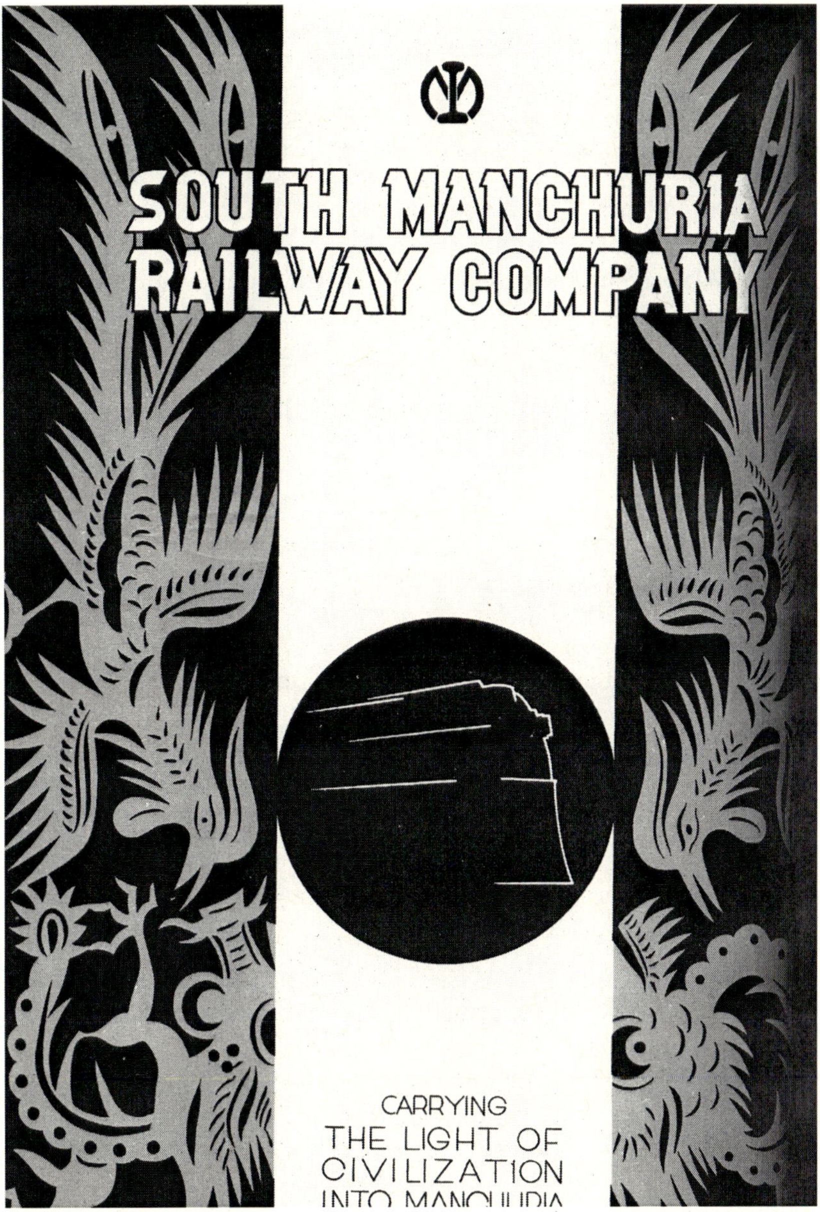

Figure 1 SMRC advertisement in *Manchuria*, "Carrying the light of civilization," 1936, University of Chicago Regenstein Library collections.

the smug Social Darwinism of the late Meiji period, and it is unclear whether he had other motives (beyond obliging his friend's hospitality) for touring Manchuria.

After Sôseki's first glimpse of the region, there were two locations that asserted a primal influence on all his future observations: (1) Dairen's commercial port, commonly known by Japanese as *Manshû no genkan* ("entranceway to Manchuria"), and (2) SMRC's Yamato Hotel. The first showed how Japanese organization and enterprise could motivate the vast Chinese labour force, and the second symbolized SMRC's civilizing mission and modernity. These two motifs would emerge as key themes in Sôseki's account of the region, and they would also establish an important model for its future portrayal, whether in writing, photography, or painting.

On arriving by ship in Dairen's port, the Japanese visitor's first stop would have been the city's busy commercial wharves, where coolies toiled to load and unload Manchurian agricultural products, natural resources, commercial goods, and baggage onto ships leaving for or arriving from other parts of the Japanese Empire or China proper. This bustling place made an unforgettable first impression on Japanese observers like Sôseki, with guides pointing out the sheer strength and unceasing activity of the Han Chinese coolies, who were more robust than their working-class Japanese counterparts. Then, at the wharf, a late-model automobile would arrive, and the driver would take its passengers up several streets and over the Tokiwa Bridge, now known as Shengliqiao (Victory Bridge).

After a straight passage along Ôyama-dôri (Oyama Boulevard), the car would then circle around the centrally located Dai-hiroba (Grand Circle), or round point, which, with its spokes of avenues radiating out from a large monument of Gotô within the surrounding park, is similar to Paris's Place de L'Étoile. In the city's design, the original Russian urban planners emulated the French style popularized by Baron Haussmann in the late nineteenth century. Ornate Western buildings surrounded this central hub, including the Yokohama Specie Bank, the city police department (and secret headquarters of the *Kempeitai* military police during the Manchukuo period), municipal offices, and the Yamato Hotel. In the centre of the great circle stood a statue of Gotô perched on his horse – a dignified memorial to the man who, after 1905, took over city planning from the Russian blueprint.

Following a short car ride from the port and along the boulevards, Sôseki's (or any other Japanese visitor's) next destination would be Dairen's newly constructed Yamato Hotel. Opening for business in 1909, it served as the original flagship of a chain of hotels soon to be built along SMRC rail lines and located close to ports or train stations (like the one in Harbin, where the Korean nationalist An Jung-geun [1877-1910] assassinated Itô Hirobumi [1841-1909] in October of the same year). The hotel's name communicates Japanese imperial grandeur and uniqueness in that it invokes the birthplace

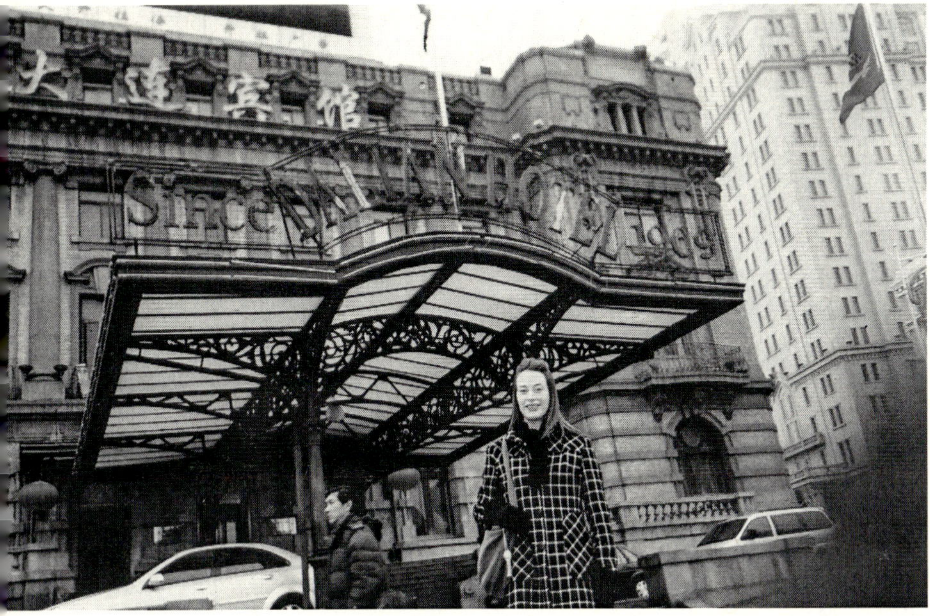

Figure 2 Yamato Hotel façade *[Dalian Binguan]*, Dalian, PRC, 2005, author's personal collection.

of the imperial ancestors in the Kyoto-Osaka, or Yamato, region. These architecturally baroque and ornately decorated hotels lost money for the corporation, but they served as important showcases of Japanese civilization and progress. In the year of Sôseki's visit, the hotels lost 19,148 yen, with the most acute losses of hundreds of thousands of yen per year occurring from 1920 to 1927. Indeed, profits only surfaced in 1917, 1918, and 1934.[18] Though the least profitable sector of SMRC, these establishments nonetheless impressed their guests, and Dairen's much-praised hotel boasted gold-leaf crown mouldings and pink marble walls in its grand foyer. This five-story edifice occupied a commanding presence in the city's centre, featuring a red limestone façade, wrought-iron detailing around the entrance, and a grand staircase framed by generous hallways cushioned in red carpet.[19]

Despite any personal misgivings about SMRC's "civilizing mission," Sôseki dutifully described his five-week tour of Manchuria in a 1909 serialized newspaper account of his travels entitled *Man Kan tokoro dokoro (Here and There in Manchuria and Korea)* – a result that Nakamura had rightly anticipated.[20] The title is misleading, since the author never made it to Korea (most likely due to his gastric distress and fear of Korean unrest in the wake of Itô's Harbin assassination), and the series was terminated at the end of the year. Nevertheless, Sôseki's often pejorative reflections on Chinese in the popular

Japanese daily, the *Asahi Shimbun,* aided in producing the groundwork for future Japanese descriptions, which featured a persistent dichotomy between a culture that was civilized (Japan's) and one that was moribund (China's). Japanese news media, like the *Asahi Shimbun,* profited from Japan's imperial thrust into the region and thus devoted much copy to related topics. Deep into the Manchukuo period, accounts by Japanese intellectuals continue to echo this civilized/moribund dichotomy.[21]

In *ManKan tokoro dokoro,* Sôseki depicted a vision of China that, on the one hand, revealed his sympathy for the poverty of the lower classes (including coolies and rickshawmen), but, on the other, decried their abjection as yet another aspect of China's elemental backwardness and unyielding traditionalism. Uchida Michio believes that the author's equivocal gaze accurately represents the contradictory attitude toward imperialism shared by many Japanese intellectuals at the time.[22] Further, he includes the author's work in a common discourse of national superiority representative of Japanese elites and their education.[23] Thus, it is not surprising that Sôseki remarked negatively on Chinese labour and that his unnerving encounter with a rickshaw driver led him to feel even more ill at ease with his country's poor and "backward" Asian neighbours.[24]

Rickshawmen and coolies were among China's poorest individuals, suffering the harsh economic vicissitudes of renting a cart or hiring out their physical labour. Yet, they also intrigued middle- to upper-class readers and, in the 1930s, were the subjects of several works that gained international acclaim, such as Manchu writer Lao She's (1899-1966) 1937 novel *Rickshaw Boy,* which portrayed the trials of these workers.[25] This text, popular in the United States in unofficial translation before 1945, also garnered sympathy and support for China during the Second Sino-Japanese War, as did Pearl S. Buck's (1892-1973) Pulitzer- and Nobel Prize-winning work (1932 and 1938, respectively), *The Good Earth* (1931), which dramatized the hardships of Chinese peasants and whose protagonist, Wang Lung, worked as a rickshawman.[26] From the early twentieth century onwards, an equivocal view of Chinese labour is an important theme in the reports of most Japanese and Western observers, regardless of their political sympathies.

In the late 1920s and early 1930s, conflicted descriptions of Manchuria are echoed in the poetry and short stories of avant-garde and/or left-wing Japanese writers such as Kitagawa Fuyuhiko (1900-90), Anzai Fuyue (1898-1965), and others, who depicted the region and its peoples in a multivalent fashion.[27] Such writings include Itô Takeo's memoirs, in which he reveals an obsession with Chinese coolies: "I remember being deeply moved by my impressions of the group of coolies working at the Dairen harbor and wharf, and as soon as I entered the SMR, I set my mind on studying the Chinese laborers at the Fu-shun coal mines."[28] In contrast to the Dairen-based poets Kitagawa and Anzai,[29] who were not financially supported by SMRC, the writer Sôseki, the researcher Itô, the photographer Fuchikami, and the artist Fukuzawa and his group were brought over or invited by the corporation and therefore had a reason to create positive impressions of Japanese development schemes. They also made a conscious choice to come to Manchukuo and, in doing so, partially fulfilled various personal dreams. Even so, like Sôseki, these cultural producers were struck by their "colonial encounter," witnessing the juxtaposition of the modern and the archaic in a Manchurian "contact zone" marked by both development and abject poverty.[30]

For Japanese like Sôseki, viewing the premodern conditions in China – conditions that Japan itself had so recently addressed – was like viewing the spectre that haunted the imperial mentality (or, more fittingly, viewing that mentality's dark shadow side). Like Freud's proverbial "return of the repressed," the trauma of the imperial project often manifested itself in Japanese intellectuals in the form of an unease toward an "other" that was so like the "self," yet just different enough to be uncanny, symbolizing "the narcissism of small differences." These observers sympathized with the plight of impoverished Chinese labourers and the harsh conditions they endured, but they also portrayed the Chinese lower classes in a fashion that undermined empathy or sympathy, and, in an ambivalent "colonial gaze,"[31] they implied an inherent Japanese superiority. Oguma Eiji asserts that imperial subjects were often included in the Empire when convenient and excluded when not (e.g., consider the ambivalent treatment of Koreans in Japan after annexation).[32] For Japanese observers, Chinese abjection in Manchuria seemed like something elemental and irremediable rather than like something that could be surmounted by the individual will (or by adopting Japanese ways). Thus they highlighted this tension between inclusion and exclusion.[33]

This played directly into Imperial Japan's civilizing mission, with its adherents believing that the hand of the Japanese colonizer (i.e., the Kantô Army-supported SMRC) ultimately had to use force to motivate the Chinese in Manchuria to develop their own region. The writings of Japanese intellectuals invariably supported this rhetoric during a time when various actors increasingly began to view northeast China as valuable to the Japanese Empire. Moreover, by the late 1920s, Japan's path was diverging from Taishô democracy and, in the 1930s, embraced certain characteristics of the political experiments of fascist Italy and Germany. In fact, the Manchukuo state that emerged out of Kantô Army violence followed the fascist example even more closely than did Japan.

Japanese Intellectuals and Manchukuo's Fascist State Formation

Following the economic and political upheaval of the First World War, intellectuals in early 1920s Italy, such as Gabriele D'Annunzio (1863-1938), developed the political philosophy of fascism. Characterized by a corporatist, organic society and state, individuals would work together for the common good. The negative aspects of this new ideology included its adherents' willingness to use violence to effectuate their ends (e.g., Mussolini's 1921 March on Rome and his blackmailing his way into Italian leadership through the use of his Brown Shirts). Following their violent protests in Japan, Japanese proponents of Kita Ikki's (1883-1937) proto-fascist philosophies – encapsulated in his *Nihon kaizô hôan taikô (General Measures for the Reconstruction of Japan),* which emphasized an "organic and indivisible" family state – sometimes found a safe haven in Manchukuo under the Kantô Army. However, in the 1930s, Japanese interpretations of fascism had more in common with "statism," or *kokkashugi,* which contained elements in line with the Meiji state's earlier authoritarianism. Indeed, the 1889 imperial Constitution never guaranteed the Japanese people "rights" as citizens (as would be the case in a liberal, constitutional monarchy) but, rather, granted them "duties" as imperial subjects.

In a 1947 postwar essay, Maruyama Masao stresses that scholars cannot discount the "distinctive undercurrent in thought and social structure that had existed in Japanese political life since the Meiji Restoration and that sanctioned the advance of Japanese fascism."[34] He argues that Japanese fascism shared with its Italian and German counterparts such characteristics as "rejection of the world view of individualistic liberalism, opposition to parliamentary politics[,] ... insistence on foreign expansion, a tendency to glorify military build-up and war, a strong emphasis on racial myths and the national essence, a rejection of class warfare based on totalitarianism, and the struggle against Marxism."[35] However, it also diverged from these models due to its state structure, which focused on the Emperor and the family system as well as on agrarianism[36] – a characteristic that arose in mid-1930s Manchukuo after the state encouraged the mass migration of Japanese rural immigrants. Thus, with the Concordia Association as its mass political organization and the Kantô Army as its military force, Manchukuo more closely approximated the Italian model than the German model of fascism.

After the establishment of Manchukuo in 1932, the form of fascism espoused by the new state's Japanese framers attracted many formerly left-wing Japanese intellectuals with promises of a developmental utopia that would protect native workers, along with Japanese rural immigrants, from capitalistic excesses. Previously, in the 1920s and 1930s, the Japanese proletarian literature and proletarian arts movements had gone mainstream, thus becoming one of the dominant currents of representation in the arts. An interesting facet of this movement is that, even before mass conversions, while its proponents critiqued capitalism's underpinnings, many still supported the concept of a Japanese nation and its empire. However, those familiar with Lenin's writings understood that capitalism and its relentless search for new markets went hand in hand with the state's imperialistic impulses – one of Japan's key reasons for establishing an economic and cultural foothold in Manchuria after 1905. Beginning in 1928, and intensifying after the 1931 Manchurian Incident, the movement was increasingly persecuted by a Japanese government that viewed it as a threat to domestic political stability and, through the Comintern, as an external challenge from communist Russia. Yet, internal divisiveness and ambivalence toward Comintern directives all indicated the heterogeneity of Japanese Marxism, factors that also contributed to the fascist state's success.[37] Following Japan's increasing flirtation with fascism after the Manchurian Incident, left-wing intellectuals who could no longer publicly decry the state's encroachment on their freedom often found their utopian society in Manchukuo, which, in a political experiment engineered by Japan, soon became a space for the projection of various ideological and cultural dreams. For converted or avant-garde Japanese intellectuals visiting Manchuria or Manchukuo, certain ideological and aesthetic aspects of the proletarian movement remained in their works as an important legacy.

Several factors prompted the political shift toward a more fascist system in Japan and the initiation of a fascist satellite state in Manchuria. Indeed, by the late 1920s and early 1930s, Japanese intellectuals of all political stripes turned toward varying forms of socialism as potential models for assuaging the nation's social divisions and economic ills.[38] Moreover, for right-wing proponents, the success of fascist Italy after Mussolini's March on Rome, and of Nazi Germany after Hitler's rise to power, allowed these nations to serve as economic and social templates that stood at some distance from the liberalism of the Anglo-Saxon West, and that, prospectively, could soothe domestic tensions in Japan – also a late-developing industrial nation with a recent history of political unification. In addition, after the 1929 onset of the global Great Depression, Japanese intellectuals of all political orientations increasingly viewed capitalism and liberal democracy as bankrupt. Sometimes the protests and strikes they supported even became violent. For example, in the early 1930s, ultranationalist activists assassinated *zaibatsu* (conglomerate) chiefs like Dan Takuma (1858-1932) in a flagrant attack on capitalism.

Ironically, Manchuria, long viewed as Japan's *seimeisen* (lifeline),[39] and then Manchukuo, helped solve Imperial Japan's economic woes through its own kind of corporatist capitalism, which allowed it to escape the Depression by 1933. Therefore, due to the vital natural (and soon political as well as spiritual) resources of the new state, the Japanese government deemed it necessary to more closely integrate Manchukuo with Japan. Despite Japanese claims to its fully independent nationhood, Yuma Totani argues that Manchukuo was a "satellite state of the Japanese empire" and that, following

Japan's 1937 entrance into the Second Sino-Japanese War, it could also be termed a "client state."[40] However, when, how, and why did this chimerical entity originally develop?

A 1931 plot by the Kantô Army, euphemistically referred to as the Manchurian Incident, provided an excuse for establishing Japanese military rule over the entire Manchurian region.[41] Roughly a year of intense military operations brought large portions of Manchuria under Japanese control. Following glowing reports of battle successes, Hirohito accepted the rapid takeover of the region. In a belated imperial rescript, issued on 4 January 1932, the Emperor even praised the Kantô Army's valour in suppressing "bandits." Hirohito's top-down official support of the Manchurian campaign preceded popular propaganda that had been diffused among the public and, later, provided strong justification for Japanese intellectuals and others to back the eventual establishment of Manchukuo.

Despite tacit imperial approval, from the outset Japanese recognition of Manchukuo was fraught with inconsistencies and conflicting political aims. Growing tensions with the United States and other Western countries perpetuated this. Amidst a climate of self-determination sanctioned by US president Woodrow Wilson after the First World War, territorial takeover in the imperialist fashion of the late nineteenth and early twentieth centuries was no longer ideologically feasible. Prasenjit Duara notes that Manchukuo evolved out of this postwar atmosphere, in which "imperialism became increasingly illegitimate and political and economic competition among states was expressed through forms of nationalism."[42] Akira Iriye, in an important study of Japanese foreign policy, even characterizes the war-weary interwar years as "after imperialism."[43] Thus, in the light of Wilsonian appeals for colonial self-determination, government leaders decided to establish an independent, multi-ethnic state rather than annex it to the Japanese Empire (as they had done with Korea).

Therefore, even though he was noted for what Herbert Bix calls his "indulgence of the military concerning Manchuria,"[44] Prime Minister Inukai Tsuyoshi (1855-1932) delayed legal recognition of Manchukuo due to his desire not to alienate the United States and his wish to find a proper way of working with currents of Chinese nationalism. Nonetheless, on 7 January 1932, in his "non-recognition principle," as part of the "Stimson Doctrine" which opposed Japanese expansion, US Secretary of State Henry Stimson (1867-1950) condemned any political change to Manchuria. Following this, when pressed by the West, Inukai was sympathetic to Manchukuo and allowed the Kantô Army to install Chinese collaborators as leaders. Despite the Japanese prime minister's conciliatory attitude, on 15 May 1932 he was assassinated by a dissatisfied young naval officer. A succession of prime ministers followed, all with ties to the Japanese imperial family and armed forces, thus marking the end of parliamentary rule, the gradual uncoupling of Japan from Western conceptions of modernity, and the rise of fascism. The "Manchurian Question" was an important part of this shift.

On 15 September 1932, Admiral Saitô Makoto's (1858-1936) cabinet finally recognized the new state with the signing of the Japan-Manchukuo Protocol Agreement, which assured that Manchukuo would be defended by Japan.[45] The 1932 founding of the nominally "independent" state of Manchukuo under Japanese directives was soon accompanied by Japan's 1933 withdrawal from the League of Nations and its progressive military involvement in China south of the Great Wall.[46] Despite its early legal link to Japan, according to Thomas David DuBois, Manchukuo can be viewed as an example of a "partially sovereign state," at least in the years from 1932 to 1937.[47] Though most Chinese scholars and left-wing Japanese cultural historians (such as Kobayashi Hideo and Tusukase Susumu) characterize Manchukuo as a puppet state, DuBois argues that it maintained considerable independence from Japan: "Manchukuo handed over to Japan the power to staff and ideologically mold its judiciary, while the tutelary attitude that Japan took toward the state was concretely manifested in aspects of Manchukuo penal and civil law, and a surprisingly contentious path to the abrogation of Japanese extraterritoriality."[48] Thus, DuBois contends that Manchukuo was a nation characterized by a framework of laws but that, in accordance with these laws, Japan treated some of its ethnic groups (e.g., the Chinese and, especially, the Koreans) differently than it did others – much as, prior to Philippine independence, US citizens were treated differently than were citizens of the Philippines. However, with the 1937 outbreak of the Second Sino-Japanese War, political conditions on the continent necessitated Manchukuo's further integration with the imperial metropole, and, as DuBois points out, "Manchukuo effectively surrendered its national sovereignty to the needs of the Japanese empire, sacrificing its jurisdictional integrity as well."[49]

In the 1930s, while debates raged in Japan about the nature of Manchukuo's statehood under Japanese auspices, Japanese officials and members of the Kantô Army began to create an ideological framework for the new state. Visiting intellectuals from Japan would compose an important part of this endeavour, just as they had for SMRC. Despite Japan's increasing isolation from the international diplomatic community, Manchukuo was founded on the ideals of Pan-Asianism and liberation from the West, which were seen as an antidote for an "Asia oppressed by the white West." These ideals developed out of an earlier right-wing critique of capitalism popularized, after Zhang Zuolin's 1928 assassination, under Colonel Ishiwara Kanji (1889-1949), the Kantô Army operations officer who also masterminded the Manchurian Incident. Bix asserts that he and his adherents viewed Manchuria as "a laboratory to create a new social order based on principles of social equality and loyalty to the state rather than selfish capitalistic profit seeking."[50]

Moreover, Manchukuo would serve as a testing ground for new political, economic, and social policies that could also later benefit the *naichi* (domestic Japan).[51] Here, the new state's framers soon adopted an anti-capitalist, right-wing version of socialism – in other words, fascism – to prevent the social disorder, strikes, and economic upheaval that plagued late Taishô and early Shôwa Japan. In addition, the framers of the Manchukuo experiment, like Ishiwara, hoped to combine a modern infrastructure and material culture with traditional Asian values as expressed in the Confucian-inspired slogans *Odôrakudô* and *minzoku kyôwa*.[52] However, in Manchukuo, the Japanese-led corporatist government desired the implementation of an East Asian modernity that would avoid the ravages of Western capitalism and ensure the following goals: corporate benevolence toward the most productive workers, harmonious cooperation of multi-ethnic peoples through mass organization, and security and defence against the encroachment of Soviet communists from the north. Thus, in accord with this initiative, SMRC and affiliated governmental organizations encouraged the Japanese observers who flooded into Manchukuo soon after its establishment to depict these ideals in their works.

However, in domestic Japan, barely three years after the Tanaka cabinet's ignominious fall after having urged expansion on the continent, the public had to be persuaded to accept further military operations in Manchuria between 1931 and 1933. Thus, following the Manchurian Incident, fervour for supporting Japanese intervention in Manchuria was ignited by the (often forced) cooperation of popular news media outlets.[53] In other words, organized attempts to coordinate and promote a positive vision of Manchukuo through propaganda created by intellectuals engaged in cultural production was preceded by public mobilization brought on by government-orchestrated war fever.[54] In addition, Sandra Wilson notes that, in the media, Japanese increasingly began to hear about the costly legacy of the 1904-5 Russo-Japanese War, which was presented as a justification for establishing Japanese control over the region.[55] Tsukase also stresses that Japan's "sacrifice" in that war served as a way for the Japanese government to justify Manchukuo's existence.[56] Indeed, former Japanese colonists in Manchuria, like Kimura Ryôji, underscored Japan's responsibility to those who lost their lives fighting for this territory: "The Liaodong Peninsula was a place built on the precious blood of [our] fathers and sons. We are the ones who inherited it and [it is up to us] to make it great!"[57] The repeated evocation of prior hard-won Japanese victories helped to strengthen the idea that Japan now had a moral duty to support the potentially advantageous Manchurian campaign waged from 1931 to 1933.

As a result, Japan "entered the 1930s with a view of war as essentially a positive and profitable undertaking, with little public memory of the enormous burdens it could bring, and with an assumption that going to war was a *modern* thing to do."[58] In addition, radio, newspapers, and popular songs – like the "Manchurian March" and "Song of a Mounted Bandit" – soon stimulated ideas of Manchuria as a romantic land of opportunity.[59] Thus, various types of informal propaganda intended for a domestic Japanese audience, both justifying the existence of the new state and highlighting its potential wealth, preceded the formal propaganda intended for foreign and regional audiences.

From Japanese Avant-Gardism to Fascism[60]

After the establishment of Manchukuo in 1932, SMRC's cultural initiatives, as well as those of the Concordia Association, helped support the new state's official propaganda efforts. However, without the formal and informal participation of members of the Japanese avant-garde who arrived from Imperial Japan to legitimate these endeavours in their works, such efforts would have been hollow. In Japan, many of the writers and artists associated with the avant-garde – including Anzai, Kitagawa, Takiguchi Shûzô (1903-79), Fukuzawa, Migishi Kôtarô (1900-34), and Kawabata – chose surrealism as their mode of representation and were attracted to images of an external "other," whether in France, China, or Manchuria.[61] Prior to the mid-1930s, their connections to these outside spaces furthered their careers and legitimated their activities as members of a cosmopolitan, politically advanced avant-garde that was attracted to Marxism. However, after 1931, domestic Japan's increasingly fascist political climate negatively influenced cultural production and led to intellectuals' making tough choices in order to retain their status as critical cultural producers.[62] Raymond Williams's definition of culture as "the works and practices of intellectual and especially artistic activities" could be applied to modernist and avant-garde cultural production in interwar Japan and to modernism in wartime Japan.[63]

In order to understand Japanese avant-garde propagandists in Manchukuo it is necessary to understand exactly what "avant-garde" and "modernism" meant in interwar Japan. In the two decades after Japan rose to great-power status following its 1905 victory in the Russo-Japanese War, innovations in transportation and communications throughout an expanding empire vastly changed popular perceptions of time, space, and everyday lived experience in Japan. Moreover, events in the Japanese Empire destabilized the domestic political and cultural environment while, at the same time, stimulating various forms of modernist and avant-garde production. In his essays on urban modernism in Europe and, specifically, Great Britain, Williams views the urban metropolis as a locus of empire in which "new social and economic and cultural relations, beyond both city and nation in their older senses, were beginning to be formed."[64] This was especially true in Tokyo, Japan's political and cultural capital in the interwar and wartime periods, as well as in Shinkyô, the capital of the Manchukuo "empire" after 1934. The city's stimulating, and at times alienating, environment allowed for what Williams terms the "simultaneous cosmopolitan access to a wide variety of subordinate cultures."[65] This access to a plethora of trends and ideas from all parts of the globe in imperial capitals and cosmopolitan locations such as Tokyo, Dairen, Shanghai, southeastern Manchuria, and (after 1932) urban Manchukuo rendered them "contact zones,"[66] or an "artistic contact nebulae"[67] – places that allowed for the creation of complex, hybrid visions of modernity on the part of Japanese intellectuals.

Modernism arose in the nineteenth century as an apolitical and anti-bourgeois reaction to high art by disaffected artists residing in the imperial capitals of the world. These people had encountered a cosmopolitan mix of subject cultures during the height of Europe's quest for empire.[68] The avant-garde, by contrast, appeared a few decades later, in the 1910s, and had a radical political agenda. For Raymond Williams, in the context of Europe, modernism "began" when cultural producers assimilated art and literature into specific movements, which he views as "the products, at the first historical level, of changes in public media."[69] In the late nineteenth century, in both Europe and Japan, due to innovations in information technology and communications (such as the telegraph, telephone, railway, and trans-oceanic steamship routes), artistic and literary ideas began to flow with ease across political boundaries and to transgress national borders. The perpetual search for the new, even in the realm of literary and artistic expression, was a direct offshoot of broader national trends linked with the discourse of civilization. As the Social Darwinist catchphrases of both European and Japanese imperialism at the turn of the century, "modernity" and "progress" served as the civilizational directives for economic development and political reform, and they were used as justifications for imperial rule over colonized peoples. Despite its inherently exploitative nature, European imperialism, like Japanese imperialism during the mid-Meiji period, allowed for the hybrid mixing of goods, peoples, and cultures while stimulating global exchanges of various kinds. Thus, the colonized "subordinate cultures" with which intellectuals came into contact in the cosmopolitan space of the imperial capitals generated visions of a reality beyond that of the normative, elite bourgeois social sphere. These capital cities served as contact zones, which Mary Louise Pratt defines as "multidimensional spaces within which subjects on all sides are constituted in and by their relations with others."[70] In the interwar years, the search by Japanese avant-garde writers and artists for a "distant reality," or a truth beyond the state-promoted rhetoric of modernity, also formed part of the aesthetic of modernism.[71]

In imperial capitals, a figure whom Williams refers to as "the internationally anti-bourgeois artist" became the main progenitor of various forms of modernist expression that coalesced into movements that explicitly repudiated the past and countered various "traditions." Eventually, modernism, in the context of nineteenth-century Europe, bifurcated into what Peter Bürger views as two distinctly anti-bourgeois currents with different approaches to the increasingly complex notion of politics: (1) an aesthetic formalism that emphasized the "formerly aristocratic valuation of art as a sacred realm above money and commerce" and (2) "art as the liberating vanguard of the popular consciousness."[72]

However, by the turn of the century, and in the years preceding the First World War, writers and artists in Europe as well as in Japan turned increasingly to the creation of works that, according to Bürger, did not repudiate the styles before them but, rather, criticized art itself as an institution and challenged the course of its development in bourgeois society.[73] These individuals then became the avant-garde, of which Dadaism, in its self-critical mode, is a prime example.[74] According to Bürger, the avant-garde revolted against the idea of art as an institution divorced from the praxis of everyday life.[75] While concurring with Williams's general thesis on modernism, Bürger defines the avant-garde as a modernist group that rebelled against art's distance from the everyday while, at the same time, protesting against its institutionalized status. Therefore, the avant-garde constitutes "an attack on the status of art in bourgeois society. What is negated is not an earlier form of art (a style) but art as an institution that is unassociated with the life praxis of men."[76] Operating from this definition, he labels Dadaism, which arose during the First World War, as a "true" avant-garde movement that later coalesced into other movements that had a more radical political slant. Bürger thus reveals the connection between a work of art and history – something that he believes actually began with Dadaism rather than in the late nineteenth century (as implied by many Western art historians).[77] His theoretical statements do not apply neatly to every aspect of the avant-garde in the Japanese context, but they are useful as a theoretical framework for a general discussion.[78] In Japan, Dadaism can be viewed as a radical precursor to a more obviously avant-garde surrealism. However, because the revolutionary poet Takahashi Shinkichi (1901-87) and, to some extent, Tsuji Jun were its sole practitioners, its importance stems not from its strength as a movement but, rather, from its experimental attack on the nature of poetics and its ability to inspire later avant-garde expressions of poetry.[79] In applying Williams's and Bürger's theories, I also differentiate the Japanese avant-garde from practitioners of modernism in terms of their radical social (or political) engagement with the masses.

I concur with Williams's premise that modernism is inextricably linked to imperialism, with the avant-garde as its radical offshoot. Hewitt further develops Bürger's ideas, viewing the avant-garde as an outgrowth of modernism and, like Williams, situating it within the context of imperialism. In addition, according to his study of the Italian Futurist poet Filippo Tommaso Marinetti (1876-1944), Hewitt posits that, "imperialism ... implies an aesthetic of transgression and incompletion, an aesthetic of the avant-garde."[80] Marinetti, like the individuals whom I investigate, was an avant-garde cultural producer who later supported fascism – maintaining the aesthetic formalism of the avant-garde (modernism) while professing (or supporting) a radically different politics. Hewitt argues that, in their works, the European avant-garde, initially including Marinetti, communicated the existence of the "simultaneity of the radically disparate," where contradictory aesthetic forms and political thought coincided in a volatile suspension: for example, left-wing and right-wing versions of socialism (Marxism and fascism), or proletarian and bourgeois arts and politics.[81] I find that this characterization of the avant-garde as promoting an aesthetic that highlights this "simultaneity" is especially relevant to my discussion not only of Japanese avant-garde production before 1931 but also of Japanese cultural producers who depicted Manchukuo after 1932 (regardless of their politics).[82] In the imperial context of Japan and Manchukuo, global trends and ideas entered the marketplace relatively quickly due to the rapid, though often uneven, pace of development. Arguably, the European and Japanese avant-garde both emerged as a response to the depredations of imperialism and its corresponding rhetoric of modernity and progress.[83] In Japan, the historical context of modernism and the avant-garde was directly affected by imperialism's transformation of the domestic cultural and political landscapes.

Like Japanese art historian and curator Mizusawa Tsutomu, Williams believes that the avant-garde can be categorized as a series of movements dating from around 1910 into the late 1930s.[84] However, for the Japanese context, I adopt Bürger's definition of the avant-garde as a literary/artistic "movement," with a generally left-oriented politics critical of mainstream society/culture, that views itself as rebelling against the bourgeois values that made art into a status-based institution. In defining the advent of a Japanese avant-garde, scholars in Japan (such as Wada Hirofumi) view this moment as arising after the 1923 Kantô Earthquake and, like Bürger, point to a left-oriented politics sympathetic to Marxism as one of its determining factors.[85] I also contrast the avant-garde with practitioners of modernism, who might have expressed either a left- or a right-wing aesthetics or who did not follow a distinct political orientation.

As noted by North American scholars, including Miryam Sas and William Gardner,[86] Japanese modernism and avant-garde movements should not be viewed as miming, or as derivative of, their European counterparts. Gennifer Weisenfeld refers to the MAVO group as "a Japanese manifestation of a worldwide avant-garde movement in the visual arts in the 1920s."[87] Wada concurs with her but sees the avant-garde as originating in poetry in the early 1920s, with a post-earthquake efflorescence of other avant-garde forms that engaged in a more radical politics.[88] Due to the global scale of transnational trade and political interactions in the post-First World War era, it is difficult to assign an authentic locus or specific time for any one avant-garde movement, though many began in Europe and their ideas soon diffused to places like Japan and even Dairen. Current works on Japanese modernism and the avant-garde in the interwar period, including mine, focus on the unique social and political realities present in domestic Japan, as well as in colonial outposts of the Japanese Empire, like Dairen, and examine how they affected cultural production. Gardner, for example, views the emergence of Japanese modernism in its own socio-historical context: "While certainly inspired by Western avant-gardes, [it] developed and attained meaning in relation to domestic practices and institutions that, although also partly appropriated from the West, had already established their own shape and trajectory in Japan."[89]

Moreover, because the term *zen'ei,* or "avant-garde," was not in common use in Japan until the 1920s (when it usually referred to artists), it appears, somewhat anachronistically, in the contemporary period. For example, art historian John Clark identifies three moments that he believes define the artistic subjectivity of the avant-garde in Japan: "The inception of avant-garde groups from around 1910 to 1914; the social positioning of artists and art objects of the Dada and Proletarian Art movements from 1920 to 1934; and the rise of Surrealism and abstract art as a permitted, tacitly anti-establishment practice from 1929 to 1941."[90] However, according to Tanaka Atsushi, the artist, theorist, and poet Kanbara Tai (1898-1997) first used the term in April 1923 in his "*Action* Members Declaration" for the catalogue of the first exhibition of the Action group, composed of the anti-art establishment members of *Nika-kai* (Second Section).[91] Thus, in Japan, the term *zen'ei* was originally applied to avant-garde art in the Taishô period (1912-26) as a direct translation of the French word for "advance guard," which is the military terminology that was once employed to describe the mid-nineteenth-century social, political, and cultural revolution in France.[92] Therefore, in the French context, the original term harboured connotations of progress and radical change, and this was expressed in the arts as a measure of advanced civilization.[93] This places the historical meaning of "avant-garde" squarely within a discourse linking socio-political events to cultural production. And this, I argue, was the case in Imperial Japan.

However, Japanese writers and literary groups only rarely used the term "avant-garde" to describe themselves. Indeed, it became more common in Japan in the late 1920s – possibly due to the influence of an increasingly porous and interdisciplinary art world – and acquired a radical, left-wing political currency. One example of its expansion into generalized left-wing cultural production involves the publication *Zen'ei* (in this context, best translated as *Vanguard*), Yamada's left-wing magazine dedicated to the proletarian arts. Therefore, in scholarly studies investigating literary production in 1920s and 1930s Japan, terms such as "avant-garde," "modernism," and "modernist" have, with few exceptions, been applied retrospectively.[94] This is also the case in the Manchukuo context.

Like Williams, I view the (Japanese) avant-garde as a subset of (Japanese) modernism in the late 1920s to early 1930s, with the proletarian literature and proletarian arts movements (represented by Yamada) and surrealism (practised by Ai Mitsu, Fukuzawa, and Kawabata in his early career) as avant-garde forms of literary and artistic production that fit the radical political nature of Bürger's definition. Using Hewitt's notion of an avant-garde connection to imperialism through the "simultaneity of the radically disparate," I argue that the avant-garde in Japan was well suited to an aesthetic of imperialism. While I am not implying a fundamental opposition between the literary/artistic works of the Japanese avant-garde in the interwar period and the modernists during wartime, I view politics and culture as being in a discursive and dialogic relationship. This continued to be true in Manchukuo; however, after 1932, these writers and artists were producing in a right-wing, fascist context, which, intriguingly, allowed for mild critique and equivocation. Yet, as I argue in the following chapters, their works also supported a fascist regime and, thus, were no longer politically oppositional in character.

In Manchukuo, art and literature support a right-wing version of radical politics, which, according to Hewitt's and Williams's definitions, continues to be modernist. Meanwhile, what Tansman calls an "aesthetic of fascism" (see Chapter 3) also begins to develop.[95] However, does the avant-garde *have* to be left-wing? Bürger implies that it does, while Hewitt suggests that it does not. I interpret these Japanese intellectuals who once belonged to the avant-garde as maintaining a certain continuity with their earlier aesthetic and literary styles while, at the same time, following a very different politics – one that is (tacitly or overtly) supportive of Japanese imperialism, the Manchukuo state, and wartime Japan. In what follows, I focus on the cultural production of these formerly avant-garde or left-wing Japanese writers, artists, and photographers, who jointly portrayed the new state in modernist imagery that retained many of the antecedents of their earlier "avant-garde" moment.

The 1931 Manchurian Incident sparked renewed interest in Manchuria among the avant-garde. However, back in domestic Japan, in the wake of the March 1928 mass arrests of individuals suspected of supporting communism and the Manchurian Incident, attacks on the left continued after the Japanese state intensified its surveillance over Marxists and socialists through the increased censorship of cultural production.[96] Moreover, the ensuing emphasis on national unity in the Japanese press branded these people as "dissidents"; therefore, support of the Manchurian project became a convenient way for Japanese intellectuals to recant their political ideals and to exert them in a different and, ironically, freer context. Converted former left-wing Japanese intellectuals like Yamada and avant-garde cultural producers like Fukuzawa and Fuchikami thus distanced themselves from their erstwhile interest in Marxism and became integral to the construction of a constellation of popular modernist myths about Manchuria.

Kantô Army officials like Ishiwara, in fact, welcomed these political converts to Manchukuo to work in the SMRC research department and other state organizations, as long as they geared their socialism toward cultural, economic, and/or social science-oriented endeavours. Their writings and images reveal an intriguing conjunction between the new state of Manchukuo and an older, romanticized notion of *Manshû* (Manchuria), inspired by earlier accounts of SMRC-funded observers of Japanese development in that region. The impressions of Japanese observers like Sôseki and even Itô had led to stereotypical conceptions of the region based on the rhetoric of modernization and development. Their works juxtapose a Japanese-led civilization with an elemental Chinese backwardness. They depict run-down, exoticized Chinese areas in contrast to efficient Japanese cities that exude order and organization (long symbolized by SMRC).

After 1932, the term *Manshû* is ubiquitous in all kinds of printed materials and literary journals such as *Manshû roman (Manchuria Romance),* 1937-44.[97] Thus, *Manshû* became a virtual blank space for the projection of idea(l)s and utopian forms of modernity not realizable in Japan. And this is where the original avant-garde project of social reform begins to intersect with the Japanese state's fascist agenda for Manchukuo. In the title of this book, I put "avant-garde" in quotes because the modernist form of these artists' representations remained continuous, while their radical political agenda did not. Thus, the following chapters address Japanese cultural producers who discuss Manchukuo in works that could easily be defined as "informal," or what I refer to as "avant-garde," propaganda.

Because of earlier persecution for their political beliefs, former resistance to the imperialist project, or suspected sympathy for the working classes in Japan, the individuals I discuss were apt to accept the Manchukuo tour/sojourn and then enthusiastically depict the new state as part of the *tenkô* (political conversion) experience. Though their accounts were not always positive, they left a compelling literary or visual narrative of what drew them to participate in the attempt to create a new culture for a utopian state under Japanese auspices.

2
Literature in Service of the State: Yamada Seizaburô and Right-Wing Proletarianism, 1931-43

This chapter investigates Yamada Seizaburô as an example of how a prominent, formerly left-wing intellectual became involved in the construction of a new culture in Manchukuo. His 1943 text *Manshûkoku bunka kensetsuron (Discourse on the Construction of Culture in Manchukuo)* encapsulates his ideas on culture, but his efforts to stimulate a thriving literary culture and multiethnic literature began in 1940. In the late 1930s, Yamada's successful "conversion" from being a former left-wing writer and proponent of proletarian literature to being a supporter of Imperial Japan and Manchukuo provided a template for others to follow. The writer's reflections offer compelling reasons for why so many left-oriented Japanese intellectuals were attracted to producing cultural narratives in support of the Manchukuo project.

Even prior to Manchukuo's 1932 establishment, Manchuria was an important venue for Japan's culture wars of the late 1920s and early 1930s. According to Prasenjit Duara, Japan used culture to disembed "the project of national homogenization from race and its associations with imperialism ... culture introduced a paradigm of voluntarism (at least in theory) for the process of assimilation and homogenization."[1] Envisioned as a "blank slate" incorporating cosmopolitan versions of modernism alongside nativist impulses, this region attracted adherents of all political stripes, including right-wing extremists as well as those fleeing political persecution in Japan. Louise Young notes how "the vision of social transformation in Manchuria became a kind of magnet for displaced Japanese revolutionaries. Frustrated by the increasingly repressive atmosphere within Japan, left-wing intellectuals were drawn by opportunities for social activism in the new empire."[2] The main reason the region and its Japanese-led regime were so compelling to disgraced leftists like Yamada was that it offered them a renewed sense of personal agency. Young also asserts that the new state stimulated their careerism and inspired grandiose dreams: "Proximity to the absolute power of the colonial state did not corrupt the leftists or lead them astray from the righteous path of revolution. Instead, it nurtured delusions of grandeur."[3]

Although Yamada was somewhat chastened by his three-and-a-half-year imprisonment and subsequent *tenkô* experience, he was warmly welcomed by Manchukuo's state planners, who provided him with unprecedented opportunities to exercise his talents. His aims, pursued in service of the state, maintained some continuity with his earlier political beliefs. In effect, they constituted a new type of political ideology specific to many converted Japanese who came to Manchukuo – an ideology that I refer to as "right-wing proletarianism." Indeed, the wartime period made Yamada even more prolific, thanks to the frequent trips he took throughout China in the early 1940s. This increased travel within Japanese-occupied China had an invigorating effect on Yamada, and he seemed to envision himself as a kind of Japanese Lu Xun (1881-1936), viewing Manchukuo as a cultural template first for the Chinese and then for the newly conquered multi-ethnic areas of Southeast Asia.

Manchuria, Manchukuo, and the Early Shôwa Political and Intellectual Climate[4]

In order to better understand Yamada's intriguing career trajectory, we must first examine the intellectual and political climate of interwar Japan. In the critical time period of the late 1920s and 1930s, when Yamada developed into an earnest left-wing writer, cultural historian Minami Hiroshi asserts that, in Japan, domestic events and foreign affairs became inextricably linked.[5] Concurrently, Japanese intellectuals at both ends of the political spectrum increasingly envisioned Manchuria as a utopian hope for the future of a domestic Japan in crisis. Several developments led to such views.

Domestically, a series of bank failures and the ensuing fall of the Wakatsuki cabinet sparked economic depression in 1927 – two years earlier than the global Great Depression.[6] The consequent consolidation of medium-sized businesses into cartels under the principle of *gôrika* (rationalization) spurred the growth of pro-expansionist *zaibatsu,* which mechanized their workers through Taylorism and the Fordist assembly line in Japan and the colonies. In Japanese cities, strikes became frequent phenomena, and tenant unrest marked the blighted countryside. Though steps toward democracy and popular representation progressed throughout the Taishô (1912-26) and early Shôwa (1926-89) periods, the authoritarian apparatus of the Meiji state was still very much in control of Japanese subjects and their discontents. As a result, the 1925 universal manhood suffrage law, actualized in the 1928 election, was tempered by the *Chian iji hô* (Peace Preservation Law) of the same year, whose subsequent revision in 1928 promulgated the death penalty for crimes against the state.

In foreign affairs from 1927 onwards, the Japanese government under Tanaka Gi'ichi pursued a proactive foreign policy that discarded the peaceful internationalism of the post-First World War era and early 1920s and, instead, colluded with the army, politicians, and capitalists who favoured imperial expansion in Manchuria and on the continent. In the years leading up to the 1931 Manchurian Incident, Japanese policies toward Manchuria became more overtly imperialist in terms of legislation and military policy, in contrast to the former "informal imperialism" of furthering economic interests in the region. In Japan, these domestic and foreign economic or political changes combined with a turbulent intellectual climate to form the backdrop to Manchukuo's incipient creation.

The late 1920s and 1930s of the early Shôwa period also saw a growing critique of modernity on the part of Japanese intellectuals of diverse political orientations who witnessed the upheaval and dislocations caused by Japan's rapid, forced modernization.[7] They also noted how their government increasingly promoted imperial expansion on the continent and in Manchuria in order to ensure domestic unity and economic prosperity. Both left-wing and right-wing groups not only became concerned with domestic social issues but also offered differing opinions on how control over Manchuria might affect them. Adherents of left-wing socialism asserted that artistic and literary expression could change their world, while right-wing groups advocated violent action and immediate military engagement in Manchuria. For intellectuals of both political viewpoints, this time period was marked by apprehension about the social problems generated by state-sponsored capitalism, and many debated what role the Japanese state should play in developing Manchuria. It was this intellectual climate that led Yamada to become more deeply involved in questions concerning his country's future.

In the late 1920s, while literary surrealism gained momentum in Japan,[8] adherents of the proletarian literature and proletarian arts movements stimulated and organized a left-wing intellectual critique of Japanese society and imperialism through groups like *Nappu* (NAPF, or *Nippona Artista Proleta Federacio* [Esperanto]), which was founded in March 1928 (following the mass arrests of leftists on 15 March), as well as the *Nihon puroretaria sakka dômei* (NALP, or the Japan Proletarian Writers League). Left-wing activists strongly believed in literature as a means of effecting social change; consequently, by 1930, for many intellectuals proletarian literature became one of the most popular forms of literary expression.[9] In this year, Yamada published *Nihon puroretaria bungei undô shi (A History of the Japanese Proletarian Literature and Arts Movements)*.[10] In 1931, he also published *Nihon puroretaria bungei riron no hatten (The Development of the Theory of Japanese Proletarian Literature and Arts),* which features theoretical discourse related to the proletarian arts.[11] Later in the same year, NAPF was renamed *Koppu* (KOPF, or *Federacio de Proletaj Kultur-organizoj Japanaj*), replacing the term "arts" with the more inclusive term "culture."[12] The fact that the movement developed its own self-proclaimed proletarian culture, which merited the publication of two books on its history and theory, indicates that it had successfully entered Japanese intellectual consciousness.

Moreover, the possibility of changing society through a cultural movement very much appealed to Yamada and his leftist associates. In 1932, despite having been arrested in the previous year for violating the Peace Preservation Law, Yamada joined with Akita Ujaku (1883-1962) to publish *Bunka undô-shi (A History of Cultural Movements)*.[13] Inspired by socialist ideals and Leon Trotsky's (1879-1940) and Vladimir Lenin's (1870-1924) essays on literature and revolution, writers and activists such as Yamada, Nakano Shigeharu (1902-79), Kobayashi Takiji (1903-33), Sata Ineko (1904-98), Tokunaga Sunao (1899-1958), and Kitagawa Fuyuhiko believed they could change social consciousness through their literary efforts, which were aimed at reforming a culture that no longer served the people. (Even after his political conversion several years later, Yamada continued to believe it was possible to realize these ideals, albeit in a different political context – the fascist space of Manchukuo.)

In 1928, after Yamada helped found NAPF, under his editorship the magazine *Senki (Battle Flag)* became (along with other, smaller journals) the main venue of organized literary expression for adherents of the proletarian literature and proletarian arts movements. Prior to this, Yamada served as editor of *Bungei sensen (Literary Front)*. However, in 1927, he left with, among others, the novelist Hayashi Fusao (1903-75) and the constructivist artist Murayama Tomoyoshi (1901-77) to found the *Zen'ei geijutsu-ka dômei* (Federation of Avant-Garde Artists).[14] Following *Senki,* NAPF's new journal, called *Nappu,* also published proletarian literary works. However, by 1930, many writers also published in what Gregory Kasza calls "integrative magazines" like *Chûô kôron (Central Review)* and *Kaizô (Reconstruction)*.[15] Having attained an immense popular success, proletarian writers thus became the dominant force in major Japanese journals and magazines that combined "political and social criticism, literary contributions, and neutral reportage."[16] Writers like Nakano and Kuroshima Denji (1898-1943) showcased issues relating to strikes and self-determination movements in Korea and colonized parts of China, while Tokunaga and Sata described the daily life and mundane struggles of domestic Japan's working class. In these same publications, after Japan's proletarian movements had been crushed, Yamada would become renowned for his descriptions of Japanese-led rural cooperative schemes in Manchukuo. In the works of proletarian writers like Yamada, Kitagawa, and others, Manchuria/Manchukuo served as a place to critique Japanese capitalism and to achieve political and/or developmental aims that had failed in domestic Japan.[17]

However, despite its initial success, this popular movement soon encountered several challenges that led to its dissolution by the mid-1930s. These included an internal struggle over whether to adhere to Soviet-led Comintern directives or to take a path more suitable to Japan. In addition, the government's 1928-29 mass arrests of socialists in Tokyo generated a diffuse climate of political repression against left-wing intellectuals who espoused socialist and communist ideals. Against this background of suppression and the Japanese government's turn toward fascism, the 1931 Manchurian Incident initiated a wave of political conversions that would peak two years later. Moreover, on 8 June 1933, two Communist Party leaders, Sano Manabu (1892-1953) and Nabeyama Sadachika (1901-79), issued the *Kyôdô hikoku dôshi ni tsuguru sho* (Letter to Inform Our Fellow Accused Comrades), sparking the *tenkô* phenomenon, which saw 70 percent of all imprisoned communists renounce their affiliation, with most others soon following suit.[18] This incident profoundly affected the now struggling proletarian literature and proletarian arts movements.

By February 1934, the Japan Proletarian Writers' League disbanded, with writers soon engaging in what Hasegawa Izumi calls "*tenkô* literature," in which formerly leftist intellectuals distanced themselves from their earlier political affiliations.[19] Citing Honda Shûgo, Keene estimates that – haunted by police persecution, the hounding of their families, and Takiji's 1933 murder in police custody – 95 percent of all socialists, communists, and left-wing intellectuals recanted their beliefs.[20] In addition, factionalism and suspicions of embedded police informants plagued the last year of the communist party's existence before it disbanded in 1935. For example, on 23 December 1933, Miyamoto Kenji (1908-2007) and his allies attacked Oizumi Kenzô and Obata Tatsuo after suspecting they had betrayed a fellow comrade, Noro Eitarô, to the police. Working on principles, Miyamoto and his group lured Oizumi and Obata into a trap and brutally cross-examined them where only Oizumi escaped alive due to his confession. Obata was buried under the floorboards to hide the evidence, but the story soon came to light in the press as the "Red Lynching."[21] Two other party members were tortured and killed in February 1934, and by 1935, the communist movement finally dissolved. Moreover, after the eruption of the Sino-Japanese conflict and the initiation of the total war system, Yamada himself published his *Jigo zange (Personal Confessions)* in 1938 following his imprisonment.[22]

In the 1930s, many converted socialist writers, including Yamada and the avant-garde poet and former Dadaist Nogawa Takashi (1901-44), went into exile in Manchukuo, where, until the early 1940s, repression of Japanese nationals was less severe than in domestic Japan. Under Ishiwara's relatively liberal policies, Manchukuo, curiously enough, became a safe haven for both left-wing activists and right-wing extremists, including those involved in literary and artistic production.[23] Ishiwara welcomed converted communists and socialists (as well as militarists) from the Japanese archipelago who joined organizations like SMRC's *Mantetsu chôsabu* (SMRC research department), the Concordia Association, or the *Manshû eiga kai* (Manchurian Film Association) headed by the notorious former Tokyo police chief Amakasu Masahiko (1891-1945).[24] Their works, which were published in domestic Japan, served to showcase the success of Japanese development and cultural influence in Manchukuo.

Kawamura Minato asserts that, especially for left-wing writers or artists, the trip to Manchukuo and its subsequent depiction in various media was equivalent to a renunciation of communism and socialist ideals – that is, *tenkô* – as a show of support for the imperial regime based in domestic Japan.[25] The experience of *tenkô* changed the political meaning of, and motivation for, their work, especially in the context of their impressions of the new state.[26] For example, after his political conversion, Yamada encapsulated his ideas for Manchukuo culture in his 1943 text, *Manshûkoku bunka kensetsuron,* in which he envisioned a utopian space in which a multi-ethnic culture could arise through mutual cooperation with the Japanese.[27] After undergoing at least a nominal political conversion and witnessing the establishment and subsequent development of Manchukuo, Japanese intellectuals expressed increasingly utopian ideas about colonized labour and rural peasants (e.g., see Yamada's and Nogawa's writings as well as those of Shimaki Kensaku [1903-45]).

Formerly proletarian and/or avant-garde writers such as Yamada, Tokunaga, Shimaki, Haruyama Yukio, Hayashi Fumiko (1904-51), and Kawabata were enlisted to depict Japan's attempt to fashion a new state out of the Manchurian space. These writers, as well as avant-garde photographers such as Fuchikami Hakuyô (1889-1960) and Kimura Ihei (1901-74), were invited by various media organizations, ranging from Manchukuo government associations to SMRC's publicity department to local and regional Japanese-language newspapers. Interestingly, many of their accounts and photographic images continued to use socialist realism (or even surrealism) to portray Chinese workers, Chinese cultural customs, and the lives of Manchukuo's lower classes. While these writers and artists often depicted proletarian subjects and labour, the political import of their work changed in that it began to depict the working classes as actively participating in stimulating Manchukuo's development, thus supporting Japan's imperial project.

However, by the late 1930s, critiques other than those of former socialists and communists had also emerged in relation to Japanese imperialism and the massive economic, political, social, and cultural transformations that had occurred in Japan in mere decades. Permeating debates on both the left and the right was an uneasy acceptance of modernization and a desire to divest it from the grip of the West. Conservative literary critics such as Kobayashi Hideo (1902-83) mourned the loss of connection to one's hometown due to urbanization and its concomitant atomization of human relations, while the ethnologist Yanagita Kunio (1875-1962) yearned for a return to Japanese traditions in order to recover a primeval past untouched by the ravages of a predominantly Western modernity.

A similar yearning for an essentialized nativism appeared in the works of the *Roman-ha* (Romantic Group) writers, whose literary offshoots were also active in Manchukuo. For example, as a member of this group, Kitamura Kenjirô (1904-82) came to Manchukuo and helped initiate the *Manshû roman (Manchuria Romance)* literary journal.[28] His writings later appeared in a 1940 short story collection edited by Yamada, as well as in two editions of Manchurian literature that he co-edited with Yamada and Kawabata in 1942 and 1944, respectively.[29] Yamada, despite his earlier left-wing inclinations, served along with Kitamura and the former proletarian writer Shimaki as co-editors of these collections. The Manchurian space allowed these writers to realize dreams that had failed in Japan.

In contrast to left-wing Japanese intellectuals, who limited the expression of their concerns to the written page, right-wing extremists often used violence to critique capitalism, modernity, and the aims of Japanese imperialism, for example, in the form of officers' rebellions and political assassinations in the spirit of Saigô Takamori (1827-77). Elise Tipton believes that, in the early Shôwa period, discontent at both ends of the political spectrum was "the result of dissatisfaction with industrialization and its sociopolitical consequences. Both represented attempts to solve social and economic problems arising at the end of the First World War which were seen to be the consequence of modernization and the development of capitalism."[30] Echoing the intellectuals involved in the proletarian literature and proletarian arts movements, right-wing extremists blamed big government, big business, and the imitation of Western societies for Japan's rural crisis, which was manifesting itself alongside increasing urbanization and social dislocation.[31] Yet, in contrast to leftists, who supported colonial self-determination, rightists favoured military engagement in Manchuria and complete Japanese control over the region in order to further domestic economic interests and to prevent the encroachment of Soviet communism.

The militarist proponents of this political philosophy were responsible for manufacturing the bloody political events of the early 1930s, including the 1931 Manchurian Incident, the 1932 assassination of Prime Minister Inukai Tsuyoshi (heralding the end of party rule), and the 1936 Young Officers' Revolt led by the right-wing national socialist theorist Kita Ikki. Inukai's murder silenced the last vestige of "Taishô democracy" and marked the beginning of joint military and bureaucratic rule. From Inukai's death until the end of the Second World War, Japanese prime ministers ceased to come from civilian backgrounds and were connected either to the military or to the imperial family. Thereafter, young right-wing military officers fanned the flames of nationalism and advocated a proactive imperialistic policy toward Manchuria, which had been viewed as Japan's *seimeisen* since the end of the First World War and was now seen as an outlet for the archipelago's domestic problems.

Increasingly, the political climate of the early Shôwa period was marked by a struggle between these left- and right-wing interpretations of socialism; however, in Manchukuo, it was a right-wing political vision of Manchuria that eventually prevailed. According to Kobayashi Hideo, much of Manchukuo's political and economic structure was based on a socialist form of organization similar to that found in Kita's right-wing interpretations, which inherently served to support Imperial Japan.[32] As noted previously, Manchukuo could even be considered a fascist state after the Italian model. Despite Manchukuo's nominally independent status after 1932, the Japanese government and many intellectuals increasingly viewed the state as an integral part of the Japanese Empire and its cultural endeavours. The changing intellectual climate surrounding these historical developments provides the background for the Japanese-led establishment of Manchukuo and serves to illustrate some of the underlying reasons for a growing Japanese interest in its attractions.

The Expansion of Japanese Culture in Manchukuo's Modernist Utopia

The Japanese government had long viewed Manchuria as a critical part of the Japanese Empire not only for economic reasons but also because it symbolized the strength of Japan's civilizing mission and cultural dominance within the framework of modernization and, later, paternalistic Pan-Asianism. Until the Manchurian Incident, Manchuria's economic, military, and cultural ties to Japan through SMRC, the Kantô Army's connections to the Japanese military, and peripatetic colonial settlers ensured that the region remained firmly entrenched in the Imperial Japanese cultural sphere. For nearly three decades, the narratives of visiting Japanese intellectuals supported the spread of Japanese economic development and cultural rhetoric in Manchuria. This trend continued into the Manchukuo period as writers' and artists' depictions of the new state evolved along with the goals of Imperial Japan.

From the 1930s onwards, in various media, Japanese cultural producers created works that depicted Manchukuo's relationship to domestic Japan as culturally crucial. Citing Yano Torû, Faye Yuan Kleeman characterizes "the 1930s as the turning point for this shift from a commercial, entrepreneurial approach toward the colonies to a politicized, imperialistic approach," which, she argues, also had an impact on Japanese literature.[33] The Japanese government, as well as its client regime in Manchukuo, made great efforts to create for the new state a separate culture with its own individual character. Yet, this attempt to emphasize cultural independence and uniqueness could be achieved only partially. This was because, officially, Manchukuo was promoted as an integral part of Imperial Japan's cultural sphere and, thus, as representing the success of Japanese cultural and political guidance. Visiting domestic Japanese writers, photographers, and artists sponsored by the SMRC conglomerate and, increasingly, by Manchukuo government organizations ensured this by producing various writings, photographic collections, and paintings, all of which represented the new state in a positive light.

Through culture, Manchukuo soon came to symbolize the successful political initiatives of Imperial Japan, while cultural producers like Yamada and others concerned themselves with "finding in Manchuria a frontier where they could realize a vision that many considered impossible to achieve in the established society of Japan."[34] It is against this epistemological backdrop that visiting intellectuals from domestic Japan used Manchuria as a utopian canvas for the depiction of a Japanese-led East-Asian modernity sustained by traditional Confucian principles. Louise Young notes that the tour of Manchuria, and later Manchukuo, served as a form of "cultural legitimation of those who aspired to the high arts."[35] Thus, not surprisingly, the region and new state were subsumed within the imperial project of the Japanese nation – with the arts as an important component. According to Prasenjit Duara: "As a national *idea,* Manchukuo was predictably weak, because the commitment of its makers to independence from Japan was weak and variable."[36] Clearly, Manchukuo could not have survived for almost fifteen years without, on the one hand, the sustained aid of the onsite SMRC,[37] and, on the other, the leadership of local Chinese elites who chose to collaborate with the Japanese.[38] Moreover, its central political infrastructure was based on a Japanese model under Japanese guidance from Tokyo. This was also the case with the multi-ethnic culture and literature: these were superimposed on Manchukuo by Japan through visiting and/or sojourning intellectuals like Yamada, Kitamura, and Kawabata, whose purpose was to expand the Japanese cultural sphere.

Young notes how, in the 1930s, such "unofficial propagandists" generated interest in the region, and in the subsequent new state, through a "cultural deluge" of media: "Books, magazines, movies, records, and other forms of popular entertainment took the sense of national crisis primed by the press and radio, and infused it with the boisterousness of a carnival."[39] In other words, informal media showcased Manchukuo to both Japanese and Western audiences, advertising its legitimacy both at home and abroad. One example of this is the photographic collection *Manchukuo: A Pictorial Record,* published for a bilingual English and Japanese readership by the prominent Tokyo daily, *Asahi Shimbun*. In its foreword, the 1934 edition states grandiloquently: "This volume of photographs may justifiably be said to enjoy the distinction of representing *the first attempt yet made either in Japan or abroad to portray the life of the Manchukuo people in all its phases without the slightest tinge of political bias.*"[40] These now quaint-sounding captions describe images of "Manchurians" (usually Han Chinese) of all social classes going about their daily lives, benefiting from the regime's peaceful rule, which ensured prosperity for all. A prostitute thus becomes "an attractive young Manchu employed as a professional entertainer like the geisha in Japan,"[41] and an intellectual displaying his well-appointed traditional home becomes "a member of the Manchukuo intelligentsia *voluntarily posing* for a picture with his wife and two children in front of the entrance to his courtyard."[42] The volume satisfied readers' curiosity about Manchukuo while informally supporting the state's ideal of a utopian society free of class conflict or other social problems.

Thus, in this pictorial published by a leading newspaper of the imperial metropole, all Manchurians are depicted as happy, well-cared-for subjects living in an ultramodern urban environment in which each person fulfills a role as a productive member of the new state.[43] Photographs featuring robust rural natives cheerfully displaying their local customs also appear in this collection, communicating a prevailing impression of peace and prosperity under a Japanese-led administration, whether in the cities or in the countryside. Taking advantage of the media hype surrounding Manchukuo, several publications portrayed a similar vision that appealed to many, including former left-wing intellectuals in Japan.

Yet, the question remains: Why did domestic news organizations like the Tokyo-based *Asahi Shimbun* newspaper, the Japanese handlers of the Manchukuo experiment, and SMRC devote so much financial and intellectual capital to depicting the new state and its culture to audiences in the archipelago and abroad? How did Yamada, through his initial journalistic activities for the *Manshû Shimbun (Manchuria News)* in the late 1930s, become actively involved in collaborating with the regime to describe, and then to help create, a uniquely "Manchurian" culture? A clue can be found in Homi Bhabha's characterization of "nations as narrations," which explains a state's need, in its infancy, to continuously reiterate its (fictive) history as this is how (through continuous self-definition) it comes to authenticate itself.[44] This can be further explained by the process of transculturation, which Mary Louise Pratt claims is an unavoidable offshoot of the imperialist project.[45] I argue that this also pertains to Japan's official stance toward Manchukuo as well as to the efforts of intellectuals like Yamada, who supported the utopian aims of the new state through their cultural initiatives. The sheer volume of Japanese printed materials featuring colonial Manchuria and Manchukuo still found in libraries throughout Japan and the United States attests to the "obsessive need" of the imperial centre to perpetuate the self-narration and compulsive description of its colonial (or semi-colonial) periphery.[46]

Yamada's Support of a New Literary Culture in Manchukuo, 1939-41

After nearly three and a half years of imprisonment for his left-wing activism as part of the proletarian literature and proletarian arts movements, Yamada was finally released in February 1938. The writer completed his *tenkô* process with the publication of his confession *Jigo zange,* which appeared in the same year. His subsequent trip to Manchukuo in April 1939, and his initial employment as a journalist with a state-run newspaper, served to provide him with a further means of proving his loyalty to Imperial Japan. Yamada would remain in Manchukuo for over six years, developing *Manshû bungaku* (Manchurian literature) by working with Han Chinese writers and detailing Japanese rural development initiatives. Eventually, in August 1945, he was taken prisoner by invading Soviets.

Undoubtedly, Yamada's new role had been intricately planned by state propaganda organizations, with much Kantô Army collusion. Scholars like Mark Peattie characterize the Manchukuo regime as "military fascist," with many of the state's decisions emanating from the Kantô Army.[47] Former Manchukuo propaganda chief Mutô Tomio (1904-98), in his 1988 revisionist memoir *Watakushi to Manshûkoku (Manchukuo and Me),* notes that any journalist hired by a newspaper in the new state first had to receive his permission through the Manchukuo Publicity and News Bureau, and then he (Mutô) had to seek final approval from the General Affairs Board and the *Kantô gun dai yokka* (Kantô Army's Fourth Section).[48] This was the case for both Yamada, who was appointed in 1939, and Kawabata, who was invited in the early 1940s and whose tours were sponsored by the *Manchukuo Daily News* as well as by the Kantô Army. In another example, even before SMRC recruited the photographer Fuchikami to edit its *Manshû gurafu* pictorial in 1933, the Kantô Army hired him to work on technical aspects of propaganda for the 1932 establishment of Manchukuo. Indeed, the Kantô Army made many of the state's decisions regarding who should be invited to Manchukuo, thus influencing how it would be portrayed.[49]

The Kantô Army headed up the state's hierarchical propaganda apparatus, and it made final decisions even on matters related to the hiring of journalists. According to Yamamoto Taketoshi, the review process of these important state employees intensified after 1937 and became even more stringent in late 1941 following the eruption of the Pacific War.[50] Imperial Japan's wartime needs soon necessitated the closer integration of Manchukuo's propaganda and cultural initiatives with those of domestic Japan: loyalty to the regime and the propagation of its ideals were essential. Clearly, Ishiwara and the Kantô Army made a conscious decision to invite a rehabilitated Yamada to Manchukuo to write for *Manshû shimbun (Manchuria News)* and later allowed him, through literature, to direct the construction of the state's multi-ethnic culture.

Yamada was an incredibly prolific author on behalf of the Manchukuo regime, professing a right-wing proletarianism that differed from his earlier ideas in that it did not criticize the Japanese Empire and its paternalism toward Chinese and Southeast Asians. Yamada was first attracted to Manchukuo in 1939 by an offer of employment from the *Manshû shimbun,* headquartered in the capital city of Shinkyô. His writings indicate that he only intended to stay six months to a year at most, but he ended up staying years beyond 1940, when he edited his first collection of short stories by multi-ethnic writers.[51] Initially, Yamada worked as a journalist, beginning his reportage at the end of 1939. Interestingly, at that time, he worked for the same media organization whose English-language newspaper *Manchuria* had published a special edition on "Concordia and Culture" in 1938.[52] Clearly, journalists like Yamada helped the state disseminate its ideals and, thus, served as unofficial propagandists.

Wada Hideyoshi, as bureau chief of the *Manshû shimbun,* asked Yamada if he would like to observe the growth of Manchuria's culture, plan cultural exchanges between Japanese and Manchurians, and stay to inspect the conditions of the new state.[53] At the same time, Yamada attended all of the Concordia Association's national conferences, usually held in Shinkyô.[54] These conferences promoted a cultural vision of the state that, in its insistence on harmony, cooperation, and state-sponsored peace and prosperity, much resembled that of Italian fascism. Yamada now felt that he could best contribute to Manchukuo's new (fascist) culture by dedicating his talents to stimulating a new literary culture that would promote the ideals of the Concordia Association.[55] Yamada noted that, while serving as a journalist, and having just viewed the association's deliberations, he decided to compile a short story collection.

Despite his past as a left-wing activist in Japan in the 1930s, Yamada humbly wrote in 1940 that he could still be of use to the new state: "Of course, just because I have 'little strength and no talent,' this should be no reason to not consider what I might be able to contribute. Even so, I still have my work in literature."[56] Yamada's career in fostering multi-ethnic literary pursuits in Manchukuo began in earnest with his 1940 editing of a short story collection by "Manchurian" writers. In his introduction, he describes, in apparently sincere, emotional, and impressionistic language, just how he intends to contribute to the creation of a new, multi-ethnic literary culture:

> "If only I could directly get closer to the writers of each of the races living in this country" – that's what I thought. In this country known as a racially pluralistic nation *[fukugô minzoku kokka],* to mobilize writers of each race in the newspapers, along with introducing them to the wider world, and for each writer of different bloodlines to mutually encourage and compete with each other, will improve the literature of this country; and, if I can to some

> degree contribute my resources to make abundant, multi-faceted, literary results truly suitable to this country – I also considered this. To really sum it up, I am now truly happy ... doing this, being able to publish this short story collection by writers from each race.[57]

Caught up in the emotionalism of what Alan Tansman evocatively calls the "fascist moment,"[58] Yamada revels in an endeavour "in which the individual is depicted as merging with, or is called on to merge imaginatively with, a greater whole."[59]

The volume initially intended to propagate Yamada's mission is entitled *Man Rô zai Man sakka tanpen senshû (Anthology of Short Stories by Manchurian and Russian Authors in Manchuria),* even though four Japanese, two Russians, and only two Han Chinese are listed as authors, with Yamada, of course, contributing the introduction. This early attempt at literary multiculturalism seems to be a primarily Japanese effort, featuring the *Rôman-ha* writer Kitamura Kenjirô's critically acclaimed story "Kinuta" ("Anvil"). However, it also includes selections by two of Manchukuo's most prominent Han Chinese authors from the *Bungei kyôkai* (*Wenyi xiehui,* or Literary Arts Association): Wu Ying (1915-61) contributed the somewhat morose piece "Baigu" ("Bleached Bones"), and Jue Qing penned "Daikan'en" (*Daguan yuan,* literally "Expansive View Garden [Daoist Monastery]").[60]

In the volume's introduction, Yamada notes that he hopes writers of each race will mobilize their literary efforts in newspapers, the primary media organs of the state. However, the serialized publication of short stories in papers and literary journals was characteristic of early Shôwa literary culture in Japan and, thus, was not unique to Manchukuo. By the early twentieth century, famous Japanese journalists, like the *Asahi Shimbun* writer Sôseki, had become some of Japan's most brilliant literary talents. Perhaps, as Young notes, the new state "nurtured delusions of grandeur"[61] in Yamada, who, now entrusted with the important task of building a multi-ethnic literary culture on behalf of Manchukuo, may have viewed himself in a similar vein as Sôseki: as about to achieve renown in the seemingly freer political climate of Manchukuo.

The early 1940s were also a time when Japanese state planners deemed culture of the utmost importance in the development of a thriving multiethnic state that, ultimately, was to serve as a template for other Japanese-occupied areas. Literature became one of the key arenas for the description and development of Manchukuo's unique culture. The March 1941 issuing of the *Geibun shidô yokô (Prospectus for the Guidance of the Arts and Culture)* revealed this deepening trend. In June, a star-studded round-table discussion in Tokyo focused on the *Prospectus,* with Manchukuo propaganda and media chief Mutô Tomio complaining about the lack of specialists and the immaturity of "Manchurian literature."[62] Here, Kawabata, as a renowned Japanese establishment author, designated *Roman-ha* author Kitamura's *Shunren (Spring Festival Couplet)* as a masterpiece – one that Manchurian writers should emulate. Mutô's solution to the need to foster professionals was to have the state create organizations that would scientifically manage the arts (including literature). These organizations would be headed, with the help of Manchurians, by key Japanese figures. Clearly, he had Yamada in mind when he made this statement.

As a now prominent Japanese writer in Manchukuo, Yamada jumped on Mutô's bandwagon on 27 July 1941, when he accepted an invitation to direct the *Manshû bungei-ka kyôkai* (or, in Chinese, *Manzhou wenyi-jia xiehui*) (Manchurian Writers Association). He soon engaged in forming the Manchurian writers under his purview into Mutô's desired "professionals." This Shinkyô-based organization was established after the state's issuing of the *Prospectus,* and its members included Gu Ding (1909-60), Jue Qing, Liang Shanding (1914-95), Wu Lang (1912-57), Wu Ying, Xiao Song (1912), and Yi Chi (1913-unknown).[63] Yamada already knew Wu Ying and Jue Qing as they had contributed to his 1940 story collection. Through working within official Japanese cultural channels, these Han Chinese writers soon rose to become Manchukuo's most prominent authors.[64]

Prior to the much publicized, early 1940s Manchukuo tours taken by literary giants like Kawabata, the state had deemed that Yamada, being a reformed leftist who also appealed to Chinese writers, was valuable for stimulating literary pursuits in Manchukuo. Prominent enough in Japan to have secured strong literary credentials, he served as an important example of an intellectual who could be brought back into the fold to support the sacred mission of wartime Japan.[65]

Yamada's Idealized Writings on Japanese Rural Development, 1940-44

Although Yamada was initially attracted to Manchukuo as a journalist interested in covering the affairs of the Concordia Association, the writings of Shimaki (a former proletarian writer) on Japanese settlers in rural development areas motivated him to engage in his own literary endeavours while fostering Manchurian literature in general. Arriving in 1939 like Yamada, Shimaki came to Manchukuo to inspect Japanese rural settlements and then published *Manshû kikô (Manchurian Travelogue)* in 1940. As Keene notes, "he had been inspired to make this journey by the great interest he had discovered among the farmers, especially in the poverty-stricken northeast, in the possibilities of a more rewarding life in Manchuria."[66] Shimaki presented an idealistic view of settler endeavours and noted that any criticisms of the Manchukuo regime were intended to improve the lives of these Japanese immigrants.[67] This is similar to Yamada's attitude toward the settlements.

Inspired by Shimaki, Yamada spent two months at a village in northern Manchuria comprising Japanese agricultural settlers. In late summer 1940, he published "Kaitaku zuihitsu: Hoshi to niji to" ("Essay on Rural Development: With Stars and Rainbows"), which appeared in *Manshû gurafu,* sandwiched between photographs shot by Fuchikami and his crew showing young Japanese brides lined up for mass weddings at the local shrine in Tetsuryô (Tieli, PRC) and settlers enthusiastically ploughing land planted with cabbages.[68] Yamada's piece in SMRC's propaganda magazine was followed by two volumes, both published in April 1941 (after the state's March cultural reorganization directive): *Kita Man no hito-yo (A Night in Northern Manchuria),* a collection of writings that includes reportage, short stories, and personal impressions;[69] and *Hito-tsubu no come wo ai-suru kokoro (A Spirit That Loves a Grain of Rice),* which focuses on the cultural and spiritual ideals of the Japanese settlers, the development of Manchurian literature and culture, and the wildlife and geographical features of the region.[70]

In 1942, Yamada felt he knew enough about these Japanese-run *kaitaku-chi* (rural development districts) to publish a vaguely nostalgic memoir, *Watakushi no kaitaku-chi shûki [My Memoirs of the Frontier].*[71] Stories in the multi-ethnic literary collections he helped edit, along with Shimaki, in 1942 and 1944 also display a rural focus. Consequently, by the early 1940s, Yamada revealed himself as a prolific author determined to capture the rugged nature of Manchukuo's rural development, which was being carried out by intrepid Japanese farmers. No doubt, their struggles and hardy spirit symbolized the best of Japan's rural proletariat, now made prosperous through their toil as immigrants in the Manchurian region. Thus, Yamada's proletarian utopia was realized not within the realm of domestic Japan's crowded and overly Westernized urban cities but, rather, in the wide-open rural spaces of Japan's Manchuria.

Cultural Construction in Manchukuo, 1943-45

Throughout the early 1940s, Yamada wrote about rural development, helped edit two collections of Manchurian literature, and articulated a cultural framework for Manchukuo. The latter culminated in his 1943 opus *Manshûkoku bunka kensetsuron (Discourse on the Construction of Culture in Manchukuo).*[72] This work outlines Manchukuo's cultural policies, issues related to the life and culture of Manchukuo's (non-Japanese) citizens, the mission of the Japanese and their culture, and the fostering of Manchurian literature and the arts, concluding with Yamada's personal reflections.[73] In the early 1940s, *bunka kensetsu* began to be used as a generic term for Japanese intellectuals eager to profess their loyalty to either Imperial Japan or to its efforts in Manchukuo. For wartime Japan, Manchukuo served both as a space for the realization of ideals not attainable in the archipelago and as a model for nation building in occupied territories in Southeast Asia. This being the case,

Japanese intellectuals soon imported Japan's culture wars into Manchukuo, and the term *bunka* took on a nationalistic tenor that it had lacked in the late 1920s and early 1930s.[74]

It is evident that Yamada's witnessing of the Concordia Association's meetings slowly led him to internalize the ideals of this fascist association. By 1943, we can see that the writer, a former leftist, had become a firm imperialist. In many ways, Yamada's new role represented the success of Ishiwara's *tenkô* program, with one of its important ramifications being his willingness to rehabilitate his career by serving as an ideologue. In his discourse, Manchukuo's culture is based on uniquely East Asian principles arising from a neo-Confucian tradition, of which Japan was the ultimate curator. Such a culture arose from marrying *kyôwa* (harmony) with East Asian modernity in Manchukuo, and potentially, in lands newly assimilated into the Japanese Empire. The moral strength of Japanese rural pioneers, as well as the idealism of Manchukuo's urban Japanese intellectuals, gave Yamada and others hope that Japan could export this vision elsewhere.[75]

Following *Manshûkoku bunka kensetsuron,* Yamada published four volumes of a series entitled *Kenkoku retsuden (A Biography of the Construction of the Country),* with two volumes appearing in May and October 1943, and the last two appearing in July 1944 and March 1945, despite the intensification of the Japanese war effort.[76] This multi-volumed collection detailing Manchukuo's short history appears to link the construction of the country to culture in a physical as well as ideological sense. It presents a classic case of Bhabha's "nation as narration."

To put Yamada's mission of "cultural construction" into a broader East Asian context, it must be noted that, in the spring of 1943, the author spent about forty days travelling in China and even attended the *Chû'Nichi bunka kyôkai dai kai* (Sino-Japanese Culture Association Congress). Yamada hoped to investigate what measures Japan was taking to improve the outlook of the "New China" during the third year commemoration celebration of the establishment of Wang Jingwei's (1883-1944) collaborationist government. This China junket culminated in his August 1944 travel essay, *Shinsei Chûgoku yûki (New China Travelogue),* in which he explicitly argues in favour of integrating Manchukuo and China into a greater cultural sphere.[77] In his introduction, he states: "The New China is filled with the light of hope, the New China has become Manchukuo's and Japan's two wings, and is rising up in the construction of Greater East Asia."[78] Here, intriguingly, the word "construction" appears again, in a kind of mantra that seemingly indicates Yamada's support of the Greater East Asia Co-Prosperity Sphere. Appearing undaunted by reports of the worsening China conflict and growing anti-Japanese resistance movements in Manchukuo, Yamada continued to publish literary collections containing works by authors of the five ethnicities until the last year of the war, an example being *Zai Man sakka shôsetsu-shû:*

Rô Shû (Collection of Novels by Authors in Manchuria: Lao Song), published in January 1944.[79]

Conclusion

When the Russians invaded Manchukuo on 8 August 1945, Yamada remained behind. He was eventually caught by the Soviet military and, as an active collaborator of the Japanese-led Manchukuo regime, spent several years imprisoned in labour camps in the Soviet Union, where he professed his former leftist ideas. However, by 1950, he was able to return safely to Japan, where he continued his literary activities in the postwar period and became a member of the *Shin Nihon bungaku-kai* (New Japan Literature Association).[80] Yamada's sojourn in Manchukuo would continue to haunt him in the postwar years, leading him to pen his 1958 work of self-reflections entitled, *Tenkô-ki: Hyôsetsu no jidai (Record of a Political Conversion: Period of Ice and Snow [Purification]).*[81] Nearly two decades later, one of his pieces was published posthumously, thus evincing a further sense of expiation suitable to the postwar climate.

Before his death, Yamada became interested in the December 1949 Khabarovsk Trials, which focused on prosecuting the Japanese who carried out biological weapons experiments on political prisoners and POWs in Manchukuo. In the 1970s, following the journalist Honda Katsuichi's travels through China and the publication of writings about Japanese war crimes, such issues generated much public interest. Yamada's posthumous book on the topic, *Saikinsen gunji saiban (Military Tribunal on Biological Warfare),* was published in 1974, a few years after the "Nixon Shock" (i.e., the United States of America's official recognition of the People's Republic of China).[82] Twelve Japanese soldiers were prosecuted by the Soviets in a sixteen-day war crimes trial, which addressed their participation in a 1939 bio-weapons unit connected with the infamous *Ishii butai* (Unit 731) located in Pingfang, near Harbin.[83] Yamada felt that he was at least partially responsible for supporting a regime that had sponsored such atrocities, which had been perpetrated in the year that he came to Manchukuo, and when he decided to serve in the capacity of a journalist who had attended the mass meetings of the fascistic Concordia Association. This exposé was written in a spirit similar to *Jigo zange,* which had absolved him of his proletarian left-wing past after his 1938 release from prison and which, in 1939, had allowed him to embrace right-wing proletarianism on behalf of Manchukuo. However, through *Saikinsen gunji saiban,* Yamada's further renunciation of his work on behalf of the Japanese-led Manchukuo state enabled him to embrace a fully "liberated" communist China, which, in its own Cultural Revolution, expressed some of the author's earlier proletarian literary ideas.

3
Surrealism in Service of the State: Fukuzawa Ichirô and Associates, 1935-36

> The function of the artist is to express reality as *felt*.
>
> – Robert Motherwell

In 1935, attracted by invitations from the *Nichinichi shimbun* [Manchuria Daily News], the South Manchuria Railway Company headquarters, and *Mitsui bussan* [Mitsui Trading Company], Japan's foremost theorist of surrealism, the artist Fukuzawa Ichirô, and two of his associates, who were also influenced by the Japanese surrealist movement, Shimizu Toshi (1887-1945) and Suzuki Yasunori (1891-1974), embarked on a tour of Manchukuo. In the mid-1930s, Japan's Tokyo-based art world considered surrealism to be one of the most modern, cutting-edge forms of representation. Thus, Fukuzawa's arrival from the metropole lent legitimacy to the birth of a uniquely "Manchurian" culture – under Japanese auspices yet with a cosmopolitan, global reach. He and his two companions came to enjoy artistic inspiration in an exotic locale while lecturing or exhibiting in SMRC employee clubs and touring Manchukuo's modern cities and rural development areas.

Moreover, the Manchukuo tour, usually sponsored by SMRC and the Manchukuo Publicity and News Bureau (the state propaganda organization) or its media organization, and after 1938, the Kantô Army, often gave Japanese intellectuals like Fukuzawa an opportunity to not only show the imperial government that they had renounced their allegiance to Marxism but also boost their careers by increasing their profiles. In the mid-1930s, Fukuzawa and others attempted to distance themselves from their Marxist connections, creating ambivalent images that romanticized the Manchurian region and its people while still mildly critiquing the Manchukuo experiment. They depicted the region as a multi-ethnic utopian space but also as a site of numerous contradictions. Intriguingly, the commissioned large canvases produced by Fukuzawa and his associates sometimes made their way into Japanese government buildings and military headquarters, despite the multivalent nature of their images. This was due to Shimizu's army connections, and included a painting each by Shimizu and Suzuki for the Manchukuo embassy residence in Shinkyô, and one by Fukuzawa for the Shinkyô-based Kantô bureau presidential office.[1]

Envisioning a Rural Paradise in Manchuria: Artists and the State

From the mid-1930s to the early 1940s, Japanese artists, as well as photographers like Fuchikami Hakuyô, "discovered" in Manchuria a utopian rural paradise that Japan had lost due to rapid modernization and urbanization after the First World War.[2] At the same time, media like *Manshû gurafu (Manchuria Graph),* 1933-44, continued to focus on construction and trade in the cities (including the coolie labour that sustained urban development) and often depicted scenes such as productive factories belching smoke while including articles on Japanese rural settlers. Notably, the modern and the urban remained inherent characteristics of depictions of the new *state* of Manchukuo, while the Manchurian *region* was portrayed as vast and largely uninhabited. This opposition of the modern state and the traditional region complemented Japan's aims.

A romanticized Manchuria supported the imperial government's vision of a bucolic countryside ripe for Japanese settlement – the perfect solution to the problems of over-urbanized regions and blighted rural landscapes in domestic Japan. The widespread promotion of rural development schemes whose purpose was to entice immigrant Japanese farmers to come to Manchuria began in 1933 and intensified after 1936.[3] Japanese observers collaborated with the Imperial Japanese and Manchukuo governments to construct and promote a popular Confucian-inspired fantasy of a vast, rural paradise, or *Ôdôrakudô* (Paradise of the Kingly Way), in which all five official ethnicities lived in harmony. These ideals were enshrined in the propaganda efforts of the Concordia Association, which sought to organize (and mobilize) Manchukuo's people for the needs of the state.

It seemed that, in Manchuria, the contradictions of Japan's modernity and its rural crisis could be resolved by the application of uniquely Asian ideals and Japanese exceptionalism. Here, one senses the multifaceted intellectual influence of Tachibana Shiraki's (1881-1945) post-Manchurian Incident exhortations favouring a Confucian worldview,[4] coupled with Tachibana Kôzaburô's (1893-1974) agrarian communalism, which held that class divisions could be assuaged through the restoration of village autonomy and communal values.[5] Aspects of the thought of Yanagita Kunio and the *Romanha* literary group further infused the volatile mix of ideologies comprising Japan's view of Manchuria, forming a vision that later culminated in such official initiatives as the 1942 *Kindai no chôkoku* (Overcoming Modernity) symposium.[6] However, the kind of interpretations of Confucianism that the Japanese sought to impose in Manchukuo had been largely replaced by the Westernized ideals promoted by Chinese intellectuals following the May Fourth 1919 anti-Japanese protests and resulting cultural movements. So, in reality, for most inhabitants of the region, these ideas remained in the realm of rhetoric. Moreover, the depictions of a rural utopia fashioned by Japanese observers contradicted the fact that certain areas of Manchuria (especially in the southeast) were overwhelmingly urban (suffering the usual problems associated with rapid development) and that Manchukuo's cities were often more modern than any in domestic Japan.[7] In addition, most rural land had already been claimed by Chinese or Koreans, with landlords and local warlords controlling much larger plots of land than was the case in either China proper or domestic Japan.[8]

So what prompted Japanese artists and others to produce these utopian representations of a rural paradise? For example, Kimura Ryôji, a resident of the port city of Dairen from the 1930s to the early 1950s, explains that Manchuria was "a fertile land that gave rise to the individuality of the one who wields a brush."[9] In emphasizing Manchuria's uniqueness and its difference from Japan in terms of spatial use and its largely Han-Chinese cultural customs, Kimura states: "It can be said that according to those who enjoy the brush, Manchuria is blessed with a large scale and the rich *peculiarities* unique to the continent."[10] Both of his retrospective comments give the impression that Manchuria is, for the artist, a largely empty landmass with vast horizons that could be fashioned into any kind of utopian vision. In emphasizing that the region itself inspired an aesthetic vision particular to the Japanese artist, Kimura's words represent yet another projection of the contradictory desires of the colonizer (Imperial Japan) onto the colonized (the Manchurian region), with the latter presented as entirely separate from the state of Manchukuo (which is characterized by its efficient modernity).

Indeed, after either touring the region or settling there on a long-term basis, Japanese artists often chose to depict peaceful rural landscapes with simple dwellings in which natives (and sometimes Japanese settlers) lived by the herding of sheep or the ploughing of fields. Aside from supporting Japanese ideology, there were also compelling commercial reasons to focus on such subjects. In the 1930s and early 1940s, paintings and illustrations of Manchuria in media printed in Manchukuo or Japan were avidly consumed by Japanese readers. For example, a small book entitled *Harubin to fûzoku: Genchi shashin shû (Harbin and Its Customs: Photo Collections of the Colonies),* along with photographs of the City of Harbin and its local attractions, included sketches and images of paintings.[11] This artwork, not surprisingly, mostly focuses on rural scenes. In an image typical of this time period, the cover features a sketch of rudimentary cooking pots hanging from a hearth, with simple kitchen implements like a cup, plate, and teapot standing on top. This could be the home either of a Chinese villager or, more likely, considering that the book was published at a time when the state was exhorting Japanese rural settlement, of a Japanese "pioneer."[12] The table of contents is framed on the left with the reproduction of paintings of a wooden Russian Orthodox chapel and of mules ploughing in late winter. On the following page is a photograph of Japanese praying "day and night" before a Shintô shrine.[13] In this text, the Japanese artists Furushima Matsunosuke, Akatsuka Tokio, and Hirata Kafû represented Manchuria's distinctive rural scenery, with Russian churches, donkey carts, New Year's stilt walking, and other regionally specific subjects – despite the urban locus of the photographs.

Other favourite scenes depicted by Japanese artists in various media featured the multicultural and multi-ethnic particularities of the area, whether Chinese or Russian.[14] These included visions of exotic local Han Chinese (termed "Manchu") culture (e.g., the Niang Niang festival, extensive New Year's celebrations, and Chinese women in traditional dress). More modern versions of "Chineseness" supported the state's conservative agenda by communicating the desirable characteristics of a model populace. For instance, the inside cover of a special 1938 edition of the *Manchuria Daily News (Manshû nichi-nichi shimbun)* English-language publication *Manchuria,* entitled "Concordia and Culture in Manchukuo," is graced with S. Ikebe's sketch *Ku-niang (Manchoo [sic] Girl)*. The illustration depicts a young Chinese woman wearing a green high-collared dress with red polka dots, red pumps, and a watch. She sits in a modern, upholstered chair, with her eyes downcast in a modest, almost subservient fashion.[15] This is a posture that, according to Norman Smith, represents the regime's *Wangdao* (*Ôdô,* or "kingly way") ideals regarding the role of women, which is to be submissive and reserved.[16]

In addition to these elements of local colour, representations of picturesque but slightly dilapidated Russian Orthodox churches in urban areas were also popular. They, too, were non-threatening and symbolized the vestiges of Russia's lost imperial past (in contrast to rising Soviet strength to the north). Mention of these relics of Tsarist rule in cities like Harbin, along with depictions of peaceful, traditional, but impoverished White Russian agricultural settlements in Binjiang province, served to reinforce for the Japanese viewer the modern strength of the Japanese national character, which had clearly surpassed this once powerful Western nation and its largely Caucasian peoples.[17] Such picturesque images predominated artistic work, while SMRC-sponsored publications, including *Manshû gurafu,* were more likely to feature snapshots of Manchukuo's modern cities, crammed with construction sites teaming with hardworking coolies (along with images of rural Manchuria). Such images were in line with the aims of Imperial Japan, the demands of the market, and the Japanese thirst for exoticism.

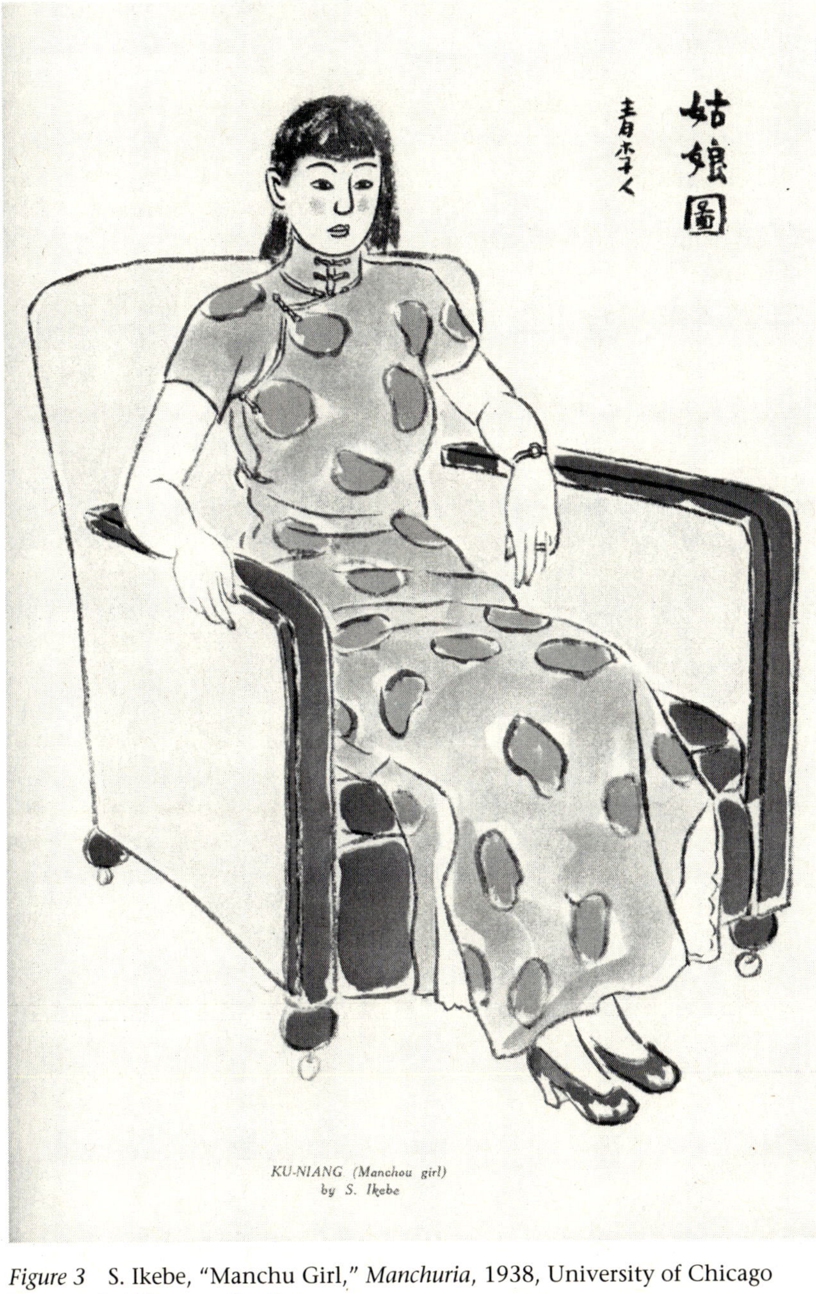

Figure 3 S. Ikebe, "Manchu Girl," *Manchuria*, 1938, University of Chicago Regenstein Library collections.

Large-scale oil paintings depicting the themes elaborated above sold exceptionally well in Manchukuo, where elite Japanese and wealthy Chinese bought these distinctive scenes to decorate the empty walls of their spacious Western brick houses. Here, there was a great demand for all kinds of oil paintings, which were believed to be more modern and Western than were traditional Japanese or Chinese watercolours and scroll paintings. Also, according to Tsuruta Gorô, a Japanese artist who exhibited and sold his works in Manchuria, painters from Tokyo often sent their works to colonial Manchuria and then, after 1932, Manchukuo.[18] There, they sold better than in domestic Japan, where the art market favoured *nanga* (Chinese-style watercolour paintings on scrolls) and oil paintings of higher quality and more daring subjects.[19] Many avant-garde artists like Shimizu, Suzuki, and Ai Mitsu, who might not have sold their canvases so easily in the metropole, displayed their works for sale in Manchukuo. Though Fukuzawa was independently wealthy and worried little about earning a living from his paintings, many of his colleagues had very real economic concerns. Exhibition venues, where art was sold, included the top floors of department stores like Dairen's Mitsukoshi, wall space in the grand entrances of the region's Yamato hotels, and even SMRC employee clubs. Obviously, the conflicting forces of the market and personal freedom of expression posed a dilemma for Japanese artists with regard to their choice of what to represent. Moreover, the fact that their tours of the region were often financed by organizations with definite political agendas also played a part in how they portrayed the new state.

From the 1930s into the early 1940s, the visits of Japanese artists served the Manchukuo state's goal of fostering the creation of a unique Manchurian culture – a pursuit that intensified after 1937 in order to set the region apart from war-torn China proper. Various kinds of propaganda media promoted an image of peace and cooperation, where the arts arose out of a previously barren region now made fertile under the auspices of the new state and its Japanese handlers. In the 1938 essay "Fine Art in Manchuria" published in the "Concordia and Culture in Manchukuo" special edition of the *Manchuria Daily News*, Fujiyama Kazuo, as deputy director of the newly established Manchukuo National Central Museum, uses this agrarian imagery to paint a picture of Manchuria's potential for artistic endeavours:

> Manchuria can be considered virgin land for the growth of art and culture. It was almost turned into a desert as far as art and culture were concerned, during the course of its history in which warfare, conquest, and subjugation predominated. Such conditions existed even in very recent years, as the despotic rule of the Chang warlords differed little from that of past conquerors. Even under such adverse circumstances, the creative spirit of Manchuria's

> art and culture was not killed, for today, after the restoration of peace and the dawn of a prosperous age in the new State of Manchoukuo, we again see the long neglected seeds of art and culture sprouting in the soil of Manchuria.[20]

Naturally, Japanese artists, as representatives of Asia's most culturally advanced imperialist nation, would take the lead in sowing these new endeavours in Manchukuo's as yet culturally "untilled" soil. If invited by SMRC, the state's propaganda organizations, or any of the newly formed artistic associations under the purview of the Concordia Association, many artists jumped at the chance to boost their careers and to increase their publicity back home in Japan. Fukuzawa and his colleagues were among a large number of artists who travelled to Manchukuo and whose works were often shown to its citizens before their arrival, seemingly to inspire viewers with a "modern" vision of art emanating from the imperial capital under Japanese auspices.[21]

Some of these visits arose out of invitations to display works in large-scale, state-sponsored exhibitions whose purpose was to build a new Manchurian artistic culture. For example, as early as October 1932, the Manchuria Fine Art Institution sponsored an exhibition of paintings that were chosen from over one thousand entries.[22] Fujiyama notes that this highly publicized event helped to accelerate Japanese influence in the arts and spurred further government-supported exhibitions:

> With the holding of this first exhibition, *Japanese artists and experts began to visit Manchukuo in an endless stream,* and in March, 1934, the joint Japan-Manchoukuo Art Exhibition supported mainly by the Eastern Japan Artists Association, to commemorate the glorious advent of the Chief Executive as Emperor of Manchoukuo took place. Among the exhibits were *twenty paintings by famous Japanese artists which were solemnly presented to His Majesty the Emperor of Manchoukuo,* while together with these, numerous works of Japanese and Manchurian artists were placed on exhibition [sic].[23]

These transnational interactions, which ensured that Fukuzawa and his colleagues' works were exhibited before they (the artists) even arrived in Manchukuo, reveal the interactive flow of culture, ideas, and images between domestic Japan and its "colonial" periphery in northeast China. This asymmetry provides further evidence of transculturation in the arts.[24] Fukuzawa and the other artists, photographers, and writers I examine were all part of what Karen Thornber describes as an "artistic contact nebulae."[25] The tours of Japanese artists and other cultural producers typify these unbalanced exchanges, in which Japan played a leading role in the guidance of

Manchukuo's cultural activities. During his visit to Shinkyô, Shimizu even met with Zheng Xiaoxu, Manchukuo's prime minister, to express his wish for an exhibition of Japanese establishment artists to come to Manchuria.[26]

In part, the sponsors of these cultural figures, whether SMRC or the various news outfits connected to the Manchukuo Publicity and News Bureau, could influence the image they created by choosing the attractions they would view. The Japan Tourist Bureau, which cooperated with the Manchukuo government and had its own independent offices in Dairen and other Manchurian cities, recommended various destinations.[27] Thus, by representing a Japanese-led modernity, Russian exoticism, and Chinese traditionalism (often linked to a Manchu past), Dairen, Mukden (Hôten), Hsinking (Shinkyô), Harbin, and other urban sites served to highlight a simplistic view of the peoples involved in the cultural construction of the region.[28] Yet, the Manchurian scenes that most attracted the attention of SMRC, government sponsors, central art circles, and bourgeois patrons in domestic Japan and Manchukuo were those that reflected the Japanese government's official rhetoric, which emphasized the region's backward, agrarian nature and indicated that proper development and security could only occur under Japanese supervision. These scenes were located in the liminal areas situated between the urban and the rural, areas that were in the process of either being developed (by Japanese) or being allowed to decline (by the Chinese and/or Russians). Therefore, the idyllic simplicity of depictions of Chinese roofs protruding from millet fields, Harbin's Russian vestiges, northern Manchurian birch forests (near Japanese Youth Corps camps like Tetsuryô), Chinese New Year's stilt costumes, bucolic Chinese villages, peaceful views of grazing sheep (at the fringes of Japanese settlements), and other themes were not innocent in their insistence on Manchuria's inherent exoticism and pacified nature.

On the macro-level, the saturation of the Japanese art world and marketplace with these utopian visions of Manchuria helped obscure the Kantô Army's violent involvement in the creation of Manchukuo and allowed Japanese observers to mythologize the Empire's goals in a vast region that, for years, had been deemed Japan's lifeline. According to Young, these simplistic visions of the region (whether in art or other media) contributed to the political obfuscation of Japan's aggression on the continent: "Mass culture industries flooded their marketplace with Manchurian-theme products, and in the process disseminated a specific package of information and a set interpretation of themes on the continent ... When representations of Manchuria moved from the factual, if selective reportage in the news to fictionalized dramatizations on stage and screen, the complex realities of the military occupation were reduced to the simple and sanctifying patterns of myth."[29] Within the space of a picture frame, artists condensed Manchuria into a

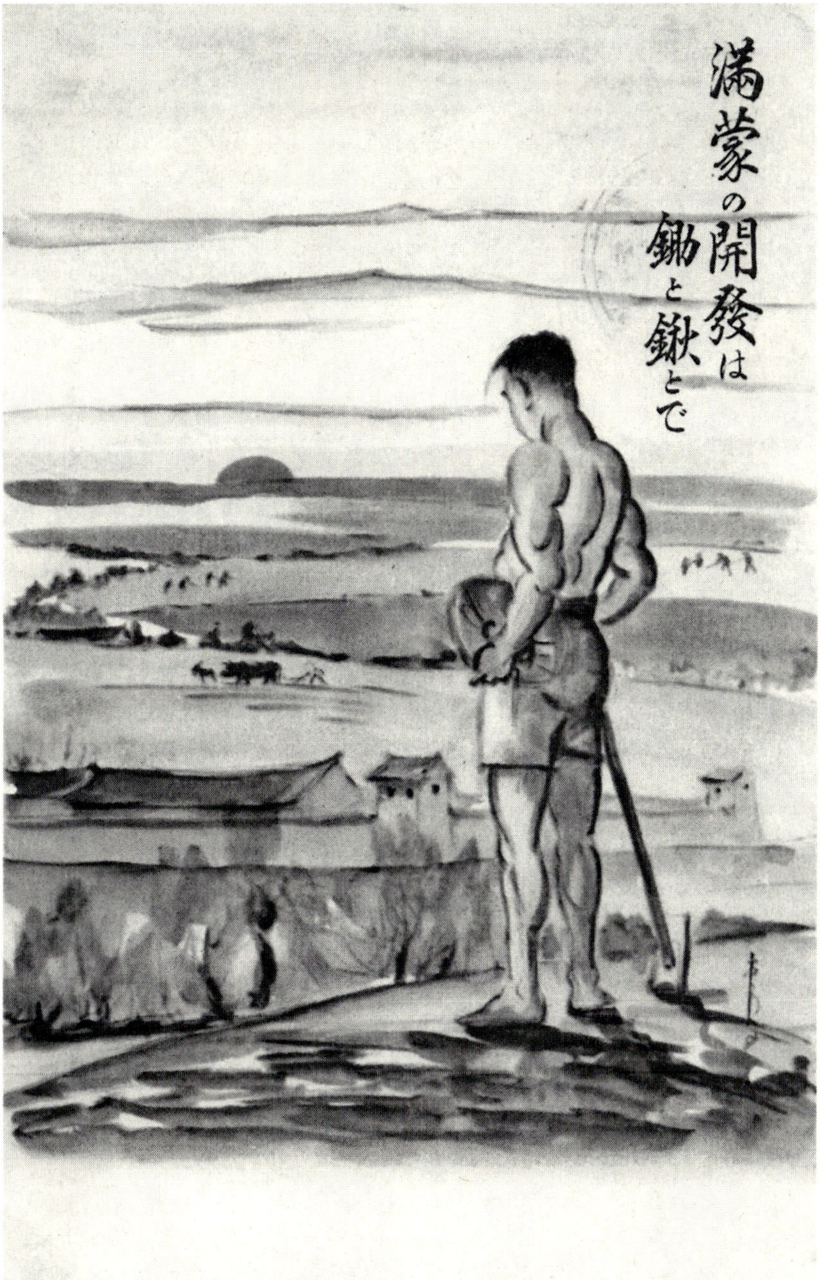

Figure 4 Manmô no kaihatsu wa suki to suki to de [The development of Manchuria and Mongolia proceeds from plough to hoe], late 1930s, early 1940s, author's personal collection.

comprehensible and attractive form, despite the fiction of Manchukuo's full independence from Japan.

The power of these images lies in their ability to generate a certain atmosphere in the collective imagination, where they can perpetuate an emotional allure beyond rational comprehension. Alan Tansman, in his study of Japanese fascism and aesthetics, warns that, "through a shared experience of beauty, epiphanic representations provoke spontaneous consensus and aesthetic cohesion."[30] The transcendent force of these bucolic images, described as "epiphanic representations," therefore served as "unofficial propaganda,"[31] with their power coming from a shared vision of empire that, nevertheless, nicely complemented the goals of the Manchukuo state. Indeed, the less a cultural product appeared to the cosmopolitan Japanese observer like manufactured propaganda, the more potential it had to prompt the desired effect: "To Japanese officialdom in the 1930s, propaganda meant the cultivation of cultural values and attitudes that would be held so deeply they would appear innate and not imposed."[32] The ideological battle for (Japanese) hearts and minds in Manchukuo would, then, be fought, at least in part, by artists who might not even have noticed that they had been enlisted.

Thus, carefully fashioned images prompting spontaneous moments of the sublime could have a healing effect on the unsettled domestic Japanese individual while grounding him or her in the shared experience of consuming the beauty of the Japanese Empire: "Art can thus serve as a model for political and social wholeness that not only fuses the atomized subject with the whole of society but also finds freedom in necessity. Though repressive, this ideology of the epiphany offers pleasure and spiritual meaning to a deracinated bourgeoisie, as well as relief from the miseries of commodification."[33] The amusing irony of Tansman's assessment of art's role in supporting Japan's ideological goals is that the marketplace was the venue in which these shared "epiphanic representations" were disseminated. The popular depiction of the sublimity of the Manchurian space on canvas, which appeared in exhibition halls, in department store galleries, on grand hotel entrance walls, and in individual Western-style living rooms, thus represented ever-increasing possibilities for the Japanese viewer, like a blank screen for the projection of dreams.

It is true that not all Japanese observers, including artists, depicted such peaceful scenes or unquestioningly played into the regime's agenda for Manchukuo. However, the saturation of various media and exhibition venues with these serene depictions confirmed for viewers back home the stability of northeast China under a Japanese-led regime, along with the fact that the new state offered vast tracts of agricultural land to incoming Japanese settlers. These peaceful views of bucolic rusticity in the Manchurian landscape hid the fact that many of these lands had been forcibly seized from

Chinese or Korean peasants.[34] They also obscured the reality of growing Chinese resistance movements and how, with the advent of the Second Sino-Japanese War in 1937, Manchukuo was increasingly being used as a military base to attack China proper. The images produced by these visiting Japanese artists left an interesting visual testimony to their views of the region – views that stood in sharp contrast to the Manchukuo state's rhetoric of modernity and progress as represented in the new capital city of Shinkyô.

Surrealism on Display: Fukuzawa's Manchurian Tour and Related Exhibitions

I now turn to a specific example of how the Manchukuo state, working in tandem with SMRC and news organizations, helped to promote itself in the eyes of cultural producers working in the mode of one of Japan's newest and most cosmopolitan forms of artistic representation – surrealism. I examine three Japanese artists' views of Manchuria, and in doing so, provide a more in-depth investigation of the issues discussed above. The impressions of these men are important in that, as surrealists, their vision of Manchuria comes from an avant-garde critique of the artistic establishment. Moreover, like their proletarian counterparts in the late 1920s, they also emphasized labour and depicted natives in multivalent forms. An artwork can be interpreted in different ways: it can symbolically criticize, and, at the same time, superficially express a commonly held official political paradigm. An interesting aspect of the art of Fukuzawa and his colleagues is its focus on rural subjects and vistas whose large horizons emphasize the region's empty lands. Their work came at a time of increasing interest in Manchukuo and corresponded with an acceleration of Imperial Japan's plans for settlement. By winter 1936, they had obligingly created enduring images in oils that captured the impressions of their sojourn in 1935.

In April 1935, the prominent Japanese artist and theorist of surrealism Fukuzawa Ichirô, accompanied by Shimizu and Suzuki, left Tokyo and, invited by the SMRC headquarters, the Manchuria Daily News, and Mitsui Trading Company, went on a tour of Manchuria. As they lectured or exhibited in SMRC employee clubs and toured Manchukuo's modern cities and rural development areas, Fukuzawa and his two companions came to enjoy the artistic inspiration provided by this exotic locale. Suzuki stayed until the end of May, Fukuzawa left around August, and Shimizu remained until September of the same year, visiting rural or undeveloped areas in Manchuria and Mongolia as well as urban sites, including the Japan-Tourist-Bureau-recommended cities of Dairen, Shinkyô, and Harbin, where all of them held joint exhibitions.[35] Shimizu even staged an individual exhibition of his work in Beijing. While the artists collected their impressions of the region, their works, brought over from domestic Japan, showed Japanese colonists and others in Manchukuo's cities the latest trends in the Tokyo art world.

Fukuzawa and his colleagues brought their modern, transnational artistic vision to this part of the *gaichi* (colonies). As members of the Tokyo-based *Dokuritsu bijutsu kyôkai* (Independent Artists Association), working in the mode of surrealism, they also represented the newest art form to arise in Japan.[36] All of the artists' Manchurian-themed works would be exhibited in the group's 1936 show in Tokyo, thus adding an imperialist flavour to the Japanese surrealist moment. Moreover, as a successful artist who had been in Paris during the heyday of Andre Breton's (1896-1966) surrealist group from 1924 until his 1931 return to Japan, Fukuzawa represented an authentic Japanese tie to this global avant-garde movement.[37] In the mid-1930s, Japan's art world considered surrealism to be one of the most modern, cutting-edge forms of artistic representation. Japanese artists, who, since the 1920s, had viewed the crackdown on their counterparts in the proletarian arts movement, increasingly downplayed the original Marxist connotations of the movement associated with Breton. Further, as discussed in Chapter 2, Manchukuo had become a space for formerly left-wing intellectuals to realize their ideals while, at the same time, letting the imperial Japanese government know that they supported its political experiment in Manchuria. Thus, Fukuzawa's arrival from the metropole lent legitimacy to the birth of a uniquely Manchurian culture whose global reach did not threaten Imperial Japan.

On the artists' return to Tokyo in the fall of 1935, they displayed their sketches of images collected in Manchuria and Mongolia in an exhibition in the city's fashionable Ginza area. The *Manmô sobyô ten* (Exhibition of Sketches from Manchuria and Mongolia) was held at the *Seijusha garô* ("Green Sapling" Art Gallery) in early November 1-5.[38] At the same venue, they also held the *Manmô miyage shôhin ten* (Exhibition of Souvenir Sketches of Manchuria and Mongolia), at which they displayed pieces like Shimizu's *Shirakaba to ushi (White Birch and Ox), Môko kôgen (Mongolian Steppes), Chôjô (Great Wall),* and *Môko fûkei (Mongolian Scene);* Suzuki's *Tsukiyo no uma (Horse on a Moonlit Night), Kokuto kensetsu fûkei (Scene of the Construction of the Capital),* and *Nyûkoku no bôshi (Mother and Son Entering the Country);* and Fukuzawa's *Ame (Rain), Fuantejî (Fantasy),* and *Dokuhaku (Soliloquy),* among other works.[39] Common themes included the region's distinctive scenery, development in rural areas, and native peoples. In this well-heeled venue in Tokyo, for their bourgeois domestic Japanese audience, Fukuzawa, Shimizu, and Suzuki captured the exotic curiosities of the continent in preliminary drawings. It was a preview show that no doubt generated consumer demand for their later oil paintings.

Not long after the successful Ginza exhibition, in February 1936, Fukuzawa, Suzuki, and Shimizu held an exhibition in oils called the *Manmô yôga ten* (Exhibition of Oil Paintings of Manchuria and Mongolia) in Osaka's *Sankakudô* (Triangle Hall).[40] The Tokyo display of their sketches of Manchuria, which served to advertise coming attractions, was followed by their works' being diffused throughout various venues in regional Japanese cities. In addition, Shimizu, also featuring oil paintings of Manchuria and Mongolia, exhibited on his own in neighbouring Kobe from 9 to 12 February 1936. Critics noted: "As usual, Shimizu makes efforts to capture the development of the new frontier." One also commented: "Suzuki in his own particular artistic style describes much of Manchuria's and Mongolia's scenery and people, with a strength in depicting horses as a subject." But there were also complaints: "In Fukuzawa's distinctive style, an intimate connection to Manchuria and Mongolia does not *obviously* appear except in a few works."[41] The last comment probably stems from the fact that Fukuzawa's less "readable" works often emphasize the unconscious, dreams, and a very personal vision of the Manchurian space, in contrast to the nostalgic realism apparently sought by the critic. Clearly, evidence of the exoticism of the continent, with its cultural peculiarities and its unique spatial scale, was much prized by both Japanese critics and their domestic audience. The numerous exhibitions mounted by these three artists in both Japan and Manchukuo also point to the popular Japanese interest in viewing representations of the continent and Manchuria. The latter formed a romantic space that, in the imagination of these viewers, was usually set apart from Manchukuo.[42] The artists were thus able to bring a cosmopolitan atmosphere to the new state (and Japan) by depicting the region in their own particular modern style, which was clearly influenced by European surrealism.

In Japan, by the mid-1930s, surrealism was a transnational art movement with offshoots in the colonies, including in Manchukuo,[43] and was thus representative of an artistic contact nebulae.[44] When Fukuzawa returned from Paris to Tokyo in 1931, he became, along with Takiguchi Shûzô (1903-79), Japan's most prominent surrealist painter and theorist. Therefore, when Fukuzawa first visited Dairen as part of his tour of Manchukuo in April 1935, he was proud to be hosted by the surrealist group *Gokakai* (the Five Fruits Group [pear, almond, date, peach, and chestnut]),[45] whose exhibition he also visited.[46]

In 1932, five artists in Dairen – Hamano Nagamasa, Sakaiya Kazuyuki, Yamamichi Eisuke, Ichimura Chikara, and Yonetani Shinobu – had formed *Gokakai,* which fostered avid cultural exchanges with the city's avant-garde writers, who also dabbled in literary surrealism. The poet Takiguchi Takeshi (1904-unknown) and *Gokakai* member Yamamichi frequently visited the writer Anzai Fuyue in his home, where Yamamichi would criticize the latter's artworks.[47] *Gokakai* remained in existence until the early 1940s, when it was subjected to political repression and lack of funds.[48] In 1934, the avant-garde magazine *Kasasagi (Magpie)* began publication in Dairen under Takiguchi's leadership, along with the writers Koike Yoshio, Inoue Rinji, and Yagibashi Yûjirô, who promoted surrealism and its imagery as a dominant form of poetic expression. *Kasasagi*'s contributors expressed a strong interest in art and theoretical explorations of surrealism, while maintaining intimate connections with the members of *Gokakai. Kasasagi* ran until the early 1940s and was one of the last avant-garde journals to remain true to its internationalist ideals of free expression.[49]

In mid-1935, as an advisor to young avant-garde artists in Tokyo, Fukuzawa was astonished to see such progressive paintings in Manchukuo, in the midst of what he somewhat disparagingly called *inaka* (the countryside).[50] In spring 1936, he recommended five *Gokakai* painters for admittance to the prestigious *Ecole de Tokio* (School of Tokyo) in the imperial capital, where surrealism was at the height of its popularity as a form of artistic expression.[51] March 1936 saw the founding of *Ecole de Tokio,* then composed of thirty surrealist artists who published a magazine by the same name. Ozaki Shinjin believes that this marks the point at which the foreign art movement of surrealism became firmly "nativized" in Japan.[52] The school's magazine included contributions from Dairen-based painters like Ichimura and Yamamichi, who were also members of the group and who had formed the Dairen-based surrealist art association *Gokakai* four years earlier.[53] As a representative of a leading Japanese art movement who had lived and worked in the Parisian birthplace of surrealism, Fukuzawa brought legitimacy to the surrealist endeavours of the Japanese avant-garde in Dairen and exposed Manchukuo's "nascent" art world to a cosmopolitan vision emanating from the imperial centre.

Manchurian Vastness on Canvas, Mid-1930s

The pastoral tranquility portrayed in Japanese paintings of Manchuria echoed that found in the paintings of nineteenth-century Western European artists, whose works also saw a resurgence of popularity in Japan in the late 1930s and early 1940s. Interestingly, the pastoralism of the European Romantics arose out of an intellectual climate that renounced the ravages of the Industrial Revolution. In this way, it was similar to the "epiphanic representations" of rural simplicity captured in Japanese artists' renditions of the plains of Manchuria. With regard to its rapid development of Manchuria, Japan experienced the same sort of critique in the early twentieth century as had Western Europe in the nineteenth century. Still, Kimura Ryôji's insistence on the "large scale" of the country assured viewers that Manchuria's agricultural lands were largely empty, just waiting for the hand of the enterprising Japanese colonist. This distinctive portrayal of space emphasized Manchuria's difference from Japan and China proper.

These cultural producers exaggerated the geographical, cultural, and even physical differences between Japan and the continent. This is true even of the oneiric paintings of Japanese avant-garde artists like Fukuzawa, Shimizu, and Suzuki, though their works lacked the sentimentality of other popular depictions and sometimes offered a critical view of Manchuria/Manchukuo. Even so, Manchuria's sublime "large scale," or its dream-like vastness, is strikingly

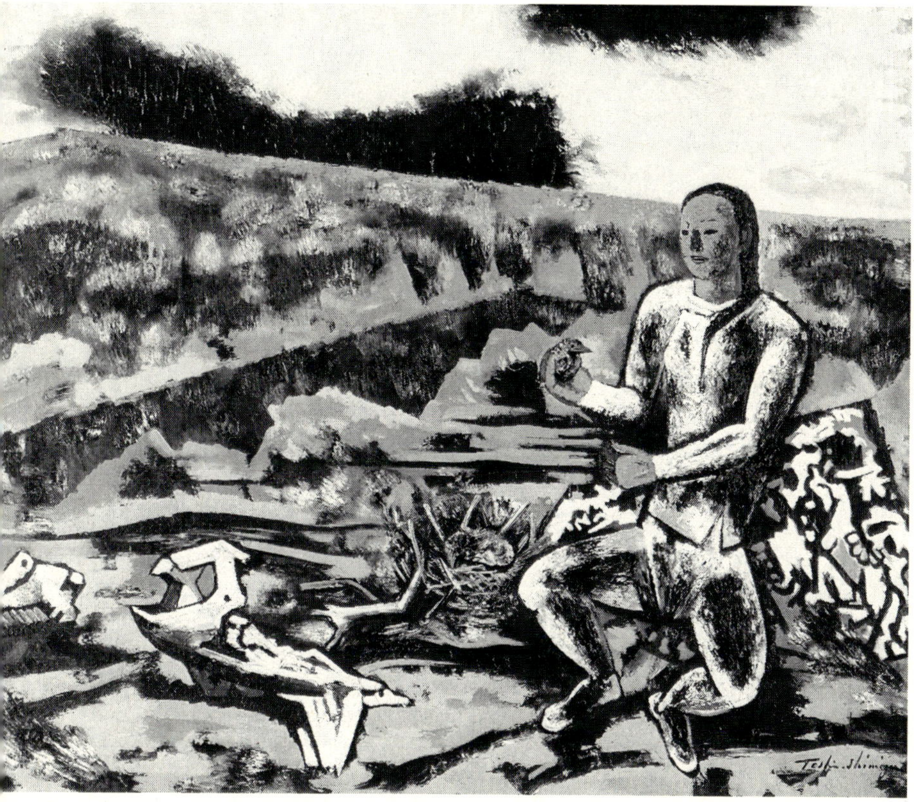

Figure 5 Shimizu Toshi, *Kyûchô Môkôjin* [Mongolian Saving a Bird], 1936, Tochigi Prefectural Museum of Fine Arts.

evident in Fukuzawa's and the other artists' paintings, not only in their emphasis on the distance implied by the horizon line but also in their generous use of canvas. For example, Shimizu's 1936 painting *Kyûchô Môkojin (A Mongolian Saving a Bird)* is 180 by 225 centimetres in size, while Fukuzawa's surrealist 1936 image *Ushi (Oxen)* measures fully 192 by 260 centimetres.[54] The three artists' paintings all range from more than a metre high to over two metres long.

Japanese curators, including Otani Shôgo, believe that these painters' fantastic visions of the vast spaces and horizons of Manchuria clearly owe something to Salvador Dali (1904-89). Otani believes that, beginning in 1935, the works produced by Fukuzawa, Shimizu, and Suzuki were somewhat influenced by Dali, whose works had been familiar to Japanese artists and poets since the early 1930s.[55] In March 1935, before the artists went on their tour of Manchuria, Takiguchi Shûzô translated Salvador Dali's ground-breaking essay entitled "The Object in Surrealist Experiments," which appeared in

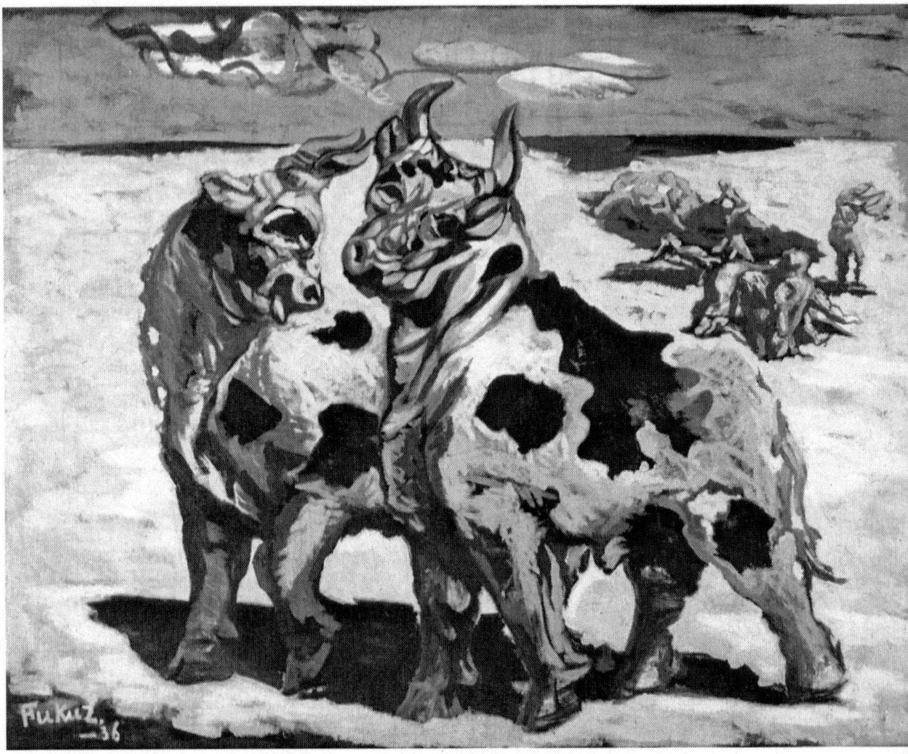

Figure 6 Fukuzawa Ichirô, *Ushi* [Oxen], 1936, The National Museum of Modern Art, Tokyo.

Shihô (Poetry Methods), thus giving writers and artists like Fukuzawa further access to Dali's interpretations of surrealism.[56]

Regardless of Dali's influence, this vision of vastness clearly reflects the colonialist contention that Manchurian lands were largely empty and ready to be developed and organized by a stronger power – namely, Imperial Japan. Despite the fact that Fukuzawa and the other artists subscribed to a left-oriented politics, they were not immune to recognizing Japan as the imperial centre and its colonies as the exotic periphery. This is reinforced by their repetitive accounts of coolie labour in Manchurian ports and urban construction sites as well as by their depiction of the pervasive yellow dust of vast, dry northeastern Chinese plains (to be settled by Japanese immigrant farmers). The sketches and paintings of these avant-garde artists constantly emphasized Manchuria's difference from Japan.

Fukuzawa's Oxen and Equivocation, 1936

The large oil paintings painted by Fukuzawa, Shimizu, and Suzuki portray a much more complex picture of the region than that lauded in the accounts of various other propaganda media. For instance, while emphasizing Manchuria's distinctiveness from Japan, Fukuzawa, a socially critical artist, hints at the superficiality of the utopian ideals of the new state of Manchukuo, where suffering and pleasure coexist. In his most critically acclaimed work, *Ushi,* Fukuzawa depicts Manchukuo as a vast land of startling contradictions and jarring juxtapositions (see Figure 6).

In the foreground, *Ushi* shows two frolicking black-and-white oxen. They look like they are made of paper-mâché due to the gaps in their structure, which reveal the roseate colour of the land. In the top right of the painting are two groups of people, one a skeletal bunch of grey, seemingly nude labourers toiling at a worksite and, below them, a group of muscular pink-skinned bodies sitting closely together. From this group a portly man emerges, taking off his clothing. According to Otani, the people in the first group are coolies who are working hard to develop Manchukuo, while the people in the second group are well-nourished men enjoying themselves at the seashore. The individual who is removing his clothing is a Russian whom Fukuzawa had observed and sketched by the edge of the Sungari River in Harbin.[57]

It can be argued that the artist's Marxist inclinations and his tendency toward social critique are reflected in his juxtaposing starving indigenous labourers with well-nourished (White Russian) bourgeoisie. Otani also believes that the curious structure of the oxen, whose image was inspired by Fukuzawa's glimpse of a Greek frieze on a golden wineglass, represents the hollow nature of the puppet state of Manchukuo.[58] Perhaps, like the golden ideals of the West, which are built on the foundations of classical Greek civilization, the new state's ideals would, in the memory of later Japanese generations, themselves eventually come to enshrine a static antiquity. Though it is not known whether prewar Japanese viewers of the artists' various exhibitions in the mid-to-late 1930s were able to decipher this message, Otani mentioned that he based his assumptions on close readings of Fukuzawa's postwar writings and contemporaneous sketches.[59] However, the artist's personal view of labour in Manchukuo, at least according to his writings in prominent domestic Japanese art magazines, reveals a much more complicated, even equivocal, attitude toward Manchukuo's largely Han Chinese workers. In an essay in *Mizue (Watercolour),* Fukuzawa makes comments that clearly replicate the colonial gaze, despite the avant-garde nature of his art. The two artists with whom he travelled also exhibited such contradictions in their work, and it is to these that I now turn.

Manchurian Labour in Surrealist Eyes, 1936

During his roughly four-month visit to Manchukuo with Shimizu and Suzuki, Fukuzawa sketched Chinese workers resting. One month after his return, he remarked dryly: "Manchukuo is probably the Manchukuo of construction and production, but ... I was surprised by how so many people took naps by the side of the road."[60] Fukuzawa's words, published in *Mizue,* seem to reflect the contemporary Japanese cultural bias of inferring inherent continental laziness among Manchurians, in contrast to Japanese efficiency. Fukuzawa's statement carries the assumption that working-class natives should be productive rather than at rest and that they are all in robust health and receive adequate nourishment. Of course, the artist's own image of the skeletal labourers in *Ushi* contradicts this. Also, Fukuzawa may not have been aware of the common Chinese cultural convention whereby all social classes (even today) rest after the noon meal, which is generally the largest of the day and is heavily based on carbohydrate intake (e.g., from *mantou* [wheat buns], noodles, millet, or rice).

Of course, this negative impression of indigenous labour stemmed from largely superficial observations since it is doubtful that Fukuzawa or any of the other artists in his group ever personally approached a Han Chinese worker to ask him or her about his or her life (usually characterized by deprivation, loneliness, and scarcity). Due to crushing poverty, the largely uneducated Han Chinese working class had limited access to education; consequently, these people would not have had the opportunity to acquire more than a rudimentary grasp of pidgin Japanese. Even if Fukuzawa, Shimizu, and Suzuki had wanted to talk to these labourers without the interference of the guides who were no doubt provided by hosting organizations, they would have been constrained by linguistic, cultural, and social differences.

This idea of persistent Chinese lassitude in the face of a powerful Japanese drive for the development of Manchukuo is also depicted in Suzuki's painting *Yokotawareru Manshû dojin (Reclining Manchurian Native),* which shows a man dressed in cotton-padded Chinese-style clothing lying on the earth, with a black dog beside him.[61] The horizon likely depicts the ocean in early spring, with three rooftops (it is unclear whether they are buildings on the wharf or whether they are factories) appearing in the distance beyond, with white smoke rising from one of them. As a coolie, possibly at the edge of the ocean near the wharf, the reclining man's face is blackened from the sun and harsh climate, and he looks down and away from the viewer. (This posture resembles the non-threatening, subservient gaze of the Chinese woman sketched in Ku-niang.) Yet, there is little to indicate that the scene is situated at the wharf, except for what looks like waves, because the background is largely empty and undeveloped, with the human figure and the dog being the main parts of the composition. The emptiness of much of the painting framing the image of a worker at rest seems to support Fukuzawa's impression of the inherent laziness of lower-class Chinese, leaving Manchukuo as a state that can only be developed through a Japanese-led effort.

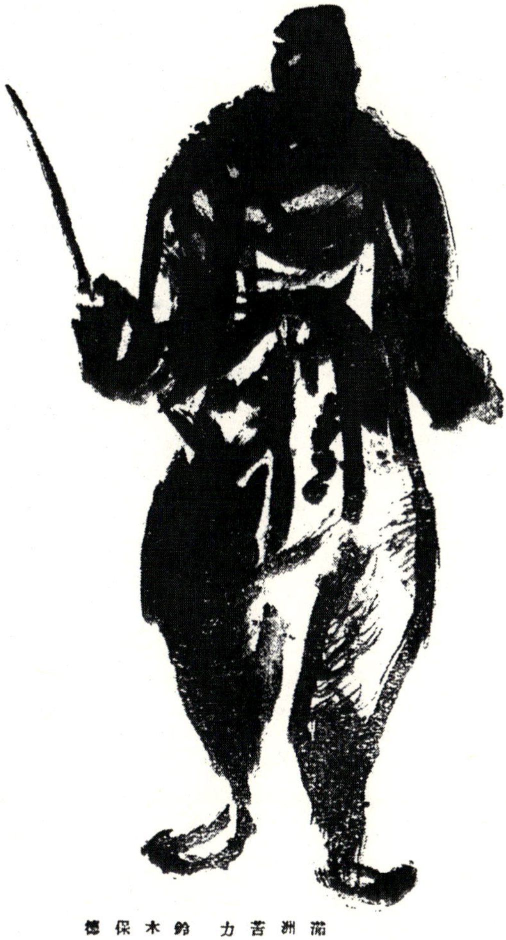

Figure 7 Suzuki Yasunori, *Manshû domin* [Manchurian native]. Original image published in *Atorie* [Atelier] (Tokyo: Atorie-sha, 1935), 26-27. The reprint is a scan of the microfilm by Kristina Troost, Duke University Perkins-Bostock Library, from the microfilm reprint of *Atorie* by Yûshûdô (Tokyo, 1993).

Suzuki's August 1935 article in *Atorie (Atelier),* entitled "Manshû domin to dôbutsu" ("Manchurian Natives and Animals"), actually reveals an attitude toward labour that contrasts with Fukuzawa's, but it is still redolent of a prewar Japanese preoccupation with race, lineage, eugenics, and bloodlines – common to many imperialist (and fascist) powers at the time.[62] He lauds how the small Manchurian horse (actually a Mongolian pony) can work much harder than a Japanese horse *(koku-uma),* even though they are of the same lineage. It is not difficult to extrapolate from this assertion an idea about the productivity of the region's human workers. Indeed, this short essay appeared during a time when there was an increased focus on eugenics, when prominent authors like Kawabata, in his 1933 story "Of Birds and Beasts" featured in *Kaizô (Reconstruction),* even hinted that humans, like dogs, exhibit behaviours based on their pedigrees.[63] The conflation of Manchuria's animals with people shows Suzuki's distance from his subject and his view of the coolie as someone at a vast remove from his own realm of experience. Here, on canvas, a Japanese observer conveniently relegates the Chinese labourer to the background of Japan's development project.

This concern with the surfaces of colonialism was also common to the view of labour in the late 1920s works of the Dairen-based avant-garde poets Anzai Fuyue and Kitagawa Fuyuhiko. Six years prior to Fukuzawa's description of the "phenomenon" of Chinese laziness, a similar image of an indigenous labourer sleeping at the roadside in colonial Dairen appears in one of the surrealist poems in Kitagawa's prescient 1929 poetry collection *Sensô (War)*. This short poem ironically describes the bliss of a sleeping coolie, who, like a dust rag, is lying near a rowhouse:

> "Flowers"
> Buried in the midst of flowers stolen from the row of streets, and snoozing in the sunlight, an old Chinese man like a dust rag, is happy.
> Happy.[64]

In the late 1920s, Kitagawa, as a self-consciously Marxist poet, attempted to undermine the notion of Japanese capitalism's economic development in Manchuria through this satirical image of a happy worker who subverts the system by stealing and napping. He also translated Breton's *Second Manifesto of Surrealism* and, in 1930, proclaimed that surrealism should be used to further a left-wing political agenda.[65] This poem, read alongside Fukuzawa's, Suzuki's, and Shimizu's images, shows the equivocation in depictions produced by surrealist writers and artists in prewar Japan. By contrast, in the *Mizue* essay, Fukuzawa seems astonished that his former impression of Manchukuo as a progressive worksite did not quite live up to reality. It is notable that, even in the works of the Japanese avant-garde, the Han Chinese coolie becomes a blank surface on which is projected Japan's desires and anxieties related to development in the colonial space.

Obviously, not all inhabitants of Manchukuo expressed hope for Japanese-led economic development, despite the government's best propaganda efforts. Based on the impressions of his tour with Fukuzawa and Shimizu, Suzuki completed a work entitled *Kokuto kensetsu (Constructing the Capital),* which depicts an angry-looking, well-dressed young bourgeois Han Chinese man in traditional blue silk clothing turning his back on a construction

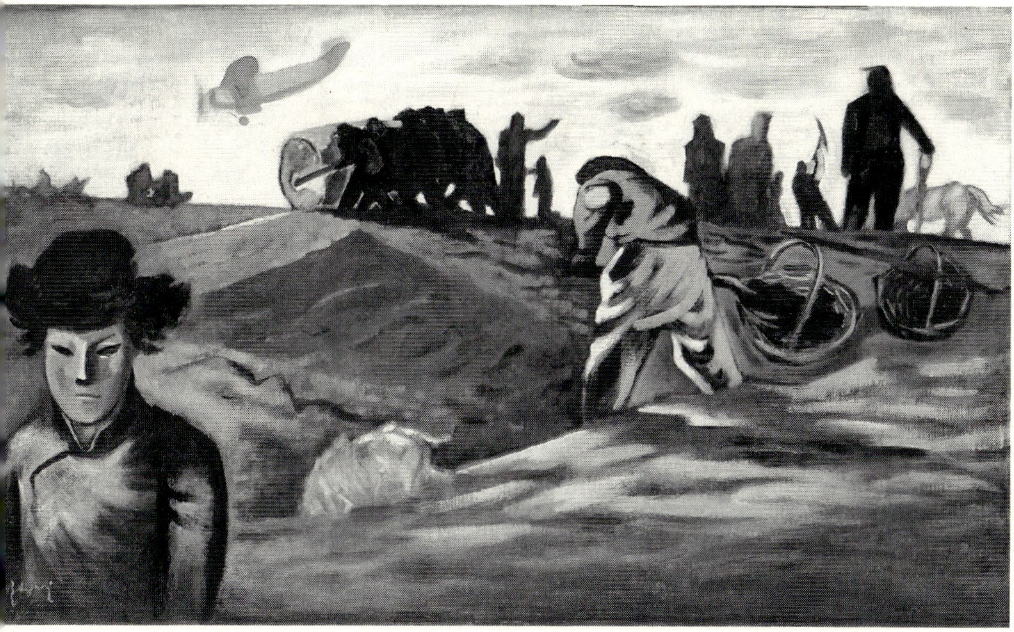

Figure 8 Suzuki Yasunori, *Kokuto kensetsu* [Constructing the capital], 1936, Tomioka City Museum, Fukuzawa Ichirô Memorial Gallery.

site.[66] Here, faceless coolies use primitive tools like baskets, hoes, and manual stone rollers to dig up and level the earth near Shinkyô, the new capital of Manchukuo. An airplane flies above, in stark contrast to the archaic building methods, possibly a metaphor for the Japanese presence and its corresponding modernity as being superior to (above) the back-breaking toil performed by the Chinese workers (below). Indeed, by 1936, the Manchuria Air Transport Company, established in 1932 by the Manchukuo government, operated fifteen civilian routes and two military routes, with 7,645 kilometres covered.[67] Suzuki, Shimizu, and Fukuzawa certainly could have profited from the Dairen-Mukden-Hsinking-Harbin route, possibly flying from Tokyo to Dairen within a day.[68] Though they came by ship, these acclaimed Japanese artists could have had the chance to view some of the development projects in the nation's new capital from the air, arriving like gods blown in on the favourable winds from Japan to bring culture to Manchukuo.

This painting, as well as Suzuki's *Yokotawareru Manshû dojin* described above, show Han Chinese refusing to be productive members of the new state (even if they are members of the former elite, the upper-class landed gentry) and call into question the utopian designs of Manchukuo's Japanese-led economic development, which obviously do not benefit all five ethnic groups equally. Similarly, Chinese women's popular literature of the time highlighted "the predominance of darkness, pessimism, disorder, and destitution in portraits of Manchukuo society."[69] These were not the most flattering depictions of a nation created in the image of the "land of the rising sun." Norman Smith argues that these dark views of Manchukuo society were allowed to be published due to the Japanese censors' low regard for the power of women's literary production.[70]

Yet, unlike the works of the Chinese women writers who belonged to Manchukuo government-supported writers' associations, *Kokuto kensetsu* and its intriguing depiction of a worksite was created by a Japanese painter, whose corporate and newsmedia hosts most likely expected him to praise his country's involvement in the region. As an artist attached to Fukuzawa's entourage, Suzuki's critique would not have been anticipated because surrealism's style (though not radical politics) had been largely accepted by the mainstream Japanese art world, which also had begun to distance itself from the more overtly left-wing political manifestations of the movement. Moreover, this multivalent image featured a young Han Chinese man who was turning his back on the Japanese-led modernity and development in Shinkyô. While these depictions reveal the contradictions of the largely "colonial" space of the new nation of Manchukuo, they nonetheless support the state's propaganda message, which was that, if Japan did not control Manchuria's rich natural resources, then they would be squandered by an inefficient, lazy Han Chinese population bound by feudal traditions and/or family pride.

Manchurian Natives as Elemental Aspects of the Region, 1936

For Shimizu, on the other hand, peoples native to the region either blend into a vast landscape of yellow dust blown in from the dry Manchurian plains or serve to symbolize the harsh incongruities of a frontier space marked by a latent elemental violence inherent in the land itself. This viewpoint is also found in the works of other Japanese avant-garde artists and writers who were producing at a time when workers and lower-class natives in Manchuria often appeared as exotics blending into a wide, empty landscape or as symbols of lower-class abjection.

Shimizu's *Môko fûkei (kôgen. onna. uma) (Mongolian Scene [Steppes. Woman. Horse])* depicts, on the left side of the canvas, a nude woman with Chinese-cut bangs posing in a Western pinup style and superimposed over a grassland scene next to the partial shadow of a horse.[71] Sketched over the right half of the painting, an attractive young Mongolian man on horseback and wearing a traditional queue appears next to her. In contrast to the indigenous Mongolian ponies grazing in the background, these figures look like artificial, ghostly forms projected onto the surface of the land – a conceit that is echoed in their serene, slightly smiling faces. Only the three horses in the far background seem to have a volume and depth that anchors them

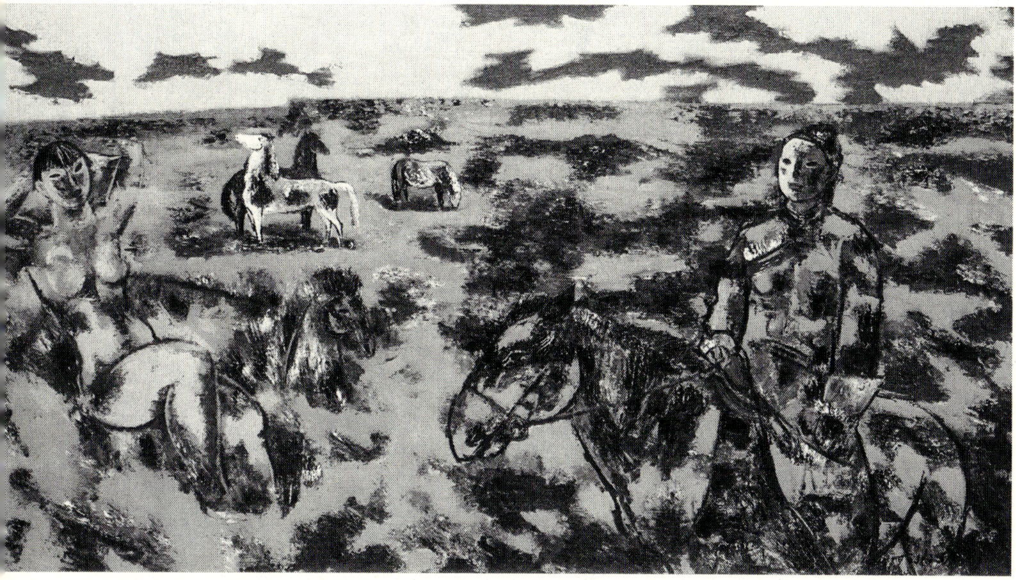

Figure 9 Shimizu Toshi, *Môkô fûkei [Kôgen. onna. uma]* [Mongolian scene: (Steppes. woman. horse)], 1936, Tochigi Prefectural Museum of Fine Arts.

to the land. Shimizu's painting reflects the various contradictory desires projected onto the surface of the largely empty grasslands of the steppe. It thus depicts the lonely, harsh, and illusory expansiveness of a strange region marked by exotic peoples and wild horses – a region in which the potential Japanese colonist, or *kaitaku-sha,* seems an alien intruder.

In Shimizu's *Kyûchô Môkojin (A Mongolian Saving a Bird),* a man in the garb of a coolie – again wearing a queue – sits beside the broken skull of a horse (see Figure 5). He leans against a rock that looks eerily like the fossilized remains of human skulls, while tenderly holding a small bird of prey near its displaced nest. The man's placid expression (he is smiling softly) and the smooth roundness of his figure contrast disturbingly with the jaggedness and unease of his alien surroundings, which hint at past violence. Could it be that one day, he, too, will be displaced from a landscape in which he no longer belongs? This would parallel the violent, imperialist displacement of nomadic indigenous peoples worldwide throughout the nineteenth and early twentieth centuries. Or is it that the region itself cannot easily support human inhabitants of any ethnicity – whether Mongolian, Han Chinese, or Japanese? Ominous black clouds seem to rise threateningly in the horizon. Shimizu appears to have viewed Manchuria, and especially its borderlands with Mongolia, as a savage land of startling contradictions, where the erotic projections of the mind could populate the space with often-violent desires. Rather than portraying it as a rapidly transforming land imbued with the physical shifts of economic development, Shimizu views Manchuria as a space for dystopian dreams – a space that, in the scattered remains of uninterred bones, contains a latent violence and features few indications of human life or habitation.

Conclusion

In the mid-1930s, the inherent contradictions expressed in the Manchurian-themed works of formerly left-wing Japanese surrealist artists and writers accurately reflect the tensions within the avant-garde forms of representation created in Japan during a politically turbulent time. Coolies and their abject, though sometimes romantically rustic, situation in Manchuria had also been a favourite literary topic of Dairen-based avant-garde poets like Kitagawa and Anzai in the late 1920s.[72] The existence of a ragged, exploited labour force in the colonial space uncomfortably reminded these cultural producers of the ruinous human cost of Japanese-led development and modernization. In contrast to travel writers and surrealist artists, proletarian authors and artists in late 1920s domestic Japan never exoticized the worker or the poor. Yet, in the mid-to-late 1930s, the setting apart of the world of Manchukuo's lower classes as "alien," "exotic," and outside the realm of Japanese experience and, therefore, in need of the paternalistic guidance of Japanese overlords, became a common feature of the works of visiting avant-garde Japanese artists, writers, and photographers.

In the paintings of Fukuzawa, Suzuki, and Shimizu, the coolie, through his labour, physically embodies the process of Japanese development in Manchukuo.[73] However, the usually Han Chinese working-class labourer himself benefits little from this progress, and, therefore, the destitution and hardship of his life symbolize the latent contradictions in the utopian rhetoric of the Manchukuo state, which touts the supposed harmony of the five ethnicities. In reality, Japanese culture reigned supreme in artistic representations, with modernity and development clearly being Japanese-generated in this new, nominally independent nation. For the Japanese artist, photographer, or writer, the Han Chinese coolie, through his labour on behalf of the modernization and development of the Manchurian region (and, by extension, the state of Manchukuo), served as a metaphor for the conflict between the modern and the traditional.

SMRC – or news media – sponsored tours of the Manchurian region ensured that prominent domestic Japanese artists, photographers, and writers would create works that reflected appropriate visions of the continent for later public consumption in domestic Japan. This linked Manchuria, and later Manchukuo, with domestic Japan and strengthened the Japanese government's imperial influence. Yet, in the eyes of the avant-garde artists, their representations of the continent had a contradictory, and even anti-bourgeois, aspect that rendered their works far more complex than was ordinary state propaganda.

In the mid-1930s to early 1940s, following the establishment of Manchukuo, images of the widespread use of Han Chinese coolie labour on worksites and in ports, along with depictions of the vast emptiness of a largely rural land, saturated various media produced by the Japanese avant-garde. In these works, it often seemed as though the utopian concept of "Manchuria" was kept separate from the idea of the modern state of Manchukuo – a conceit further discussed in the following chapters. The representations of the development and modernity of Manchukuo in contrast to the largely utopian fantasy of a rural Manchurian region were reflected in the intriguing images of the surrealist artist Fukuzawa and his associates as well as in the works of the avant-garde photographer Fuchikami.

4

The Lure of Artistic Vision and Commercial Prerogative: Ai Mitsu and the Burden of Representation, 1935 and 1943

> Art does not reproduce what is visible, but renders [it] visible.
>
> – Paul Klee

In the 1920s and early 1930s, northeast China, known as "Manchuria" by Imperial Japan, drew Japanese observers, especially artists, with its romantic image as a place of wide open spaces and quaint local customs. After the 1932 founding of Manchukuo, Japanese artists soon became part of the Japanese-led cultural mission to disseminate images of the new state to domestic Japanese, regional, and foreign audiences – mainly to those from English-speaking countries who did not officially recognize Manchukuo. Thus, whether actively or passively, they became collaborators in producing propaganda on behalf of the new state. SMRC employees and other Japanese urban colonists provided an important market for the works of these artists, who often found it difficult to subsist on their métier in their home country. Because they were Japanese artists, most of whom came from Tokyo, consumers considered their works in oils to be more prestigious than the works of local artists. Thus, in a phenomenon to which I refer as the "commercial prerogative," their works commanded the highest prices.

This chapter investigates the career of the Japanese avant-garde painter Ai Mitsu (1907-46),[1] along with the personal concerns that so often brought him to Manchukuo: the invitations of close relatives who had settled in the region and the desire to practise art in his own introspective fashion while maintaining financial stability. I examine his exhibitions in Manchukuo department stores and SMRC employee clubs and discuss the places, people, and themes he chose to represent. I also discuss how Manchukuo served Ai Mitsu's purpose as a formerly left-wing artist interested in furthering his professional vocation while, at the same time, satisfying his romantic fascination with the continent.

Ai Mitsu's career, along with his transnational travel as a surrealist artist, exemplifies the "artistic contact nebulae" that arose out of the cultural interactions between the metropole and the colonial periphery, encouraged by the Manchukuo government and SMRC's promotion of domestic Japanese artists who exhibited in Manchukuo from the mid-1930s to the early 1940s. The fact that these artists from domestic Japan would often paint subjects related to what they saw in Manchukuo was not lost on the government, news media, and entities such as SMRC. Ai Mitsu visited Japanese colonial territories in Manchukuo, Korea, and China (Shanghai) three times to sell his works and to gain inspiration by viewing the distinctiveness of the landscape and the Japanese-led development of the continent.[2]

Ai Mitsu's Early Career and Emergence as an Artist, 1920s to Early 1930s

On 24 June 1907, Ishimura Nichirô was born, the second son out of four children, to a small-landholding farming family in the mountains near Hiroshima. Komisa, his younger sister with whom he was especially close, arrived two years later. She became a favoured subject for his early art, and her later invitations to him to come and see her in Manchukuo would serve as a compelling reason for his 1935 visit. Until he was seven, the artist remained in this rural venue, but his uncle then "adopted" him as the family heir and moved him to the City of Hiroshima. Already displaying prodigious talent in drawing in elementary school, Ishimura, at age fifteen, expressed an interest in becoming an artist. However, the members of his adoptive family firmly blocked this move, although they finally let him work as an apprentice with Taniguchi Printing in the hopes that he would become a graphic designer. Nevertheless, in late 1922, armed with the techniques that he had learned at this business, the intrepid youth moved to Osaka with the desire to become a true artist who lived outside the profit-driven dictates of commercial art.[3]

In the spring of 1924, Ishimura went up to Tokyo and began to study art with Nakamura Fusetsu (1866-1943) at the *Taihei yôga-kai kenkyûjo* (Pacific Arts Institute), where he met Inoue Chôzaburô (1906-95) and Tsuruoka Masao (1907-79), both of whom would later join him to form the *Shinjinkai* (Newcomers Painting Society) in 1943. Very early on Ishimura revealed a formidable artistic talent, rendering a male torso reminiscent of Austrian expressionist Egon Schiele (1890-1918) in almost photographic detail by age eighteen. Human figures were clearly his forte, but as the 1930s progressed, he increasingly focused on scenery and still lifes. (In later works, human images would make an appearance only in his self-portraits and those commissioned by Manchukuo patrons.)

In 1926, Ishimura also became a member of the avant-garde, anti-establishment art exhibition venue *Nikkaten* (Second Section) and began to use the name Ai Mitsu. Thus, by the late 1920s, the once countrified artist acquired a new identity and became part of the flourishing avant-garde art scene in the Ikebukurô area on the margins of Tokyo. This area was called "Ikebukuro Montparnasse," so-named for its large concentration of artists' studios. Here, rent was relatively cheaper than it was in the emerging *sakariba* (bustling places) of Ginza or Shinjuku.[4] This appears to have been a difficult time financially, when the artist was under great pressure to succeed while relying on the support of various friends and relatives. He also sought to prove that his uncle's practical considerations for his adopted son's livelihood were misguided.

During Ai Mitsu's early career as an artist, his friends described him as much noted for his eccentricity and his relentless pursuit of his art, despite his poverty and (often) ill health. Neither his rural biological nor his urban adoptive parents could afford to support him in an activity they viewed more as a bourgeois hobby than as a true profession. This made it easy for Ai Mitsu to gain sympathy for the working classes, with whom he identified in interwar Tokyo, where the proletarian literature and proletarian arts movements flourished. During his late teens and early twenties, the young man associated with friends who performed in the left-oriented Tsukiji Little Theatre, populated by such iconoclastic types as the androgynous MAVOists, who were presided over by the constructivist artist Murayama Tomoyoshi.[5]

The delicate youth sometimes took on female roles in plays put on by his artistic friends, even wearing his Pierrot-like make-up with rouge, eye shadow, and lipstick long after his performance was over.[6] Ai Mitsu was apparently fascinated with how clothes affected the performance of gender and nationality, as evidenced in his 1934 caricature-like self-portrait *Jigazô [joshôshita jigazô]* [Self-portrait (Self-portrait in women's clothes)] in which he appears in Western-style women's clothing with his hair in a schoolmarm-like bun.) His earlier photographs show a somewhat effete, thin, wide-eyed, handsome young man with floppy hair cut in the continental European style of the interwar period. Dazzled by Tokyo's thriving avant-garde art scene, the artist would later broaden his horizons with three trips to Japan's neighbouring countries. These served as a mixed blessing, both financially and in terms of his artistic development.

Ai Mitsu's Shanghai Visit, 1933

In the late 1920s and early 1930s, the semi-colonial Chinese city of Shanghai served as yet another node in the East Asian nexus of modernity, which included Tokyo. Shanghai's International Settlement harboured underground leftists and gangsters of all global and national affiliations, along with the ever-present Western and Japanese capitalists who circulated in companies and banks near the Bund, facing the Huangpo River. The city also attracted Japanese artists and intellectuals, as it was often the closest they could get to Europe; moreover, it harboured a community of left-oriented activists. Since its 1917 inception, a thriving group of left-wing Chinese writers, dramatists, and artists who had studied in Japan – including Tian Han (1898-1968) and Guo Moruo (1892-1978) – circulated in and around the bookstore owned by the Japanese Christian socialist bookseller Uchiyama Kanzô (1885-1959). This location became an important rallying point for avant-garde and left-wing Japanese artists and intellectuals who wanted to meet their Chinese counterparts.

For example, in 1926, the avant-garde artist Migishi Kôtarô (1900-34) travelled in the entourage of the famous Japanese writer Tanizaki Junzaburô (1886-1965), touring Shanghai and the Jiangnan region. In 1930, he published the influential prose poem "Shanhai no ehon" ("Shanghai Picture Book") in the August edition of the "mixed-media avant-garde poetry magazine *Serekuto (Select),* featuring sketches, poems, essays, and articles by writers and artists working in the mode of Surrealism. In this magazine, images were often coupled with text in frequent collaborations between Tokyo-based poets and artists."[7] In November, following Migishi's publication of "Shanghai Picture Book," he joined the newly created *Dokuritsu bijutsu kyôkai* (Independent Artists Association) (founded in 1930), to which, by 1933, Ai Mitsu would also belong. It is possible that Ai Mitsu, after becoming familiar with Migishi's work, met him in Tokyo, and he may even have heard about Shanghai from him.

Up until 1933, Ai Mitsu regularly displayed his work with the Second Section exhibitions of avant-garde artists in Tokyo as well as in various Hiroshima-based exhibitions. From 10 to 31 March of the same year, when the Independent Artists Association held its third exhibition in Tokyo, Ai Mitsu took part for the first time and displayed one of his paintings. The members of this association were now beginning to evince a progressive tendency toward surrealism, no doubt bolstered by the influence of its leading member Fukuzawa Ichirô, who had returned from Paris in 1931. Ai Mitsu's only featured painting, *Shiro kabe (White Wall),* was said to resemble the work of the Russian émigré artist Chaïm Soutine (1894-1943), the most representative artist of the *Ecole de Paris* group.[8] After arrangements were made to display this painting, the artist immediately returned to Hiroshima and set off for Shanghai, where he would stay for about two months, touring and painting.[9] Around this time, Ai Mitsu's work would begin to transform due to contact with this group as well as his growing exposure to the traditional Chinese painting of the Song and Yuan dynasties, which he viewed in the homes of Japanese art patrons in Hiroshima and Shanghai.

At age twenty-five, Ai Mitsu made his first trip to the continent, visiting Shanghai in the spring of 1933. According to Fujisaki Aya, this jaunt was not undertaken without trepidation on Ai Mitsu's part. In a brief note written in one of the guest books at an in-house art exhibition held by the Hiroshima physician and local patron of the arts Kurokawa Setsuji (1890-1945), the artist left the following terse comments:

> March 15, 1933
> I am going to Shanghai. I must go although
> I do not want to.
> Not at all, for some reason. Ai Mitsu[10]

Kurokawa, a collector of traditional Chinese art and modern Japanese oil painting, may have suggested the Shanghai trip to Ai Mitsu to help stimulate his career. The artist paid his passage with a loan from his foster father Ishimura Umezô, who, as part of Hiroshima's traditional merchant class, probably saw the lucrative potential of the trip.

Ai Mitsu's Shanghai sojourn appears to have been taken out of duty or "commercial prerogative" rather than out of a desire to increase his artistic inspiration. In letters to his future wife, he complained bitterly about his lack of creative progress and made cynical comments about the commercial prospects of his stay.[11] Regardless of these misgivings, for about two months he sketched the city and held exhibitions in Japanese venues located in the Japanese colonial quarter of the city. For example, he gave a special one-man show in the Hongkou district's elite commerce-oriented *Shanhai Nihonjin kurabu* (Shanghai Japanese Club). Here, he exhibited independently from 13 to 14 May, featuring such historically perceptive and dark works as *Fû'un kyû (Crisis Situation), Kôhoku senseki (Ruins at Jiabei), Ho-kake bune (Sailboat),* and *Shin kôen fûkei (Scenery in the New Park).* During these months, the chilling, damp cold of the city gave way to a mild spring climate favouring the flowering of the plum and cherry trees so common to southern China – something that never failed to stimulate the creativity of traditional painters. Nevertheless, in contrast to subjects such as those depicted by the avant-garde artist and poet Migishi in his sentimental, traditional scenes of the Jiangnan region (produced following his 1926 visit), Ai Mitsu daringly portrayed the ruins of the 1932 Jiabei conflict in Shanghai, while in other paintings he depicted images that hinted that further trouble was brewing for domestic Japan, an island of modernity in a sea of building turmoil.[12] Apparently, the show garnered positive reviews in the press, and this enabled him to sell quite a few of his works.[13]

Ai Mitsu presciently sensed the growing Sino-Japanese tensions in China and starkly portrayed them to his Japanese audience, which was composed of ex-patriot capitalists from domestic Japan. Ai Mitsu's use of dark colours and deep shades dates from this period, when he became increasingly interested in the political events in the colonies. At the same time, he was inspired to combine traditional "realist" Chinese Song and Yuan dynasty painting techniques with the emerging surrealist forms of expression that were growing in popularity in Tokyo. According to John Clark: "His detailed brushwork, which owes much to his interest in the works of the Chinese Song and Yuan academies, and various other self-taught techniques, represent Ai Mitsu's personal and simultaneous discovery of characteristically Surrealist techniques of automatism, *frottage,* and possibly the knowledge of *décalcomanie.*"[14] His frustrated perfectionism also contributed to the gratingly thick layers of oil paint he applied to his canvases.

This fusion of Japanese modern (Western) and Chinese traditional (Eastern) painting techniques allowed Ai Mitsu to create an important cultural synthesis, later symbolized in the Japanese-led construction of culture in Manchukuo (in which he indirectly played a part through his two later visits and exhibitions). Like Migishi, who, four years after his historic 1926 visit to Shanghai in Tanizaki's entourage, had become renowned in the Japanese avant-garde art world, Ai Mitsu gained his fame in early 1938, roughly four years after his Shanghai visit. It can be argued that each visit to the continent boosted artists' credentials and allowed them to sell more paintings, regardless of their later subject matter or aesthetic styles.

Images of Manchuria by Visiting Domestic Japanese Artists, 1932-44

According to Chiba Yoshi, the 1932 founding of Manchukuo was an unparalleled opportunity that drew artists to the new state,[15] just as it would lure Ai Mitsu in 1935. As mentioned previously, Fujiyama Kazuo revealed how, after 1932, the numbers of Japanese artists coming to Manchukuo for tours accelerated.[16] These included both establishment artists and avant-garde artists like Ai Mitsu and Fukuzawa. Incidentally, Fujiyama served as deputy director of the *Manshûkoku kokuritsu chûô hakubutsukan* (Manchukuo National Central Museum), which was established in 1938. Clearly, he knew the importance of art as a cultural symbol – something that could help to fashion a new cultural narrative for the nascent state. Besides the establishment of a network of museums, for which the Manchukuo National Central Museum would serve as a model, several art exhibitions initiated interactions between the imperial metropole and Japan's tutelary state of Manchukuo, where art was of potential national significance.

For example, in October 1932, the Manchuria Fine Art Institution presented an impressively large exhibition with over a thousand entries.[17] Fujiyama notes that it even garnered support from the last Qing emperor, who saw the Japanese-guided state as a means of reclaiming his lost political position: "Chief Executive Pu-Yi sent Mr. Liu Pao-hsi as his personal representative to the exhibition and he delivered an address stressing and encouraging national growth in the cultural field, parallel with that in other fields."[18] Here, Pu Yi (1908-67) views the mutual collaboration of Japanese and Chinese as beneficial to the growth of a collective new culture in Manchukuo, which, besides the fine arts, presumably also included literature and drama. Subsequently, with the new designation of the client state as an "empire" in 1934, the joint Japan-Manchukuo Art Exhibition, supported by the Eastern Japan Artists Association, was held in March in honour of Pu Yi's coronation as emperor of Manchukuo. Twenty paintings by Japanese artists were given to the puppet ruler, indicating strong support from the metropole and the leading role that Japanese cultural producers were to play in constructing culture in the new state.

Following this success, Fujiyama gives an example of another exhibition with national significance – this time, in a reciprocal gesture, to honour the Japanese emperor Hirohito: "In commemoration of the historic visit of His Majesty to Japan, another art exhibition was held in May 1937 under the auspices of the Japan-Manchoukuo Cultural Society, which turned out to be the forerunner of the Imperial Art Exhibitions. The standard of exhibits was relatively high, and gave a bright outlook for future progress in cultural fields."[19] Here, art is used to celebrate the Manchukuo emperor's visit to his more authentic Japanese counterpart in a series of high-level exchanges meant to encourage further top-down interactions. Just before the July outbreak of war between China and Japan, Manchukuo's art world appeared to flourish under Japanese auspices, which encouraged exchanges between the metropole and the periphery.

Back in the imperial capital of Japan, in established Tokyo art circles from 1934 to 1944, there was an increase in the appearance of Manchuria as a subject of artwork in Japanese national exhibitions sponsored by the *Monbushô* (Ministry of Education). Chiba, by looking at the titles of art exhibited in the official venues (whose name changes mirrored Imperial Japan's reorganizations of the art world as well as wartime cultural consolidations), calculated the rising numbers of Manchurian-themed works: six in the 1934 *Teiten* (Imperial Fine Arts Academy Exhibition); nine in the 1937, forty-three in the 1941, eight in the 1942, and eleven in the 1943 *Shin Bunten* (New Ministry of Education Exhibition); twenty-three in the 1940 *Hôshukuten* (Exhibition Celebrating Japan's Founding); and six in the 1944 *Senji tokubetsu-ten* (Special Wartime Exhibition).[20]

The titles of these works indicate the type of subjects commonly depicted during a period when the popular Japanese imagination had increasingly begun to orient itself toward Manchukuo. In 1934, the year preceding Ai Mitsu's first Manchukuo trip, paintings with the following titles were exhibited: *Manshû musume (Manchurian Girl), Shinkô-koku Manshû (Newly Arisen Nation, Manchuria), Harupin fûkei (Harbin Scene), Manshû shoken (Views of Manchuria), Shôtoku Karyô (Chengde Jialing),* and *Kin sôgan Manshû onikkusu takushi (Gold Inlay Manchurian Onyx Table).*[21] These images represent exotic places and items of curiosity, young Manchurian women, and scenes of the new nation and its most exotic Western-influenced city, Harbin. Incidentally, the largest number of Manchurian-themed paintings appeared in the 1940 wartime exhibition celebrating Japan's imperial founding, which featured several paintings depicting Harbin, the families of Japanese rural pioneers, rural development, Manchuria as a paradise, Japanese war heroes at the border, and so on.[22] In 1942, the year before Ai Mitsu visited for a second time, the following Manchuria-related paintings were shown in the New Ministry of Education Exhibition: *Rehe (Jehol), Môkô no onna (Mongolian Woman), Kôchi (Yellow Earth), Rakuchi (Paradise), Hokuhen (North Face), Kaitaku sengen-tai (Rural Development Pioneers),* and *Yuki no asa (Snowy Morning).*[23] Here, in their depiction of Japanese rural pioneers, native women, and particular geographical or climatic features, the titles hint at a deep penetration into northern Manchuria. These subjects reveal a preoccupation with the region's uniqueness and offer an exotic narrative of the new state, which is most often portrayed as rural *Manshû* (Manchuria) rather than as modern, urban *Manshûkoku* (Manchukuo).

In Manchukuo itself, however, art critics like Fujiyama worried about the creation of a new type of art whose specific characteristics enabled it to be identified as *Manshû bijutsu* (Manchurian art). According to Fujiyama:

> Needless to say, the writer does not contend that Manchurian art possesses special or unique characteristics, nor a distinct standard. Manchurian art must break loose from sectionalism and attain an international place for itself in the cultural world as "Manchurian Art." [The] Manchurian environment will facilitate this[,] while the factor of human agency or the mixture of various races and their cultures must also be borne in mind when speculating on the future of Manchurian art and culture.[24]

It seems as though Fujiyama wanted *more* art specifically focused on the geographical and ethnic particularities of Manchuria rather than less. Ironically, this was to distinguish "Manchurian art" from the predominant art trends prevalent in domestic Japan, which Chinese modern artists also tended to copy. As seen in domestic Japanese art magazines like *Mizue,* most of the paintings produced by both Japanese and Chinese practitioners in Manchukuo at that time could be characterized as representing various types of realism or expressionism, with a vaguely place-related theme tying them to the new state. Fujiyama also hoped that the emergent art scene would allow a fusion of Japanese and Chinese styles: "A new effect can be produced when the true spirit and beauty of Oriental expression are coupled with the qualities of western and Japanese painting."[25]

The above passage certainly sounds like a characterization of Ai Mitsu's work, which did meld a Western-inspired surrealism with traditional Chinese painting and the modern printmaking techniques he had learned in Hiroshima. Of course, it is difficult to tell to what extent the artist maintained an interest in Japan's official art scene. However, as an avant-garde artist, he would have been familiar with the themes depicted by establishment artists, and he befriended these artists despite his differing mode of representation. In Japan, for artists who worked in oils, avant-garde originally meant "anti-establishment," and those rebelling against what they called *Kokuten ideorogi* (national art exhibition ideology) created the Second Section in 1923, which Ai Mitsu joined in 1926.[26] However, his distinctive style would not fully emerge until his 1933 acceptance into the Independent Artists Association. After two important tours of Shanghai and Manchukuo, which seemed to generate for the artist the kind of East-West stylistic fusion so lauded by Fujiyama in 1938, Ai Mitsu's art developed into a recognizable variant of surrealism.

Ai Mitsu's Manchukuo Visit, 1935

From the 1930s into the early 1940s, the visits of up-and-coming Japanese artists like Ai Mitsu, as well as the more famous Fukuzawa and his colleagues, served the Manchukuo state's goal of creating a unique, new Manchurian culture – an aim that intensified after 1937 in an attempt to set the region apart from war-torn China proper. Propaganda media of various kinds promoted an image of peace and cooperation, with the arts arising out of a previously barren region, now made fertile under the auspices of the new state and its Japanese handlers. No doubt, after 1932, the increasing saturation of the official art world with Manchurian-themed art led cultural producers like Ai Mitsu to take the trip – whether for inspiration or for practical commercial purposes. Most bourgeois Japanese families, to which the artists usually belonged, had relatives living in the new state, making the visits even more compelling. They could stay with family members in the domestic comfort of a Japanese home (albeit more Westernized than those in Japan), while experiencing the romantic, unfamiliar territory so diametrically opposed to Japan.

Thus, from March to May 1935, Ai Mitsu took a ship from Yokohama to Dairen, culminating in further travels throughout Manchukuo and Korea by train on Japanese-laid tracks under the administration of SMRC. The artist made a stopover in the Japanese-developed town of Kôshurei (Gongzhuling, in Chinese), situated in Jilin Province on the SMRC line equidistant between Siping and the Manchukuo capital of Shinkyô. As part of the region's rural development initiatives, Kôshurei boasted an agricultural experiment station set up by SMRC in 1913, which featured "agricultural improvement" and animal husbandry.[27] There, Ai Mitsu visited his brother-in-law Tachikawa Katsu, a SMRC employee married to his beloved younger sister Komisa.[28] No doubt, his arrival in this developing northern Manchurian provincial town brought prestige to his relatives for hosting this renowned Tokyo artist.

Possibly through Tachikawa's SMRC connections, some of Ai Mitsu's paintings were later exhibited in Dairen's *Mantetsu sha'in kurabu* (South Manchuria

Railway Employees Club) in Manchukuo's premier port city. These included the paintings *Manshû fûkei (Manchurian Scenery),* depicting a building on the right, with an ominous dark mass to its left; and *Kôshurei (Gongzhuling),* a scene in Komisa's new Manchurian hometown depicting a large Western-style structure in the distance. Here we see the physical vestiges of the corporation's successful program of modernization, witnessed by SMRC employees in the form of modern, Western-style oil paintings by a Japanese avant-garde artist from domestic Japan. However, Ai Mitsu's images were ambiguous and of questionable market value if assessed only for their pictorial qualities. His representative landscapes roiled with turbulent, billowing clouds of dark strokes, even three years prior to his surrealist period, which was supposedly inspired by the paintings of Max Ernst (1891-1976) and Salvador Dali, which he viewed in a 1937 Tokyo exhibition.

Many avant-garde artists like Ai Mitsu, whose canvases might not have sold as easily in the metropole, displayed their works for sale in Manchukuo. It appears that, even though the dark colours may have put off some Japanese art consumers (as in Shanghai), Ai Mitsu's sales were modestly successful. The oil paintings produced by Ai Mitsu and others perfectly suited the relatively large-scale Western-style brick homes of both the Japanese and Chinese urban bourgeoisie. Their works graced the walls of individual houses, where a Western oil painting by a Japanese artist indicated the family's advanced modern taste and added a cosmopolitan flavour to the décor.

With regard to surrealism, savvy Japanese art consumers with access to the latest Japanese art magazines, such as *Mizue* and *Atorie (Atelier),* would have known about the recent trends in modern art in Tokyo. Japanese periodicals circulated throughout the Empire and in its related territories, such as the client state of Manchukuo. For example, after 1936, following Fukuzawa's 1935 visit, the Dairen-based surrealist offshoot group *Gokakai* connected with prominent Tokyo surrealists in the *Ecole de Tokio* group through the journal of the same name. It is difficult to determine whether or not Japanese art patrons in Manchukuo fully understood the political import of avant-garde works or those by Japanese surrealist artists. However, it seems as though most believed "avant-garde" meant "ultra-modern" or "cutting edge" rather than harbouring any left-wing connotations. Moreover, by the mid-1930s, Japanese artists were retreating from political radicalism due to the death knell of the proletarian literature and proletarian arts movements following arrests and the government's increasing infiltration of unofficial art groups. The process further accelerated after 1937, with wartime cultural consolidation. In any case, the works of the avant-garde were viewed as suitable to Western-style architecture and wall space and were thought of as symbols of Japanese imperial modernity.

Nonetheless, a demand rose for all kinds of oil paintings in the new state – no matter what their stylistic qualifications or even quality. Tsuruta Gorô, an oil painter who travelled to Manchuria in the 1920s, points out that Japanese artists from Tokyo often sent their works to colonial Manchuria (and, after 1932, to Manchukuo), where they sold better than in domestic Japan. According to some artists, Manchuria/Manchukuo was a commercial "paradise."[29] Curator Otani Shôgo somewhat disparagingly notes the undoubtedly mass-produced nature of some works, which concerned themselves with rather maudlin pastoral subjects and bucolic scenery and were created by Japanese artists who were only interested in the commercial opportunities of Manchuria/Manchukuo, where consumers were not viewed as being as sophisticated as those in Tokyo.[30] Exhibition venues at which this kind of art was sold included the top floors of department stores like Dairen's Mitsukoshi and SMRC employee clubs. Obviously, the conflicting forces of the market and personal freedom of expression posed a dilemma for Japanese artists with regard to what they chose to represent. Moreover, the fact that their tours of the region were often financed by organizations with definite political agendas also played a part in how they portrayed the new state and why they may have focused so insistently on *rural* themes (which inherently supported the idea of Japanese-led development).

However, Ai Mitsu's work resoundingly differs from the work of art establishment Japanese painters who worked with Manchurian themes in that it focuses on *urban* settings rather than on rural scenery or local colour. His murky and somewhat bleak Manchukuo, as opposed to a bucolic Manchuria captured via "epiphanic representations," seems overhung by ominous clouds, like the darkness perpetuated in the works of Manchukuo-based Chinese writers, where the gloom of the new state overshadows its shiny promises. These images even show a striking contrast to the brightly coloured, though sometimes equivocal, 1936 works of the surrealist artists Fukuzawa, Shimizu Toshi, and Suzuki Yasunori. Incidentally, all three belonged to the same Independent Artists Association as did Ai Mitsu. And, in 1935, beginning in April, they toured the new state in style as guests of the leading commercial and news organizations (concurrently with Ai Mitsu in Manchukuo from April to May). Yet, Ai Mitsu's memories of his sojourn, as depicted in his art, differ greatly from those of these better-known artists, who, despite their avant-garde orientation, depicted inherent Chinese laziness, natives as an integral part of the land, and the great emptiness of the northern Manchurian plains. He appears to have completed his paintings rapidly, perhaps even working on them while abroad during his stay in Kôshurei with Komisa and her family. In contrast, Fukuzawa and his crew first produced sketches, which, on their return, they exhibited in Tokyo as an advertisement for coming attractions. By February 1936, they were displaying their oils in Osaka and regional Japanese cities. This not only helped to build interest in their works but also allowed them to sell art at a more leisurely pace. In Ai Mitsu's case, it may have been that, despite his growing reputation, he needed money quickly and was at a stage in his career when he had not yet attained the renown that he would enjoy in the late 1930s.

In the artist's three extant paintings of Manchukuo, the imperial sun appears not to shine. The sample is rather small, but important judgments can nevertheless be based on them. Here, Japan's role appears purely in the vestiges of buildings, but the rays of its beneficent modernization project do not shine on the land to illuminate its potential bounty as they do in Japanese epiphanic representations of the continent. For example, in the painting *Manshû fûkei,* the structure appears astonishingly silent (rather than busily producing on behalf of the new state), as does the lonely scene of Western buildings in Kôshurei. Indeed, human figures do not appear at all in these depictions. While Ai Mitsu insistently focuses on Japanese urban development and architecture, it seems they cannot coexist with a human element; rather, these vestiges of Japanese-led modernity are ominous intrusions on the landscape, mirroring some of the ambiguities present in Fukuzawa and his colleagues' works, which could be interpreted to support both the right- and left-wing politics of the state. Ai Mitsu habitually used darkly pigmented oils, which have since faded into blots of ambiguous colour, making it difficult to distinguish what is actually pictured.

Ai Mitsu appears to have been tortured by each of his visits to Manchukuo as the works he produced afterwards visually document the psychic turmoil of a man sensitive to his fluctuating environment and hostile toward the mass commodification engendered by urbanization in modern Japan and the Manchukuo art scene (though he himself sold his paintings as commodities). However, this first Manchukuo visit does appear to have enhanced his credentials and to have contributed to his participation in the growing phenomenon of Japanese artists' travelling to the colonies to boost their careers and to increase sales. Despite Ai Mitsu's earlier poverty and aesthetic struggles, the harsh experience of earning a living appeared to stay with him, indicating his roots in first a rural farming family and then in a lower middle-class artisan family. Nevertheless, in 1938 the artist finally gained the fame he both hoped for and feared (due to a potential loss in artistic autonomy), with his monumental work, *Me no aru fûkei,* still proudly displayed in the National Museum of Modern Art in Tokyo. By the late 1930s, with the critical acclaim of this work, the Tokyo avant-garde art world soon recognized Ai Mitsu as a sublime new talent.

Surrealism, Artistic Repression, and Wartime Mobilization, 1937-45

By mid-1936, surrealism had matured as an avant-garde movement in Japan, but, with the eruption of the Second Sino-Japanese War in July 1937, many artists, including Ai Mitsu, soon faced mounting government pressure due to the exigencies of war on the continent. After this critical date, the official art world and its associations underwent a series of reorganizations that reflected the changing political climate and the growing need for national mass mobilization. In the official art world, as opposed to that of the avant-garde of Ai Mitsu and his counterparts, this centralization had already begun with the founding of *Shin Bunten* (New Ministry of Education Exhibition) in October 1937, which remained in existence until October 1944, when a special wartime exhibition was held. This venue consolidated the official art world, ensuring that it was in accordance with government control over all realms of officially sponsored cultural production.

In addition, much to the chagrin of avant-garde practitioners, private art associations came increasingly under surveillance. This included the *Jiyû bijutsu-ka kyôkai* (Association of Free Artists), which was founded in February 1937 but had to change its name to *Bijutsu zôsakka kyôkai* (Creative Artists Association) in July 1940, after government pressure due to the left-wing activities implied by its name.[31] In addition to government surveillance of official cultural organizations, the fall of 1937 marked the beginning of the draft system, with many artists being engaged to sketch the Sino-Japanese War.

Even if artists were not drafted or persecuted due to their alleged leftist connections, their activities were severely curtailed by mass mobilization and the total war system that, after 1938, included the strict rationing of art supplies (as well as food and other goods necessary for everyday life). Some, amidst a climate of rising patriotism, felt compelled to offer support to the troops and began to dedicate their art to this end. For example, on 23 to 24 October 1937, along with colleagues in his hometown of Hiroshima, Ai Mitsu took part in an exhibition honouring sick and/or wounded soldiers entitled the *Geishû bijutsu kyôkai shôbyô shôheishi imon ken gatten* (Geishû Art Association Exhibition for the Consolation of Ill and Wounded Officers and Soldiers).[32] (Hiroshima was an important sendoff point for Japanese imperial army troops who were being deployed to the continent, as the artist himself would experience in 1944.) Following the exhibition, the artist donated several of his works to the Hiroshima Army Hospital and the Hiroshima Navy Hospital.[33]

Regardless of Ai Mitsu's conflicted opinions on the war, he was respectful of Japanese troops fighting in China and hoped to boost their morale amidst a climate of massive patriotic fervour among the Japanese people. This sort of support was common at the time, when war fever, in the form of various media, advertisements, and government exhortations, began to enflame the Japanese public. Moreover, according to Kushner: "Members of Japan's cosmopolitan elite did not distance themselves from wartime propaganda; they embraced it and involved themselves in its creation. Intellectuals were not misled; they actively helped convince others because they believed in Japan's war in Asia."[34] It may have been that, because Ai Mitsu had heard of so many young men his age and younger going to war and returning with injuries or illnesses, he felt compelled to mobilize his talents on their behalf. Despite these pressures, along with the increasing duty to support the war effort, surrealist artists were not suppressed for their political views – at least not in an organized fashion – until 1939, with the beginning of the forcible consolidation of all art groups. Those who, like Ai Mitsu, worked actively to support the war through special exhibitions may have experienced a softening of surveillance and government interference, providing yet more reasons to do so.

Nevertheless, in May 1939, the *Bijutsu-bunka kyôkai* (Society for Art and Culture) was formed, comprising a group of forty-one artists, including Ai Mitsu, Matsumoto Shunsuke (1912-48), and Asô Saburô (1913-2000), and representing what Clark and other Japanese art historians have characterized as a last gasp of resistance against the tide of wartime control.[35] Both Fukuzawa and Ai Mitsu left *Nikai-kai* to join the *Bijutsu-bunka kyôkai*. Fukuzawa served as the leader of this group, now painting exclusively in the mode of surrealism, and Takiguchi Shûzô served as its primary theorist. Though both were arrested in April 1941 for violating the Peace Preservation Law, they were released from prison by the fall of that same year. This chastened them somewhat, but debates on art, and challenges to the military's influence on culture, would continue.

Not long afterwards, one of Ai Mitsu's close friends from the Hiroshima area was arrested. This was a shock that struck uncomfortably close to home. The artist's wife, Ishimura (née Momota) Kie, whom Ai Mitsu married in 1934, noted to a visiting friend that police pressure had precipitated a mental decline in her husband: "He is like a madman. He is now creating work for the Kyôkai Exhibition but he has been stuck in the atelier on the second floor for almost a month now. He only comes out to eat or to go to the restroom and does not speak – he is almost like a madman."[36] Due to this kind of pressure (not to mention the imprisonment of its leader and primary theorist) the *Bijutsu-bunka kyôkai* soon disbanded, and Japanese curators note that even an inner-focused Ai Mitsu was forced to undergo a kind of *tenkô* (political conversion/reorientation) regarding his surrealism.

Following the December 1941 attack on Pearl Harbor, the Japanese government forced the consolidation of thirty-eight art journals into only eight. Attempts to control representation and to curtail unorthodox forms of avant-garde expression like surrealism, now tainted with an alleged connection to communism, continued apace. For example, through the 1943 establishment of the Japan Fine Arts National Service Association, all official artistic activities were now ultimately consolidated into one organization, and no official venues remained in which to exhibit works free from government oversight.[37]

Despite these pressures, and in order to maintain a sense of nominal autonomy from the state, Ai Mitsu joined Matsumoto and others from the *Bijutsu-bunka kyôkai* in April 1943 to form the private eight-person coterie *Shinjinkai,* which also included Itasono Wasaburô (1911-2001), Inoue Chôzaburô, Ono Gorô (1910-unknown), Tsuruoka Masao, and Terada Masa'aki (1912-89).[38] This group, which existed until September 1944, may well have been the last truly independent artists' association outside of the government's purview, but its activities were severely curtailed by lack of exhibition venues, the drafting of members, and the inability to get adequate supplies within Japan's total war system. Nevertheless, until the fall of 1944, these artists exhibited three times in Tokyo's fashionable Ginza area. Unfortunately, with the exception of a small pamphlet from their very first show,[39] little remains of their work.

Japanese art historians or curators like Otani Shôgo note that, throughout their exhibitions, these artists insisted on depicting themes unrelated to the dominant war paintings of the era.[40] Ai Mitsu's wife Kie once said that, while her husband painted such subjects as birds and bees, he noted that there was nothing wrong with doing so, even though many artists depicted soldiers and cannons.[41] However, there is nothing peaceful or bucolic about the fauna depicted in Ai Mitsu's works between 1942 and 1943, in which glowing, bluish-greenish birds appear to have hollow skulls and ominous flying insects resemble warplanes, much as in the works of the surrealist artist Kitawaki Noboru (1901-51), who was also active during this time.[42] According to Egawa Yoshihide, Ai Mitsu's 1943 *Umi (Sea),* exhibited in the group's first exhibition, shows the influence of Fukuzawa's war record paintings.[43] This is apparently due to the black smoke on the horizon, which was commonly found in contemporary war paintings depicting the sea.[44] The work features rather depressing flat blues and greys; waves, comprising thick brush strokes with a few strokes of red and yellow in the foreground, take up much of the painting; and a wide horizon appears at the very top. As Japan's inland sea in the vicinity of Hiroshima never boasts such high, agitated waves, it appears that *Umi* was inspired by Ai Mitsu's view of the cold blue sea near the port city of Dairen during his last Manchukuo visit.[45] It is difficult to tell how this work might be supportive of the war. Even its purported realism is expressed through thick, abstract brush strokes.

Nevertheless, artists' attempts to avoid state control did not necessarily mean that they were against the regime. As already noted in Ai Mitsu's case, most Japanese artists collaborated with the state in some fashion to support the war effort. However, I argue that the process of collaboration began long before 1941, and may have already begun in the late 1930s, when a wartime climate soon affected the general Japanese population (which, in most cases, actively supported the war effort). I concur with Yoshida Yoshie's characterization of Ai Mitsu as "a living human being in anguish during the war" rather than with the prevailing assessment of him as a "resistant artist."[46] Until recently, Japanese scholarship sought to find examples of resistance rather than to analyze varying degrees of collaboration. North American scholars, including myself, are trying to unpack the complexities of this very nuanced issue.

Debates on Wartime Art: Japanese Avant-Garde and Military Views, 1941

The progressive gloom generated by repeated government attacks on avant-garde art circles did convince some of the prominent surrealists in the *Bijutsu-bunka kyôkai* to take up the pen in influential art magazines to protest on behalf of their colleagues. In a January 1941 review of the group's exhibition in the leading art journal *Mizue,* Takiguchi lamented the loss of vitality of young artists like Ai Mitsu who needed to work in an "atmosphere where they could give birth to dreams" – an atmosphere that was lacking in wartime Japan.[47] He felt that they had lost their desire to contemplate each other's art as well as their international focus, thus negating the entire reason for the founding of their group.[48] His article discusses some of the paintings of such artists as the surrealist Fukuzawa and Komekure Suijin, who portrayed images that were also popular in establishment art views of Manchuria (e.g., bucolic country landscapes filled with rocks, stylized trees, birds, and mountain villages).[49]

Interestingly, immediately following Takiguchi's article there is a transcription of a round-table discussion entitled "Kokubô kokka to bijutsu: Gakka wa nani wo subeki ka?" ("The National Defence State and Art: What Should Artists Do?") between the art critic Araki Sueo and three members of the Army Information Bureau, including Major Akiyama Kunio, Major Suzuki Kurazô, and Lieutenant Kuroda Senkichirô.[50] Araki's view was that philosophy could be used to support the nation, but he believed that when culture became ideology, it ultimately harmed artists. Major Suzuki disagreed, arguing that culture and art were necessary for the development of the nation, especially for national defence.[51] It is interesting to note how, even in art magazines like *Mizue,* members of the military were now becoming increasingly engaged in cultural debates about the role of artists during wartime.

In a February essay appearing in the same magazine only a month later, Takiguchi responds to the above comments by discussing artists' dissatisfaction over the "immaturity" of the art world's new structure and its purpose of establishing a spirit of national defence. He contended that this negated the fact that modern art was entirely informed by developments in France, which had spread throughout the world and had aided in the global initiation of modern "traditions,"[52] which, he implied, arose out of the international flow of ideas.[53] In this way, Takiguchi refers obliquely to surrealism and connects the efforts of the Japanese avant-garde to a greater European movement. However, this might not have been the best tactic at a time when government officials were promoting a break from the West and a return to traditional Japanese values. Takiguchi attempted to make a distinction between the individual political beliefs of artists and those of the state, contending that the latter should not be imposed on artistic expression, which should remain free from both political and national boundaries.

In contrast, in a *Mizue* article the following April entitled "Bijutsu bunka seisaku no kihon rinen: Ashita he no seishin sôzô to sono hôsaku" ("The Fundamental Ideology of Art and Culture Policies: The Creation of a Tomorrow-Oriented Spirit and Its Measures"), Araki strikingly contradicts the more moderate ideas he expressed during the aforementioned round-table discussion with members of the military. In a kind of *tenkô* pronouncement, he stresses the political exigencies of the time and the need for a national cultural policy for new nations, or *Shinkô kokka*.[54] No doubt, he also made an implied reference to Manchukuo and the soon-to-be conquered regions in Southeast Asia. This shows that, by the early 1940s, even the Japanese military had begun to involve itself in heated debates over culture and its connections to Manchukuo, and it managed to persuade many in the art world to take its side. Araki held up ancient Greece and Rome as past models, and Germany, Italy, and (interestingly) the Soviet Union as contemporary models, for cultural policies.[55] These indicate support of either a fascist right-wing (Germany and Italy) culture or a communist left-wing (Soviet Union) version of a socialist culture, aesthetically similar to that of Manchukuo.

In the same issue, Matsumoto published his famous essay on the cultural destructiveness of militarism, in which he refutes the ideas of Araki and the military participants of the round-table discussion, arguing that artists were "not political ideologues" and that the reality was that, in wartime Japan, they could not express themselves properly.[56] Matsumoto escaped the draft due to his deafness and, in 1942, painted a self-portrait in which he was dressed in the garb of a worker rather than in a military uniform. Prior to the eruption of the Pacific War, Matsumoto's rebuke, along with the lively debates between the avant-garde and the military over the role of art and culture in supporting nationalist ideals, showed that there was not yet a complete government moratorium on such discussions; rather, the enactment of these nationalist ideals was a work in progress.

After 1937, for Japanese artists enlisted as soldiers, China south of the Great Wall no longer served only as the subject of a yearning for a traditional culture Japan had left behind. Now, more often than not, they depicted it as a battlefield or as a venue in which Japan's cultural ambitions for the Greater East Asia Co-Prosperity Sphere could be played out.[57] Indeed, by 1942, war paintings were fairly much the norm in the official art world, but persistent representations of China and Manchuria continued to hint at Japan's mission on the continent as being part of a "sacred war."

For example, Umehara Ryûsaburo's (1888-1986) 1942 painting *Pekin shûten (Beijing Autumn)* depicts the peaceful scenery of Japanese-occupied Beijing as viewed from the artist's window.[58] From on high, the artist's gaze scans a traditional Chinese cityscape of walls, gates, pagodas, and temples, supporting the Japanese government's official pan-Asianist philosophy (which, earlier, had been applied to Manchukuo). Prior to the 1911 toppling of the Qing Dynasty (1644-1911), in order to ensure that no Chinese imperial subject could look down on the Manchu emperor Pu Yi, no civilian buildings in Beijing could be taller than one story. It is notable that Japanese troops occupied Beijing in the late summer of 1937 and that the city soon became part of a puppet regime viewed as a satellite within the growing sphere of Japanese control – a sphere that also included neighbouring Manchukuo, the former "land of the Manchus." Not long after 1942, establishment artists, who supported the state's mission of ensuring that Manchuria would serve as a site for Japan's colonial dreams, increased their depictions of this region.[59]

Manchukuo's Wartime Consolidation of the Arts, 1937-43

In Manchukuo, Japanese officials further attempted to solidify the cultural dependence of the new nation on Imperial Japan by setting up a new national art exhibition system that resembled the one in domestic Japan. For example, only a couple of months before the outbreak of the Second Sino-Japanese War, a national art exhibition was held in Shinkyô, marking the beginning of a yearly system that was institutionalized the following year (i.e., as soon as mass-mobilization became a reality in domestic Japan). Thus, the first Manchukuo state-sponsored art exhibition was held in May 1937 in honour of the Manchukuo emperor's visit to Japan for a meeting with Emperor Hirohito. In 1934, Pu Yi had been crowned the new state's emperor, supposedly putting him on equal footing with his Japanese counterpart; but, after 1937, his role was increasingly subordinated to that of Hirohito – to the point at which, in a 1940 Shinto ceremony, he was actually reclassified as Hirohito's younger half-brother.[60] Not surprisingly, Pu Yi's visit to Hirohito resembled nothing so much as an act of fealty to Imperial Japan on the part of a weaker tributary nation.[61] According to Yamamurô Shin'ichi, Pu Yi's reinstatement as emperor allowed greater Japanese control of Manchukuo and better reflected its relationship to the imperial Japanese system.[62] The fact that an official art system would be institutionalized on the occasion of an imperial visit shows that even cultural activities now had an important symbolic function for Imperial Japan and its colonies, including the nominally independent state of Manchukuo.

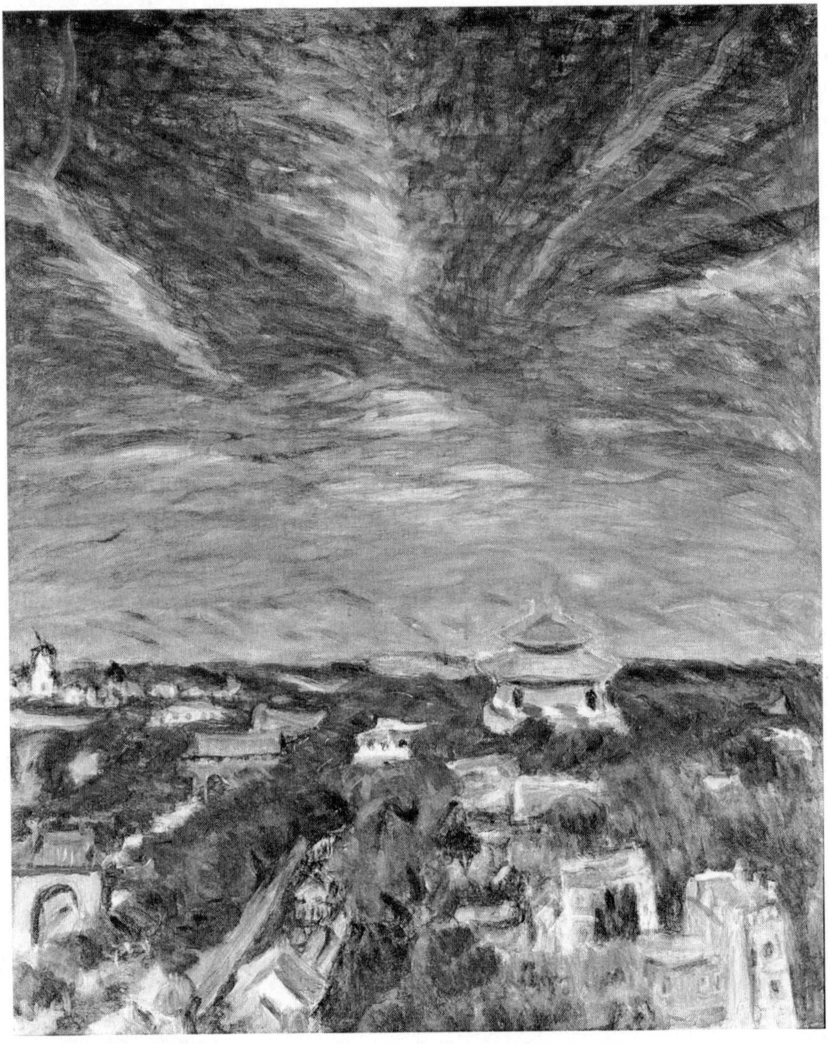

Figure 10 Umehara Ryûsaburô, *Pekin shûten* [Beijing autumn], 1942, The National Museum of Modern Art, Tokyo.

The inextricable cultural relationship between Manchukuo and the Japanese archipelago during wartime, like that of a colonial nation, was underlined in the May 1938 creation of a yearly art exhibition system called the *Manshûkoku bijutsu tenrankai* (Manchukuo Art Exhibition). In late 1939, this exhibition system was formed into a cultural association under the purview of the Japan-Manchoukuo Cultural Society, an organization supervised by the Shinkyô-based minister of people's welfare. It was intended to promote bilateral cultural relations between Japan and Manchukuo, but the former played a leading role in its guidance.[63] Thereafter, it simply became known as *Kokuten* (National Exhibition), after an exhibition system based on the Ministry of Education-sponsored Tokyo salon *Shin Bunten* (New Ministry of Education Exhibition). This official art institution accepted Western-style and traditional Asian art forms created by Japanese and Chinese painters from Taiwan and Manchukuo, thus showing the centrality of Japan's art system to the new state, which also attracted colonial painters from other parts of the Japanese Empire.

However, not surprisingly, Japanese avant-garde artists in Dairen and southern Manchuria disparagingly referred to the above initiative as *Kokuten ideorogi* (national exhibition ideology), accurately divining the propaganda-like nature of the new salon system that state media and publicity chief Mutô Tomio helped design to showcase the new state's artistic ideals.[64] The painters connected to groups like the surrealist *Gokakai* often refused to send works to exhibitions that they believed constituted an assault on artistic freedom. Indeed, the kind of art usually favoured by judges either glorified Manchukuo's ideal of *kyôwa* (harmony) or reflected the utopianism and exoticism of "epiphanic representations."[65] Manchukuo's new art exhibition system represented the state's increasingly centralized control of culture under Mutô after spring 1939, and it confirmed that it was clearly linked to the figure of the Japanese emperor (its authenticating symbol).[66]

Besides the few examples stated above, the close relationship between Japan and Manchukuo was further evinced by yet more reorganization of cultural organizations and activities. Many of the wartime transformations of various institutions in Japan were later instituted in Manchukuo. In domestic Japan, officially recognized artists' associations, exhibition venues, and even writers' groups were forcibly consolidated by the state around 1940. Not surprisingly, this process of consolidation began a year later in Manchukuo in connection with further mass mobilizations in domestic Japan and its colonies just prior to the Pacific War, and it was symbolized by the Manchukuo Publicity and News Bureau's 1941 issuing of the *Prospectus for the Guidance of the Arts and Culture*. The intensification of Japan's war efforts after 1941 marks the acceleration of the wartime consolidation of cultural activities in Manchukuo as the nation was prepared as a military base from which to attack Southeast Asia while conducting long-term operations in China proper. This state-sponsored consolidation marks a fundamental change in Manchukuo's formerly liberal cultural policies, advocated by Ishiwara since the early 1930s.

Ai Mitsu's 1943 Manchukuo Trip

After 1937, Manchukuo's relative stability, while the rest of China was at war, helped Japanese cultural activities to flourish under the propaganda of a regime that touted the cultural strength of Imperial Japan. The economy also remained fairly prosperous, allowing the products of Manchukuo factories to furnish the Japanese war effort while sustaining the comfortable bourgeois lifestyle of urban Japanese colonists. Certainly, art remained an affordable luxury for this group, and the consumption of oil paintings as purchasable symbols of status for the Western-style parlour continued apace. Ai Mitsu's artistic career shows how the occupied areas drew former avant-garde artists from Japan to depict Japanese economic and cultural developments, and it serves as an example of the cultural interaction between the "colonial" periphery and the Japanese archipelago deep into the wartime period. The Manchukuo government continued to benefit from these kinds of exchanges, through which artists indirectly served as propaganda vehicles for the success of the new state by representing its unique cultural attractions and the pace of its development.

Ai Mitsu travelled once more to Manchuria in the fall of 1943 on the invitation of Sawada Gi'ichi, a wealthy clothing retailer at the *Rôka yôkô* (Bloom Western Outfitters) Dairen department store and head of its associated art department, which sold Western oil paintings. From September to December, the artist toured with Sawada, painted, and exhibited his works, in addition to fulfilling a commission for the clothier's portrait. During his fall sojourn, the Dairen-based artist Mitsui Seishô even arranged for a personal exhibition of Ai Mitsu's works in the swank lobby of the SMRC-run Yamato Hotel. This was the hotel patronized by Sôseki and a slew of other notable Japanese guests representing much of Japan's cultural establishment. As mentioned previously, SMRC's chain of Yamato hotels, despite suffering a consistent loss of economic revenue, served to demonstrate the pride of Japanese culture to SMRC-hosted visitors as well as to independent tourists.[67] Therefore, the hotel's hosting of an exhibition of paintings by Ai Mitsu, whose 1938 work *Me no aru fûkei* had already garnered international critical acclaim, represented a great publicity coup in Japanese-run colonial Manchuria's traditional port city.

Due to the relatively good economy in Manchukuo and colonial Korea, Ai Mitsu had greater success in selling his works there than in domestic Japan, which, by then, was experiencing the exigencies of wartime. From Dairen, he continued his travels on the South Manchuria Railway to the capital city of Shinkyô and the exotic White Russian-influenced city of Harbin. In Harbin, Ai Mitsu stayed in the Hotel Moderne, the former temporary lodgings for members of the Lytton Commission, who had rejected Manchukuo's legality over a decade earlier in 1931. Here, in the middle of December, while waiting for his ship to arrive in port in Dairen, he tried to paint outdoors; however, his paints froze, so he produced his artwork by viewing the scenery through the windows of the hotel or department stores.[68] The famed Hotel Moderne was situated in the Kitayskaya district, a Russian-inspired shopping area full of boutiques, department stores, restaurants, and

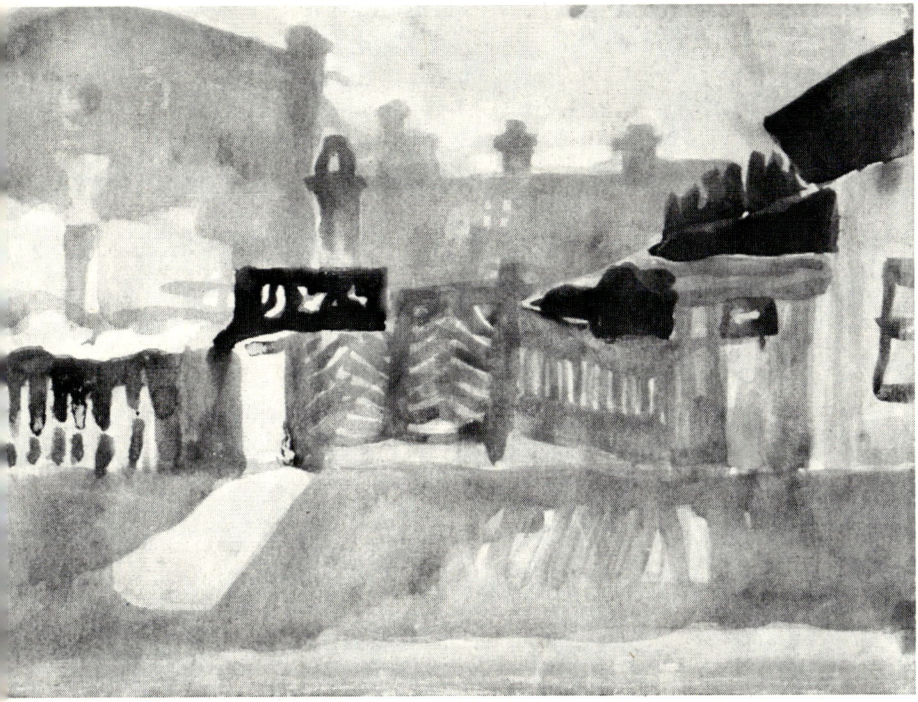

Figure 11 Ai Mitsu, *Manshû fûkei* [Manchurian scene], 1943. The Museum of Modern Art, Kamakura and Hayama.

nightclubs, now restored to a semblance of its former glory, complete with rickshaw cabs.

A painting the artist completed in 1943, *Manshû fûkei (Manchurian Scene),* shows, in bluish colours, the murky scene of a factory courtyard, with a standard gate (reminiscent of modern Republican China) allowing entrance and, within, a collection of buildings with myriad chimneys. Here, the cool, crisp air of late fall in northeast China seems hazy with the smoke of burning leaves, coal, and wood as breath, smoke, and exhaust rise up in billows. The factory itself lies shrouded against the elemental atmosphere. The harshness of the climate appears to have made a deep impression on Ai Mitsu.

Ai Mitsu's 1943 visit came at a time of great transformation in his artistic style and in his thematic focus. After 1941, the artist was forced to distance himself from surrealism due to his artistic group's voluntary renunciation of it as it was now deemed tainted by communism. Following his third trip to the continent, Ai Mitsu began to move toward self-portraits. This may have been an outgrowth of the portraits he was commissioned to paint by local art patrons in Dairen and Harbin. Possibly, while examining his subjects, he began to examine himself as an object of his own art. Besides his symbolic, surrealistic work *Me no aru fûkei,* his three extant self-portraits are his most renowned works and have garnered much contemporary critical attention. On 5 October, in a letter to his wife, Ai Mitsu comments: "Facing the great outdoors, I'm painting. In order to not be gripped by a wearying modern nervous condition *[shinkei shitsu na kindai byô],* I notice that I want to collide head-on with nature in its naked wholeness."[69] This statement hints at the kind of fascistic return to the land and native place recommended by Japanese philosophers in the wake of the 1942 Overcoming Modernity symposium. Here, the locality stands in deep contrast to the one with which the artist was familiar, and he seems to make a conscious effort to overcome (and resist) the effete, nervous urban mentality that was so separate from his rural upbringing.

Indeed, the three self-portraits completed after his last Manchukuo sojourn portray the artist, surrounded by a dark, heavy background, resolutely facing an elemental force. In each painting, his face appears in profile, looking diagonally to the right, with his chest conveying a weighty immobility and his eyes darkened and turned inward.[70] While southeastern Manchuria provided Ai Mitsu with a taste of its harsh weather, on his return to Japan, the artist experienced a deepening wartime climate of deprivation and self-sacrifice on behalf of the men at the front. During these times, when the government proclaimed that "extravagance [was] the enemy," it seemed that his Orientalist conceptions of birds, bees, insects, and flowers, along with surreal compositions of the natural world depicted in an aura of an other-worldly light, no longer fit the very real austerity of total war. His earlier self-portraits of a somewhat bohemian, even effeminate young man, contrast sharply with the self-portraits he produced after his 1943 trip. One of his last self-portraits, completed in 1944 just prior to his military conscription, shows a serious, middle-aged man in a white shirt suffused with yellow light, harbouring a stern expression and displaying the imminent growth of a beard. Apparently, the wartime emphasis on a strong masculinity along with the time he spent in the rugged Manchukuo development areas had an impact on this self-portrait.

The Artist's Military Service, 1944-45

Not long after completing the aforementioned series of portraits, Ai Mitsu would be drafted, remaining in China until the end of a war from which he would never return, languishing in a Shanghai hospital amidst the chaos of postwar China's emergent civil war. He enlisted as a soldier on 21 May 1944 and entered the second unit of the 4th Hiroshima Division, leaving Hiroshima on 26 May and arriving in Nanjing on 2 June. When Japan surrendered on 15 August 1945, Ai Mitsu was fighting in south central China, and his unit moved to Wuchang for the formal declaration of defeat. In November, while in Wuchang, the artist was interned in the 127th Military

Hospital with pleurisy (liquid had accumulated in his right lung). This was compounded by an attack of amoebic dysentery, leading to his removal to Shanghai's 175th Military Hospital.

While interned in a hospital bed next to the artist Kushida Yoshikata, Ai Mitsu's fate would be to die of these maladies at the relatively young age of thirty-eight, in the damp winter cold of 19 January 1946 in a Shanghai infirmary in a city that he had originally balked at visiting. Arguably, the artist's military service on the continent led to his illness and further mental decline. As a man already plagued by melancholy and hyper-sensitivity, it is not a stretch to assume that illness due to malnutrition, knowledge of the loss of the war, and news of the Hiroshima atomic bombing would have plunged him into a depression, thus leading to his further deterioration. Before his death, Ai Mitsu would experience a China liberated from Japanese oppression and an independent Manchuria, but then he soon saw China descend into the chaos of civil war.

Conclusion

Ai Mitsu was one of the least enthusiastic of the cultural producers under discussion, and he falls into the category of "occasional propagandist,"[71] or, more accurately, "unofficial propagandist."[72] He was not officially invited by the SMRC, news media organizations, or Kantô Army, but the venues in which his works were displayed were important to the company and its employees. The works Ai Mitsu produced for these venues fall into the category of either "commercial prerogative" or "occasional propaganda." Because they featured Manchukuo as a subject, they contributed to saturating the art market with images of the new state, thus heightening further awareness of the area among art viewers, patrons, and consumers.

Thus, while Ai Mitsu did not intentionally set out to produce a multi-pronged "avant-garde" propaganda, as did the group of artists with the surrealist Fukuzawa, who received invitations from corporate, media, and military organizations, his works nonetheless served as "propaganda vehicles."[73] Despite their dark nature and possible critique of the Manchukuo experiment, they were still products of a regime that looked favourably on Japanese artists going to the new state, regardless of their vision or how their visit was arranged, because it provided free publicity for the aims of Imperial Japan.

5
Reflections of Labour and the Construction of the New State: Fuchikami Hakuyô and *Manchuria Graph,* 1933-41

As seen in the preceding chapters, from the early twentieth century into the 1930s, Manchuria became a fascinating site where Japanese observers could view the intriguing juxtaposition of modern and traditional, of Japanese and Han Chinese culture, and of Japanese colonist and working-class native in an area of growing strategic importance to Imperial Japan. After the Japanese-led founding of the nominally independent state of Manchukuo in 1932, the semi-public/semi-private SMRC collaborated with the Manchukuo government's Publicity and News Bureau, or *Kôhôsho,* in sponsoring visits of Japanese avant-garde writers, artists, and photographers who were to describe the Japanese-led program of modernization and local cultural attractions along the rail lines.

Some, like the photographer Fuchikami Hakuyô (1889-1960), enjoyed the initial tour so much that they chose to stay and make the depiction of Manchuria their life's work. SMRC initially attracted Fuchikami to tour the region in 1927 and then, after his photographs were successfully received in Japan and the United States in 1933, hired him to direct the photography for its new magazine, *Manshû gurafu (Manchuria Graph).* This publication supported the Manchukuo *Kôhôsho*'s propaganda initiatives and, through SMRC's sponsorship of bilingual magazines and periodicals, flooded domestic Japan (and other countries) with modern visual images of Manchukuo's success. In the mid-1930s, SMRC periodicals like *Manshû gurafu,* put forth by Fuchikami and his team, created visual propaganda for the Manchukuo regime by depicting modern, efficient cities surrounded by peaceful, picturesque rural areas populated by intrepid Japanese agricultural settlers.

In the mid-1930s, the Chinese coolie and the Japanese *kaitakusha* (agricultural settler), both of whom highlight the regime's focus on productivity, increasingly became symbols of Manchukuo's desire for development. However, they also reflect the state's inherent contradictions as the growing numbers of urban labourers were the result of the displacement of native

Manchurian farmers from land that was now being used for Japanese settlement. Here, I investigate the images shot by Fuchikami and his crew and the politically complex messages they convey, with Manchuria seemingly becoming a "paradise" for both the Japanese settler and the Chinese worker.

Images and Equivocation

Mariko Tamanoi begins the introduction of her recent study on Manchuria and memory with the discussion of a 1934 photograph by Terashima Manji (1898-1983), a member of the *Manshû shasshin sakka kyôkai* (Manchuria Photographic Artists Association [MPAA]).[1] The photograph *Nan Man no aki (Autumn in Southern Manchuria)* appears in the January 1939 edition of *Manshû gurafu,* under Fuchikami's meticulous editing.[2] The image shows a pastoral scene in which sheep graze under a tree and a telephone pole and electric lines appear in the distance. The archetypal Manchurian countryside is thus linked to a broader urban communications network amidst a sepia wash of nostalgia for the rural past. The photo first captivated Tamanoi in the 1994 *Ikyô no modanizumu* (Modernism in Manchuria) exhibition organized by Nagoya curator Takeba Jô. However, she did not learn of its true history until over a decade later, when the owner of Terashima's materials noted that the image was actually a shot of the local execution ground, where Chinese political activists were killed.[3] Terashima was a SMRC employee and a former member of its photography club, which, under Fuchikami's leadership, evolved into the MPAA. Clearly, Terashima belonged to the Japanese establishment and could by no means be labelled a radical or an activist. Why, then, did he choose to capture this multilayered image for consumption by Japanese, regional, and international audiences?

It can be argued that the equivocal, compressed nature of what I term "memory strata" makes *Nan Man no aki* "avant-garde" rather than "modernist." This image could serve both as a critique *and* as an endorsement of the dominant paradigm espoused by Manchukuo's framers or the SMRC-supported publication *Manshû gurafu,* to which photographers like Terashima and Fuchikami contributed their work. The multivalent constellation of meanings reveals the mixed feelings of these Japanese observers, who, like Sôseki decades before them, saw the cracks in the rhetoric of Japanese development and domination. Yet, they were also drawn in by the appeal of a utopian vision emphasizing the attainment of goals not possible in a cramped and politically repressive domestic Japan.

In my earlier studies of the Japanese avant-garde writers Anzai and Kitagawa, who were active in the 1920s and 1930s, I argue that their equivocal descriptions of colonial Manchuria, in poems or short stories, could be both supportive and critical of Japanese imperialism.[4] Each author voyeuristically reproduces the "colonial gaze" common to contemporary observers of his time while critiquing the negative conditions issuing from Japanese imperialism. One of their common obsessions is labour in Manchuria, performed by either coolies or prostitutes. This topic was also of concern to the proletarian literature and proletarian arts movements, whose writers or artists, unlike Anzai and Kitagawa (who joined it in 1931), never exoticized the working classes.

I propose that the Japanese response to the Manchurian region prompted a complex set of reactions that mirrored the essential contradictions of the Japanese imperial project itself. Cultural production in the form of art, photography, or fiction encapsulates these deeply engrained, psychologically internalized beliefs. Many of the cultural producers attracted to Manchukuo professed vaguely left-oriented political beliefs and had flirted either with Marxism or with the proletarian literature and proletarian arts movements prior to their coming to this new state. While superficially professing their allegiance to Manchukuo by accepting a tour or employment there, some of their former ideals remained, leading to the uneasy coexistence of contradictions that were often not apparent until their images were analyzed.

Like Tamanoi, I was seduced by these photographs of a past still in flux. One of the images that most captivated me while I was leafing through original copies of *Manshû gurafu* at the Waseda University Central Library was a grainy, modernist photograph of a teapot, entitled *Still Life on Road Surface,* by Seitoku Nobuyoshi (unknown).[5] This object, sublimely evoking the essential qualities of the absent, model Chinese labourer, appears in the June 1937 edition of the pictorial dedicated to art photography of Manchuria.[6] The cover features an image of a Chinese woman spinning wool, shot by Date Yoshio (1907-46) and entitled *Ryokukage (Green Shadow).*[7] Not surprisingly, *Fûkei (Scene),* Terashima's idyllically rendered "epiphanic representation," also appears, here capturing a herd of sheep grazing, heads down, amidst an almost maternal hillock covered by bushes, seemingly rendered in brushstroke. By contrast, Fuchikami's shot of a pipe emerging from a soybean oil-processing plant,[8] along with Seitoku's image of a factory belching smoke,[9] demonstrates a contrasting modernist aesthetic not unlike the New Objectivity of German photographer Albert Renger-Patzsch (1897-1966).

The influence of pictorialism on certain images produced by Fuchikami and his team led to a particular portrayal of photographic images as paintings, where the hard edges of photographic realism blended into impressionism through a blurry diffusion of light and/or a grainy texture. As seen in the story of Terashima's image, which so intrigued Tamanoi, pictorialism obscures the murky history of hidden violence behind Japan's control of Manchuria. In these images, the sun does not shine brightly, but, like the

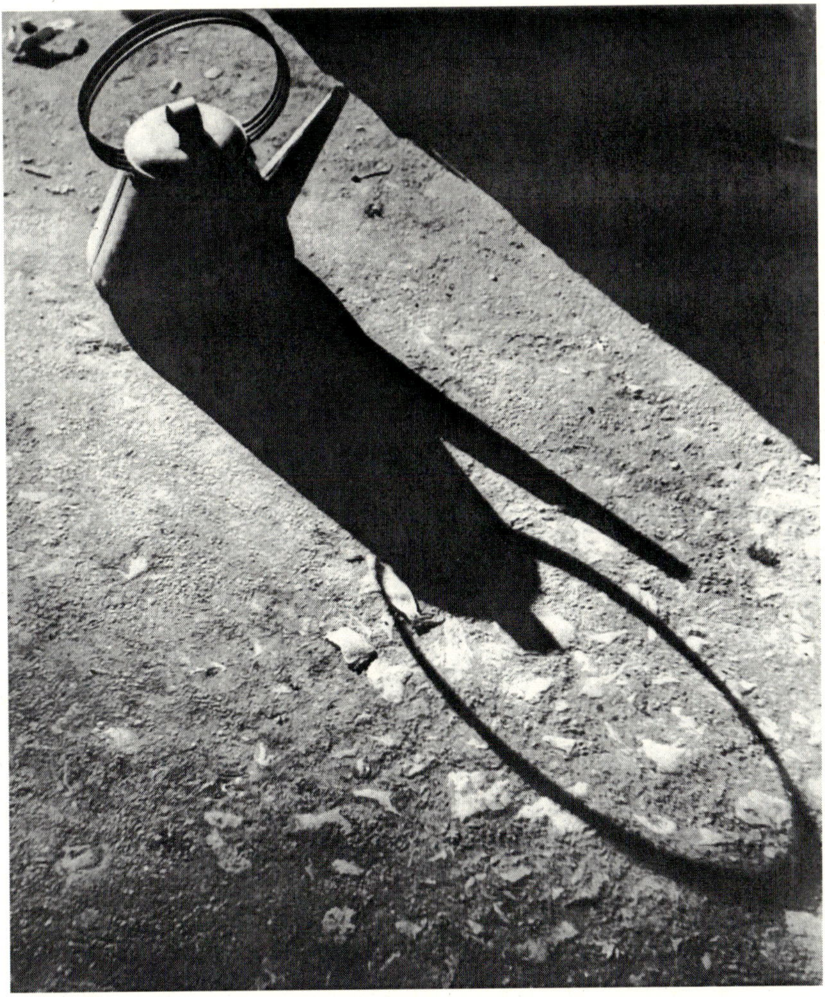

Figure 12 Seitoku Nobuyoshi, "Still life on road surface," *Manshû gurafu* [Manchuria graph], June 1937, Waseda University Central Library collection.

Dairen poet Anzai's "warped sun" in the poem "Kakô" ("Estuary"), from his 1929 collection *Gunkan Mari (Battleship Mari),* or even in Fuchikami's 1930 *Raku-hi (Nightfall),* featuring malnourished coolies (a woman, her young son, and an old man) using baskets to remove earth from a worksite,[10] Japan's imperial project in Manchuria filters through a distorted lens that obscures, but also hints at, the inherent violence of the colonial space.

By contrast, Fuchikami's similarly named image *Sekiyô (Setting Sun),* reproduced in the January 1939 edition along with Terashima's *Nan Man no aki,*

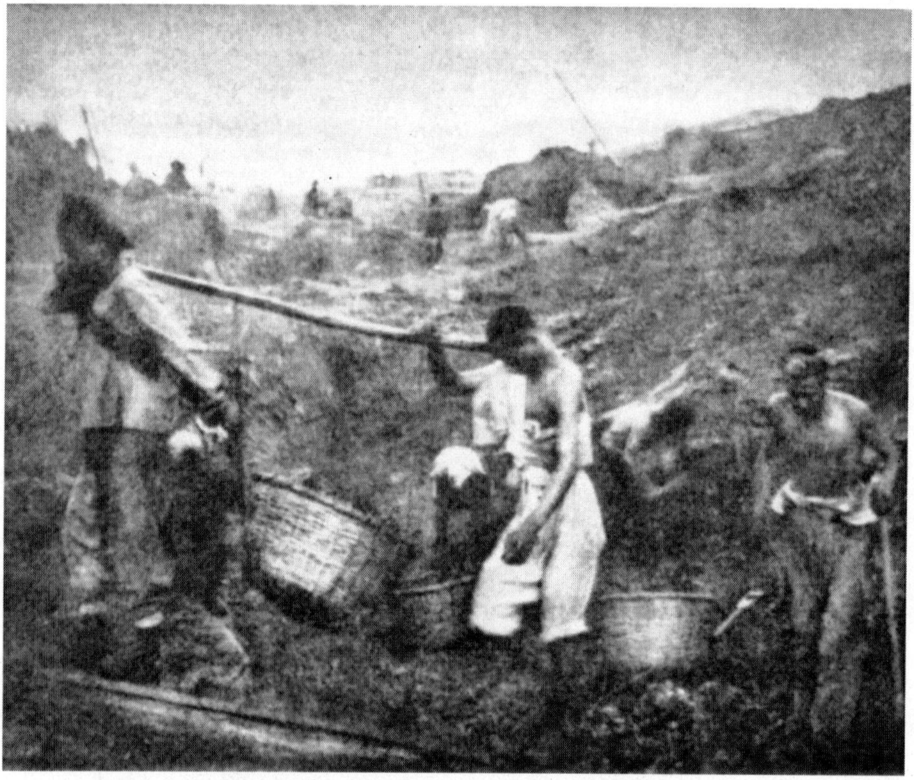

Figure 13 Fuchikami Hakuyô, *Raku-hi* [Nightfall], May 1930, *Manshû shashin nenkan* [Manchuria photography annual], Waseda University Central Library collection.

features a vast landscape with the rays of the setting sun illuminating distant, skeletal trees (near the horizon point), though without coolies (usually portrayed as robust and male in the Manchukuo period) or any other forms of life.[11] According to Norman Smith, in the works of Chinese women writers in Manchukuo – at least those not censored due to official misogyny – darkness served as a trope to criticize the "land of the rising sun."[12] According to him: "These writers manipulated the extensive focus on the dark to subvert Japanese sun-centered propaganda. The rising sun was symbolic of imperial Japan as well as being the physical embodiment of masculinity *(yang),* thus serving as a tool for the criticism of imperialism and patriarchy."[13] Somehow, epiphanic representations like *Sekiyô* or *Nan Man no aki,* both appearing in the same 1939 edition of *Manshû gurafu,* could coexist with the critique of a regime perhaps in decline.

Fuchikami and his associates' shots, which stand in stark contrast to Renger-Patzsch's socialist realist version of photography, show how the

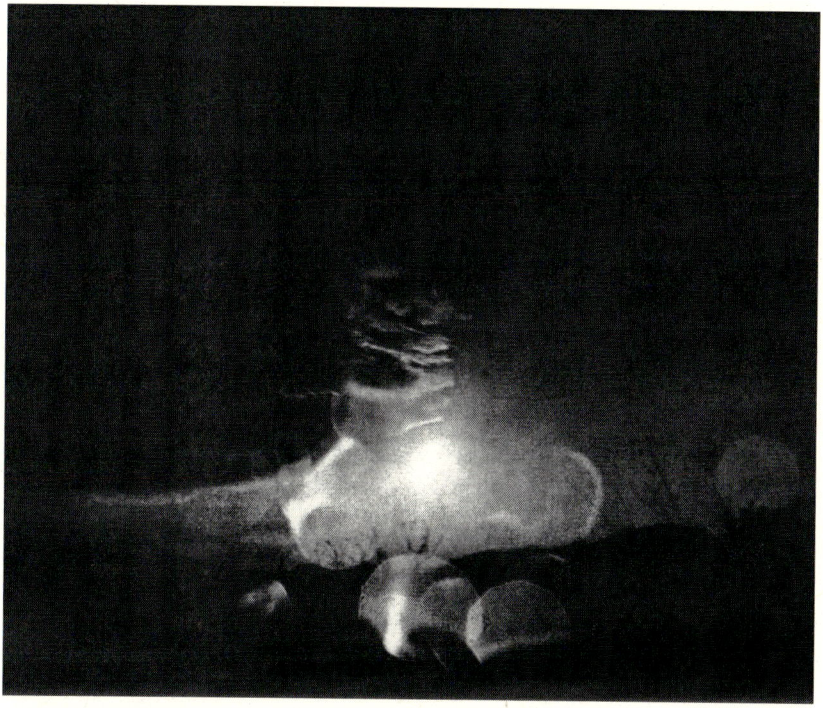

Figure 14 Fuchikami Hakuyô, *Sekiyô* [Setting sun], *Manshû gurafu* [Manchuria graph], January 1939, Yumani shobô 2008 reprint, Duke University Perkins-Bostock Library collection.

contradictions of a modern Manchukuo and a timeless, traditional Manchuria can coexist, evoking complex strata of impressions. The asynchronic, simultaneous existence of two time scales mirrors the unevenness of development in the region. The sublime portrayal of a teapot in rustic surroundings, or the setting sun in an empty landscape, can therefore exist together with the coolie worker in a factory belching smoke because they are part of a new, ahistoric entity called Manchukuo. In H.D. Harutoonian's discussion of modernist forms of cultural representation and the rise of fascism in Japan, he posits that "modernism sought to flee history at the same time that it appealed to older historical representations of the authentic cultural object as a way to replace abstraction and fragmentation with concreteness and wholeness."[14] While Renger-Patzsch's images were used to support German fascism in the 1930s, those of Fuchikami and his team were used to bolster support for the Manchukuo regime, which can be seen as following a fascist model even more successfully than Japan (though one more resembling Mussolini's fascist Italy than Hitler's Germany – at least with regard to its relative lack of racialist polemics).

Alan Tansman describes how cultural production can be diverted into supporting political aims through the concept of the "fascist moment,"[15] which he defines as "an aesthetically cathartic epiphany susceptible to being politically channelled into the creation of a fascist mood."[16] Its insidiousness lies in the fact that it "represents the dangerous alignment of aesthetics and politics. It provides the possibility of conversion by positing and taking advantage of an 'expressive vacuum' and filling it with the misleading promise of a new way of being."[17] This "promise" of a utopia, as reflected in the photographs of Fuchikami and his crew in *Manshû gurafu,* led the pictorial's readers to believe that the new state was modern (yet comprising empty land for rural settlers) and that it was made productive through coolie labour (but populated by native peoples who would otherwise squander its potential). However, as indicated above, the memory strata evoked in these photographs connote deeper layers of meaning, which contrast with the obvious dominant paradigm – hence, due to their complexity and their equivocal nature, these images can be termed "avant-garde propaganda." However, before we can fully unpack the potential meanings contained in these photographs, we must examine SMRC's promotion of a photography club that later evolved into the MPAA, and, from 1933 to 1944, its orchestrated effort to use the talents of these photographers for propaganda purposes in *Manshû gurafu.*

SMRC Tours and the Promotion of Colonial Manchuria as a Site of Difference

Early twentieth-century Japanese accounts often portrayed the Manchurian space as being vastly different from that of domestic Japan in terms of culture, customs, and development; however, in the 1930s, Manchukuo's Japanese leadership tried to link the region to domestic Japan by establishing in it a Japanese cultural presence. Though rarely explicitly referenced as doing so, the SMRC conglomerate played a key role in promoting such descriptions of Manchuria through its presentation of the railway as a symbol of Japanese-led progress. As discussed in Chapter 1, immediately after its 1907 establishment, SMRC invited Japanese cultural illuminati like Sôseki to visit Manchuria on guided tours that differed little from those it later orchestrated for Manchukuo in the 1930s. These figures brought the culture of domestic Japan with them and, on their SMRC-hosted tours, often gave lectures along the rail lines for Japanese audiences.

All these cultural producers notably focus on the Chinese working classes (and their labour) as participants (or as those who *should* be participating) in the Japanese effort to modernize colonial Manchuria and/or the independent state of Manchukuo. The region thus becomes a space onto which Japan projects conflicting desires: it should be a successful example of Japanese-led modernization and development while also functioning as a rural utopia for Japanese agrarian settlement. These two phenomena went hand-in-hand as Chinese and Korean farmers were increasingly removed from their land to make way for Japanese rural colonists. These farmers then had to work as coolies in Manchukuo's newly arising cities.

Led on choreographed SMRC tours, Japanese observers like the writer Sôseki (in 1909) and the photographer Fuchikami (in 1927) often exaggerated the differences between Japan and the continent. Indeed, they were presented in almost diametrically opposed terms: continental laziness and old-fashioned Chinese traditions versus Japanese efficiency and modernization. It was implied that, because the Han Chinese were inherently lazy, only Japanese control over Manchuria could make the region productive. This productiveness would be accomplished by subjecting the incredible labour power of the coolie to the superior methods of Japanese management and organization. In the decades spanning the SMRC-sponsored tours of Sôseki and Fuchikami, Japanese reactions to colonized natives changed little, even though they may have been mildly critical of *how* the SMRC conglomerate undertook the development in Manchuria or, later, evinced some concern as to whether the artistic depiction of Manchukuo accurately reflected its reality.

Fuchikami's Early Career and SMRC Recruitment

From the 1930s to the early 1940s, the SMRC conglomerate actively collaborated with the Manchukuo government and its propaganda organization, the Manchukuo Publicity and News Bureau, to promote travelogues, novels, art, and photography collections based on touring Manchukuo to show its potential for development under Japanese auspices. This would serve as a template for other Asian nations. It is significant that, in 1932, the Kantô Army officially decided to hire a photographer with avant-garde tendencies to represent the construction of the new state to the Japanese public as well as to regional and foreign audiences. After working for a few months on behalf of Manchukuo's Japanese military, Fuchikami returned to his post with SMRC and continued colluding with state aims. SMRC initially courted the avant-garde photographer to take artistic photographs of the region using the latest, most modern techniques – first by funding his tour in 1927 and then by hiring him as a temporary employee in 1928. Following the founding of Manchukuo, in 1933 Fuchikami was put in charge of the company-sponsored pictorial *Manshû gurafu,* which was to become SMRC's (and the regime's) primary propaganda publication.

Born in Kumamoto Prefecture and educated in the Saga area and Nagasaki, Fuchikami became active in Japanese photography circles in his mid-thirties.[18] After organizing the *Nihon kôga geijutsu kyôkai* (Japan Photographic Art Association) in 1922, he initiated and edited the Kobe-based art photography journal *Hakuyô (White Willow),* which remained in circulation until

1926. Following the rebuilding of Tokyo in the aftermath of the 1923 Great Kantô Earthquake, various forms of avant-garde representation infused the cultural landscape, and Fuchikami turned to avant-garde forms of expression, experimenting with Dadaism, surrealism, and montage.[19] In grainy, sepia-toned images, he even photographed the androgynous, bobbed members of the constructivist MAVO group, headed by Murayama Tomoyoshi.[20] Along with his contemporaries, Fuchikami helped to promote art photography as a new form of artistic representation in mid-1920s photography circles. However, he was to achieve far greater success by leaving Japan and devoting a sizable part of his career to photographing Manchuria.

In November 1927, SMRC's new *Sôsaishitsu jôhôka* (Presidential Office Information Division) led Fuchikami on a fateful tour of company-administrated areas in Manchuria and northern China,[21] its hope being that he would be inspired to shoot a modern, positive view of these areas colonized by Japanese. Fuchikami soon obliged the corporation by giving a lecture in Tianjin a month later, and, in 1928, he displayed his photographs in the exhibit *Manshû ryôkô sakuhin ten* (Exhibition of Works from the Trip to Manchuria), held in Osaka's *Asahi kaikan* (Asahi Meeting Hall).[22] His photographs allowed viewers in domestic Japan to see the exotic vistas of the continent, in addition to the modern improvements that SMRC had brought to the region. Due to the successful reception of his images in Osaka, in October 1928 Yaginuma Jôbu – editor of the company's employee magazine *Kyôwa (Concordia)*[23] and former Harbin bureau chief of the *Asahi Shimbun*[24] – hired Fuchikami to be a part-time photographer for the Dairen-based SMRC Presidential Office Information Division. At this time, Yaginuma spearheaded SMRC's invitation of important Japanese cultural figures to Manchuria, including the poets Kitahara Hakushû (1885-1942), Nî'i Kaku, and Saitô Mokichi (1882-1953), and the artist Ka'i Mihachirô.[25] During his employment, Fuchikami would help organize a photography tour of Manchuria and Korea for seven Japanese photographers, including Yamamoto Makihiko, Fukumori Hakuyô, and Sakakibara Seisô.[26]

By the late 1920s, Fuchikami's efforts at running an avant-garde photography journal in Tokyo had failed after his patron's company went bankrupt, so the photographer looked forward to crossing over to Manchuria with his family in the hope of changing his fate.[27] As a new employee of SMRC, he soon moved his household to the cosmopolitan port city of Dairen, a locus of Japanese colonial modernity and a hotbed of amateur interest in the developing new medium of photography. For example, in 1931 alone, the *Ryaoton shakôkai* (Liaodong Photography Society) and Shinkô Club were formed, with *Manshû shadan (Manchuria Photography World)* beginning publication as a monthly magazine for amateur photographers.[28] From 4-5 February 1933, the Ashiya Camera Club held an exhibition in the Mitsukoshi department store's Dairen branch, and then travelled to other Manchukuo cities.[29] Club activities, such as photography and baseball, helped to promote the solidarity of SMRC employees and allowed them to socialize outside of the workplace in a relatively informal environment. However, due to SMRC's importance as a colonial enterprise, even these seemingly casual activities often took on a nationalistic flavour, as when SMRC photographers exhibited their images to much acclaim at the Chicago World's Fair in 1933 and in SMRC ballplayers' regular trouncing of their Tokyo opponents.[30]

During his initial period of employment, Fuchikami was responsible for the yearly publication of the *Manshû shashin nenkan (Manchuria Photography Yearbook),* which first came out in 1930 and was edited by SMRC's Presidential Office Information Division.[31] The twenty-five photographers featured in this publication would later become the founding members of the *Manshû shashin sakka kyôkai,* along with those in the SMRC public-relations staff and the Japan Photographic Art Association.[32] Immediately following Manchukuo's establishment in 1932, Fuchikami was hired by the Kantô Army as technical head of the *Shisei-kyoku kôhôsho* (the resource administration department's publicity and news bureau) from March to June to carry out the propaganda activities surrounding the founding of the new state, while Yaginuma served as chief of the same bureau.[33] After June, Fuchikami and Yaginuma both returned to their employment with SMRC.[34] December of the same year also heralded Fuchikami's founding of the MPAA, with his serving as the group's leader along with three other associates – Yoneki Zen'eimon (1908-74), Sakakibara Masa'ichi (1897-1980), and Yora Sei'ichi.[35] In 1933, six others joined, namely: Date Yoshio, Doi Yûji (1906-69), Isshiki Tatsuo (1908-86), Okada Chûji (1909-77), Nakata Shiyô (1901-90), and Baba Yashio (1903-74).[36] At various points in its existence, the group also included Saotome Tôru, Aoyama Shunji, Mizuma Tetsuo, and Terashima Manji. In Dairen, the MPAA published the journal *Hikaru oka (Shining Hills),* which ran from November 1937 until June 1939.[37]

Featuring modernist photographs with an avant-garde sensibility, the group even exhibited its works in domestic and international venues in Manchukuo, Japan, France, and the United States. Notably, under the auspices of SMRC, the MPAA held the *Manshû fûbutsu shashin-ten* (Exhibition of the Natural Features of Manchuria in Photographs), featuring one hundred photos shown at the Chicago World Exposition from 27 May to 12 November 1933.[38] Because of the popularity of this exhibition, the MPAA decided to show part of the collection throughout the United States, touring major US cities in February 1934.[39] The international showing of their images of Manchuria in cosmopolitan venues in the United States made Fuchikami and his photographers' association into representatives of modernity for the new state of Manchukuo. Thus, they came to serve as model figures of Manchukuo's propaganda organization – the Manchukuo Publicity and News Bureau. Not surprisingly, Fuchikami would continue to successfully carry out this endeavour for Japanese and foreign audiences after he was recruited to direct shoots for a popular new magazine developed by SMRC in 1933 – *Manshû gurafu*.

In September of that same year, Fuchikami began his tenure as chief editor of *Manshû gurafu* and directed the photographic images compiled for the newly created propaganda pictorial published by the Dairen-based SMRC conglomerate. This magazine ran from September 1933 to January 1944 and flourished under Fuchikami's editing until his 1941 return to Japan. Though the photographer had initially been attracted to the company due to its generous part-time offer to depict the region using the latest aesthetic techniques, including montage and surrealist images, he ended up staying in Manchuria for thirteen years until his return to Japan following the death of his wife. Fuchikami's success story is similar to that of many Japanese colonists who settled in Manchuria in the 1920s and 1930s to improve their career prospects – something that no doubt contributed to their utopian view of the region, which influenced their idealized vision of the worker or peasant.

Fuchikami's photographs, dating from his early Manchurian sojourn, reflect the influence of pictorialism, avant-garde forms of cubism, constructivism, and futurism, as well as straight photography.[40] In these images, it is evident that he reifies the difference of the exotic native in a manner that distances the viewer.[41] According to Takeba Jô, this form of representation continued under Fuchikami and his team in *Manshû gurafu:* "As pictorialist expression waned in the 1930s, its legacy of lyrical distance from the subject was inherited by the work of the Manchuria Photographic Artists Association."[42] Takeba further notes that this "lyrical distance" was suffused by a type of realism, with, in 1938, Fuchikami's "declaring that the ideal, significance, and existential value of photography were to be found in 'being thoroughly real.'"[43] While flirting with realism, his often grainy images continue to emphasize the difference of the colonial native in shots that capture Chinese and Russian workers or peasants from the side, back, or with faces turned away from the camera, while those of Japanese settlers show them looking directly toward the camera. This allows the presumably Japanese viewer to identify with his or her compatriots and hence with Manchuria's development. Such photographic framing would soon have great importance in Fuchikami's creation of media that were supportive of the Manchukuo regime.

Fuchikami's Idealized Vision of the Chinese Coolie in *Manshû gurafu*, 1936-38

Manshû gurafu, like other booklets, bound photo collections, or illustrated travel narratives of Manchuria from the 1930s and into the early 1940s, included vivid depictions of Manchurian customs or cultural distinctions, the beauty of its wide-open rural spaces, and the coolies of Dairen. These topics appeared in varying degrees in each issue, with these markers of difference reinforcing how Manchuria, unlike Japan, possessed a vast amount of still-undeveloped territory. However, of special note were the Chinese coolies in the cosmopolitan port city of Dairen. Apparently, for Japanese readers, Manchuria's working class was more picturesque, exotic, and docile than that of domestic Japan – despite bearing almost inhumanly heavy loads for the new nation's development. In the mid-1930s, periodicals like *Manshû gurafu* created visual propaganda for the Manchukuo regime, which displayed a fascination for the labouring colonial native, similar to Dairen's Japanese avant-garde in the late 1920s and early 1930s.[44] These images were disseminated throughout Japan via *Manshû gurafu,* which was distributed through the *Sen Man annai-jô* (Korea Manchuria Information Office) in Tokyo, Osaka, and Nagoya. However, unlike the poets who revelled in revealing the physical and psychic violence of Japanese colonialism in Manchuria, Fuchikami's pictorial depicted a working-class utopia for the Chinese coolie in modern, efficient cities and a peaceful, culturally picturesque rural countryside populated by Japanese agricultural settlers.

In this section, I investigate Fuchikami's recurring image of the Chinese labourer, or coolie, as a symbol of Japanese-led development. The figure of the coolie serves as an important site of critique because, through his labour, he embodies the physical transformations of Japanese progress without directly profiting from it, thus representing the contradictions of Japan's civilizing mission in Manchukuo. For the Japanese writer, artist, or photographer, the image of the coolie – in his role as a mechanical agent of the physical development of the Manchurian region and Manchukuo – becomes a symbol of the conflict between the traditional and the modern. The coolie's experience also reveals how a rural farmer becomes an urban worker due to forced displacement through famine, military orders, and/or the hope of finding better work opportunities in developing areas.

In *Manshû gurafu,* Fuchikami and his team show an orderly, rational workforce under SMRC's paternalistic protection and, by extension, that of the Manchukuo state, where work, food, and stability await the largely Han Chinese working class in contrast to the deprivation and political instability of China south of the Great Wall. Naturally, as propaganda supporting a benevolent state, these images elide the violence of Manchukuo's imperialistic development and the eviction of Chinese and Korean farmers from their land. However, these photographs provide an interesting glimpse into how, in its visual propaganda, the Manchukuo government and SMRC, its commercial conglomerate, framed the construction of the new state.

After Japanese economic interests began to dominate Manchuria in the wake of the Russo-Japanese War, cheap coolie labour provided by working-class Shandong and Hebei immigrants flooding into the region became a primary reason for Japanese economic productivity, continuing into the Manchukuo period until 1945.[45] However, many of the Chinese, Korean, and even Japanese coolies were formerly farmers or vagrants who had been forced into hard labour by poverty, poor land conditions, or eviction. Workers in Dairen's port were largely male Han Chinese but included men and women from China, Korea, and even Russia. Japanese accounts of Manchuria portray these labourers simply as "Manchurians," a term synonymous with Han Chinese, but that actually includes uneducated people of all ethnic groups in Manchuria who became coolies due to reduced economic circumstances.

Following the Japanese takeover of Manchuria in 1931, many fled to protect their freedom as the Kantô Army forced Chinese and Korean peasants off their land to make way for Japanese settlers. These indigenous farmers were concentrated into collective villages to stop communist-led anti-Japanese activities.[46] The Kantô Army's military operations in Manchuria essentially supported the growth of Japanese capital in the region by ensuring a steadily increasing cheap labour force comprising poor and desperate lower-class Manchurian natives. This was also the case in Korea, where, after 1919, the land reforms under the General Protectorate left many Korean families without the land to sustain their livelihood. Some fled to Manchuria, only to suffer the same fate there. These human indices of the brutal history of Japanese imperialism in the colonial space added an uncomfortable element to the accounts of Japanese observers witnessing the supposed glories of development and the furthering of civilization in East Asia under Japanese auspices. This history is further obscured by *Manshû gurafu* images and text, whose purpose was to portray the SMRC and its development of Manchukuo in a positive light.

In a representative example, the May 1936 special edition of the pictorial, entitled "Kuri no seikatsu" ("The Life of the Coolies"), features images of Dairen's coolies shot by Fuchikami and his team of photographers.[47] The cover, incidentally, shows boughs of cherry blossoms – a harbinger of spring in the Japanese imagination and an important symbol of Japanese identity.[48] Beginning with a quasi-erudite discussion of the etymological origins of the word "coolie," stemming from a Dravidian language of Ceylon, the magazine shows the Japanese reader a sanitized glimpse of Manchuria's famed Han Chinese labourers and their history. The magazine states that, starting in 1897 with Imperial Russia's construction of the China Eastern Railway, and continuing after its completion in 1902, thousands of Chinese labourers emigrated from Shandong Province to join other Han settlers who had arrived in the late Ming or early Qing dynasties.

This process accelerated during the Manchukuo period, when Japanese media increasingly featured the new state as a utopia for the working classes. For example, a cheery August 1938 two-page montage in *Manshû gurafu* enthusiastically proclaims, "Earthly Paradise Nears!"[49] In Japanese, the cap-

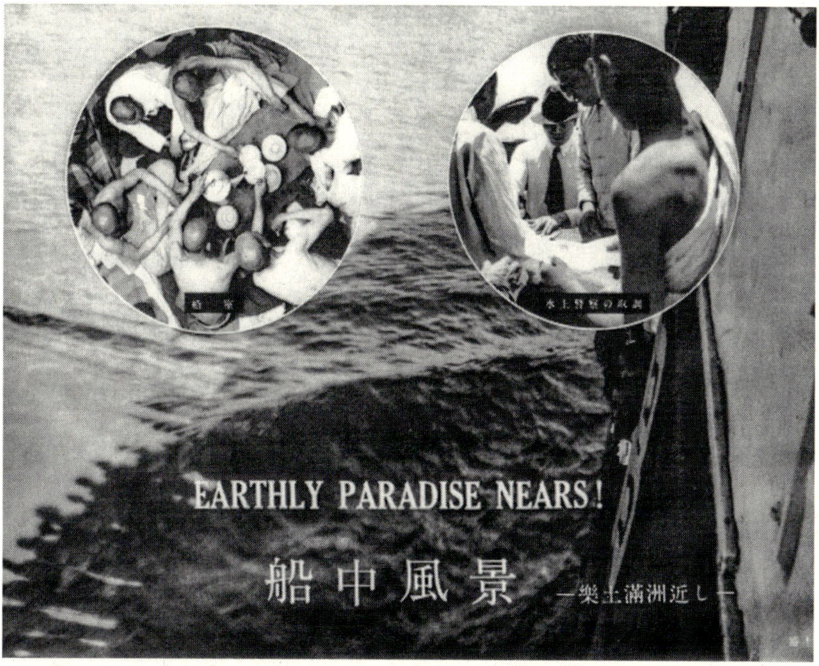

Figure 15 "Earthly Paradise Nears," *Manshû gurafu* [Manchuria graph], August 1938, Yumani shobô 2008 reprint, Duke University Perkins-Bostock Library collection.

tions read, "Scene within the Boat: Nearing the Manchurian Paradise."[50] The photos also show disembarked coolies undergoing physical examinations at the Dairen-based Datong (Tatung) Company and applying for work certificates – indications of how the government subcontracted with private companies to organize its labour needs and how it ensured that its workforce was healthy before hiring.[51] The English-language description gives further details about this process, even indicating from where in China the coolies were recruited by satellite branches of the firm, and noting their bureaucratic processing through labour permits: "The Tatung Kungssu *[sic]*, which has its head office in Dairen and branches in Tientsin, Tangku, Tsingtao, Chefoo, Lungkou and Shanhaikwan, is entrusted by the Manchukuo government with the transportation of coolies to Manchuria and the supplying of coolie labor. It also issues identification certificates to coolies which enable them to emigrate to Manchuria."[52] The pictorial hints at some of the more personal reasons the coolies came, and even stayed: "Among the coolies migrating to Manchuria[,] most of whom have invariably suffered for many years from civil wars and floods in China, there are many who wish to settle down in the new Empire as farmers or merchants. The number of coolies establishing

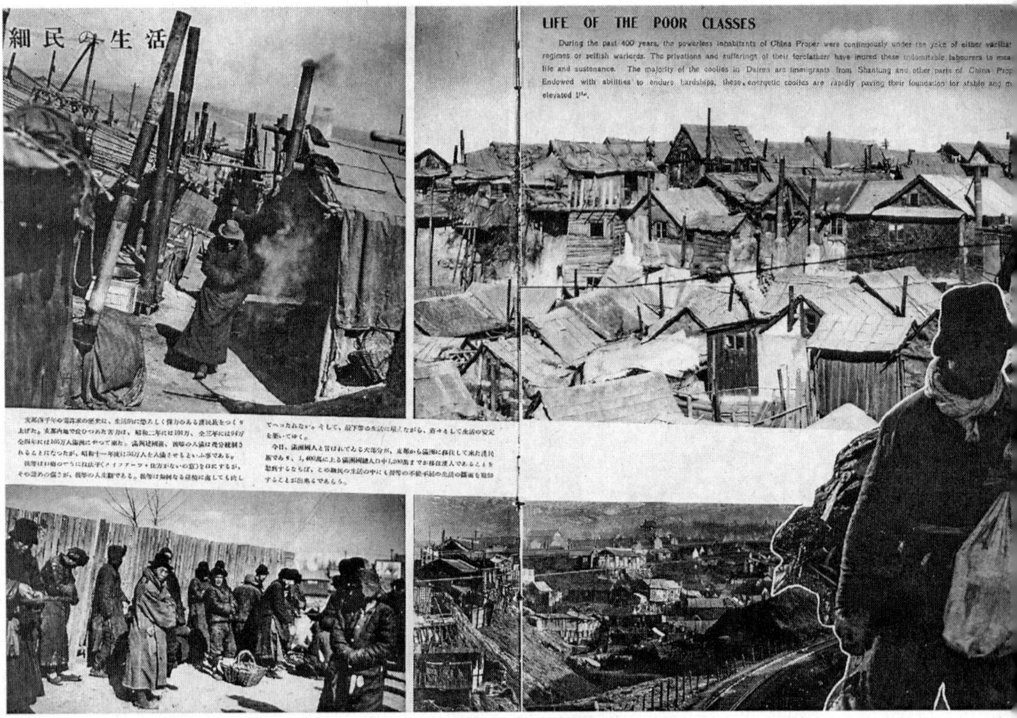

Figure 16 "Life of the Poor Classes," *Manshû gurafu* [Manchuria graph], May 1936, Waseda University Central Library collection.

permanent residence in the country has considerably increased in recent years."[53] Here, Manchukuo is portrayed as a nation that would allow personal advancement for the Chinese working class fleeing civil strife south of the Great Wall.

The Japanese caption in the "Life of the Poor Classes" section in the same May 1936 special edition highlights this message. It portrays Manchuria as providing work, food, and stability for working-class labourers in contrast to the deprivation and political instability they face in China proper:

> Four thousand years of China's severe and punishing history have formed the surprising lifestyle flexibility of the Han race. From domestic China, destitute coolies came over to Manchuria, with 1,010,000 arriving in 1927, 940,000 in 1929, and 1,050,000 in 1930. After Manchukuo was established, their entrance into Manchuria has been numerically controlled, but in 1936, 360,000 will still be let in. They have a habit of saying "it can't be helped," and a strong grasp of this saying has become their view of life. But

> they are not discouraged from deciding to leave a place for another environment. And so, while enduring the lowest standard of living, they little by little begin to build stability in their lives.[54]

The English caption on the next page condemns the political climate of domestic China and implies that these working-class Chinese immigrants are benefiting greatly from the stability and economic prosperity of the new state of Manchukuo.

This echoes the government's official rhetoric, which is that the state was established to "liberate" the "Manchurian" people from the political oppression of Chinese warlords. The implication is that even the working class can share in the improved standards of living promoted by a fair and just government run according to Confucian "Kingly Way" principles:

> During the past 400 years, the powerless inhabitants of China Proper were continuously under the yoke of either vacillating regimes or selfish warlords. The privations and sufferings of their forefathers have inured these indomitable labourers to meager life and sustenance. The majority of coolies in Dairen are immigrants from Shantung and other parts of China Proper. Endowed with abilities to endure hardships, these energetic coolies are rapidly paving their foundation for a stable and more elevated life.[55]

Here, Manchukuo is seen as a privileged refuge for these workers, a place whose political stability and economic conditions offer them more opportunities than can be found in domestic China. The statistics and tables in the pictorial concerning these coolies are intended to provide a scientific basis for Japan's contentions.

SMRC depicts these immigrant workers, who thronged into Manchukuo for its job opportunities, as well taken care of and as being lodged in Spartan, but neat, housing. In its images, the May 1936 issue displays a brilliant work of propaganda in photomontage form. It documents the fictive life of the robust model coolie inured to hardship in his humble physical surroundings, while also showing picturesque scenes of the Chinese working class consuming street foods and enjoying outdoor Peking Opera. In addition, the issue features SMRC's special dormitories, which boasted plumbing and sanitary living quarters and were described as a "paradise" for its model coolies, who were able to lift sixty-eight kilograms.[56] The visual imagery of these almost superhuman workers,[57] and their strange living environment, interested investors as well as ordinary people in domestic Japan (and, presumably, English-speaking Westerners), who were curious about the exoticism of the continent and the life of its working-class poor. Yet, it is evident that these photographs tell only part of the story.

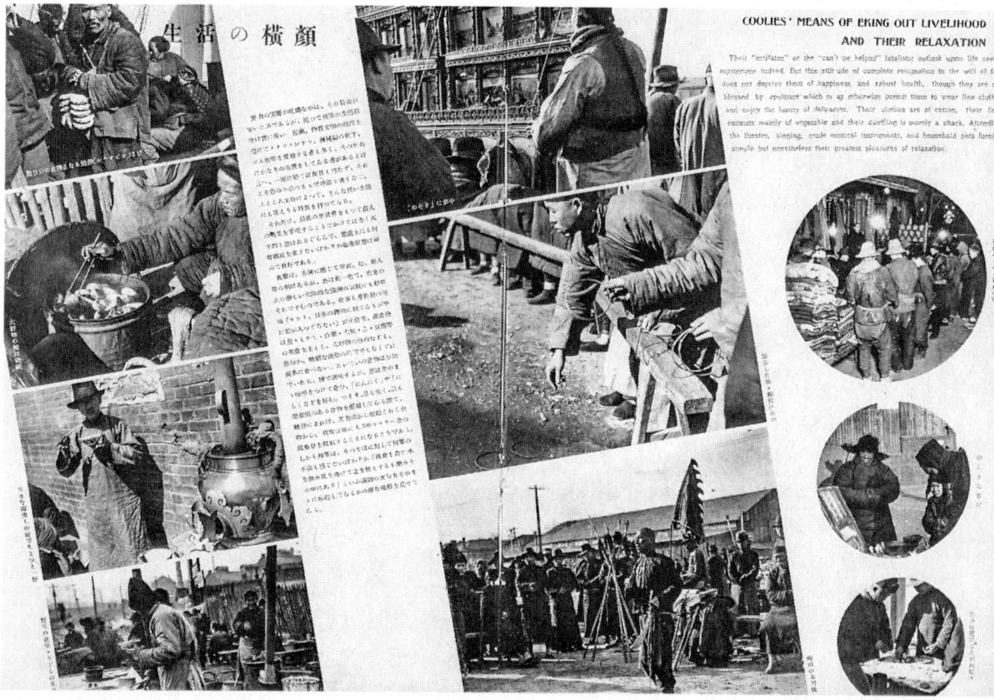
生活の横顔
COOLIES' MEANS OF EKING OUT LIVELIHOOD AND THEIR RELAXATION
Their "meifatze" or the "can't be helped" fatalistic outlook upon life seems mysterious indeed. But this attitude of complete resignation to the will of fate does not deprive them of happiness and robust health, though they are not blessed by opulence which may otherwise permit them to wear fine clothes and enjoy the luxury of delicacies. Their clothes are of cotton, their food consists mainly of vegetable and their dwelling is merely a shack. Attending the theatre, singing, crude musical instruments, and household pets furnish simple but nonetheless their greatest pleasures of relaxation.

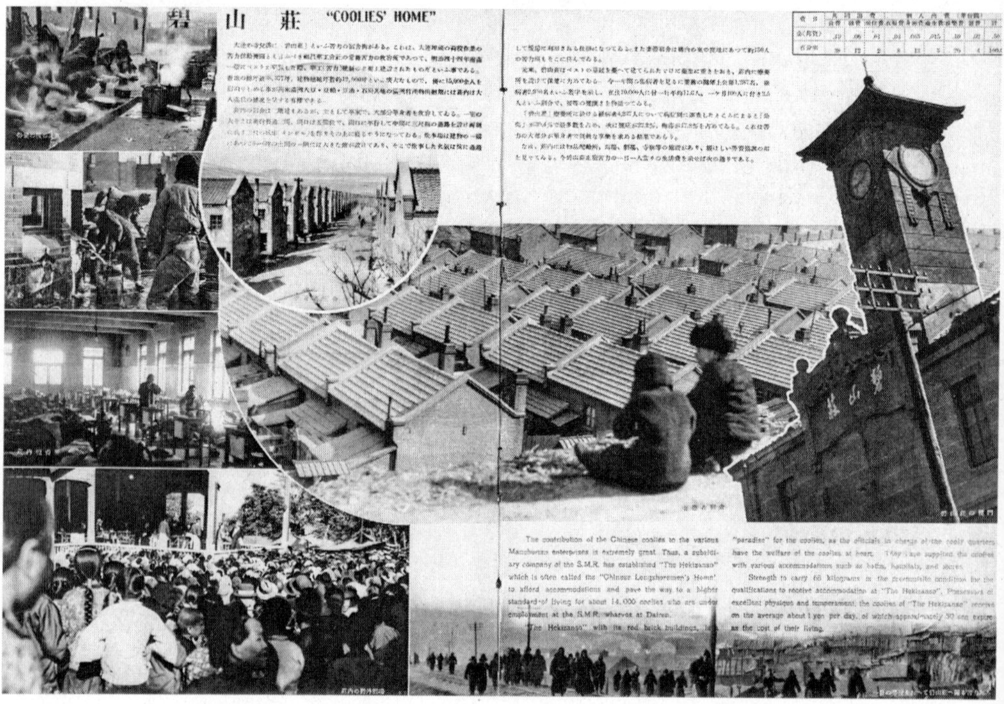
碧山荘 "COOLIES' HOME"
The contribution of the Chinese coolies to the various Manchurian enterprises is extremely great. Thus, a subsidiary company of the S.M.R. has established "The Hekizanso" which is often called the "Chinese Longshoremen's Home" to afford accommodations and pave the way to a higher standard of living for about 14,000 coolies who are under employment at the S.M.R. wharves at Dairen.
"The Hekizanso" with its red brick buildings, is a "paradise" for the coolies, as the officials in charge of the coolie quarters have the welfare of the coolies at heart. They have supplied the coolies with various accommodations such as baths, hospitals, and stores.
Strength to carry 68 kilograms is the prerequisite condition for the qualifications to receive accommodation at "The Hekizanso". Possessors of excellent physique and temperament, the coolies of "The Hekizanso" receive on the average about 1 yen per day, of which approximately 30 sen expire as the cost of their living.

Facing page:

Figure 17 Montage of Chinese street scenes, *Manshû gurafu* [Manchuria graph], May 1936, Waseda University Central Library collection.

Figure 18 Bishanzhuang coolies' home, *Manshû gurafu* [Manchuria graph], May 1936. Waseda University Central Library collection.

The incredible work potential of the Chinese male coolie and his simple but healthy living conditions sponsored by SMRC and other corporations are constantly reinforced by *Manshû gurafu's* images and tables, which neglect to mention that these men were often worked to death or succumbed to disease in cramped conditions for artificially low wages. Published in the 1940 edition of the *Manshû rôdô nenkan (Manchuria Labour Yearbook),* Japanese statistics arising from an August 1939 investigation by the *Rôkô kyôkai* (Labour Association) note the extreme wage differentials for Korean and Chinese male workers in industries run by Japanese. These disparities also serve to explain how the unequal *economic* treatment of the "five races[/ethnicities]" continued to allow ethnic Japanese to reap the true profits of Manchukuo. For example, in factories, Koreans earned 40.2 percent and Chinese earned 28.8 percent, respectively, of the salary of a Japanese male worker; while in mines, Koreans earned 39 percent and Chinese 29.4 percent, respectively, of a Japanese male worker's salary.[58]

Moreover, both the size and quality of living quarters differed drastically for (1) the bourgeois Japanese colonists and their Westernized upper-class Chinese counterparts and (2) lower-class Han Chinese immigrants. In the late 1930s, when the Japanese population was at its largest but accounted for only 25 percent of the population of Manchukuo, Japanese inhabitants of all social classes took up approximately 60 percent of all available living space.[59] On average, Japanese colonists (and some ethnically Korean-Japanese subjects) were afforded twenty to thirty square metres of living area per person, while Han Chinese coolies in the Laohutan section of Dairen had only one to two square metres in which to sleep and leave their meagre belongings.[60] Chinese scholars vividly describe working-class living quarters as consisting of fetid, filthy, and cramped flats, with Si'ergou and Bishanzhuang as the main areas in which coolies were assigned work and lodging.[61]

The Fuchang Chinese Labour Corporation,[62] run by Japanese colonial management even before the Manchukuo period, and one of the means through which SMRC obtained its labour force, housed over thirty thousand labourers at one point.[63] According to Fang Jun and Wang Shengli, several tens of thousands of men died from highly communicable diseases during the corporation's lifetime.[64] Cramped, dirty conditions contributed to the spreading of epidemics and caused general ill health in crowded quarters, where the men had little space for rest.[65] Fang and Wang decry the living conditions endured by the Han Chinese coolies, characterizing it as an "inhuman lifestyle" inflicted on workers by the Japanese and their Chinese capitalist counterparts.[66] However, the peaceful image of the "coolie's paradise" as depicted in *Manshû gurafu* was not always quietly endured by the "docile" Chinese working class. On 11 April 1938, in a violent statement against the exploitation of both Japanese management and wealthy Chinese capitalists, Chinese communist arsonists torched Fuchang's employment headquarters, which Chinese scholars, including Fang and Wang, describe as "an organization [that] enslav[ed] Dalian's port workers."[67]

Thus, in colonial Dairen, and into the Manchukuo period, deep ethnic and class divisions separated the experiences of the Chinese labourers – who ensured the prosperity of the port – from the urban middle-class Japanese expatriate community.[68] From the early 1920s into the 1930s and beyond, the existence of two very different spatial realities related to class and ethnicity in the same urban location highlighted the tensions and fragility of the colonial atmosphere. By contrast, Fuchikami and his team depicted the coolies as an orderly, rational workforce under the paternalistic protection of SMRC and, by extension, the state.

By the careful manipulation of historical realities through the use of images and captions, SMRC's state propaganda, manufactured by photographers such as Fuchikami, depicted the Chinese worker as a heroic figure in the service of the state. The caption to Fuchikami's image *Kureen to kuri (Coolie and a Crane [Dairen Wharf]),* which ran in the June 1936 special "art photographs of Manchuria" edition of *Manshû gurafu,* even refers to the worker as a *chôjin* (superman):

> The Dairen port, which has the ability to process 11,000,000 tons of cargo per year, is the Far East's top free port, and moreover, it is newly arisen Manchukuo's front door. Out of Manchukuo's annual trade of about 800,000 yen, roughly 5/7ths goes through Dairen. Concerning the disposal of the yearly ever-increasing import and export of cargo, which proceeds without a hitch, it is truly because the superhuman-like coolie's energy and the sophisticated loading device are partnered together.[69]

Here, the hook of the crane mirrors the curved back of the coolie in an interesting juxtaposition of mechanized and human labour. In this balanced photographic composition, the man's back is facing the viewer and, rather than appearing as a human worker, he seems to be an elemental part of the industrial landscape of the wharf. Indeed, his body is dwarfed by the monumental size of the crane, which is shot in extreme close-up with an angle pointing upwards to highlight the size of the cargo load. While the image lauds the coolie's superhuman power to carry these loads,

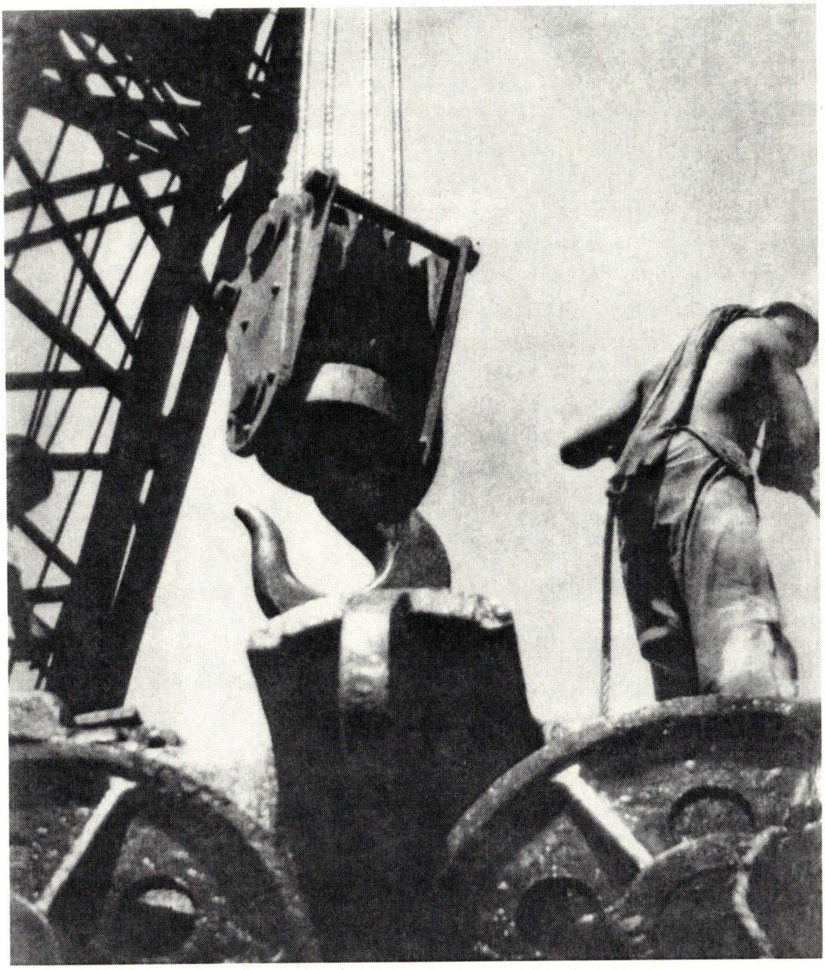

Figure 19 Fuchikami Hakuyô, *Kureen to kuri* [Coolie and a crane], *Manshû gurafu* [Manchuria graph], June 1936, Waseda University Central Library collection.

the worker himself is denied agency because the viewer cannot see the expression on his face and, therefore, cannot fathom how he really feels about his work. He is objectified as an artistic figure and kept at what Takeba calls a "lyrical distance."

Other photographs, under Fuchikami's editing, show how the hard-working coolie is satisfied with the simple implements of a non-bourgeois lifestyle that would certainly fit Tansman's notion of an epiphanic representation. These images do not show the worker at all but, rather, hint about his lifestyle and workaday preoccupations by depicting the objects he utilizes in everyday life. A key example of this conceit appeared one year later in the pictorial's second collection of art photographs of Manchuria, which was featured in the June 1937 special edition. This edition of *Manshû gurafu* was issued only a month before the outbreak of the Second Sino-Japanese War.[70] Here, a beautiful still-life photograph by Seitoku, entitled *Still Life on Road Surface,* represents this ideal in a modernist image of a simple tin teapot that casts a larger-than-life shadow on the textured surface of the road (see Figure 12). The Japanese caption reads:

> Manchuria, with a continental climate, has winters of almost unbelievable coldness, but summers are also especially hot. And thus, for people who do physical labor, thirst-quenching drinks exist as inseparable companions to this sort of lifestyle. Just like Russian peasants heading out for the fields with their samovar, Manchuria's common people, including laborers, don't let a tin teapot with tea leaves and water in it leave their hands for a moment. According to the Manchurians, who would never let unboiled water into their mouths, this one teapot filled with tea leaves and water is truly nothing but the sweet dew from Heaven.[71]

In its simplicity and sturdiness, the teapot is seemingly intended to capture the essence of the absent Manchurian labourer. Further, it generates "an aesthetically cathartic epiphany susceptible to being politically channelled into the creation of a fascist mood," indicative of what Tansman calls the "fascist moment."[72]

Interestingly, Fuchikami had based the utopian aesthetics of *Manshû gurafu* on the left-wing Soviet propaganda pictorial *CCCP* [Soyuz Sovietskikh Sotsialisticheskikh Respublik in the Russian Cyrillic alphabet, or the USSR, the Soviet Union], while urging his group to utilize the experimental avant-garde camera techniques he had developed in the 1920s in Tokyo.[73] These photographs of Chinese coolie labour show that a modernist aesthetic does not necessary translate into left-oriented politics, even though it may criticize bourgeois excess and corporate paternalism while communicating a simple rusticity divorced from capitalism.[74] In fact, through the fascist moment, these images may be co-opted to meet the demands of a right-wing version of socialism, such as that practised by the Manchukuo regime.

The Image of the Japanese Settler in a Rural Utopia, 1933-40

In this section I discuss an aspect of labour that shows how the romantic concept of *Manshû* (in the agricultural development of wide open rural spaces) merged with that of *Manchukuo* (a utopian state characterized by urban modernity and industrialization). In *Manshû gurafu,* we see not only how the images of the two very different spaces inhabited by the Japanese rural settler and the Chinese urban coolie can coexist in the new state, but also, how they communicate two very different symbolic meanings. The idealized depictions of the *kaitaku-sha,* which display a perfect marriage of pictorialism and Renger-Patzsch-like objectivity, show how the fictive utopian rural space developed by Japanese settlers can persist alongside the highly urban productivity of the cities presided over by the Chinese coolie (made productive only under Japanese auspices, of course).

The images of the Japanese settlers in *Manshû gurafu* can best be understood against the background of Japan's deepening imperialistic war on the continent, begun first with the military manoeuvres associated with the Kantô Army in Manchuria after 1931, then, following the 1933 Tangu Truce, tensions in this demilitarized zone between Manchukuo and China proper from 1933 to 1937.[75] These small-scale skirmishes finally erupted into the Second Sino-Japanese War by July 1937, which resulted in what later commentators have called the "China quagmire" (1938-45). Amidst this climate of ever-increasing operations in China south of the Great Wall, the Japanese government's rhetoric focused on its need to be ever more involved in other East Asian nations. By 1940, this had culminated in a discussion of the "Greater East Asia Co-Prosperity Sphere." As early as 1938, the diplomat and foreign ministry spokesman Tatsuo Kawai (1889-1965) argued: "The objective of Japanese expansion is neither the attainment of capitalistic supremacy nor the acquisition of colonies, but the realization of harmony and concord among the nations of East Asia and their common happiness and prosperity."[76]

"Harmony" and "concord," or *kyôwa,* were, of course, ideals that were first articulated in Manchukuo by proponents of a right-wing version of socialism (like that of Ishiwara Kanji), in which capitalism supposedly took a backseat to the aims of a utopian, Confucian-inspired paternalistic government. In 1940, the Greater East Asia concept grew out of a proposal voiced by Foreign Minister Arita Hachirô (1884-1965), whereby Japan would guide the nations of East Asia based on the Manchurian experiment. His successor, Matsuoka Yûsuke, a former president of SMRC, would soon coin the term "Greater East Asia Co-Prosperity Sphere." In April 1943, Shigemitsu Mamoru (1881-1957) proclaimed the liberation of East Asia as Japan's primary war objective. If we view the images of the rural pioneers against this background, we can finally begin to grasp the important role the Japanese settlers played in the geopolitics of East Asia.

The photographs of the *kaitaku-sha* thus serve as examples of the intrepid Japanese settler who developed the northern Manchurian frontier amidst Japan's deepening conflicts on the continent. By the early 1940s, Manchukuo was even lauded by Japanese officialdom as a template for the Southeast Asian nations into which the imperial army "advanced" in order to help "liberate" them from Western colonial rule.

In *Manshû gurafu,* emphasis on labour and productivity in the rural and urban spaces of Manchukuo remained a constant theme throughout its roughly eleven years of existence. However, in this section, I concentrate on how Fuchikami and his crew portray the developmental agricultural space of the rural fields tilled by the Japanese pioneer rather than the urban space of the factory or ports. An evident evolution of themes that contrast with those of previous years can be seen in the roughly three historical phases of images featured in the years from 1933 to 1937, 1937 to 1940, and 1941 to 1944. This is due to political developments in Japan and the Empire as well as to the eruption of the war in China (1937) and the Pacific (1941). Nineteen thirty-seven was also the concluding year of the first five-year plan for Manchukuo, while 1942 was the concluding year for the second. Thus, the placement of the images in *Manshû gurafu* is important in terms of how they are framed and juxtaposed with other events taking place in the Japanese Empire. Here, I focus on the images in the publication from 1933 to 1941 because it is these years that feature Fuchikami's tenure as editor.

Early images of the *kaitaku-sha* appearing in the year of *Manshû gurafu*'s inception helped to communicate the area's vast potential for settlement, while later editions, appearing after Fuchikami's 1941 return to Japan, focused almost exclusively on the northern Manchurian Japanese pioneers or military operations in north China. From 1936 onwards, individual editions were more likely to feature Japanese *kaitaku-sha,* but they were just one of many topics related to Manchuria. From the late 1930s onwards, individual editions increasingly devoted more spreads to these farmers, while a December 1940 special edition entitled "Kaitaku-chi wo meguru" ("Touring the Rural Development Areas") was the first to focus exclusively on their efforts.

Naturally, it would be a big undertaking for the governments of Manchukuo and Imperial Japan to attract the settlers and to convince them to immigrate, in accordance with state aims, from 1933 to 1936. Therefore, all of the media in charge of propaganda in both countries, including the SMRC-funded *Manshû gurafu,* were mobilized. In the two years following the Manchurian Incident, the Japanese public had consumed songs, images, and all kinds of mass culture products (including war songs, film melodramas, "human bullet" candy, and even odd Manchurian-themed restaurant menus) induced by the climate of "war fever" and thus had developed a great appetite for news with a Manchurian theme.[77] In addition, printed materials related to Manchuria also took off during this time, fortuitously jump-starting the flagging Japanese publishing industry. An industry yearbook even happily touts: "Brisk sales of books on Manchuria have breathed new life into an utterly stagnated publishing industry."[78] Nonetheless, prospective Japanese farming families had to be convinced that the area was fertile as well as safe and that it presented them with a better life than they had in the cramped and resource-poor archipelago.

SMRC quickly mobilized Fuchikami and his crew to create seductive representations on behalf of the settlement project. For example, just inside its

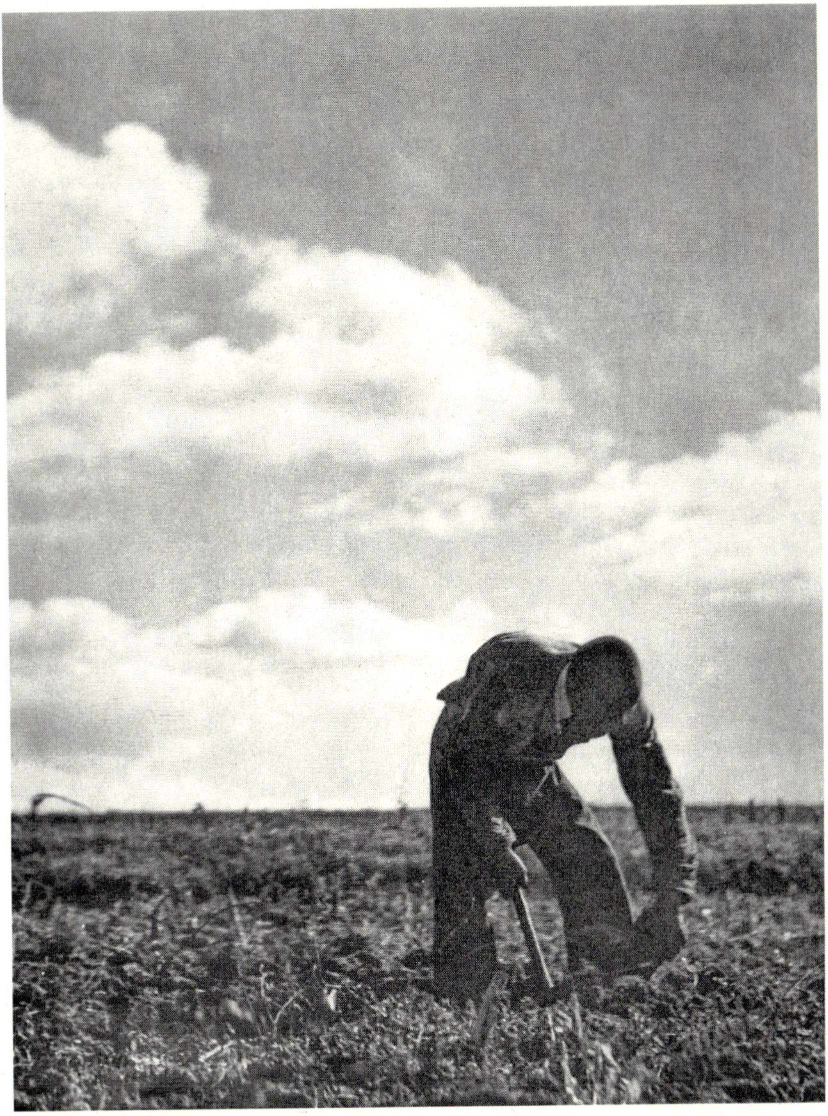

Figure 20 Inside cover image of farmer in field, *Manshû gurafu* [Manchuria graph], November 1933, Waseda University Central Library collection.

cover, the November 1933 edition of *Manshû gurafu* contains an image that depicts a pastoral scene of autumnal fields being harvested by a lone farmer, thus highlighting the region's peaceful and bucolic nature – only two years after the Kantô Army's military takeover.[79] The farmer performs his labour in a seemingly vast area, with the sky taking up most of the photo.[80] By contrast, on the two following pages, more urban-themed images appear, featuring a montage of Japanese soldiers holding *Hinomaru* flags, commanding officers, military formations, a ceremony to pacify the souls of dead soldiers, troop ships returning to Dairen, and a parade in front of a school, all under the heading *Kagayaku gaisen: Jihen kinenbi* ("Shining, Triumphant Return: Anniversary of the Incident"), with the English title "Victorious Return of Japanese Heroes: Anniversary of the Manchurian Incident."[81] Celebration, dignified sorrow, national pride, and Japanese desire for future development are symbolized in these photographs. Though the publication makes it seem as if the Kantô Army's military operations were finished, in 1933, there was still active guerrilla resistance near the Yanbian border of Korea.

The path toward planning for the colonization of northern Manchuria was formulated in the early to mid-1930s in both Tokyo and Shinkyô. In Manchukuo, Shinkyô hosted a colonization conference in November 1934 for a group of fifty experts and interested parties to discuss the settlement of this part of the region by Japanese farmers.[82] In December 1935, in the same city, the Manchuria Colonial Development Company was organized with start-up capital of 15 million yen.[83] It assisted settlers in acquiring suitable land; supervised and distributed that land; and provisioned financial aid, equipment, and facilities: "One-third of the authorized capital was provided by the Manchukuo government, one-third by the South Manchuria Railway Company, and one-third by the general public in Japan."[84] Interestingly, even this joint venture represented the corporatism of Manchukuo in its even division of responsibility for the endeavour among the new state's government, SMRC (as long-term developer of the region), and the Japanese people. SMRC's *Fifth Report on Progress in Manchuria to 1936* notes: "In April, 1936, it [the Manchuria Colonial Development Company] decided to settle 20,000 Japanese farming families in ten years and 1,500 families during 1936, and the Department of Colonial Affairs in Tokyo placed at the disposal of the Company 1,135,000 yen and the Manchoukuo Government the necessary land. The settlements will take place in Pinkiang Province."[85]

Instant success did not seem the case during the first wave in 1933-36, when five groups of five hundred farmsteads attempted colonization. The message conveyed in *Manshû gurafu* seemed to be that colonization was hard work and required *gaman,* or endurance, but that, in the end, Japanese perseverance would prevail. Despite the efforts of the Manchuria Colonial Development Company, a December 1936 special edition of *Manshû gurafu* entitled *Nihon yimin no sôbô* ["The Faces of Japanese Settlers"] notes that 40 percent left the settlements, either "dying of illness [or] quitting their new land owing to some unavoidable circumstances."[86] What these "unavoidable circumstances" were is never explained, but in northern Manchuria, Chinese landlords often hired local mercenary militias consisting of young Han Chinese peasant men who would cultivate the land during the growing season and defend their territory (and raid others) in the fallow season and in severe winters.[87] Not surprisingly, if Chinese gentry were not properly compensated for their land, these militias might come to rectify matters. These armed peasants were often characterized as "bandits" by the Japanese settlers, who were led to support an increased Kantô Army presence (in collusion with SMRC, whose tracks they were ordered to patrol) and also to arm their own young men. This lent an almost militaristic character to these isolated villages, which were connected only by a growing railway network built by SMRC.

By November 1938, captions in *Manshû gurafu* insistently focus on security and "peace," much of it provided courtesy of SMRC. This hints at the fact that personal safety might have been a very relevant concern for the growing numbers of settlers: "In addition, immigrants in the South Manchuria Railway Company's Self-Protective Villages, free immigrants encouraged by various prefectures, and immigrant groups of religious and social organizations will, [sic] shortly settle in Manchuria. These groups are expecting to build up peaceful farm communities within their respective settlements and will strive to develop agriculture, advance culture, and maintain peace and order."[88] The caption continues, with a hopeful description of some of the paternalistic, Confucian-inspired slogans of the new state, which are intended to ease tension in the locals: "No doubt, the native inhabitants will receive much benefit from the newcomers, and the two will effect a strong, cordial relationship full of inter-racial harmony and peace in the new born [sic] land, Manchoukuo."[89] The repetition of words such as "peace," "harmony," and "cordiality" appearing in the pictorial's pages in the late 1930s ring hollow to the contemporary reader, who benefits from hindsight.

In addition to a less-than-welcoming reception by the local Han Chinese population, the Japanese settlers also had to deal with the powerful presence of the Soviet Union, which loomed as an ever-present threat to the Japanese rural settlements in northern Manchukuo. Even if fear of the Russians and Chinese bandits could be overcome, the Siberian winter challenged even the hardiest Japanese recruits from mountainous regions in Nakano.[90] The food, as well, would have taken much getting used to since northern rivers only provided muddy-tasting fish that had to be thoroughly cooked, and cabbages and other vegetables tasted coarse to the Japanese palate. Added to this, rice was not one of the staples (these were millet porridge and wheat flour for buns and noodles).[91]

Nevertheless, the cover of the December 1936 edition of *Manshû gurafu* shows a heartening image of robust young women in *monpe* (loose work trousers), with adorable babies in knit caps strapped to their backs, harvesting wheat or millet (no doubt this photograph was shot at the beginning of autumn). The magazine clearly indicates that it is possible to raise a family in rural Manchukuo and that "even" women can easily perform the necessary farm work.[92] Along with this hopeful cover-image, an inside caption on the volunteer Youth Corps, who preceded these immigrants, encouragingly notes: "The remaining 60 percent, the picked youths, however, has [sic] conquered every difficulty and has proved the possibility of Japanese emigration to Manchuria."[93]

The accompanying article is headed, "The Utopia of Japanese Settlers in North Manchuria," with a circular insert of a Japanese shrine built by settlers at the left and, at the bottom, a map of rail-linked settlements in Sanjiang Province, currently part of the PRC's Heilongjiang Province, with Tieli City (Tetsuryô, a former training centre for the Youth Corps) as its county seat. Tetsuryô's Shintô shrine, of course, serves as the spiritual nerve centre of the community, as a place where marriages are conducted and subsequent offspring are blessed and receive their names. Traditional Japanese values, thus reproduced in the rural Manchurian space, are coupled with modern communications and transportation networks. The pictorial highlights the modernity of the settlements by stressing the fact that all of them are (or will be) connected via telephone, road, and rail access courtesy of SMRC. Fuchikami's photographers portray the settlements as well-organized, with the Japanese farmers using mechanized McCormick-Deering tractors purchased from the United States; and villages are peopled with well-fed families in which no woman appears without a child on her back. Hence, the scenes emphasize the fertility both of the land and of its new immigrants and, thus, the potential reproducibility of the entire rural development scheme on a grand scale.

A further two-page spread in the same edition, entitled "Peaceful Life at a Settlement," features bucolic scenes similar to those explored by the Japanese artists who depicted Manchuria (see Chapters 3 and 4). Here, we see empty lands illuminated by the sun, clear streams full of ducks and fish, and the ever-present woman with an infant on her back.[94] According to Michael Baskett, this image of "real" women in the Manchurian space was also very common in films of the era, such as the 1937 Japanese-German co-production *Atarashiki tsuchi (New Earth)*.[95]

After the mid-1930s, Japan's colonization schemes in northern Manchuria began to accelerate, with the government aiming for the mass migration of Japanese farmers into Manchukuo. This is made clear in the November 1938 edition of *Manshû gurafu:* "The Japanese government completed recently a plan calling for the immigration of a million families or a total of 5,000,000 individuals within 20 years, but at the present time the First Stage Five Year Program which aims at the sending of 500,000 people is being pushed."[96] The pictorial elucidates much of this plan, which was developed during the intensification of the government's efforts to exhort settlement amidst a global political climate in which Japan's Axis ally, Nazi Germany, favoured extended *Lebensraum* (living space) for its ethnic population.[97] A caption emphasizes the archipelago's need for more land for its burgeoning population:

> The average area of land available for farming in Japan is about 1 *chobu* per household. In comparison to other countries this average is about 1⁄60 of the United States, 1⁄90 of Canada, 1⁄7 of Germany, and approximately 1⁄16 of Denmark. To make matters worse, Japan is being pressed with an annual increase of 900,000 in population, which make [sic] living more difficult for the people who are already stricken with poverty.[98]

The cover of this same November 1938 edition shows two robust young Japanese women smiling and holding plump infant sons, with a young toddler in the foreground. As on the cover featured two years earlier, the women and children depicted create a picture of well-fed good health. The following two-page spread, with the English title "Japanese Immigrant Settlements in North Manchuria," is underlined by the Japanese caption *Hirake'iku shojo-chi (Tilling Virgin Land)* spread in white lettering over a photo of two strong young Japanese men from the Tetsuryô Youth Training Camp. The photo appears on a diagonal, with one-half of the land remaining as prairie and the other half having been ploughed into rows with the metal fingers of a tiller pulled by an American Caterpillar tractor – in an image reminiscent of John Steinbeck's *East of Eden* and the American West.[99] Through the recurring juxtaposition of symbols evocative of the fascist moment, which highlight the productivity of both land and family, readers are constantly regaled with the high fertility of northern Manchuria's soil and its settlers.

A few months later, *Manshû gurafu* readers could enjoy an example of the simple implements of the *kaitaku-sha*, symbolizing the spiritual qualities of the absent Japanese pioneer. In the photograph by Yagi Akio (1903-46) entitled *Asa no hikari (Morning Light)*, which appears in the January 1939 special art exhibition edition, farm tools are shown arranged outside a humble but sturdy dwelling.[100] This photo is startlingly reminiscent of the symbolism of Tansman's fascist aesthetic evoked in Seitoku's photo of the tea-kettle, which represents the absent Chinese coolie labourer and his implied simple satisfaction with working-class implements and a non-bourgeois lifestyle. Yagi's similarly epiphanic representation shows a standard wattle-and-earth house representative of Japanese settlements. It consists of daub walls, double-framed glass windows to keep out the cold, and a thatched roof. A pitchfork, shovel, and rake are arranged against the outside wall of the house, along with a metal wash tub resting on rocky soil covered with autumn leaves. The shadows at the break of dawn transmit a feeling of peace. Despite the rustic simplicity of the surroundings, each implement has its place and

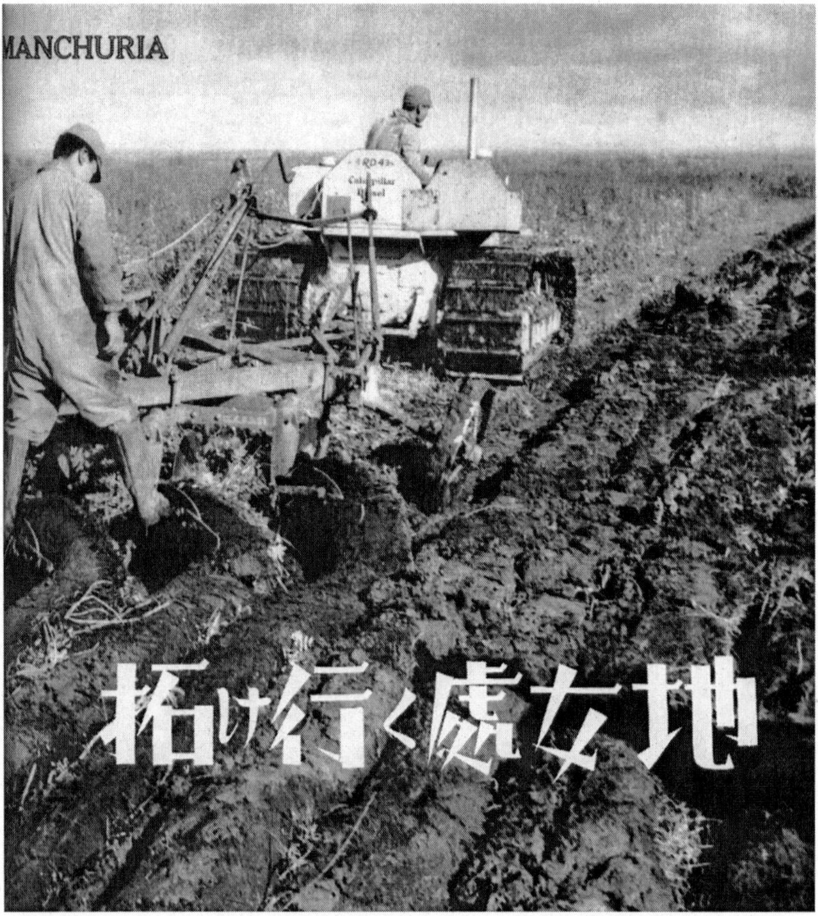

Figure 21 "Tilling Virgin Land," *Manshû gurafu* [Manchuria graph], November 1938, Yumani shobô 2008 reprint, Duke University Perkins-Bostock Library collection.

is essential to the livelihood of the settler. Together, they represent the absent *kaitaku-sha,* who inhabits the rural space of Manchuria rather than the urban space of Manchukuo.

Indeed, this anti-bourgeois right-wing version of socialism, or what I call "right-wing proletarianism," captured in the photographs examined above, appears also throughout the works of the converted proletarian writers Nogawa Takashi and Yamada. Since 1938, when squadrons of youth labour corps pioneers, like the two young men in the *Tilling Virgin Land* image, were sent over, writings about Japanese pioneers and settlers began to proliferate. According to the November 1938 edition of *Manshû gurafu:* "7,000 families

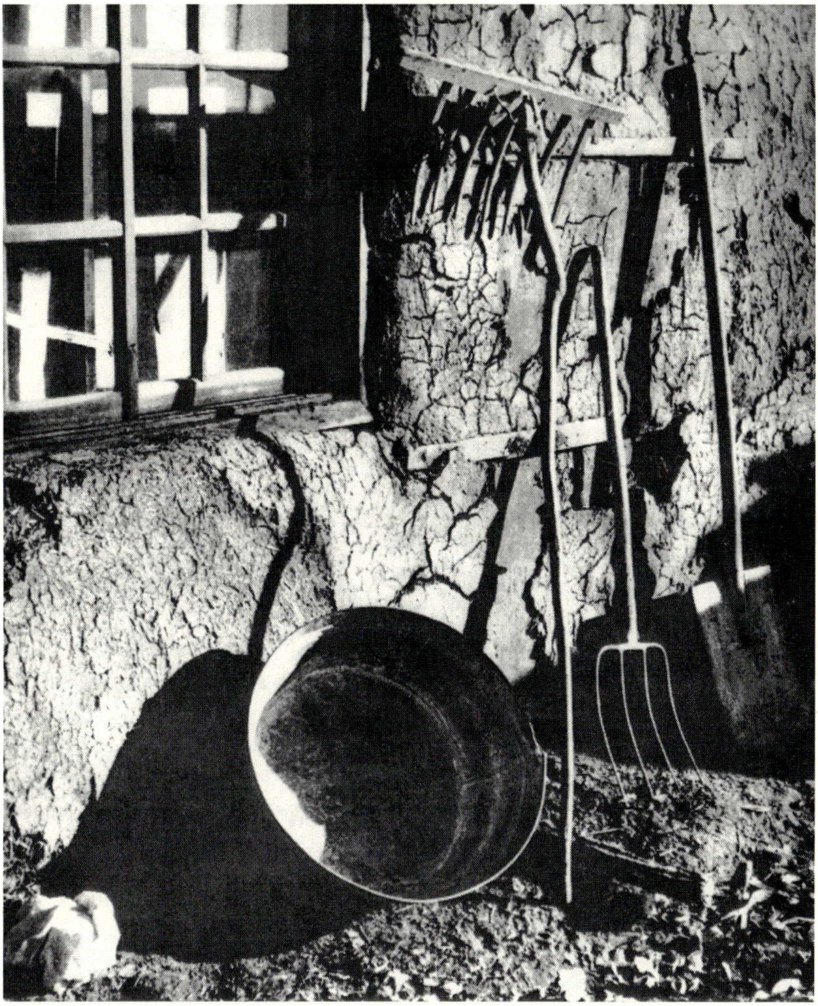

Figure 22 Yagi Akio, *Asa no hikari* [The light of day], *Manshû gurafu* [Manchuria graph], January 1939, Yumani shobô 2008 reprint, Duke University Perkins-Bostock Library collection.

have settled in 50 localities so far under governmental sponsorship (total for April, 1939), but besides this total, the Young Men's Training Camp capable of accommodating 30,000 boys from Japan will be established in North Manchuria within this year."[101] Like Shimaki and Yamada, who began the trend of writing about the pioneers in 1939-40, formerly proletarian authors like Nogawa and even Tokunaga Sunao also published works dedicated to this topic. Tokunaga's 1939 novel *Sengentai (The Pioneers),* in fact, focuses on the youth labour corps and contains scenes of young Japanese teenagers astounded at the labour productivity of Han Chinese coolies hired for the settlements.[102]

After Fuchikami left for Japan following the death of his wife in early 1941, *Manshû gurafu* began to change its focus, seemingly evincing a less artistic inclination in favour of the new orientation of the Manchukuo regime as a base for Japanese military operations in China proper and Southeast Asia. However, one of the continuities with earlier editions of *Manshû gurafu* is an intensification of the obsession with production from 1943 to 1944. Amidst the darkening wartime climate, agricultural productivity and the creation of large families remain an all-consuming idée fixe for both the state and its propaganda organizations. Even the advertisements featured in the pictorial in the 1940s emphasize productivity for the Manchukuo regime. For example, patent medicine ads targeting Japanese men liberally pepper these later editions, promising to increase their labour power and virility (thus ensuring the production of more crops as well as children). The emphasis on production is reinforced in ads for medicines ranging from the energy promoter Vitamin B to several strangely named *horumon* (hormone) concoctions, one for each gender, which supposedly boosts either male or female hormones. In fact, in the early 1940s, an obsession with birth and breeding of all kinds, whether of humans or livestock, appeared in mass-consumed propaganda films as well as in more highbrow forms of art. For example, in the short documentary entitled *Manchukuo: The Newborn Empire,* the commentator discusses initiatives focusing on the cross-breeding of native Manchurian sheep with varieties from Japan to increase the production of wool.[103] After leafing through numerous editions of these later volumes of *Manshû gurafu,* one sees that this fixation becomes increasingly ominous and ever more indicative that Imperial Japan is losing its overextended war.

This theme of high productivity of both crops and children in the Manchurian space even permeated fine art. Consider, for example the formerly surrealist artist Asai Kan'emon's (1901-83) striking 1943 painting featuring a Madonna-like Japanese mother (complete with wispy, halo-like clouds near her head) dressed in blue, with her red kimono-attired toddler son, in an image entitled *Hôshû (Homare no kazoku) (Abundant Harvest [Family of Distinction]).*[104] The promised "abundant harvest" appears to be the production of one blessed child, who looks toward the viewer, while his mother modestly casts her gaze downwards at the child's jacket, which he will later wear at his first *shichi-go-san* shrine visit.[105] At the *monpe*-clad mother's feet rests a teapot reminiscent of that in Seitoku's 1937 photograph, while, portentously, a dog resembling a red fox, or *kitsune,* in the lower right corner gazes at the matriarchal family. In Japanese folk wisdom, the red fox is a trickster, and his presence casts an ironic shadow over this family that is missing its traditional head, the absent father likely having been called to war. The peaceful scene of maternal harmony is disrupted by the flame-like

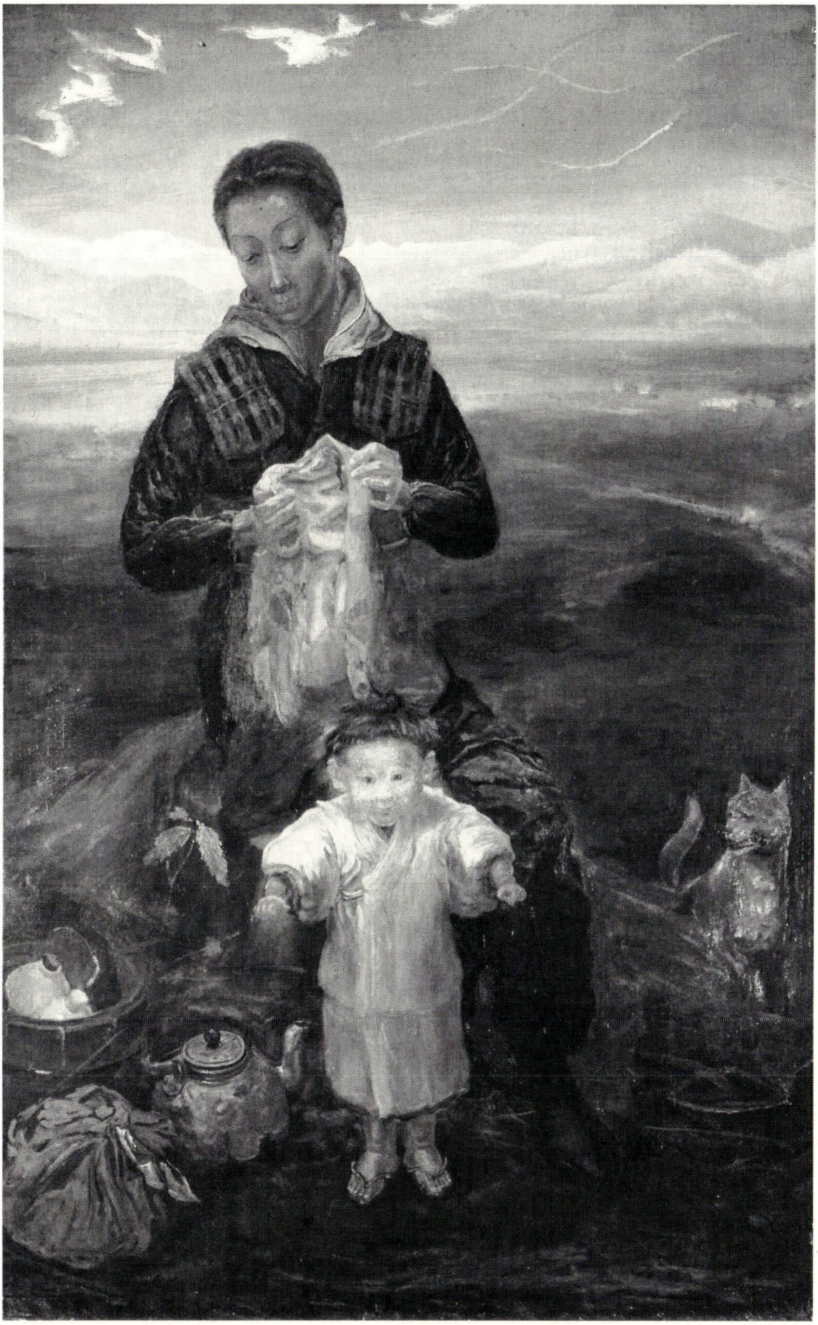

Figure 23 Asai Kan'emon, *Hôshû [Homare no kazoku]* [Abundant harvest (family of distinction)], 1943, Yokosuka Museum of Modern Art. Oil on canvas, dimensions: 117cm x 73 cm.

ochre of the soil and the turbulence of the rolling clouds in the background. Similar equivocal messages appear in the shots of the Japanese *kaitaku-sha* but with a different political import. The latter show that frenzied agricultural production in the rural space proceeds in an efficient and scientific manner, with the land's being worked by self-consciously smiling Japanese families who eagerly produce both a bounty of agricultural products and children – helpful in repopulating the ranks of soldiers killed amidst the intensifying Sino-Japanese conflict, the burgeoning war in the Pacific, and extended operations in Southeast Asia.

Conclusion: Manchuria/Manchukuo as a Site of Contradictions

In their images, Japanese observers like Fuchikami and his team attempt, with varying degrees of success, to differentiate the romanticized idea of Manchuria as a utopian space for the projection of Japanese colonial desires from the utopian multi-racial modern state of Manchukuo. This trend parallels the contradictory messages propagated by both the Manchukuo government and the partially state-sponsored South Manchuria Railway Company. On the one hand, the government and SMRC used many resources to link the region to domestic Japan while promoting Japanese culture and language; but, on the other, the cultural figures they sponsored focused on the distinctiveness of the Manchurian region in terms of both culture and physical factors. This is reflected in the contrasting depictions of the Chinese coolie workforce in urban areas and the Japanese settlers in rural locations. However, the two are linked in the photographers' ability to generate a fascist moment, as in the symbolic images of the coolie's teapot and the *kaitaku-sha* implements, both of which represent right-wing proletarianism.

From the mid-1930s to the early 1940s, while still focusing on the prevalence of coolie labour involved in trade and construction in the cities, Japanese photographers and artists "discovered" a utopian rural paradise in Manchuria that had been lost in Japan's rapid modernization and urbanization, and it is the north Manchurian *kaitaku-sha* that they increasingly featured in their works. Interestingly, the modern and the urban remained inherent characteristics of the new state of Manchukuo, while the broader Manchurian region continued to be portrayed as vast and largely uninhabited and, therefore, ready for colonization. This representation of a bucolic countryside ready for Japanese settlement as a solution to the problems of an over-urbanized domestic Japan contradicts the fact that certain areas in Manchuria (especially in the southeast) were overwhelmingly urban and that Manchukuo's cities, with a sophisticated rail and telecommunications network, were often much more modern than many in Japan.[106]

The 1938 initiation of the total war system, and the paper shortage due to the worsening conflict with the Allies after 1941, was reflected in a climate that favoured the consolidation of journals in domestic Japan. This trend began to affect Manchukuo in the last year and a half of the Second World War and even extended to the successful *Manshû gurafu*. In May 1944, the SMRC-sponsored journal and *Kaitaku gahô (Rural Development Pictorial)* were merged into one publication – *Manshû (Manchuria)*.[107] Despite, for over a decade, the pictorial's repeated insistence on the Manchukuo government's message of peace, racial harmony, and empty lands ripe for development, it was to end publication in January 1944 due to Imperial Japan's wartime exigencies.

6
The Manchukuo Publicity and News Bureau's War of Words and Images: Mutô Tomio and the Discourse of Culture, 1938-43

In the early 1940s, Manchukuo's Japanese leaders intended the country to serve as a cultural template for newly conquered nations in the Greater East Asia Co-Prosperity Sphere. In this chapter, I investigate Mutô Tomio's (1904-98) role as director of the *Manshûkoku kôhôsho* (Manchukuo Publicity and News Bureau) from 1939 to 1943 and discuss how his organization chose intellectuals to promote the new state's interests in Imperial Japan's project of nation building in Southeast Asia. Mutô was impressed by Nazi Germany's successful use of images in film, art, and literature in support of Adolf Hitler's (1889-1945) fascist regime (a right-wing version of socialism), and he also considered the activities of Joseph Goebbels (1897-1945) as a model for Manchukuo. While Goebbels's frustrated literary ambitions led to his obsessive organization and control of Nazi Germany's culture, Mutô, a former judge, was able to both control Manchukuo's culture and publish his own literary pursuits in various propaganda materials in Japanese, Chinese, and English. However, the literary talent of both ideologues was very low, and they were best at exhortations, speechmaking, and displaying their organizational skills. Mutô also served as a church elder in Manchukuo and felt that his Christian beliefs were fully compatible with the new state's paternalistic Confucian ideology.

I examine Mutô's personal writings and analyze his attraction to Manchukuo's cultural project, along with his tendency to support controversial figures from both sides of the political spectrum – like Amakasu Masahiko (1891-1945) and Yamada Seizaburô. While Mutô helped construct Manchukuo's new culture, he also engaged in cultural production, first in his role as propaganda director of the Concordia Association and then as state propaganda chief. For example, he wrote plays such as his 1937 "Invention and Free Love" (appearing in the 1938 Concordia issue of *Manchuria*),[1] as well as poetry and numerous essays compiled in 1941 in *Manshû sanka (Song in Praise of Manchuria)*.[2] These pieces were intended to serve as literary models for the new utopian society promoted by the Concordia Association, their author believing that literature could be used to achieve social transformation, though now in a right-wing proletarian, rather than in a left-wing socialist, guise.[3]

Mutô's Christian Conversion and Rapid Career Ascent, 1921-39

Originally from a poor peasant family in Shizuoka, Mutô harboured ambitions to further his education after graduating from his local high school in Fujioka-mura and, at age fourteen, went up to Tokyo, where he began working as a lawyer's servant while studying at night school.[4] He soon decided to study law, purportedly as a means of serving social justice and defending the oppressed. By the early 1920s, he had also become interested in Christianity. In April 1921, Mutô succeeded in entering Tokyo's First Higher School, a preparatory school dedicated to steering its aspirants into Japan's most prestigious imperial educational institution. After his studies in the Faculty of Law, funded by a group of businessmen, Mutô graduated from Tokyo Imperial University in 1927 and thus joined a small and highly connected elite. Incidentally, this university (and its law department) served as the primary feeder school for the Japanese government as well as the Empire's top colonial bureaucracy. It thus greatly aided the ambitious young man in generating the contacts he needed to succeed in his endeavours. Thus, it was not surprising that, only two years after graduating, Mutô passed the highest qualifying law exam and became a judge for the Tokyo regional courts in July 1929.

In the same year, the brilliant young judge was baptized a Christian, following six years of instruction by the American Methodist medical missionary and English teacher Samuel H. Wainwright (1863-1950), and the Japanese Presbyterian labour organizer Kagawa Toyohiko (1888-1960). Kagawa was Mutô's spiritual mentor, a Christian socialist who, beginning in 1909, and for the better part of a decade, had applied his religious beliefs to encouraging labour activism in the Kobe slums. In 1921, he founded the *Iesu no tomo kai* (Friends of Jesus Movement) to foster what he called a "redemptive love," or *shokuzai ai no jissen,* leading to economic, psychological, social, physical, and political emancipation for the practitioner who devoted his or her life to ministering to those in greatest need (usually, the poor).[5] In the Kansai region, Kagawa had also been involved with the *Yuaikai* (Fraternité Association), which maintained connections to farmer and labour unions and, in 1928, helped organize the Japanese Federation of Labour. This background of concern for the agricultural and working classes resonated with Mutô, who himself had come from an impoverished peasant family. By adopting a strict Protestant work ethic coupled with the service-oriented values of his emerging Christianity, the jurist rose to a prominent position and believed he could utilize his talents for society's betterment.

In 1929, Kagawa organized the idealistic *Kami no kuni undô* (Kingdom of God Movement).[6] In an initiative lasting until 1934, he hoped "to bring into fruition the Kingdom of God on earth."[7] Under the influence of his Christian socialist mentor, Mutô was drawn toward Kagawa's vision of a new world in which utopian social planning could address all kinds of social and economic ills.[8] He later attempted to bring these same ideals to fruition in the corporatist state of Manchukuo, where he accepted a bureaucratic position in the same year that Kagawa terminated the Kingdom of God Movement. Mutô, while obviously an opportunist and social climber, was drawn to a mission larger than himself and saw parallels between the revamped Confucian ideals of the fascist Concordia Association and Kagawa's utopian socialist Christianity. Intriguingly, in the postwar period, a presumably pro-US Kagawa (who, in 1940, even apologized for Japan's invasion of China), now on his deathbed, dramatically said to Mutô: "If you do nothing else, please write about Manchukuo's history to leave it for posterity. In the invasion carried out by Japan, only Manchukuo is worth a novel."[9] Kagawa's lack of contrition regarding his role in fostering an illusory utopia in Japanese-occupied Manchuria reveals the quasi-nostalgic attitude of many Japanese intellectuals on both sides of the political spectrum.

According to Stephen C. Mercado, Manchukuo's Japanese framers were well aware of the strong influence of Christianity in the American political sphere. Therefore, once friction with the United States began, following the 1932 League of Nation's refusal to recognize Manchukuo, appointments were made to put Japan's most prominent Christians (including Mutô) into important positions. According to Mercado: "Hoshino Naoki, Japan's top civilian official in Manchukuo, made Mutô Tomio the puppet empire's propaganda chief with the expectation that Mutô would put his Christian background to good use in dealings with the West."[10] In July 1932, Hoshino (1892-1978) had been appointed director general of the Manchukuo Finance Department and, by 1936, worked as the State Council's chief bureaucrat. After 1937, he served as the Manchukuo cabinet's vice-minister of financial affairs.[11] By 1940, he also headed the new state's planning board. Moreover, Hoshino's father was a Christian pastor at the Shiba Church in Tokyo's Minato district, and, according to Mutô, Hoshino himself secretly professed Christianity during his time as a Manchukuo official.[12] Therefore, it was in Hoshino's, and the new state's, interest to attract like-minded allies who could wholeheartedly back Manchukuo's ideological construction and, perhaps, explain their actions in a fashion that the (largely Christian) Westerners would understand.

In the Manchukuo context, Mutô's rapid career ascent was nothing short of remarkable for a young Japanese bureaucrat from humble origins, and it attests to his passion and hard work as well as to the savvy manipulation of his connections with Japanese officials and the Kantô Army. After five years as a judge, in April 1934, Mutô acquired a position as a Manchukuo bureaucrat, serving as chief of the first section of the Ministry of Justice's criminal bureau and, one year later, as counsellor to the Legislative Bureau of the State Council's Management and Coordination Agency.[13] Both positions allowed him proximity to those in power, who swiftly promoted the enthusiastic young man when he was in his early thirties. Through his friendship with Hoshino, Mutô then quickly rose to postings outside the realm of law, where his strong rhetorical skills remained key – for example, in his service as consultant to the Management and Coordination Agency, where he first met Amakasu, and, of course, in his later work for the *Kôhôsho*.

As a member of the *Kempeitai* (Japanese military police), Amakasu had earlier gained notoriety for his role in authorizing the brutal murder of Osugi Sakae (1885-1923), Osugi's common-law wife Itô Noe (1895-1923), and his five-year-old American nephew in the ruthless police attacks on leftists following the 1923 Kantô Earthquake. He served only three years of a ten-year prison sentence following his court martial, whereon he spent several years in exile studying in France – paid for by the Japanese Imperial Army, which no doubt helped engineer his much-truncated prison term.[14] A position in Manchukuo allowed Amakasu to distance himself from his humiliating miscalculation in engaging in a supposedly justified "war" against communism and to work with supportive accomplices. Moreover, he garnered much respect among extreme nationalists and Japanese military circles for his iron tactics, and he was rumoured to have aided in planning the 1931 Manchurian Incident.[15]

Amakasu soon re-emerged in Manchukuo, where, by the mid-1930s, he served as director of the Concordia Association's General Affairs Division and, in this position, appointed Mutô to work on the organization's behalf.[16] Starting in December 1937, Mutô thus took up his new post as chief of the propaganda section of the Concordia Association's central headquarters, while maintaining his earlier position as counsellor to the Legislative Bureau.[17] Despite their political differences, the two men worked well together following this appointment, and Amakasu's close Kantô Army connections no doubt smoothed Mutô's career path and propaganda efforts.

While heading the Concordia Association's propaganda activities, Mutô accompanied Amakasu as one of Manchukuo's emissaries on a 1938 tour of Europe in early September, during which they also arranged Japan's goodwill delegations to fascist Italy and Germany. As the ship docked in Shanghai en route to Europe, Mutô, while observing the ruins of the 1932 Jiabei Conflict, had the following opportunistic thoughts: "If one day soon the China Incident ends, and then the chaos of war breaks out in Europe, Japan will protect its neutrality in the case that the US goes along with the venture. Japan will invest this economic power garnered through neutrality into Manchukuo, and will allow it to prosper as a utopian country."[18] On 5 September, their vessel stopped at the Italian port of Naples, and, by train, they soon proceeded to Rome, where they met Mussolini and toured the Vatican. Via Trieste and Vienna, Mutô and Amakasu arrived in Munich during the infamous Munich Conference. To their dismay, only one of their delegation, Han Yunjie, actually met Hitler at the 29 September conclusion of the conference.[19] In Nazi Germany, Amakasu toured the film studio Universum Film-AG, a seminal event that determined his support of Mutô's propaganda efforts as well as the style of films and materials to be used by the *Manshû eiga kyôkai* (Manchurian Film Association, or *Man'ei*).[20] The successful tour of Japan's European fascist allies, in an atmosphere of appeasement following the Munich Conference, gave the two propagandists the impression that Mussolini and Hitler offered superior political, economic, and social models for Manchukuo.[21] Proximity to these charismatic leaders and the opportunity to witness their fascist states gave Mutô, in 1939, the distinction of rising to head Manchukuo's propaganda activities; after 1943, he headed all Japanese propaganda efforts. After Mutô's return, on 22 March 1939, Hoshino promoted him to the position of propaganda director of the *Kôhôsho,* serving under the State Council's Bureau of General Affairs.

Mutô's first initiatives were to improve the new state's coordination of propaganda activities during the intensification of the war effort in China, to stimulate new cultural activities supportive of the regime, and to reform *Man'ei* (a film company established in 1937 after two years of planning with the Kantô Army).[22] Through the support of Kishi Nobusuke (1896-1987), deputy director of the Management and Coordination Agency, Mutô paid back Amakasu's favour by recommending him to serve as managing director of *Man'ei*.[23] Thus, in November 1939, Amakasu replaced Negishi Kan'ichi, the former studio chief of Nikkatsu Tamagawa, and, on behalf of the "Manchurian people," purportedly set out on a mission to create films with a specifically "Manchurian content and focus."[24] A year earlier, in support of propaganda efforts, *Man'ei* had already planned the distribution of government films in various localities by equipping these places with sixteen-millimetre projectors and thus stimulating local film corps. Mutô and Amakasu's joint propaganda initiatives also included nurturing an avid local film culture by initiating travelling film shows at sixty-six rail stops in towns and cities along SMRC tracks, in *kaitaku-sha* (Japanese rural pioneer) villages, and at Manchurian Youth Corps training centres (like Tetsuryô, or Tieli).[25] This plan was soon followed by the rapid proliferation of five thousand small-scale movie theatre outlets located in sixty-two towns with populations of over ten thousand each.[26] According to Mark Driscoll, as a result of such endeavours Amakasu, as "chairman of Manchukuo's propaganda film company Man'ei, was considered the most powerful cultural broker in Japanese-controlled Manchuria in the early 1940s."[27] Thus began Mutô's interest in fostering films with Amakasu, along with other cultural initiatives to bolster the Manchukuo people's "moral" culture; however, he himself favoured sponsoring literary and artistic pursuits.[28]

Beginning in the late 1930s with his work for the Concordia Association, Mutô began to produce "literature," even writing edifying dramas and essays that expressed his ideals, such as a 1938 article explaining the philosophy of "concordia" (see below).[29] In another example, he wrote a one-act play in 1937 entitled "Invention and Free Love: A Play in One Act," with the Chinese title of "Faming yu ziyou lian'ai." This play, which parallels his own life, was performed in Shinkyô with Chinese actors.[30] Its narrative features an ambitious young man from a peasant family who heads to the imperial capital to acquire an education while working as the servant of a bourgeois family (in the play, the story is set in Shinkyô rather than in Tokyo). Mûto, like the enterprising working-class Chinese servant Fan Tzu-chun in the wealthy Chu household, educated himself through night school and thereby gained the notice of his well-connected patron.[31]

In the end, Fan's invention, which was able to prevent smoke and soot from rising out of the city's chimney pots (possibly an electrical chimney scrubber), was so effective that he won the right to court Chu's daughter, Ma-li, who remarked ecstatically: "In China there has not been in the past anything worth calling an invention. In our Manchoukuo, we should make many inventions such as would astonish the world."[32] Before Fan earns ten thousand yuan for his patent from the Manchukuo Invention Association and the Patent and Information Bureau, Chu contemptuously remarks: "It is impossible that a man not educated at a university in Japan, America, or in Europe could have invented such a wonderful machine."[33] Later, however, after Fan brings acclaim to his household, Chu is contrite and offers him his support. When a representative from the two organizations comes to the Chu mansion, Ma-Li further exclaims to Fan: "I wonder why I didn't notice that you are such a great scholar. Frankly speaking, until today I looked on you as a slave. Or a coolie. I made a great mistake. We look down on the coolies and house-boys with contempt, but some of them may be great men, though I don't think a man like you could be found elsewhere."[34] Thus, the play ends with a budding romance, representing Manchukuo's new modern ideal of "free love," which emerges outside the parameters of social class and the traditional Chinese arranged marriage system. The play also evinces the benefits of a strong work ethic, humility, and selflessness. Here, Mutô's moralistic story mixes an urban right-wing proletarianism with Kagawa's Christian socialist utopianism in the form of a corporatist state (represented by Chu and his daughter, the progressive younger generation) that takes a paternalistic interest in its subjects.

As for Amakasu, his ultranationalist ideology was motivated by a deep desire to serve the emperor and Imperial Japan by creating a successful state that would bolster his home country.[35] However, though his aims were skewed in favour of Japanese goals, the type of films he advocated and the nature of his leadership were, according to Peter High, "marked with a certain interest in social justice,"[36] and it is possible that they demonstrate Mutô's influence. Exposure to the charismatic Mutô's youthful zeal may have enabled Amakasu to believe that he could atone for earlier indiscretions by serving the state in waging a propaganda war through peaceful but effective means. He was convinced that, through films made for entertainment and instruction, he could garner the support of Manchukuo's ordinary people.[37] Whatever their political differences, Mutô and Amakasu worked well together due to their common goals, and they even collaborated on the formulation of the 1941 *Geibun shidô yokô (Prospectus for the Guidance of the Arts and Culture)*. However, before we focus on this important late stage in Manchukuo's wartime cultural construction, we must examine the state's earlier cultural initiatives (i.e., during the intensification of the conflict with China) and look at how the continuous reorganization of Manchukuo's propaganda apparatus worked in tandem with them.

The Concordia Association's Creation of a Fascist Culture, 1932-38

Arguably, Manchukuo was more thoroughly fascistic than Japan itself. Because the Kantô Army took over the region and imposed an administrative structure on over 30 million Chinese and other native inhabitants, it was a relatively simple matter for Japanese planners to develop existing structures rather than to create an entirely new apparatus under state-sponsored corporatism. Indeed, the SMRC conglomerate and its military arm, the Kantô Army, were conveniently in place and cooperating with Imperial Japan prior to the 1931 "Incident." The new state would have corporatism as its base, a military ensuring its "protection," and a mass organization – the Concordia Association – to communicate its ideals to the people. It followed a utopian fascism resembling the Italian model under Mussolini in the early to mid-1930s, and, after 1937, it followed Nazi Germany's "neo-corporatism." Mark Peattie characterizes the Manchukuo regime as "military fascist," with Ishiwara Kanji having a guiding hand in promoting the state's new culture according to the ideological aims of the military shadow-regime.[38]

The Concordia Association became one of the primary disseminators of official and unofficial propaganda to the Manchukuo people, the Japanese, and people abroad. In his memoirs, Mutô, as its former propaganda director, reveals that the new state's moral virtues and values were to be maintained through the Concordia Association, which evolved out of the former Manchurian Youth League.[39] Founded in July 1932, its goal was to preserve unity and harmony among the five officially recognized ethnic groups, while organizing the Manchurian people into communities to surmount class differences and to oppose both communism and Western capitalism.[40] This fascist organization's aims evoke the words of Slavoj Žižek: "The fascist dream is simply to have capitalism without its 'excess,' without the antagonism that causes its structural imbalance."[41] The discourse of a common "Manchurian culture" initiated by Mutô and others soon served as a palliative to eliminate social or ethnic tensions.

As Carl Cohen notes: "The word *fasciare* means to bind or to envelop, and fascism was intended by its founders as a doctrine that would, once and for all, bind the Italian nation into an organic entity, maintaining and expanding the traditions and glories of ancient Rome."[42] Like that of Italy, Manchukuo's fascism allowed a middle way between laissez-faire capitalism and communism, seemingly without their apparent excesses.[43] In the case of Nazi Germany, also increasingly a model for Manchukuo's Japanese state planners after 1938, Alan Steinweis argues that "neo-corporatism represented a non-Marxist alternative to a failing liberal social and economic order."[44]

Indeed, the two fascist countries of Italy and Nazi Germany were among the few nations, including the Vatican, that reluctantly recognized Manchukuo after 1932. In 1936, due to rising trade with Italy, a consulate was set up in Hôten (Fengtian). However, it was not until 1938 that the new state received an Italian ambassador and thus established full diplomatic relations between the two countries.[45] On 25 April 1938, after visiting Japan, Baron Giacomo Paolucci di Calboli came to Shinkyô for two weeks.[46] Mutô wrote that this created a great sensation for the Manchukuo people and, especially, for the heads of the Concordia Association since they hoped to apply Italian fascist principles to the new state.[47] On the Italian delegation's arrival, the Concordia Association headquarters, as well as the Kantô Army, staged a big welcome.[48] The importance of this fascist organization to Manchukuo's existence can be seen in a September 1938 meeting with Mussolini in Italy, when Ambassador Zhang Jing'en extended an initial message on behalf of Manchukuo's president and a second one on behalf of Mutô, the Concordia Association's director.[49] Zhang explained to Mussolini that the Concordia Association worked hard to ensure the country's proper construction and development and that its bureaucrats hoped that it would soon have an even greater role in world affairs.[50]

According to Prasenjit Duara, state-sponsored organizations such as the Concordia Association formed in order "to realize a visionary modern polity" and to carry out the political and cultural ideals of the new state, blending Western modernity with Eastern values[51] – a purpose corroborated by various media under the direction of the Manchukuo Publicity and News Bureau, the organization's top-level propaganda arm.[52] The Concordia Association was directly connected to this bureau, which was headquartered in the Shinkyô capital under the purview of the Manchukuo General Affairs

Board. In English-language materials, the *Kôhôsho* appears as the innocuously named "Information Bureau" or "Publicity Department."[53]

There are certain key phases in the propaganda bureau's development and its collaboration with the Concordia Association. For example, 1932 marked the beginning of the first Five-Year Plan, according to which the *Kôhôsho*'s focus was on growth and development, with SMRC playing a leading role in providing an important model for its nascent propaganda activities (co-ordinated by the Concordia Association). The end of the first Five-Year Plan coincided with the 1937 eruption of the Second Sino-Japanese War. In tandem with the total war system enacted in Japan, 1938 culminated in a flurry of propaganda publications produced with the collaboration of the Concordia Association. In 1940, the linkages with the Greater East Asia Co-Prosperity Sphere were intensified, while in 1941, Mutô envisioned Manchukuo's culture as a potential template for Southeast Asia. In the same year, the Manchukuo Publicity and News Bureau issued the *Geibun shidô yokô*. Nineteen forty-two soon heralded the end of the second Five-Year Plan and the beginning of the third, but it also included an attack on leftists, many of whom had collaborated with the Manchukuo culture-making enterprise. In the early 1940s, the Concordia Association required compulsory membership, something that the *Kempeitai* used in order to root out dissidents.

Mutô's 1938 Essays on the Concordia Association's Ideals and Culture

In the late 1930s, Mutô, as propaganda director of the Concordia Association, wrote two lengthy essays: "The Spirit of Hsieh-Ho (*Kyôwa,* or "harmony"): A New Philosophy" and "An Outline of the Manchoutikuo [Empire of Manchukuo] Hsieh-ho-hui [Concordia Association]." They form the introduction to a special July 1938 edition of the English-language publication *Manchuria,* entitled "Concordia and Culture in Manchoukuo."[54] This bi-monthly magazine, published by the *Manchuria Daily News* (or *Manshû nichinichi shimbun*) under the direction of the Manchukuo Publicity and News Bureau, was geared to a broad audience outside the confines of the Japanese Empire, thus illustrating the kind of propaganda initiatives that the new state's Japanese handlers hoped to convey to Western readers. Here, Mutô attempts to communicate the Manchukuo "empire's" ideological framework in a clear, exportable fashion, lest misunderstandings arise among Westerners.

The Concordia Association was intended to foster and cultivate the state's neo-Confucian values (which were to set it apart from the individualism of the West) in a corporatist society in which each individual served as part of a whole. According to Mutô: "The spirit of Hsieh-ho is the collective will to attain social perfection by suppressing the human instinct for struggle and by enhancing human affection. It aims at creating things valuable and a moral world through the cooperation and harmony of the people. It is morality and in this it resembles Stoicism or Confucianism."[55] These values were based on Asian principles as interpreted by Japanese. This is because most Chinese intellectuals – even prior to the influential anti-Japanese May Fourth Movement – had by the 1930s already rejected Confucianism as leading to a "backwards" feudal society, like that decried by Lu Xun as a *chiren de shehui* (cannibalistic society) in "Kuangren riji" (Diary of a Madman), 1917.

Reinforcing the imperial Japanese client state's paternalism, the ideals Mutô expounded included "the establishment of inseparable relations between Japan and Manchoukuo – oneness in spirit and virtue, the concord of races, the creation of a moral world through racial concord, and the bringing into practice of an original Wangtao ["Kingly Way"] government."[56] A 1933 English-language handbook published by the Publicity and News Bureau explained that, as a political philosophy, "'Wangtaoism' [Kingly Way-ism] is neither nationalistic nor communistic but represents the golden mean between fascism and bolshevism."[57] Moreover, Manchukuo's people supposedly supported this middle way, which stemmed from their own native Chinese traditions:

> The great masses of Manchoukuo, tired of the imported ideas of Republicanism, Nationalism, or Dr. Sun Yat-Sen's "Three People's Principles," which have all proved gross failures in China, quite naturally turned their minds to their own traditional political ideas inherent in Confucianism. The golden age of such ancient sage-kings as Yao and Shun loomed large and fascinating in their eyes and the result was the unanimous voice of 30,000,000 people, "Back to Wangdao."[58]

Here, we can see the Publicity and News Bureau's desire to harken back to a nostalgic, legendary Chinese past – "the golden age" underlying Manchukuo's fascist utopia.

In the various official propaganda materials disseminated by the state through the Publicity and News Bureau, the hybrid culture in Manchukuo, described as a "Paradise of the Kingly Way," or *Ôdô-rakudo,* was represented by the slogan *gozoku-kyôwa* (harmony of the five races/ethnicities), reflecting a modern, Westernized, multi-ethnic nation rationally ordered by traditional (East Asian) Confucian principles. Illustrations of racial harmony, or *minzoku kyôwa,* were often coupled with corresponding descriptions of these five races/ethnicities, as we saw in the *Asahi Shimbun* example. However, this ethnic/racial harmony was difficult to define, with Kita Sadakichi even positing that *minzoku* seemed to be a matter of ideology.[59] Tessa Morris-Suzuki argues that, in the Japanese context: "Like *Volk, minzoku* has powerful overtones of communal solidarity, but is equivocal about the basis of the solidarity. While race is clearly based on inherited physical characteristics, a minzoku may be held together by blood bonds, nationality, culture or some combination of these things."[60]

Mutô's essay "The Spirit of Hsieh-ho: A New Philosophy" elaborates on these nebulous concepts in its discussion of *Hsieh-ho,* or *kyôwa,* which he defines as cooperation and harmony within a kind of Confucian-inspired corporatism.[61] Yet, in his orientation toward Westerners, Mutô's words also evince a kind of Protestant work ethic involving self-denial, with the Concordia Association's emphasis on *kyôwa* functioning as a quasi-religion: "The power that can break through this outer covering of the soul is religion, and Hsieh-ho *(kyôwa)* is that power."[62] The propagandist also notes that "the politics of Hsieh-ho wish to combine the will of the people with that of the officials," much resembling the aims of a typical fascist organization.[63] However, the term *kyôwa* originally evolved out of a Meiji period misunderstanding of such political processes as American federalism. For example, Peter Duus argues that, for the Japanese government in the late nineteenth century, the word *kyôwa* meant "republic," often referring to the type of governance practised by the United States.[64]

While Mutô initially touted the harmony of the five races, the "ideal society" proposed by the Concordia Association would actually lead to the ultimate extinction of these once celebrated cultural differences: "The ultimate goal of the Hsieh-ho-hui movement is the establishment of an earthly paradise, an ideal society ... That will be the time when the entire nation will be one in spirit, and when a language indigenous to Manchoukuo will have been born by the disappearance of all distinctions among Japanese, Manchurians, Mongols, and Koreans."[65] It is difficult to discern whether Mutô meant this metaphorically or literally since, in 1938, there was no means of instituting any common language other than Japanese. Obviously, Chinese would have been a clear choice, but this would have threatened the nominal *cultural* independence of the nation. In fact, after 1937, Japanese was the primary language of instruction in both Manchukuo and an annexed Korea, now deep into the 1938 *Naisen ittai* (Japan and Korea as One Body) campaign begun during the intensification of the war in China.

Obviously, the vision of a multicultural utopia disseminated by the Concordia Association and other official propaganda organs was created through a Japanese lens, though Westernized Chinese elites were also courted for their support. Japanese nationals in Manchukuo and visitors from the archipelago received the majority of funding and support from a state obsessed with representing itself and that, despite its nominal independence, was largely a part of the Japanese cultural and linguistic sphere.

After 1938, Mutô and Amakasu, as director of *Man'ei,* would play an important role in constructing the state's new culture by binding people together through the Concordia Association and, after 1941, through various centrally located literary and artistic associations in Shinkyô. Of course, these initiatives, whose purpose was to lead to a higher moral order, would be furthered by the association's organizational and monetary support: "Furthermore, the Hsieh-ho-hui is giving encouragement, by offering prizes, to music, drama, art and literature with the ultimate aim of fostering a new culture indigenous to Manchoukuo which would be the product of united efforts of the entire races *[sic]*."[66] In this manner, even local cultural production could be subordinated to the regime's propaganda needs.

Mutô emphasized the primacy of Japan's role and that of the Emperor in Manchukuo's guidance. In addition, he noted that, in his ideal state, relations between people would be ordered by a Japanese-inspired hierarchy of loyalty and respect: "In every individual there must also be engendered a feeling of loyalty to the Emperor, of love for his country, piety toward his parents, and of friendship toward his neighbour and the world at large, so that as an individual as well as a member of society and the State, he will have a personality that will command respect."[67] Here, we see a melding of the Imperial Japanese virtues of loyalty to nation and Emperor – ideals also inculcated in Japanese youth since the 1890 implementation of the Imperial Rescript on Education, which was accompanied by a morning reading and obeisance to the portrait of the Japanese emperor. This began in the late Meiji period and continued until 1945. After 1937, Manchukuo also adopted this daily ritual.

Liu Shanzheng, a high school student in a provincial town near the Japanese training camp of Tetsuryô (now Tieli) during the 1930s, vividly remembered how Japanese teachers routinely checked Han Chinese students' desks and notebooks to see whether they had carved or drawn any caricatures of a supposedly divine emperor.[68] In addition, two portraits, one of Hirohito and one of Pu-Yi (albeit in a slightly smaller frame than his Japanese counterpart), were prominently hung next to each other in the front of the room and stared down at the students.[69] Thus, although Manchukuo's integration with domestic Japan became a clear and definite goal during wartime, it actually began as early as the 1934 imperial coronation of Pu Yi as emperor of Manchukuo. This was followed by mutual imperial visits, albeit with Pu Yi first going to Japan, thus showing his fealty to the Japanese Empire and emphasizing his subservient role.

With regard to the Concordia Association's work helping to construct the new state's Japanese-guided culture, Mutô comments: "The activities of the Hsieh-ho-hui [Concordia Association] may be classified into three general categories, namely, spiritual, political and cultural."[70] However, the most emphasis was placed on the latter category as it had the ability to assimilate the two preceding ones. Mutô's supposedly informative essay focuses on the primacy of culture and its role in promoting a fascist aesthetic that easily translates into social harmony: "Besides being a spiritual and political organization, the Hsieh-ho-hui is a cultural body on which devolves the great task of enlightening the people so as to lead a better, healthier and more beautiful life."[71] Nevertheless, the most important aspect of Mutô's cultural program was the following: "Through the advancement of culture the spirit of Hsieh-ho-hui will be simultaneously enhanced, for culture softens and refines human feelings.[72] Here we see the culmination of what Alan Tansman refers to as "fascist moments" in which "the individual is depicted as merging with, or is called on to merge imaginatively with, a greater whole."[73] In an assessment of fascist Japan, which can also be applied to culture in Manchukuo as expressed by spokesmen of the Concordia Association such as Mutô, Marilyn Ivy cautions: "It is the fantasy of culture itself that gives shape to many of the aesthetic and philosophical enterprises circulating around the fascist sign. That is culture – the notion of culture – emerges as that which *also* works precisely to erase the political (that is, class division and unevenness) and the traumas of capitalism (the commodity form itself)."[74] It is through culture that, in Manchukuo, we see the Concordia Association attempting to assuage the social divisions and economic conflicts that had so plagued Japan in the 1930s.

Tang Xiang, a teacher at one of Harbin's elite public schools and part of a northeastern history study group, argues that it was easier for the Japanese to pacify the Manchukuo people through culture or civilization (*wenhua* or *bunka*) than through purely political means.[75] In his opinion, the *Wangdao* philosophy and the *tonghua* concept (*dôka,* or assimilation to the ideals and culture of the state) were used by state organizations like the Concordia Association to "relax the rebellious intentions of the Chinese" who might otherwise have risen against their Japanese occupiers.[76] Mutô's own characterization of culture as an entity that "softens and refines human feelings" is certainly in line with Tang's assertions:

> When the country is governed in an ideal manner, and the economic state of the people leaves nothing to be desired, culture will flourish, and life will become beautiful. Scientific research will become popular, great scholars and scientists who will astonish the world with their erudition and discoveries [sic], and inventions will appear. Literature, music, and art, all indigenous to Manchoukuo will claim the attention of the world. The building up of an earthly paradise such as that pictured above, is the ideal for which the Hsieh-ho-hui is striving. Every Hsieh-ho-hui member is inspired with this ideal. Faith in the sublime mission of the Hsieh-ho-hui propels its members towards great achievements.[77]

Here we have an encapsulated image of the ideal world that Mutô and his associates were hoping to create, based on the premises of Mencius (372-289

BCE): only when the economic livelihood of the people is satisfied could they focus on cultural pursuits. This utopian vision was so compelling to intellectuals of all political stripes in Japan that they willingly accepted invitations for tours and sojourns in Manchukuo.

Two Japanese Bureaucrats on Propaganda in Manchukuo, 1938

I now investigate the role of propaganda in Manchukuo's integration with Japan's wartime empire. In the context of Imperial Japan's war efforts, Barak Kushner notes: "Japan's wartime propaganda centered on one major goal: unifying the battlefront with the homefront."[78] He further argues that propaganda served as "a tool for integrating Japan's wartime empire"[79] – also relevant to Manchukuo. In order to support my assertions, which concur with Kushner's argument, I analyze select essays by high-level Japanese bureaucrats, in which they discuss the meaning and importance of official propaganda for Manchukuo. These offer a sampling of how Japanese ideologues thought about their own propaganda efforts in the wake of Japan's 1938 total war system. After becoming familiar with their understanding and use of official propaganda as disseminated in an internal journal used by a privileged group of government employees, we can view the similarities and differences between the "informal" and "unofficial" propaganda produced by formerly left-wing or avant-garde cultural producers. It also allows us to develop a more nuanced understanding of Mutô's ideologically informed literary efforts.

The following writings come from *Senbu geppô (Pacification Monthly),* a top-secret internal publication labelled *toriatsukai shu'i* ("handle with care"), which was in circulation from the mid-1930s until the end of the war and which devoted lengthy passages to propaganda-based discussions. *Senbu geppô* boasted a select group of subscribers among Japanese government bureaucrats and the military. Mutô avidly read the journal and even helped choose the type of articles appearing in its pages. The *Kôhôsho* issued this periodical under the purview of the State Council, with which, as a legal counsellor, Mutô maintained close connections. Later, he served on its behalf as Manchukuo's propaganda chief and then as Japan's.

According to Japanese media scholar Yamamoto Taketoshi, who also edited the 2005 edition of *Senbu geppô* reprints, "The magazine carried articles on American and British theories and studies related to propaganda that had been rejected in mainland Japan."[80] The right-wing ideologues drafting such essays read German, British, American, and Russian examples, and they assimilated what they felt best applied to Japanese needs in the Manchukuo context. This differs from the strategy of adherents of the underground Chinese Communist Party, who followed Soviet agit-prop strategies to the letter in occupied China and Manchukuo.[81]

For example, in March 1938, Tôzawa Tetsuhiko published the article "Senden no igi" ("The Meaning of Propaganda"), hoping to clarify for his elite readers the meaning of what he believed to be an elusive term.[82] It had originally appeared a month before in the February edition of the integrative magazine *Kaizô,* accessible to the general public – but perhaps it now merited a special version in *Senbu geppô,* minus the censorship. After Tôzawa devoted several sections to investigating the term's history, even citing the Vatican's early sixteenth-century attempts to "propagate" its own religious ideas during the Reformation, he examined the more recent uses of propaganda during wartime. He predictably praised German propaganda efforts (conducted during a climate of appeasement on behalf of the Nazi Party), but he also lauded American and British propaganda from the First World War because he felt that it could effectively touch the emotions and thus had a great ability to reach the common people. Tôzawa then cited Vireck's *Spreading the Germs of Hate* as an example.

More importantly, Tôzawa stressed that the most effective propaganda was the kind that did not seem obvious – indeed, throughout Amakasu's tenure as director of the Manchurian Film Association, he never admitted that the films were meant for propaganda, just for entertainment or "information" purposes. In his strongest commentary, Tôzawa reveals that the Japanese government was now attempting to imitate the German *Reichsministerium für Volksaufklärung und Propaganda* (Reich Ministry for Popular Enlightenment and Propaganda), but he emphasized that this attempt was superficial. He held that a more useful measure would be to investigate Germany's propaganda activities and that it would be even better to focus on witty British and American First World War propaganda ditties that had so captured the popular imagination and were sung frequently.[83] He does not mention specific songs, but in 1914, songs such as "It's a Long Way to Tipperary," "Pack Up Your Troubles," For the Honour of Dear Old England," "March on to Berlin!" and "Your King and Country Want You" circulated throughout Britain and helped spur recruitment and heighten morale. Here, Tôzawa notes how propaganda had been creatively assimilated into everyday life.[84] The article also points out that, in the early 1930s, the Germans believed their First World War defeat stemmed from superior British and American propaganda efforts, which relied on the common people. Therefore, Tôzawa argues, Hitler hired Goebbels to serve as his propaganda minister, and he expanded these efforts to reach all sectors of the German population. It was very likely that Mutô avidly studied such commentaries in *Senbu geppô* and patterned his own efforts on close readings of articles like Tôzawa's, which elucidated the best German, British, and American propaganda of the past few decades.

However, we might ask, how could the propaganda be most effectively disseminated, and what was unique about Manchukuo that enabled it to have effective dissemination channels? In the provocatively titled September article "Zentaishugi kokka ni okeru senden hôshin" ("Propaganda Policies in Totalitarian Countries"), which appears in the same restricted-access publication, Tamura Toshio, the head of the Bureau of Education under the Ministry of Home Affairs, viewed Manchukuo as part of a globalized network of modern cities, including New York, Paris, Berlin, Tokyo, and Shinkyô, which were all connected by modern communications and transportation systems such as shipping, rail networks, and telephone lines.[85] In a section entitled "Senden-sen ni okeru: Bunkajin no batteki" ("The Selection of Cultural Figures for the Propaganda War"),[86] he views intellectuals as important disseminators of information about the new state. Here, Tamura argues in favour of enlisting cultural figures from "among the people," or *minkan,* because of the fear that, militarily, Japan was already experiencing difficulty gaining support for its cause.[87]

Presumably, for Tamura, "unofficial" propagandists in a "civilian" role would be more persuasive than would official propagandists in communicating the state's ideas in a manner that people could understand. Later, in 1941, with the issuing of the *Prospectus for the Guidance of the Arts and Culture,* Mutô believed that the arts served as an effective way of "proletarianizing" propaganda with the collusion of the locally based, fascist Concordia Association. In his 1938 article, Tamura views the use of intellectuals as important in that, as eloquent spokespeople and cultural producers, they and their works are an integral part of winning the hearts and minds of the common people.[88] Ostensibly, these individuals could be either Japanese or Chinese, though attempts to mobilize Chinese intellectuals on behalf of the Manchukuo state were not very effective until after 1940. From 1938 onwards, the Concordia Association attempted to stimulate propaganda efforts by issuing prizes for cultural endeavours, but this initiative was not as successful as state planners had hoped.

Tamura lamented that, in 1938 in Shanghai, there was only one newspaper loyal to Japan, the *Xin shenbao (New Newspaper).* This was not surprising, considering that the November 1937 battle for the port city nearly a year earlier had been particularly vicious, with Chiang's best Nazi-trained troops fighting valiantly against the Japanese invaders, despite their eventual loss. In contempt, imperial Japanese units soon marched up the Yangtze River to pillage and rape the republican capital of Nanjing for six atrocity-filled weeks, from December 1937 until January 1938. Tamura rightly feared that the growing anti-Japanese animosity from below the Great Wall might filter up into Manchukuo. However, though avidly debated in 1938, the skilful use of Chinese and others in Manchukuo to engage in the cultural efforts that Tamura advocated did not become a reality until 1940, beginning with such initiatives as Yamada's compilation of a volume of multi-ethnic literature, which conformed to the ideals of the Concordia Association.

It certainly seems that, in 1939, Mutô and Amakasu took Tamura's ideas to heart when they rose to their respective high positions in the Manchukuo Publicity and News Bureau and the Manchurian Film Association, hoping to use these organizations to their best advantage in fighting the "thought war." For them to reach Japanese, Manchurian, and foreign publics most effectively, they believed they had to organize their efforts by couching them in the rhetoric of "culture."

The Wartime Organization of Cultural Propaganda in Manchukuo, 1937-41

Aside from being a key year in which mutual hostilities erupted in earnest between Japan and China, 1937 marked the end of Manchukuo's first Five Year Industrial Development Plan and saw the centralized management of propaganda as part of broader administrative reforms marking the consolidation of existing government offices.[89] In the same year, the Manchukuo government's Information Board *(Manshû jijô annai-sho)* was reorganized for incorporation into the *Kôhôsho,* which Kishi Toshihiko translates as the "Propaganda and Intelligence Board."[90] Moreover, an information section was added as a third section to the supervisory and propaganda sections. "Intelligence" does not seem to be clearly indicated in the *Kôhôsho*'s Japanese name, but Kishi is probably referring to how, in 1934, the *Manshû jijô annai-sho* began working to assist other intelligence agencies in their efforts to quell anti-Japanese resistance in Manchukuo.[91]

In clarifying this term, Kishi comments: "The word 'information' here was used in the sense of information on disinformation, communist propaganda, anti-Manchukuo activities, heretical missionary activities, and public opinion and public sentiment toward the government and its policy measures."[92] Other Japanese scholars, such as Yamamoto, simply call it the "Information Board," which confuses matters for those reading his and Kishi's otherwise excellent articles in English.[93] However, in English-language materials, Manchukuo officials themselves often referred to it as the euphemistically named "Bureau of Information." For example, Obama Shigeru, chief of the publicity section in the Manchukuo Foreign Office, notes in 1939 that it is under the prime minister's direct supervision and that it "controls and directs the various cultural organizations and their general activities."[94] In 1940, it appears in English as the "Publicity Bureau," under the control of the General Affairs Bureau and, therefore, also under the prime minister's direction.[95] Duara, who primarily works with Chinese materials, avoids confusing translations by romanizing its Chinese characters to arrive at *Hongbaochu.*[96] Because of the plethora of names in English-language materials and translations referring to the *Kôhôsho,* I take Duara's cue and refer to it as the Manchukuo Publicity and News Bureau – a more fitting translation according to its Japanese nuances (and the desire of Manchukuo bureaucrats to hide its growing role in their support of Imperial Japan).

Article 22 of the State Council's new regulations, promulgated on 5 June 1937, allowed the *Kôhôsho* to take charge of any propaganda as well as pacification activities, centralizing its control so that it could properly co-ordinate activities between associated intelligence and propaganda organizations, such as those connected to the Kantô Army or the Foreign Office.[97] The *Kôhôsho's* close ties to the Concordia Association were also strengthened at this time – ostensibly allowing the state's exhortations to more effectively reach various localities. However, while later sustaining Japan's war effort against China, these trends actually *preceded* organized attempts to coordinate such measures during wartime and hinted that, at higher levels in the Kantô Army, trouble was brewing among impatient officers who were viewing what they perceived to be the increasingly intractable "China situation."[98] Moreover, Kobayashi Hideo argues that, because the imperial family invested so heavily in the South Manchuria Railway Company, they also had every reason to support the expansion of the "China Incident" in order to extend SMRC's railway lines.[99] As noted before, after Manchukuo's 1932 establishment, prime ministers increasingly came from either the imperial family or the military – both groups with strong interests in expanding further into China.

Barely three weeks after negotiations with the Chinese republican government failed to terminate further escalation of the 7 July 1937 China Incident, the *Kôhôsho* convened its first propaganda and intelligence liaison meeting on 27 July to coordinate the propaganda and intelligence activities "of organizations in areas such as printed materials, motion picture(s), religion, and fine art, as well as with outreach activities aimed at various ethnic groups, and maneuvering operations to counter disinformation."[100] In Manchukuo, better coordination of these fields was much needed, including in the realm of culture, to rein in an octopus-like system of control only nominally more organized than that of Japan, where propaganda agencies often competed or worked at cross-purposes. Bureaucrats like Mutô and Amakasu, in charge of media and other information, presided over a hierarchical flow chart of power, allowing the issuing of propaganda and "cultural" directives into the most remote localities. This downward diffusion often resembled arteries of "culture," following main SMRC rail lines from major cities down into the smallest towns. However, in the regime's interests during a time when negative fallout from hostilities below the Great Wall could spur resistance activities in Manchukuo, further measures had to be taken to ensure loyalty to Shinkyô rather than to Nanjing.

Thus, with the strengthening of the *Kôhôsho*'s role in its central Shinkyô headquarters, directives were sent directly to provincial and county-level offices in a supposedly clearer chain of command.[101] At the provincial level, the deputy chief handled the dissemination of "information," for which there were four subsections under the section entitled General Affairs: General Affairs, Propaganda and Intelligence, Information, and Motion Pictures – each of which was headed by a (likely Japanese) section chief. On the municipal level, the usually Han Chinese mayor, deputy mayor, and county or banner head directed a similar bureaucracy. These officials then coordinated their activities with local branches of the Concordia Association and other organizations such as agricultural cooperatives, trade unions, labour associations, and educational and charity groups. At the lowest city district or village level, local dignitaries and minor government officials (e.g., school principals, local elites, and Concordia Association notables) also served as officials, representing the final stage of the *Kôhôsho*'s reach. Many of these Han Chinese, or Manchu, elites received their appointments through voluntary application, which allowed them a modicum of power through collaboration with the Japanese-held power structure.[102]

Thus, we can see how deeply this hierarchical organization penetrated the everyday lives of the Manchukuo people, with propaganda often being clothed in the trappings of a "culture" in which Japan played an increasingly leading role. This process intensified after February 1938, when the Manchukuo government promulgated the National General Mobilization Law. This was prior to the total war system in Japan, which also enhanced its cultural consolidation. Further cultural integration between Japan, China, and Manchukuo occurred soon thereafter, ostensibly to stimulate cultural exchanges between Japan, Italy, and Germany in a move that indicated stronger connections to Japan's fascist allies and a desire to emulate their emergent fascist cultures.[103]

In domestic Japan, there were also wartime attempts to coordinate propaganda and associated cultural activities, but many government agencies and institutions often acted at cross-purposes, while civilian organizations were subcontracted to engage in unofficial propaganda efforts, often in a cultural guise, on behalf of the Japanese (or foreign) public. Kushner argues that wartime propaganda on the archipelago could get quite messy, even for the "official channels" at the top of the Japanese government: "The Japanese military and the government frequently encountered obstacles because of Japan's multi-faceted approach to propaganda. Since no single agency had control, different agencies often competed with divergent messages for the same target audiences."[104] Moreover, Japan had no mass culture organization like the Concordia Association until the 1940 advent of the politically and national-defence oriented Imperial Rule Assistance Association, which was intended to absorb all previous political parties. Ostensibly, in Japan, at the top of this propaganda apparatus was the *Gaimusho jôhôbu,* or the Ministry of Foreign Affairs' Public Information

Bureau. However, other parallel agencies also engaged in disseminating "information" or attempting to control it.

For example, in 1938, Home Ministry directives clarified what topics the Japanese government wanted to censor in the news media – topics often concerning Manchukuo, the deepening conflict in China, and the fear of growing anti-Japanese resistance there and in the new state. Gregory Kasza's study notes sixteen categories prone to censorship, including: "Differences of opinion with the government or military on the nation's basic China policy, a lack of unified public support for China policy, and indications that we have territorial ambitions in China or that the new states in central and northern China are Japanese puppets, or doubt about the significance of this as a holy war."[105] However, in terms of the Home Ministry's wartime initiative to control news dissemination throughout the archipelago, it was not always apparent which organizations were targeted or of whom their audience consisted. In Manchukuo, this endeavour clearly fell under the *Kôhôsho*'s jurisdiction.

In comparison with those of Japan, Manchukuo's post-1937 attempts at coordination were better organized due to the more easily recognizable hierarchical chain of command. Thus, parallel to the Japanese Ministry of Foreign Affairs' Public Information Bureau was the Manchukuo News and Publicity Bureau under the General Affairs Board, headed by the State Council and presided over by the prime minister. In August 1937, as indicated by Manchukuo central government flow charts, the individual at the very top of this apparatus was "His Imperial Majesty" Pu Yi, served by the State Council, under whose jurisdiction the General Affairs Board operated above the *Kôhôsho,* which headed the Concordia Association.[106] Nevertheless, while it was once relatively easy to pinpoint the Concordia Association as the main "grassroots" organization for the dissemination of cultural propaganda to the people of Manchukuo, as the China Incident bogged down, the new state soon began to resemble the Japanese case, with numerous reorganizations of bureaus in charge of information, publicity, and propaganda.

An example of the increasingly complicated administration of publicity and news in Manchukuo during the total war system can be found in a September 1938 *Senbu geppô* article by Takahashi Moto'ichi, a General Affairs Board administrator, entitled "Kôhô gyôsei-ron: Manshûkoku kôhô gyôsei wo chûshin ni" ("Discourse on the Administration of Publicity and News: Focusing on the Administration of Publicity and News in Manchukuo").[107] In his essay, Takahashi notes that the state has undertaken propaganda activities focusing on the nation's construction, with the corresponding need to establish a "spirit of national construction" as well as to rid the people of antiquated evil thoughts – presumably Chinese superstitions and feudal traditions that might possibly stimulate a resistant ethnic consciousness that would hamper the state's "modern" orientation.[108] However, while strongly stating his reasons for favouring increased wartime propaganda efforts in Manchukuo and fine-tuning its supposedly well-organized administration, Takahashi's essay remains vague about which organizations head what, and how directives addressing his goals should be issued.

In fact, by 1939, the situation had become so difficult to understand that, at the back of certain materials printed for Manchukuo's Japanese bureaucrats by the *Manshû jijô annai-sho* (Manchurian Affairs Information Bureau), there was a page indicating these reorganizations and name changes. For example, consider the short history of the organizational structure of this bureau from just 1933 to 1939.[109] Under the Kantô Army's special order, on 18 January 1933, the *Manshû keizai jijô annai-sho* (Manchurian Economic Information Bureau) was put in charge of disseminating economic information on behalf of the following organizations: the Manchukuo government, the Japanese embassy in Manchukuo, and SMRC – each promoting the new state's productivity and economic potential. A year later, on 2 January 1934, its name was changed to *Manshû jijô annai-sho,* indicating its growth to meet the military needs of various actors, including the Kantô Office and the Japanese Navy's command division stationed in Manchuria. On 24 March 1934, after the establishment of the *Manshû shisatsu assen i'inkai* (Manchurian Intelligence Mediation Commission), it also began aiding various intelligence agencies, and on 25 August, due to the expansion of individuals and organizations needing its services and a greater role in combatting resistance activities, the main office was moved to a larger building and more centralized location in the Shinkyô imperial capital's sixth district off *Chûô dôri* (Central Avenue). Moreover, on 1 August 1936, an imperial command incorporated the bureau into a company called the *Manshû kôhô kyôkai* (Manchuria Public Information Association) in a move representing the rise of Manchukuo's fascist corporatism – including with regard to its propaganda agencies.[110] However, on 1 January 1938, it gained independence from this company and, in the light of wartime demands, was designated as a special agency now directly under the Manchukuo Imperial Government's direction. Later in 1939, the *Kôhôsho* absorbed this bureau.

In 1938, during Manchukuo's mass mobilization efforts, the *Kôhôsho* also became further involved in the control of newspapers and other periodicals. Now under its direction was the "Manchuria Public Information Association, a joint stock concern, which ... exclusively controll[ed] the distribution of all domestic and imported news for publication in vernacular papers."[111] This association, run like a company in the fascist model, also aided the Manchukuo Publicity and News Bureau in enlisting the *Manshûkoku tsûshinsha* (Manchurian News Agency), the Manchukuo Travel Bureau, and other organizations to distribute propaganda materials both domestically and abroad.[112] As discussed in Chapter 5, these propaganda materials included *Manshû gurafu,* published by SMRC since 1933. In addition, as propaganda chief of the Concordia Association until 1939, Mutô helped disseminate its ideas overseas in Western-geared periodicals and newspapers. In the spring of 1939, he left this position and became director of the more powerful, centrally located *Kôhôsho,* which, after the outbreak of the China conflict, increasingly implemented a much-needed media reform.

However, under Mutô's command, the News and Publicity Bureau also increasingly involved itself in cultural construction, or state consolidation through culture. In other words, it began to increasingly focus on disseminating propaganda. Mutô's obsession with the malleable term "culture," and its myriad manifestations, betrays his roots as head of the fascistic Concordia Association, which expanded the state's political philosophy through its multiple and diverse cultural initiatives. Thus, Mutô's "promotion" actually allowed him to expand the association's cultural focus, which he had so carefully cultivated since 1937.[113] After 1939, with the close cooperation of the Concordia Association, new organizations dedicated to the consolidation and centralization of the regime's fostering of the arts soon proliferated.

For example, in December 1939, Obama Shigeru, chief of the Manchukuo Foreign Office's publicity section, noted in the Western-targeted publication *Manchuria* that the Japan-Manchoukuo Cultural Society was now "organized for the promotion of cultural relations between the two nations, considering the fact that the cultural development of Manchukuo hinges largely on Japan's guidance."[114] Under the supervision of the minister of people's welfare, this new society included the following eight new cultural associations: "the Manchurian Society for Protection of Places and Things of Historic Note and Specified Natural Objects, the Manchurian Academic Society, the Manchurian Language Society, the Cultural Press Club, the Women's Reading Society, the Manchurian Art Exhibitions, the Manchurian Caricature Society, and the Manchurian 'Roman' Club."[115] While most were devoted to literary and artistic pursuits, some, such as the Manchurian historical protection and language societies, indicate the regime's focus on creating a "separate" culture for Manchukuo (in contrast to China).

As Tamura notes in April 1940: "[The new Japan-Manchoukuo Cultural Society] will strive to stimulate continental literature, fine arts, music, etc.; but what is of particular importance is to develop an artistic taste or sense in the people, so that they may go about their daily life creating and enjoying. The culture of Manchoukuo must not be the monopoly of a small minority; it ought to be the common possession of all people."[116] He argues that, under Japanese guidance, a particularly Manchurian aesthetics should be cultivated among the people and that this would allow them to more fully internalize Manchukuo's ideals and, hence, flourish. This was very much a goal of fascist culture, and it was seen as a common good for all, regardless of ethnicity. In support of this, biannual government prizes would be given for "contests in various kinds of literary and artistic production," while the imperially-sanctioned Manchuria Fine Arts Exhibition would be held every year.[117]

In September 1940, after Japan's full alliance with Nazi Germany and fascist Italy, another stage in the *Kôhôsho*'s efforts began, marked by Manchukuo's further intensification of cultural control and media reform under Mutô.[118] Thus, as the model for a prototypical Pan-Asianism representative of Prince Konoe Fumimaro's (1891-1945) 1940 New Order, Manchukuo's cultural activities and its propaganda war began focusing on bolstering the nation's political strength as predicated on the Concordia Association's idea of multi-ethnic harmony.[119] Manchukuo's diverse peoples somewhat resembled the populations found in the Greater East Asia Co-Prosperity Sphere, where Japan had begun to display its military aggression and strategic interests. This initiative was, of course, followed by further *Kôhôsho* organizational reform and media control. For example, in December, to ensure that Manchukuo's inhabitants, including Japanese, read no "falsehoods" or encountered no disinformation, all newspapers and news agencies under the *Kôhôsho*'s former "guidance" now came under its direct jurisdiction.[120]

By 1941, all newspapers came under the full control of the *Kôhôsho;* therefore, any personnel changes in news organizations had to be approved by Mutô himself. Mutô selected prominent Japanese to visit Manchukuo in the hope that they would write positive reports. However, in his memoir, he notes: "Whether people recommended themselves or are recommended by others, the records of the candidates went to the chief of the News and Publicity Bureau [Mutô]. The chief then consulted with the Home Minister and the fourth division of the Kantô Army."[121] In other words, after Mutô made his decision, he had to consult the home minister, who would follow up by contacting the Kantô Army's 4th Division for approval. However, a good working relationship with Amakasu ensured that relations with the Kantô Army ran smoothly, thus allowing him unprecedented power. In the next section, I investigate a joint cultural endeavour formulated by Mutô with the collaboration of his Kantô Army ally, Amakasu.

The 1941 *Prospectus for the Guidance of the Arts and Culture*

In early December 1941, following the outbreak of the Pacific War and the commencement of hostilities with the Americans, energies were focused in a new direction to create a stronger sense of nationhood in Manchukuo – one that that would allow it to more fully participate in Japan's war effort. From 1940 to 1941, during the first forays of the southern advance preceding the war with the United States, Manchukuo's state framers saw the need to coordinate cultural activities so that the nation could serve as a template for new state structures in other postcolonial nations in Southeast Asia. Thus, this initiative corresponded with even further increases in Manchukuo's cultural control. As noted previously, prior to 1941, the Publicity and News

Bureau's intrusion into media and cultural activities had been uneven, with reorganizations in 1937, 1938, and 1940. Hence, the issuing of the 1941 *Prospectus* indicates more extensive nation-building efforts in those Southeast Asian countries that were on their way to being "liberated" by Japan.[122]

These initiatives began early in 1941, with the 1 January streamlining of Manchukuo's national and local government administrative offices, many of which were either consolidated or eliminated. However, in a move indicating the *Kôhôsho's* crucial importance to the state, the government's State Council allowed this organization to augment its staff and to increase its functions, which now included "the works of cultural administration [and] those pertaining to dynamic culture, such as literature, fine art, music, drama, record albums, and books."[123] According to Duara, the *Kôhôsho* "was originally a propaganda organ, but its office soon became the principal instrument of cultural control in Manchukuo, monitoring publications, broadcasts, libraries, news agencies, film, and the arts, among other activities."[124] After 1940, centralized power over cultural activities was transferred from the Ministry of Public Welfare's culture section directly into the *Kôhôsho*'s jurisdiction. Moreover, the *Kôhôsho* now also "absorbed the functions of the Culture Section of the Concordia Association and the Advisory Council on culture."[125] This centralization of cultural organizations allowed the Publicity Bureau to marry culture with propaganda in a more top-down, public manner – something it had been trying to do for half a decade. As Kishi points out, the result of these measures was that the *Kôhôsho* "became an organ for unilateral control not only of propaganda, but also of cultural administration as a whole."[126] Also, in a policy decision affecting literary production, all book publishers in Manchukuo were now required to join the Manchuria Book Publishers Association.[127]

However, 1941's most important event pertaining to cultural centralization was the March issuing of the *Geibun shidô yokô*. Here, Mutô and Amakasu's ideas on culture culminated in the pronouncement of an initiative that "emphasized [that] the integration between propaganda activities and creative activities in art and culture should be the guiding principles for Manchukuo's propaganda and intelligence policy."[128] On 23 March, the *Prospectus* was announced at the national *Geibundaikai* (Arts Congress) held at the Shinkyô Japan-Manchuria Serviceman's Club, which was attended by 150 people, of whom one hundred belonged to writers associations and the rest of whom were literati.[129] This initiative is an example of how the Manchukuo propaganda bureau consolidated culture under Mutô's auspices first by focusing on the centralization of cultural endeavours in Shinkyô (which enabled easier surveillance and direction).[130] According to Duara, the *Prospectus* was to "provide direction to the arts and thus coordinate the 'project of spiritual construction with the more advanced material construction of the nation.'"[131] He further emphasizes that, while these aims arose from

Japan's wartime needs, they were tied to Manchukuo's identity formation.[132] This reveals the final merging of politics and culture under the fascist regime, with culture now being geared toward Japan's wartime and nation-building efforts.

In his speech at the Arts Congress, Mutô defines *geibun*, or arts and culture, in moral tones, demonstrating Manchukuo's fascist aesthetic but also evoking Kagawa's utopian hopes for a perfect world: "First, it connotes all forms of value-creating activities, which human beings pursue with the purpose of perfecting their lives, and which include broadly politics, economics, industry, and transportation. Second, it connotes the manifestation of truth, goodness, beauty, and the sacred through the mental endeavors of human beings in sciences, morality, fine arts, religion, and the like."[133] While Mutô's use of the term "culture" is broad, and the arts appear to be one of its subsets, Kishi believes that he hoped to extract "from the concept of culture only the constituent elements" of a variety of art forms and cultural activities.[134] The arts thus functioned as a means to create a better society and to support a modern infrastructure that would ensure prosperity. This being the case, Mutô's definition of culture clearly reveals his fascistic belief that culture should be used in the pursuit of political aims.

More illustrative, perhaps, is Mutô's 1942 article, "Manshûkoku no bunka seisaku: Geibun shidô yôkô ni tsuite" ("Cultural Policies in Manchukuo: Concerning the *Prospectus for the Guidance of the Arts and Culture*") in *Dokushojin (Reader)*.[135] Here, a photograph of Shinkyô's prominent *chûreitô* (war monument), with a caption indicating that it celebrates the future send-off of Japanese and Manchurian souls (presumably returning to the imperial capital's Yasukuni Shrine in Tokyo), takes up roughly one-third of the space on the front page.[136] This image appears next to a two-page reprint of the actual *Prospectus* as it had been written (and read at the Arts Congress) more than eighteen months earlier, followed by Mutô's analysis of it in honour of the tenth anniversary of Manchukuo's founding. We see here that, for Mutô, "culture" continues to be couched in exceptionally moralistic terms, with the arts possessing the power to liberate the (divine) potential of each human being in the context of Manchukuo's corporatist society. This article serves as a clear statement of how culture and politics had now merged into the fascist state's presentation of itself in propaganda materials, and it presciently notes how, thereafter, the cultural policies of Manchukuo would be organized to aid the ever-expanding war effort engaged in by all Japanese subjects in the Empire.[137]

Mutô's "Scientific Management" of *Geibun* and Nazi Cultural Consolidation

Starting in the late 1930s, Mutô began to admire Nazi propaganda minister Joseph Goebbels, whose initiatives he read about in *Senbu geppô*. It is very likely that, in the *Prospectus,* he patterned Manchukuo's arts institutes under "scientific management" after Goebbels's 1933 efforts to bring the German arts under the purview of the Nazi Party's propaganda apparatus. At this time, Hitler and Goebbels had "moved to transform the party propaganda apparatus into a governmental organ," and, on 13 March 1933, the German "cabinet created the Reich Ministry for Popular Enlightenment and Propaganda," which, "Hitler stated, would be 'responsible for all tasks relating to the spiritual development of the nation.'"[138] Mutô certainly approved of such measures. Steinweis notes that the *Reichskulturkammer,* or the Reich Chamber of Culture, created later in September, was "designed to 'promote German culture on behalf of the German *Volk* and *Reich*' and to 'regulate the economic and social affairs of the culture professions.'"[139] This organization was further divided into seven separate culture chambers for music, theatre, the visual arts, literature, film, radio, and the press. Thus, Manchukuo's cultural consolidation under the *Prospectus* has some resemblances to the German example, with the Manchurian Arts and Culture League somewhat paralleling the Reich Chamber of Culture, and the Manchukuo Bureau of News and Publicity increasingly being modelled on the Reich Ministry for Popular Enlightenment and Propaganda.

After March 1941, in Manchukuo, the six officially recognized "arts" – literature, fine art, music, dance, theatre, and film – were now subsumed under the *Kôhôsho*'s direct control, with art activities, as well as art education, being divided into research institutes under five different categories.[140] In addition, the *Prospectus* promised the creation of four major art and culture associations.[141] Thus, a few months later, a writers' association arose out of this initiative, along with others whose leadership as well as committee members were all appointed by Mutô. For example, in July 1941, over seventy writers presided over the first meeting of the *Manshû bungei-ka kyôkai/ Manzhou wenyi-jia xiehui,* or the Manchurian Writers Association, with Mutô electing Yamada to direct it.[142] The *Kôhôsho* also hoped to create an umbrella organization that would further guide Manchukuo's arts and culture. This was finally realized on 25 August as the *Manshû geibun renmei* (Manchurian Arts and Culture League), which was to coordinate the four associations, including the aforementioned Manchurian Writers Association and the *Manshû bijutsuka kyôkai* (Manchurian Artists Association).[143] This initiative, stemming from the *Prospectus,* was intended to coordinate art and cultural activities with those of propaganda and news activities, in tandem with the aims of Konoe's 1940 New Order in Greater East Asia.

In mid-1930s Nazi Germany, cultural consolidation, or *Gleichschaltung,* was undertaken primarily for political reasons, with culture serving the goals of politics: "The arts occupied a central position in the ideology and propaganda of National Socialism."[144] A form of what Steinweis calls artistic "neo-corporatism," a term also applicable to Manchukuo, was the key to Goebbels's strategy of cultural consolidation in the Reichskammer plan.[145] He, as Mutô would in the early 1940s, concerned himself with state consolidation, which he believed could be achieved through the manipulation of cultural producers as well as the German people themselves. In terms that Mutô would certainly support, Goebbels argued: "Cultural regulation in the Third Reich ... had to be accomplished not by 'control by laws and the police' but rather through the 'intellectual leadership' of the state. The art professions should carry out their 'public tasks' in a framework of 'self administration under state supervision.'"[146] Here, we see parallels to the reorganizations taking place in the wake of the 1941 issuing of the *Geibun shidô yôkô*. Moreover, "the politics of art would be integral to the creation of the 'people's community' *[Volksgemeinschaft]*."[147] This foreshadows the post-1938 efforts of the Concordia Association to promote *kyôwa* (harmony) through the patronage of local artistic and literary endeavours.

However, while Mutô concurred with Goebbels's implementation of the Nazi propaganda apparatus, it is unclear how well he and the Japanese framers of Manchukuo understood Nazi ideology, which was based on a notion of race that excluded all those not conforming to the German fascist state's physical and intellectual criteria. As Yamamoto cautions: "It is to be noted that while the Kwantung (Kantô) Army and the Information Bureau *(Kôhôsho)* studied the theory of propaganda, they did not pay attention to the conceptual theory of Nazism."[148] Also, in Manchukuo, the Concordia Association was attempting to accommodate a multi-ethnic area through "cultural" means, not, like the Nazis, attempting to homogenize Germanic culture, solidify the power of the Nazi Party, and establish a pure Aryan race. Moreover, after 1935, Goebbels began to show more interest in Hitler's campaign of *entjüdung* (de-Jewing), which involved forcing Jews out of cultural associations, which increasingly required proof of ethnic origins. This disturbing trend corresponds to a time of "internal emigration" [focusing on personal philosophical struggles aloof from politics] on the part of non-Jewish cultural producers, many of whom rode out the Nazi period without overt protest. Only very slim parallels with the Nazi persecution of Jews can be found in the treatment of alleged Japanese socialists and communists in Manchukuo from 1941 to 1942.

Moreover, in post-1935 Germany, Goebbels had an extraordinary degree of power on three levels – that of the party (overseeing its Reich Propaganda Leadership), state (as Reichminister for Propaganda and National Enlightenment), and professional organizations (as head of the Reich's *Kulturkammer*).[149] However, in the Manchukuo case, Yamamoto views the chain of command for top policy decision making as essentially emanating from the Kantô Army through the *Kantô-kyoku* (Kantô Office), then proceeding down to the government and through the *Kôhôsho* under the General Affairs Board, issuing thereafter to the Concordia Association.[150] Also, Mutô's power was somewhat limited by the fact that he answered to the home minister and then to the Kantô Army in a two-tiered diffusion of responsibility. However, as indicated before, this was tempered by the fact that he had good relations with Amakasu and, therefore, with the Kantô Army.

The *Prospectus* and Mutô's Creation of Specialists in Art and Literature

In connection with the March *Geibun shidô yokô* directive, a six-part round-table discussion series headed by Mutô appeared from 4-9 July 1941 in the popular *Manchuria Daily News* Japanese-language newspaper. The point was to publicize the *Prospectus* to readers in Manchukuo and Japan. In his high position as *Kôhôsho* chief, Mutô served as both moderator and facilitator of these debates in Tokyo, which boasted an impressive group of Japanese cultur-al critics, thinkers, and writers – some with a formerly left-wing orientation.[151]

In the first part of the series, called "Senmonka wo tsukuru: *Geibun shidô yokô* wo megutte" (Creating Specialists: Concerning the *Prospectus for the Guidance of the Arts and Literature*), Mutô states the need to foster artists under this new system at research institutes located in central Manchukuo cities, headed by respected *naichi* artists like Ishi'i Hakutei (1882-1958):

> First of all, it is of the utmost importance that the Artists' Association *[Bijutsuka kyôkai]* has a research institute ... There is no place where artists can work, nor materials for them to work with. Therefore, as soon as the Artists' Association is established, research institutes need to be set up in important areas like Hôten and Shinkyô, for example ... In these places, artists should gather and work in their ateliers and so on, and people like Ishi'i Hakutei, for instance, should be brought from Japan and mentor them, and also, Manchurians *[Manjin]* should meet for round table discussions, and other regional exhibitions should be provided.[152]

To reflect the new state's modernity, he uses quasi-scientific terms such as *senmonka* (specialist), *kenkyûjo* (research institute), *zairyô* (materials), and *benkyô* (work) to describe the rational process of creating new artists, as though the most modern methods, if applied scientifically, could enable them to churn out a desired cultural product.[153]

By inviting important Japanese cultural figures like Ishi'i to Manchukuo, Mutô hoped to strengthen the fascist state's cultural ties to domestic Japan.[154] However, as noted previously, before he could rubber stamp decisions to invite particular individuals, he had to peruse their records, consult with the home minister, and then meet with the Kantô Army.[155] Thereafter, in the early 1940s, with the military's blessing, Mutô chose Ishi'i as a representative traditional artist from domestic Japan who could lead an artistic renaissance by "creating specialists," just as he had hoped to promote multi-ethnic literary endeavors when he had recruited Yamada and Kawabata. In 1941, Kawabata took a Kantô Army-sponsored tour of Manchukuo, obviously indicating that the military found nothing questionable about his literary production or personality. Previously, in 1938, the Japanese Imperial Army had enlisted Ishi'i to depict north China and Mongolia.[156] Clearly, his artistic vision as a conservative, respected domestic Japanese artist working in oils did not threaten Manchukuo's cultural vision; therefore, he also received the Kantô Army's endorsement. Later that year, Ishi'i even served as one of the judges for the fourth national imperially sanctioned Manchukuo Art Exhibition.[157] In 1941, to display a model for the type of art now demanded of Manchurian artists, he exhibited the work *Chôyô jôgai (Outside the Walls of Chaoyang)* at the *Shin bunten* (New Ministry of Education Exhibition) in Tokyo.[158]

Although these efforts privileged Japanese, Mutô also wanted non-Japanese inhabitants of Manchukuo, whom he calls *Manjin*,[159] to take part in this quasi-scientific process of specialization, whereby artists and writers of all ethnicities were mentored by leading cultural figures from the Japanese imperial metropole. In connection with the Manchukuo government's sponsorship of the arts, Mutô mentions that regional venues for exhibitions were to be set up along with proposed research institutes in Manchukuo's central cities.

Intriguingly, Mutô himself engaged in literary endeavours ostensibly in order to inspire further literary production. Whether or not the polemicist should be judged a "specialist" is debatable, considering the average quality of his literary production. Published three months after Mutô's historic declaration of the *Prospectus* to the Arts Congress, his writings reveal the primary themes preoccupying him at the time.

In the last stanza of the poem "Song in Praise of Manchuria," published in June 1941, the propaganda chief is already waxing nostalgic about the new utopia, which is not even a decade old. With its allusion to a "city upon a hill," its concluding phrase hints at his Christian background:

Ah, will we remember the time?
The scent of the blossoming arts
The soft spring sunshine
Reflecting on steep towers and domes
Surrounding copses of forests and villages
On Arbor Day, children will remember
Living richly under a surplus of items
At the frontier, culture broadens
Ah! We will remember this time

We and our dearest friends
Envision a "city upon a hill"
And will only cease while in the grave.[160]

Here, Mutô cites the blossoming "arts" *(geibun)* indicated in the *Prospectus* and mentions the corresponding broadening of culture at the frontier – no doubt alluding to Manchukuo's important role as a fascist bulwark against Soviet communism to the north. In the poem, material prosperity remains attainable for all in Manchukuo, while the sun (alluding to Imperial Japan) shines benevolently on urban as well as rural areas. A Japanese impulse is the primary motivator for these efforts, but they should also be undertaken with "our dearest friends," presumably Manchurians (soon to include other formerly colonized Asians in areas occupied by Japan in its southward "advance").

The last part of the poem has an ominous but prescient quality to it because, with the Soviet invasion, the Kantô Army and Manchukuo's associated Japanese bureaucrats would be the first to return to Japan, leaving their other Japanese counterparts unprotected and stateless.[161] Nevertheless, Mutô's prose poem offers us a glimpse into his utopian world and reveals the nation he envisioned as – through hard work, scientific management, and superior cultural policies – providing the example of a "city upon a hill" for those in "liberated" territories soon to be incorporated into the Greater East Asia Co-Prosperity Sphere.

Cultural Activities and Propaganda in Manchukuo from 1942-45

The tenth anniversary of the nation's establishment fell on 1 March 1942, with the result that numerous commemorative activities attached to the theme of *kenkoku* (national founding or construction) soon emerged. For example, in August, to celebrate the nation's decennial, five photographers – including Watanabe Yoshio, Koishi Kiyoshi, Kato Kyohei, Oda Matsutarô, and Aida Katsu – embarked on a tour to Manchukuo, where they each contributed images of a certain theme connected to national construction (e.g., military preparations, industry, culture, transportation, and land reclamation).[162] The *Kôhôsho* carried out cultural propaganda activities for the upcoming founding ceremony, held on 15 September 1942.

In addition, a special September edition of *Dokushojin* featured discussions of Manchukuo's cultural trends and literary works, opening with an article by Mutô, who quotes the entire *Prospectus* and analyzes its meaning for the new wartime climate.[163] He emphasizes parallels between (1) the construction of a culture and a spiritual infrastructure and (2) the construction of an economic system and a physical infrastructure – all concepts perfectly compatible with the state's increasingly fascistic orientation and Goebbels's earlier ideas for Nazi Germany.

In the same year, the Manchukuo government also began making plans for total national mobilization by enacting a national conscription law that targeted Japanese as well as other ethnicities. In tandem with this law, further efforts were made to gain the support of Manchukuo's cultural producers for Imperial Japan's war effort. Thus, on 18 January 1942, the Manchurian Writers Association held the Writers and Artists Patriotic Conference. Eleven months later, to commemorate the one-year anniversary of the Pacific War's advent, on 8 December 1942, the government promulgated the "Outline of the Fundamental National Policy of Manchukuo," which prepared Manchukuo for its national defence (conjointly with Japan), mobilized support for the Greater East Asia Co-Prosperity Sphere, and stepped up industrial productivity through the increasingly compulsory labour of the local population.[164] It also strengthened the provisions of the 1941 *Prospectus,* making it clear that writers should now "construct the national spirit, praise war objectives, and allow for a fundamental comprehension of contemporary conditions."[165] Moreover, Mutô was now under pressure to foster a style of art and culture unique to Manchukuo, with Manchurian art and culture serving the state while communicating a uniquely Manchurian quality.

By 1943, the forced consolidation of official cultural organizations had had a deep impact on Manchukuo's writers, photographers, and artists, whether Japanese, Han Chinese, or other ethnicities (with the exception of Koreans, who were noticeably absent from official channels).[166] In this year, Mutô returned to Japan, leaving his position to Ichikawa Satoshi, and in May, he began working as director of the first division of the Japanese cabinet's Information Agency – a post he retained until June 1945.[167] In Manchukuo, the "construction of a greater East Asian culture" now increasingly became the focus of cultural activities and cultural propaganda, as evidenced in Yamada's 1943-44 texts, which use the term *kensetsu.* It appears that Mutô hoped to see this process continue, despite his new posting in Japan's imperial capital. Thus, in August, Mutô chose Amakasu to serve as a special judge for the upcoming Greater East Asia Writers Congress in Tokyo, but his friend turned down the invitation (possibly because he preferred to stay in Manchukuo).[168]

Thereafter, cultural activities in Manchukuo were increasingly subsumed under total war dictates, necessary due to the worsening of Japan's material resources in its fighting of multi-front battles. In November 1943, the *Kôhôsho* issued the "Guidelines on Art and Culture in the Time of Decisive War," which forced the disbanding of all nine associations affiliated with the Manchurian Arts and Culture Association and supplanted it with the all-encompassing Manchurian Art and Culture League, which had previously served as a judicial corporate body.[169] Not surprisingly, Amakasu was elected the league's president and expressed his view that art and culture should serve as "weapons of ideological warfare."[170] Thus, by early 1944, Manchukuo's cultural production was entirely devoted to supporting Japan's war effort.[171]

Moreover, modernist artists in Manchukuo suffered from lack of art supplies since, if they worked in oils, they ordered most of their materials from Japan.[172] In addition, organized venues in which to display their work, and associations promoting their activities, also took a hit. In tandem with the November 1943 guidelines, on 4 December a national conference of artists and writers, or the *Kessen geibun taikai* (Artists and Writers Congress in a Time of Decisive War), was convened in Shinkyô's Memorial Hall.[173] Thus, even in Manchukuo, it soon became apparent that the war was not turning out as the Japanese government had hoped, with more and more Manchurian men being recruited to fight on behalf of their client state and war-related rhetoric intruding into every cultural sphere. Obviously, cultural production became less of a priority once Imperial Japan's national emergency directed the attention of Manchukuo's Japanese officials to more pressing matters.

By 1944, with the fall of the Tôjô cabinet, the losses at Saipan, Allied carpet bombing of the archipelago, and the use of *Kamikaze* navy pilots in suicide missions euphemistically termed *gyokusai* (shattering of the jewels), many Japanese government officials already knew that Japan was fighting an increasingly unwinnable war. Any remaining resources were now devoted to the "decisive battle," or *kessen,* soon to come, with women and children taking up sharpened bamboo spears as arms, while receiving increasingly lower amounts of calories from substandard government food rations. A demoralized Japanese public no longer believed the pronouncements of its government, and Mutô had already begun to plan for the inevitable.

Conclusion

In the war's final month, July 1945, Mutô began an appointment as a Tokyo-based counsellor to the General Affairs Board of the Manchukuo government's State Council.[174] It appears that the inevitability of Japan's defeat necessitated his taking this position in order to scheme for the best terms of surrender, following the issuing of the Potsdam Declaration by the United States and its allies. Thus, on 24 August 1945, Japanese prime minister Prince Higashikuni Naruhiko (1887-1990) brought Kagawa into his cabinet as an advisor. Due to his prewar studies at Princeton Theological Seminary and his organizing of a 1941 San Francisco conference to pray for peace, Kagawa was deemed a pacifist whose sentiments were believed to be decidedly pro-American. In 1941, Higashikuni had opposed General Tôjô Hideki's (1884-1948) assent to the position of prime minister, and, after Imperial Japan's 1945 surrender, he presided over the first postwar government, which ran from 17 August to 9 October.[175] Though most of Kagawa's actions on behalf of the postwar government involved restoring "popular morale," his greatest task was to exonerate the Japanese emperor, Higashikuni's nephew, by arguing to the Supreme Commander for the Allied Powers (SCAP) that Hirohito's retention as a monarch without political power would be in the best interests of assuring social unity in a newly democratizing Japan.[176] In this effort, he even pointed out that Hirohito's mother was Christian.[177] No doubt, Kagawa's high imperial connections also helped Mutô, a fellow Christian, avoid prosecution and worked to distance his protégé from his former proximity to Tôjô. SCAP eventually exonerated Mutô, but he was essentially banned from politics.

However, in 1948, Tôjô, Mutô's former boss during his propaganda work for the Japanese cabinet, was hanged following his guilty verdict as a Class-A war criminal in Tokyo at the International Military Tribunal for the Far East. The witnessing of Tôjô's execution by hanging, and MacArthur's religiously laced words renouncing war, made a deep impression on Mutô, who began a text whose focus was his reflections on his war responsibility. It is evocatively entitled *Zaigunbi wo ikidôru tsuihôsha no kokuhaku, (Confessions of an Exile Indignant Against Remilitarization),* and was published in 1951.[178] The enthusiasm Mutô expressed for propaganda activities in Manchukuo and Imperial Japan as a young legal expert was now, in the newly democratic nation, channelled toward evangelizing – an effort to which, with Kagawa, he devoted much energy.

In April 1946, Mutô had joined forces with Kagawa to initiate the *Christian News* magazine, which he edited as assistant vice-president and, by the mid-1950s, had helped increase its circulation to around thirty thousand.[179] In 1950, Kagawa invited Mutô to engage in a project that involved retranslating the Bible into Japanese to make it amenable to contemporary times through the use of modern language. The project took two years, with Mutô consulting Greek and Latin texts, and the first run of ten thousand copies sold out prior to publication.[180] In 1952, the former propaganda chief dramatically told a *Time* magazine reporter that this new focus on Christian evangelism was "to atone for [his] sins."[181] A few years later, after the end of the US Occupation, Mutô felt confident enough to publish in 1956 his memoirs of his friendship with Amakasu during his time in Manchukuo. They were entitled *Manshûkoku no danmen (A Cross-Section of Manchukuo),* with an introduction by Kagawa.[182]

In tandem with his evangelical efforts, Mutô emerged as a prominent Presbyterian minister with the United Church of Christ, leading the Ômori Church congregation in Tokyo.[183] In addition, on January 1954, the new preacher began a four-month "barnstorming" tour across the Midwestern United States to raise money for his proselytizing efforts in Japan, leading him to make the following pithy statement: "Evangelism is war ... As we fight for Christ, we must move on the scale of Alexander and Genghis Khan." He made this comment while publicizing his goal to evangelize 1 million Japanese by 1958.[184] Mutô was only partially successful in this mission, since by 2005 the number of Japanese Christians had modestly risen to about 3 million – only 2 percent of a population of 128 million.[185] However, he later became president of the elite private Christian college *Meiji Gakuin daigaku* (Meiji Christian University) in Tokyo's Minato district, where his mentor Kagawa had studied from 1905 to 1907, and he continued his efforts to reach out to Christian communities in the United States and throughout the world.[186] In 1966, among a compilation of excerpts from his writings, Mutô even published a text eulogizing Kagawa.[187] Thus, the former propagandist's collaboration with Kagawa, and his dramatic efforts to foster Japanese Christianity in a postwar democratic Japan, effectively erased from the public eye his decade of work in support of the wartime propaganda organizations that sustained Japanese fascism.

7

The Legitimization of a Multi-Ethnic Literary Culture in Manchukuo: Kawabata Yasunari's Promotion of "Manchurian Literature," 1941-44

After 1940, multi-ethnic literature composed an aspect of the Manchukuo Publicity and News Bureau's desire for broader, multi-ethnic cooperation in cultural production, symbolizing the state's ideology of *minzoku kyôwa,* or ethnic/racial harmony. This chapter discusses the popular modernist writer Kawabata Yasunari's (1899-1972) contribution to the Manchukuo project. Kawabata toured the country, publicized his composition movement, or *tsuzurikata undô,* which advocated essay writing in elementary schools, and edited two collections of "Manchurian literature" as part of a plan to promote a multi-ethnic Manchurian literary culture. I analyze Kawabata's involvement as a central literary figure from domestic Japan who became involved in formulating Manchukuo's new, utopian culture. His ideas are later echoed in *Manshû no bunka (Manchurian Culture)* 1943, written by Haruyama Yukio (1902-94), the former editor of the avant-garde journal *Shi to shiron (Poetry and Poetics).* I also suggest how Kawabata's literary preoccupation with the poor and the marginalized fed into his utopian vision for Manchukuo. Kawabata serves as an example of a figure who later became disillusioned with the cultural project and one who, in the immediate postwar period, tried to distance himself from his involvement. He won the 1968 Nobel Prize for Literature, which made him famous throughout the world, but few knew much about his wartime activities, especially in the Manchukuo context.[1]

From Avant-Garde to Pro-Japan

Kawabata's early career emerged out of an intellectual climate of concern for Japan's underclasses coupled with a critique of the rampant modernization engendered by capitalism – both representing issues preoccupying the proletarian literature movement in the late 1920s. While Kawabata never officially joined this movement, the *Shinkankaku-ha* (New Sensationist) group of writers that he helped to form in the mid-1920s with Yokomitsu Ri'ichi (1898-1947) and Kataoka Teppei (1894-1944) often flirted with proletarian themes, investigating the lives of Japan's working classes and their culture. These topics appeared frequently in their works despite the group's supposed emphasis on "art for art's sake," influenced by European modernism and avant-garde art forms. Kawabata's counterpart Kataoka soon became a member of the proletarian literature movement and garnered much success from his 1928 short story "Tsûshin kôshu" ("The Linesmen"), which centred on the work of electricians who repaired telephone poles, thus connecting the modern, up-to-date Japanese middle class and the *narikin* (nouveaux-riches). Yet, its modernist style, combining both cinematic aesthetics and what they believed characterized modernity's new sensations of speed, sound, and montage-like imagery, also had the political aim of making readers aware of social divisions in Japanese society. Kawabata was also interested in the lives and experiences of Japan's poor and marginalized, along with the social pressures they endured during a time of rapid industrialization and rural displacement. However, he never became politically engaged, as did Kataoka, who joined the leftist *Rônô-ha* (Labour Farmer Faction).

Nevertheless, the themes stressed in Kawabata's early works are similar to those expressed by proletarian writers. In 1926, Kawabata even penned the screenplay for Kinugasa Teinosuke's (1896-1982) *Kurutta ichi-peiji (A Page of Madness),* detailing the life of a woman who slipped into insanity due to the socio-economic pressures that drove her to drown her son following her sailor husband's absence and earlier mistreatment. Even now, *Kurutta ichi-peiji* is considered one of Japan's few surrealist films, incorporating a film montage depicting the parallel alternate reality of mental illness, punctuated by modern dance performances and new forms of avant-garde theatrics.[2] However, with his increasing fame due to his successful serialized novel *Asakusa kurenaidan (The Scarlet Gang of Asakusa),* which ran in the Tokyo *Asahi* from 1929 to 1930, Kawabata eventually drifted away from social literature.[3] In *Asakusa kurenaidan,* the narrative consists of a collage of events in the lives of teenagers in a youth gang led by an androgynous girl in Tokyo's colourful, plebian *shitamachi* (downtown) area of Asakusa. In later works, Kawabata continues to explore themes that involve older men in unorthodox relationships with poor, lower-class women (or girls) in situations that leave the latter vulnerable due to their gender, class, age, or economic status. In each such relationship, a man can be a saviour while, at the same time, threatening to destroy a fragile system of imperilled innocence, the sullying of which is inevitable. Seen against the background of Japan's rising engagement with China, these themes can be linked to Japanese paternalism and its assumption of cultural superiority.

This is true even of Kawabata's mid-to-late 1930s works, when he turns to a deeper exploration of Japanese identity and searches for a culture inevitably lost to Japan's modernization process. With the eruption of the "Fifteen Year War" in China after the Manchurian Incident, Kawabata's yearning to define his Japaneseness parallels the efforts of many Japanese writers and intellectuals. This desire to articulate what is truly Japanese emerged from the popular press's war fever, along with the increasing contact between ordinary Japanese and a Chinese "other" due to reading materials and popular culture.

For example, Kawabata's magnum opus *Yukiguni (Snow Country),* which began serialization in 1935 and was published in partial form as a novel in 1937, marked his increasing interest in probing a culture rapidly disappearing as Japan relentlessly advanced toward modernity.[4] This culture was seemingly found in the intricate weavings of rural women in an unnamed, snow-enwrapped town in northern Japan now famous for its hot springs. Shimamura, the main character, while pursuing a relationship with the rural geisha Komako, observes a tradition swiftly dying out amidst a local economy increasingly driven by the sex trade. Kawabata hints that, because the local weaving culture will perish with the young women who practise the craft, it is special and uniquely Japanese. Indeed, its very ephemerality makes it representative of the type of aesthetic lauded by Kawabata and, earlier, immortalized by Motoori Norinaga (1730-1801), who applied the term *mono-no-aware* (the evanescence of things) to Lady Murasaki's eleventh-century quintessentially Japanese novel *Genji monogatari (The Tale of Genji)*. Kawabata, in fact, translated this work to occupy himself amidst the increasing intrusion of the war into everyday life. This forms part of the complex background of the author's wartime works: he laments the loss of Japan's local, regional, and highly diverse traditions, which, in fact, resist the facile nature of the Japanese essentialism touted by the imperial government after 1937.

However, contrary to Donald Keene's and most Japanese literary scholars' assessments of Kawabata as a largely "apolitical" writer, he did not simply retreat into his study during the brewing darkness in China, which Japanese soldiers invaded to carry out the imperial "chastisement" of Japan's once culturally esteemed neighbour. As Sandra Wilson notes, in Japan, by the 1930s, going to war was viewed as "essentially a profitable and positive undertaking, with little public memory of the enormous burdens it could bring." It was also seen as "a *modern* thing to do."[5] Part of the success of Japan's multifaceted propaganda, both official and unofficial, was to get the public to support the China Incident. The idea was that, because Japan was modern and had become a strong regional and even world power, it had a mission to guide the politically disorganized Chinese and then to liberate those nations in Southeast Asia that remained under the yoke of Western powers.[6] In 1940, to instruct audiences throughout the Empire on these lofty goals, Kawabata joined the fifty-two writers of the *Bungei jugo undô* (Literary Homefront Campaign) who were led by Kikuchi Kan (1888-1948) and were to tour Japan, Korea, and Manchukuo.[7] Here, Kawabata and others made speeches promoting the war effort and, as ambassadors of Japanese culture, articulated the imperial state's aims to the masses.[8] Aside from his earlier tours with the Literary Homefront Campaign, Kawabata served as Manchukuo's mouthpiece, advertising the Publicity and News Bureau's new *Prospectus for the Guidance of the Arts and Culture* with his participation in a 1941 Tokyo-based round-table discussion on Manchurian culture. Yet how are we to understand Kawabata's very public actions in the context of his purported inner search for his own Japanese identity amidst the turmoil of war?

In his study on Nazi cultural propaganda, Steinweis emphasizes the structure of individual decision making in order to examine the "complicity" of cultural producers with the Nazi regime in an arena involving complex political, economic, and social choices.[9] Much of the same constellation of choices can be applied to the Manchukuo example, with writers, artists, and photographers either attracted to Manchukuo or hired by the regime to depict it. Why did Kawabata and others collaborate so willingly with the Manchukuo experiment? In the German case, Steinweis comments: "Several factors interacted: *coercion* by Nazi authorities, *collaboration* with Nazis by conservative nationalists, *psychological resignation* among liberals and socialist officers, and *opportunism* on the part of artists who hoped that declarations of loyalty to the new regime might salvage autonomy and yield material benefits."[10] These same factors of coercion, collaboration, psychological resignation, and opportunism also pertain to Japanese intellectuals – and not just artists, as Steinweis suggests – amidst an atmosphere of total war and rising support for the fascist state of Manchukuo.

At a time when Japanese intellectuals increasingly volunteered their talents to serve their country, regardless of whether they truly approved of *how* Japan was conducting the war, most agreed that Manchukuo was absolutely crucial to Japan's livelihood and that its culture must be linked to that of Japan in order to strengthen this bond. After 1941, Manchukuo's cultural consolidation began to function as a template for the Greater East Asia Co-Prosperity Sphere; therefore, it was of utmost importance to create a multi-ethnic literary culture because it had to "translate" in places other than Japan and Manchukuo. Moreover, the multi-ethnic areas in Southeast Asia mirrored the diverse conditions of Manchukuo's own population.

However, after 1937, the lingua franca of the Japanese Empire was Japanese, and political tutelage was under Japanese auspices. Therefore, the inclusion of non-Japanese members of the five ethnicities in Manchukuo's national literature project had to be mediated through the Japanese language. If the Japanese were to succeed in their mission to liberate and guide newly conquered territories, then culture would serve them as an important weapon. Regardless of what Kawabata privately felt about his mission to bring a modern, multi-ethnic literature to Manchukuo, the fact that he could help to build a thriving literary scene was very appealing to him – and this fits in well with Steinweis's argument regarding collaboration and opportunism.

Manchukuo's Insertion into Japan's Cultural Sphere

After 1932, Manchukuo's Japanese policy makers actively promoted the creation of a new national culture, art, and literature, in addition to a body of work describing the physical and symbolic construction of the new multi-ethnic nation. Military mastermind Ishiwara and others emphasized Manchukuo's cultural uniqueness and independence, despite its existing under Japanese guidance and imperial directives. According to Duara, the discourse of culture provided a unifying role for the state's ideological formation.[11] Culture, in the symbolic space of *Manshû* (Manchuria), now functioned as a means of differentiating *Manshûkoku* (Manchukuo) from Japan. Rather than serving as a gauge to measure the region's level of civilization against that of the paternal imperial state (as in earlier decades), culture in Manchukuo now became an important propaganda tool emphasizing the new nation's uniqueness and the political harmony between divergent cultures/ethnicities. However, as evidenced in the works of authors such as Kawabata, Yamada, and others, this uncoupling from Japan and its imperium through culture was only partially achieved by the discursive separation of a conceptual *Manshû* from the state of Manchukuo.

Purportedly a modern, Westernized, multi-ethnic nation organized according to rational East Asian principles, Manchukuo, as described by various propaganda media, was a hybrid culture of the "Paradise of the Kingly Way" characterized by *gozoku-kyôwa* (harmony of the five ethnicities/races) – Japanese, Korean, Manchurian (Chinese), Mongolian, and Russian. I prefer to translate *zoku* as "ethnicity" rather than "race" because, other than a small White Russian and a tiny Eastern European population, most inhabitants of Manchukuo were Asian, with most being Han Chinese.[12] Thus, there were only two "races," as such. However, it is clear that, for many of these books and articles, including those written or edited by Kawabata, the audience is Japanese, or at least Japanese-speaking. Indeed, after 1937 in Manchukuo all school children received their education in Japanese, and Japanese became the education system's primary language.

The vision of a multicultural utopia disseminated by the Concordia Association and other official propaganda organs was created through a Japanese lens, with Japanese as the dominant form of cultural and linguistic representation. As a result, Japanese nationals in Manchukuo and domestic Japanese visitors received the majority of funding for cultural endeavours (or informational tours) given by a state obsessed with representing itself. In addition to Kawabata, Yamada and other visiting Japanese intellectuals wrote in the imperial centre's language, showcasing the Japanese-led regime's cultural efforts and its ambitions for Manchukuo to serve as a utopian template for other multi-ethnic spaces that would be conquered by Imperial Japan. These include "collaborationist" Manchurian Chinese writers like Gu Ding (1909-60), who, in the early 1940s, co-edited two collections of Manchurian literature, or *Manshû bungaku,* with Kawabata and participated in literary activities with the Japanese. In truth, despite its nominal independence, Manchukuo was clearly a part of the Japanese cultural and linguistic sphere. Its regime attempted to fashion the new state's culture into one that reflected how the five official ethnicities/races harmoniously accepted *Japanese* culture, while only superficially recognizing cultural difference.

As Kawamura Minato and Komagome Takeshi emphasize, Manchukuo's culture had Imperial Japan at its centre, with the Japanese language as its official means of communication, with the Chinese and Korean languages relegated to a semi-colonial status, despite the government's official promotion of *gozoku kyôwa.*[13] Chinese and Koreans felt their ethnic insignificance to the regime through their linguistic marginalization, with their languages being subjected to translation or omission. Materials in the Korean language and/or by Korean authors are extremely rare.[14] In fact, most media/propaganda materials are printed in Japanese, with English a close second (bilingual representations are extremely common) and, occasionally, Mandarin Chinese. Japanese linguistic dominance is clearly evident. White Russians were sometimes included in Japanese accounts of the five ethnicities, and take the place of Koreans in stories translated into Japanese in the two collections of Manchukuo literature co-edited by Kawabata.

The Wartime "Japanization" of Manchukuo's Cultural Activities

Manchukuo's closer cultural integration with the imperial centre could be seen in how, after 1932, sponsorship for cultural activities progressively moved from commercial to state support. The region's literary activities and arts received financial and ideological support from the Japanese-led Manchukuo regime as well as from the imperial metropole. Yet, Manchukuo's status as an independent state became even more questionable during wartime, when events in domestic Japan and the Empire began to have a seismic effect on the new nation's political, cultural, and economic affairs. After the outbreak of the Second Sino-Japanese War in 1937, the wartime consolidation of state control and the official sponsorship of Manchukuo's cultural activities soon paralleled those in domestic Japan, though censorship and political persecution of Japanese locals were less severe in Manchukuo than in the archipelago. Although writers in Japan endured heavy censorship and surveillance from the 1920s onwards, the imperial government only targeted its own Japanese citizens throughout the imperial sphere, including in Manchukuo, from the early 1940s. This allowed Japanese cultural producers and other intellectuals in Manchukuo relatively more freedom of expression than was allowed in their home country.

Official aims to promote Manchukuo's new culture as an independent entity, as in the early to mid-1930s, were, with the 1938 advent of the total war system, or *sôryokusen taisei,*[15] subsumed within those of the Japanese state. After this date, culture and the arts in Manchukuo were aggressively manipulated to showcase a benevolent Japanese Empire's ideals, highlighting Manchukuo's interdependent relationship with domestic Japan and Pan-Asianism. Cultural activities were increasingly linked to those in domestic Japan through various state organizations. Though Manchukuo was never officially a colony of Japan, "transculturation" between the new state and domestic Japan became even more notable during wartime as Japan waged a cultural war against China.

During the intensification of the China conflict, inviting domestic Japanese intellectuals, journalists, and government officials to Manchukuo became a crucial part of state policy, the purpose being to augment the ideological mission of Japanese nation building across Asia by solidifying support for the Japanese Empire through cultural efforts. Moreover, the reinforcement of Japanese culture in Manchukuo's border regions was now of even greater strategic importance due to its geographical location between the communist Soviet Union to the north and Republican China south of the Great Wall. As revealed in earlier chapters, cultural producers invited from domestic Japan were sponsored by Manchukuo governmental organizations as well as by the SMRC conglomerate. As articulate cultural figures from the Japanese archipelago, these people were engaged to bring Japan's culture to Manchukuo while, on their return, serving as authoritative sources of information about the new state. These individuals, along with functionaries related to local government or the imperial bureaucracy, were enlisted to explain the political and strategic importance of Manchukuo to domestic Japan in cultural terms. Behind this rhetoric lies an assumption that culture, specifically Japanese culture, needed to be strengthened and expanded throughout the region to support Imperial Japan's wartime initiatives. Through these efforts in the realm of culture, Manchukuo was soon depicted as *inseparable* from domestic Japan during wartime, even though, previously, its independence and cultural distinctiveness had been emphasized.

An example of this trend of Manchukuo's political and cultural fate being increasingly linked to that of Japan appears in a 1937 travelogue by a Tokyo municipal bureaucrat named Hasegawa Magohei. The travelogue has the evocative title of *Kyokujitsu no tameku tokoro (The Places Where the Flag of the Rising Sun Flutters in the Wind).*[16] In the book's title and text, where he describes the presence of the Japanese flag proudly waving alongside that of the new state, Hasegawa consistently refers to Manchukuo as a nation claimed by Japan. As important national symbols, flags are planted in conspicuous places, claiming Japanese territory in all senses – physical, spiritual, and cultural. Hasegawa, writing in the tone of an official from the imperial capital, says that he hopes to address questions about Manchukuo asked by people in Japan.[17] Obviously, his writings serve as a mouthpiece for the Japanese government, and they dutifully persuade the reader of Manchukuo's indelible ties to the Empire. Travelling to the new state as a government functionary, Hasegawa espouses Japanese imperialist ideology by portraying Manchukuo as essential to the national defence of domestic Japan.

Within a larger framework, Hasegawa views Manchukuo as an important cultural and political bulwark against the encroachment of Soviet communism in both China and Japanese-annexed Korea as well as a nation that, simply by its geographical location, contributes to East Asian stability. In its emphasis on Manchukuo's interdependent relationship with domestic Japan, Hasegawa's narrative resembles many published the year Japan formally declared war on China. However, the message that resonates most deeply with the reader is that an intangible factor – culture – will ultimately determine the outcome of the struggle in which Japan now finds itself engaged. Hasegawa, like the Japanese government and a growing number of vocal Japanese intellectuals in the late 1930s, believed that it was now necessary, through inextricable cultural means, to couple Manchukuo with Japan. This plan was soon carried out by intensifying official transnational cultural organizations and activities linking Japan and Manchukuo, including associations for literature and the arts. In addition, important cultural figures from domestic Japan, like Kawabata and Haruyama, were enlisted to convey these ideas and, thereby, to stimulate and to legitimize them.

For example, in a 1938 essay on the nation's contemporary literature, Yamaguchi Shinichi remarks: "The Department of People's Welfare (formerly the Department of Education) and the Bureau of Information of the General Affairs Board[18] have frequently solicited contributions of literary productions in both Japanese and Manchurian in an effort to spur on cultural progress."[19] The state's efforts to grab the reins of cultural activities and fashion them into something unique to Manchukuo appears to have been difficult since Yamaguchi adds the following caveat: "Notwithstanding the good intentions of the Government, however, the results so far attained [sic], have not been very satisfactory, which in fact may have been due to the severity of the conditions imposed on such productions, which naturally tended to restrict contributions."[20] Further illuminating attempts to rectify this situation through the top-down centralization of cultural endeavours, Obama Shigeru, the chief of the Manchukuo Foreign Office's publicity section, notes in 1939 how the Manchukuo Publicity and News Bureau "under the direct supervision of the Prime Minister, controls and directs the various cultural organizations and their general activities."[21] However, it appears that the government's micromanaging of the arts was not helpful when it came to stimulating literary efforts on the part of Manchukuo's majority Chinese population. In addition, on 21 February 1941, the same bureau issued the

Hachi-bu or *Ba-bu* (Eight Abstentions), ostensibly to control subversive literary tendencies among Han Chinese writers.[22] Its prudish preoccupation with enforcing public morality by banning works that exposed Manchukuo's dark side – its decadence, brothels, and the lives of servants – not only showed the bureau's concern with eliminating anti-government rhetoric or political dissent but also inadvertently revealed some of the topics popular among Chinese authors and their readership.

The initial inability of the state-sponsored arts to thrive was one of the reasons that the central Manchukuo regime based in Shinkyô asked domestic Japanese literary luminaries to jumpstart its multi-ethnic literary endeavours and to connect with Han Chinese authors like Gu Ding who, since 1940, had had a good relationship with Japanese writers like Yamada. Indeed, one of the points made in the July 1941 round-table discussion was that, so far, no literary masterpieces had been produced in Manchukuo, with the exception of the Japanese writer Kitamura Kenjirô's *Shunren (Spring Festival Couplet)*.[23] Even so, it is ironic that a story named for a common sight in Chinese villages during the Spring Festival was penned by a Japanese *Roman-ha* writer originally from domestic Japan and that it was judged a "literary masterpiece" by Kawabata, Japan's leading *bundan* (literary establishment) writer.[24]

Even though the inland city of Shinkyô was Manchukuo's official capital, and officials made efforts to make it a cultural centre, Dairen, as a port town, had better connections to the Japanese archipelago by sea and, therefore, greater accessibility to information, books, and products from domestic Japan and elsewhere. Since 1907, Dairen, thanks to its ready access to Tokyo and the archipelago, was also the SMRC conglomerate's headquarters. In addition, prior to the Manchukuo period, Japanese bureaucrats like Kantô governor-general Miura Gorô (1870-1926) avidly fostered the regional promotion of the arts in Dairen and in the heavily colonized areas of southeastern Manchuria under his control. Consequently, in contrast to Shinkyô, from 1935 to 1940, artistic and cultural activities sponsored by SMRC or the Japanese government flourished in places that, like Dairen, were well connected to domestic Japan.[25] In efforts to tie Manchukuo's cultural activities with those in Japan, the government and SMRC invited writers to tour the new nation, while encouraging leading Japanese artists to exhibit their works in Shinkyô as well as in Dairen. The shift from Dairen to Shinkyô as a centre for cultural activities paralleled the move from SMRC patronage to more centralized government control over the arts by the late 1930s.

The reorganization of cultural organizations and activities during the Second Sino-Japanese War highlighted the increasingly intimate relationship between Japan and Manchukuo. Many of the wartime transformations in Japan's institutions were later implemented in Manchukuo. Around 1940, officially recognized artists' associations, exhibition venues, and writers' groups were forcibly consolidated by the Japanese state on the archipelago.[26] Not surprisingly, this process of consolidation, starting with the *Prospectus for the Guidance of the Arts and Literature,* began a year later in Manchukuo as part of the mass mobilization in domestic Japan and its colonies. The intensification of the war effort in 1941, prior to the attack on Pearl Harbor, marks the beginning of Manchukuo's consolidation of cultural activities – while the new state was being prepared as a military base from which to attack Southeast Asia. This state-sponsored consolidation marks a fundamental change in Manchukuo's formerly liberal cultural policies, which had been advocated by Ishiwara since the early 1930s.

The *Prospectus* and the State's Management of Literature, 1941

On 23 March 1941, the Manchukuo Publicity and News Bureau promulgated the *Prospectus for the Guidance of the Arts and Culture,* which was read by the organization's director Mutô Tomio at the Shinkyô National Arts Congress, heralding a wartime trend that saw the centralization of the arts in both Japan and Manchukuo.[27] This single propaganda organization subsumed the six officially recognized "arts" of literature, fine art, music, dance, theatre, and film. The *Prospectus* thus put the arts under the direct control of the Manchukuo Publicity and News Bureau and, under five different categories, divided cultural activities and art education into research organizations.[28] Mutô intended to manage the arts and create a modern, scientific culture supportive of the state, but he actually steered cultural production exclusively toward fascism. This reorganization/centralization of the arts would proceed along Japanese lines, according to Japanese conceptions of modernity, as expressed in the appropriate literary/artistic models.

For example, the March *Prospectus* "compris[ed] twenty-one regulations in five sections [and] dictated the adoption of Japanese literary traditions and professional organizations as models to facilitate [the] realization of Manchukuo's 'integrated independent literature.'"[29] It also designated the automatic enrolment of writers into state-sponsored literary organizations.[30] The *Prospectus*'s heavily Japanese-influenced intrusion into literature and the arts, multiple new regulations, and internal contradictions regarding the purportedly independent literature it was to foster, generated much controversy among both Japanese and Han Chinese. In fact, in the news write-up of the June round table, Mutô mentioned that the cultural policies he issued in the *Prospectus* had stimulated a flurry of critique in newspapers and magazines, which he had spent the past three months attempting (unsuccessfully) to counter.[31] He even noted that "terribly slanderous language" *(zuibun waruguchi)* had come from all quarters and that he could not completely quell it. However, Mutô did mention that he had created new literary, artistic, theatre, and music associations to address this issue.[32] Since he himself was the director of the state propaganda organization, it was doubtful that a proliferation of new groups under his purview would have had any mitigating effect on the *Prospectus*'s restrictive stipulations.

One of the most important of these new arts associations was the central, Shinkyô-based *Manshû bungei-ka kyôkai,* or, in Chinese, *Manzhou wenyi-jia xiehui* (Manchurian Writers Association), headed by Yamada Seizaburô and established on 27 July 1941, about four months after the announcement of the *Prospectus.*[33] The group included the Han Chinese writers Gu Ding, Shan Ding (1914-95), Wu Ying (1915-61), and Yi Chi (1913-unknown), whose works were later represented in Kawabata's two editions co-edited by Yamada.[34] Gu, as a member of the *Yiwenzhi-pai* (Chronicle of the Arts) faction, is usually called "collaborationist" by nationalistic Chinese scholars due to his participation in joint literary endeavours with Japanese writers in Manchukuo. However, in the postwar period, he viewed himself as closer to Japanese left-wing intellectuals, having attacked Manchukuo's literary policies since 1937.[35] Gu's complexity supports Rana Mitter's assessments of Chinese collaboration as motivated by both personal and national agendas as well as contemporary expediencies.[36]

To further publicize the *Prospectus*'s cultural policies, from 4 to 9 July 1941, a six-part series from a round-table discussion entitled "Mutô kôhôsho-chô ni kiku: Zadankai" ("Inquiring of News and Publicity Bureau Chief Mutô: Round-Table Discussion"), headed by Mutô, appeared in the widely read *Manshû nichinichi shimbun (Manchuria Daily News)* Japanese-language newspaper.[37] This intellectual round table, or *zadankai,* was actually held in Tokyo on 10 June 1941, though the newspaper published a transcription for the public nearly a month later.[38] As propaganda chief, Mutô served as both the moderator and facilitator, using rhetorical talents that later had Americans referring to him as the "Joseph Goebbels of Manchukuo." This June *zadankai,* held in Japan's imperial capital, boasted an impressive group of Japanese cultural critics, thinkers, and writers, many of whom had former Marxist inclinations:[39] Kyoto School philosopher Miki Kiyoshi (1897-1945), cultural philosopher Tanigawa Tetsuzô (1895-1989), former *Asahi Shimbun* reporter and SMRC research department employee Ozaki Hôtsumi (1901-44), and, of course, the popular novelist Kawabata.

Under the Manchukuo Publicity and News Bureau's auspices, the *Manchuria Daily News* invited Kawabata as an authoritative cultural figure from domestic Japan to take part in this highly publicized debate on Manchurian culture. In April, following the March issuing of the *Prospectus,* the same newspaper had invited Kawabata, as one of Japan's most prominent writers, to observe Manchukuo's newly reorganized cultural activities. Kawabata then stayed until May. In fact, he spent one-third of 1941 in Manchukuo, receiving another invitation from the Kantô Army in September and staying until November, at which time he also met with Han Chinese writers to discuss the future of Manchurian literature and to view the new state's educational system where he visited primary schools and publicized his composition movement. Many of these writers soon joined the Manchurian Writers Association, formed in late July 1941 and headed by Yamada, whose works would appear in the 1942 and 1944 multi-ethnic literature collections co-edited by him and Kawabata. Thus, with first-hand knowledge of Manchukuo, Kawabata lent "authenticity" to this published round-table discussion.

By inviting important Japanese figures in literature and the arts to Manchukuo, publicity chief Mutô hoped to foster a multi-ethnic Manchurian literary and artistic culture as well as strengthen Manchukuo's cultural ties to domestic Japan. Gennifer Weisenfeld notes that, in the case of Imperial Japan, "identities of the metropole/empire and the periphery/colony were mutually constitutive ... [T]he colonies by their very existence reformed Japan as much as Japan shaped colonial space."[40] The same process appears in the state-supported cultural initiatives in Manchukuo, such as the consolidation of cultural activities in the 1940s, as discussed in the above round table.

Notably, the transculturation of Manchukuo through the centralization of the arts is further revealed in descriptions of writers from domestic Japan, like Kawabata (see below) or the avant-garde critic and poet Haruyama, who, two years later, described how Mutô's *Prospectus* had inspired his own thoughts on Japanese culture and the new state. Like Kawabata, Haruyama also visited Manchukuo, once in 1940 and again in 1942, prompting his publication of two books on the natural features of Manchuria and the region's emergent culture.[41] Haruyama's impressions from his initial visit to Manchukuo appeared in his first book, *Manshû fûbutsushi (Manchurian Scenery).* In the 1943 account, *Manshû no bunka,* the former editor of the influential 1930s avant-garde poetry magazine *Shi to shiron* describes,[42] in philosophical terms, how, after the spring of 1941, the *Prospectus* fundamentally changed Manchukuo's cultural policies.[43] In this book, he assumes the role of a cultural critic, even explaining why Japan should take control of China's culture in ways resembling Mutô's scientific consolidation of cultural activities in Manchukuo.

Here, Haruyama apparently views the region of *Manshû* (Manchuria, discursively separated from the Manchukuo state) as part of China, at least in *cultural* terms. According to his book, the cultural sphere of Chinese civilization once included the Manchurian region that was now part of Manchukuo, a modern state fashioned under Japanese guidance.[44] Here, he echoes Kawabata's ideas (expressed the previous year) by arguing that China's culture had become stagnant, thus necessitating the infusion of Japanese culture.[45] Haruyama's voice resembles that of many avant-garde writers who underwent *tenkô* in the early 1930s and renounced their left-wing beliefs in order to support the Japanese government's Pan-Asianist ideology with regard to China.

According to Haruyama, one of China's faults was that it was a country that possessed *bunmei* (civilization – a fixed entity with inherent, essential qualities) but not *bunka* (culture – a mutable entity capable of changing and adopting scientific innovation); therefore, Japan should export its technological expertise to Manchukuo to supplement a traditional Chinese civilization now moribund due to national degeneration and foreign domination.[46] Haruyama's words clearly reflect the cultural ideas of the Japanese imperial state concerning Manchukuo and the key role of Japanese intellectuals in disseminating them. Not surprisingly, Kawabata had voiced Haruyama's ideas in 1942 and had established a precedent for such views with his participation in the Tokyo round table.

Kawabata's Promotion of "Manchurian Literature" under Japanese Auspices

Japan's leading role in Manchukuo's wartime cultural consolidation was evident in that the new nation's literature was represented to readers in domestic Japan by prominent Japanese cultural figures such as Kawabata and Yamada. The production of literature in Manchukuo, or with the new nation as its topic, soon became a collaborative effort for domestic Japanese and colonial Japanese writers – a process that intensified during the Second Sino-Japanese War. This included limited participation of Chinese writers in Japanese-supported literary organizations of the type suggested by the *Prospectus* and later headed by Japanese writers like Yamada. In the early 1940s, various presses in Tokyo and Manchukuo published bound editions of literary works showing how writers of diverse ethnicities engaged in cultural production supporting the new state's literary efforts. Representing the cultural interdependence between the centre and the periphery, famous *bundan* authors like Kawabata often edited these volumes in domestic Japan.

In 1941, at the height of the Second Sino-Japanese War and at the beginning of Japan's military's invasion of Southeast Asia, Kawabata was twice invited to Manchukuo by the *Manchuria Daily News* and the Kantô Army, in accordance with the propaganda prerogatives of the state-run Manchukuo Publicity and News Bureau. This organization first invited the writer for a tour of the new nation and then enlisted him to participate in the aforementioned star-studded *zadankai* consisting of Japanese intellectuals gathered in Tokyo to debate Manchukuo's culture. He visited Manchukuo from April to May 1941 to promote the nation's literary activities and learn about the June round-table discussion sponsored by the *Manchuria Daily News*. He then returned to Manchukuo in autumn, touring from September to November with Hino Ashihei (1907-60) and others invited by the Kantô Army.[47]

From 1943 to 1944, in the *Manchuria Daily News,* Kawabata wrote an unfinished serialized novel entitled *Tôkaidô (The Way East)* about a high school teacher named Ueda who lectures his daughter on the essence of Japanese culture and the importance of travel to the literary pursuits of writers in the Heian (792-1185) and other periods.[48] For Kawabata, travel in Manchukuo, China, and other parts of the Japanese Empire both affirmed his Japanese identity and helped him to feel like a literary emissary from a superior, culturally advanced nation. In the novel, the prominent Japanese author appears to communicate the belief that "Japaneseness is a special, nontransferable racial virtue," an assumption that Gavan McCormack notes is common to many endeavours surrounding the Japanese-generated culture of Manchukuo.[49] Indeed, since Kawabata's first mention of Manchuria in his 1933 story "Of Birds and Beasts," his recurring obsession with the region, and its phantom-like intrusion into his texts, parallels that of official media in Japan and other parts of the Empire.[50] In addition, Kawabata was involved in furthering Manchukuo's *tsuzurikata undô* (composition movement), for which he toured elementary schools throughout the nation in spring 1941 and gave a radio broadcast entitled *Manshû to tsuzurikata (Compositions in Manchuria).*[51] The products of Kawabata's visits to Manchukuo were published not long after his return, and they served the cultural propaganda purposes of his two hosting institutions – the new state's primary news organ and the military.

Why did Kawabata so readily travel to Manchukuo and conform to propaganda chief Mutô's cultural mission for the new state? Aside from the intrusion of the fascist state into all fields of cultural production, what personally appealed to him in this endeavour? Was Kawabata a relentless opportunist who saw his connections to the Manchukuo Publicity and News Bureau and the Kantô Army as yet another means of furthering his career?[52] Or is the reality a more complex mix of historical factors? In previous chapters, I discussed how the talents of formerly left-wing or avant-garde writers, photographers, and artists were mobilized to support a right-wing version of socialism in Manchukuo. They were attracted to Manchuria by the increased push of persecution in domestic Japan in the wake of the Manchurian Incident and the compelling pull of forming lasting narratives of the "utopian" new state. Robert Tomes, in his study on American intellectuals during the McCarthy period, provides an intriguing explanation of this phenomenon, which can also be applied to Manchukuo:

> In a society where intellectuals play a primarily affirmative role, the mutually exclusive lines between government policymaking and intellectual discourse become blurred. When intellectuals accept and ratify a society's power structure, again the lines become blurred as successful intellectuals rise in that power structure. It is not unreasonable to assume that intellectuals who

> celebrate the authorities will autonomously employ their talents and energies to forward the objectives of those authorities, whose point of view they will in some cases come to see as related to their own.[53]

Despite his early career as an "avant-garde" modernist with surrealist tendencies, Kawabata was now very much an establishment intellectual, despite his protestations to the contrary in the postwar period. He was able to further cement his status as one of Imperial Japan's most important literary figures when his aims merged with those of Manchukuo. Kawabata's role most closely approximates what O'Connor calls that of "occasional propagandists," who are generally "journalists and writers not specifically or consistently contracted to write for Japan – who found themselves drawn into official efforts to explain and justify Japan's position."[54] The questions pertaining to Kawabata's intellectual engagement with Manchukuo may never be conclusively answered, and they are part of a larger constellation of issues surrounding the wartime activities of Japanese intellectuals. However, it is possible to investigate and analyze concrete examples of his views as expressed in the introductions to his edited collections.

Kawabata's Promotion of "Manchurian" Culture and Multi-Ethnic Literature

As previously discussed, in the early 1940s, Kawabata obligingly published a serialized novel and co-edited two collections of literary works by Manchukuo's five "official" ethnicities. The novel and these collections appeared in Japanese, the language of the imperial centre. In fact, after 1937, Japanese was Manchukuo's official "national language," belying its ethnic diversity and supposed respect for the five ethnicities. In the introduction to the first volume, Kawabata warns of the Chinese "threat" while extolling the past accomplishments of the Han Chinese ethnicity, whose now-moribund nation could only be revived through Japanese guidance and cultural superiority. The 1941 round-table discussion and these two editions, compiled by Kawabata in 1942 and 1944, respectively, clearly state that Manchukuo was to serve as a template for the future establishment of Pan-Asian ideals throughout conquered areas in China and Southeast Asia.

The fact that a prominent cultural figure of Kawabata's stature from the imperial capital became a mouthpiece for the new Manchurian literature and Japanese cultural superiority is historically significant. It reveals that Manchukuo was not "independent" from the archipelago, despite official rhetoric, and that the interdependence between the two "nations" functioned in a hierarchical, paternalistic fashion. Cultural production in the form of literature served as a means of culturally integrating Manchukuo with domestic Japan – something now viewed as crucial to the wartime success of Imperial Japan. Despite Kawabata's utopian intentions, his writings and frequent trips to Manchukuo and China illustrate that the creation of an *independent* literary culture in the new state was soon subsumed by the exigencies of war. This section addresses the little-known role of this future winner of the Nobel Prize for Literature in promoting multi-ethnic literature in Manchukuo.[55]

In the early 1940s, to further foster Manchukuo's new culture and literature, Kawabata helped edit Japanese-language collections of short stories by Japanese and other Manchurian natives, including *Manshûkoku kaku minzoku sôsaku senshû 1 (Anthology of Literary Works by Each Ethnic Group in Manchukuo 1)* in 1942 and *Manshûkoku kaku minzoku sôsaku senshû 2 (Anthology of Literary Works by Each Ethnic Group in Manchukuo 2)* in 1944.[56] While Kawabata was listed as *hensan daihyô-sha* (editorial representative) on the copyright page,[57] and although he wrote the introduction, the other editors were Yamada, Kitamura, Gu Ding, Kishida Kunio (1890-1954), and Shimaki Kensaku.[58] Some of these Japanese writers, like Yamada and Shimaki, had formerly been left-wing activists or had been involved in the proletarian literature movement prior to their *tenkô* in the 1930s. Gu Ding, as the only Han Chinese co-editor, chose the other Chinese writers to appear in the collections – such as Shan Ding, Yi Chi, She Jun (1912-unknown), and Wu Ying, one of Manchukuo's most famous woman writers (known for her often decadent stories).[59]

All works by Chinese and Russians were translated into Japanese, despite the writers' multi-ethnic and multilingual characteristics. In contrast to the Han Chinese, Kawabata described the White Russian writers as retaining the true traditions of Russian culture and diverging from the path of Soviet literature. These included Boris Yu'ilski (1911-unknown) and Arseny Nesmeyelov (n.d.). Perhaps he also viewed Manchurian Chinese as the "true" inheritors of China's literary future. These editions were part of Kawabata's attempt to portray the pioneering efforts of Manchukuo's new multi-ethnic and multiracial (but not multilingual) literary culture to domestic Japan and the colonies. Cumulatively, they were known as *Manshû bungaku.*

Notably, in the first collection, Japanese authors dominate (contributing fourteen works), with a handful of Han Chinese (four)[60] and Russians (two),[61] while works by Koreans are conspicuously absent. This is also true of the 1944 collection, in which only eight Japanese authors contributed, with six Chinese, two Russians, and one Mongol.[62] Kawabata's omission of Korean authors incensed the Manchukuo-based Korean author Yom Sang Seop (1897-1963), whose criticisms appeared in *Bukwon (Northern Fields),* a 1943 anthology of Ahn Su-Kil's short stories that he edited.[63] Kim Jaeyong, a Korean colonial literature specialist, believes that this indicates a discrepancy between the Manchukuo state's *gozoku kyôwa* ideals and the reality of its treatment of Koreans. He also notes that this exclusion of Korean authors like Yom was due to the fact that it was believed "dangerous" to include

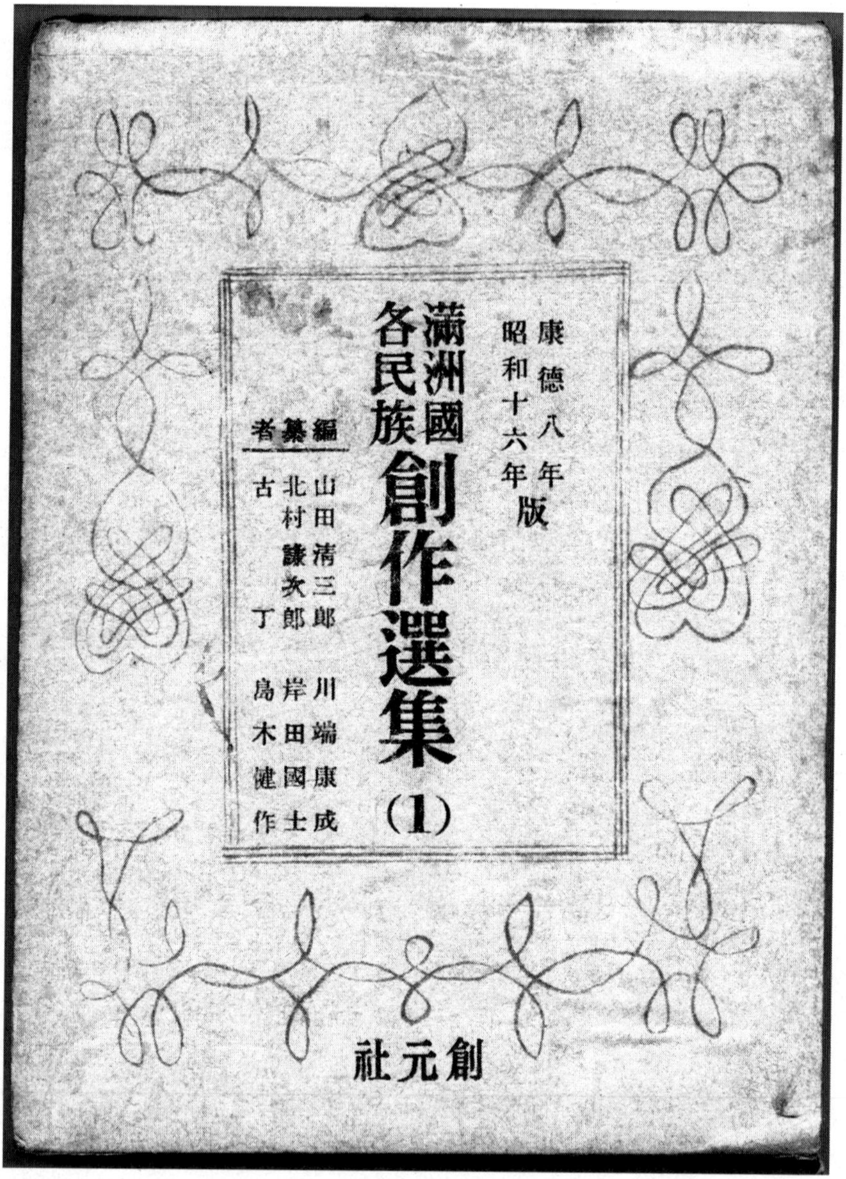

Figure 24 Front cover box, *Manshûkoku kaku minzoku sôsaku senshû* (1) [Anthology of literary works by each ethnic group in Manchukuo (1)], 1942, author's personal collection.

Figure 25 (facing page) Back cover box, *Manshûkoku kaku minzoku sôsaku senshû* (1) [Anthology of literary works by each ethnic group in Manchukuo (1)], 1942, author's personal collection.

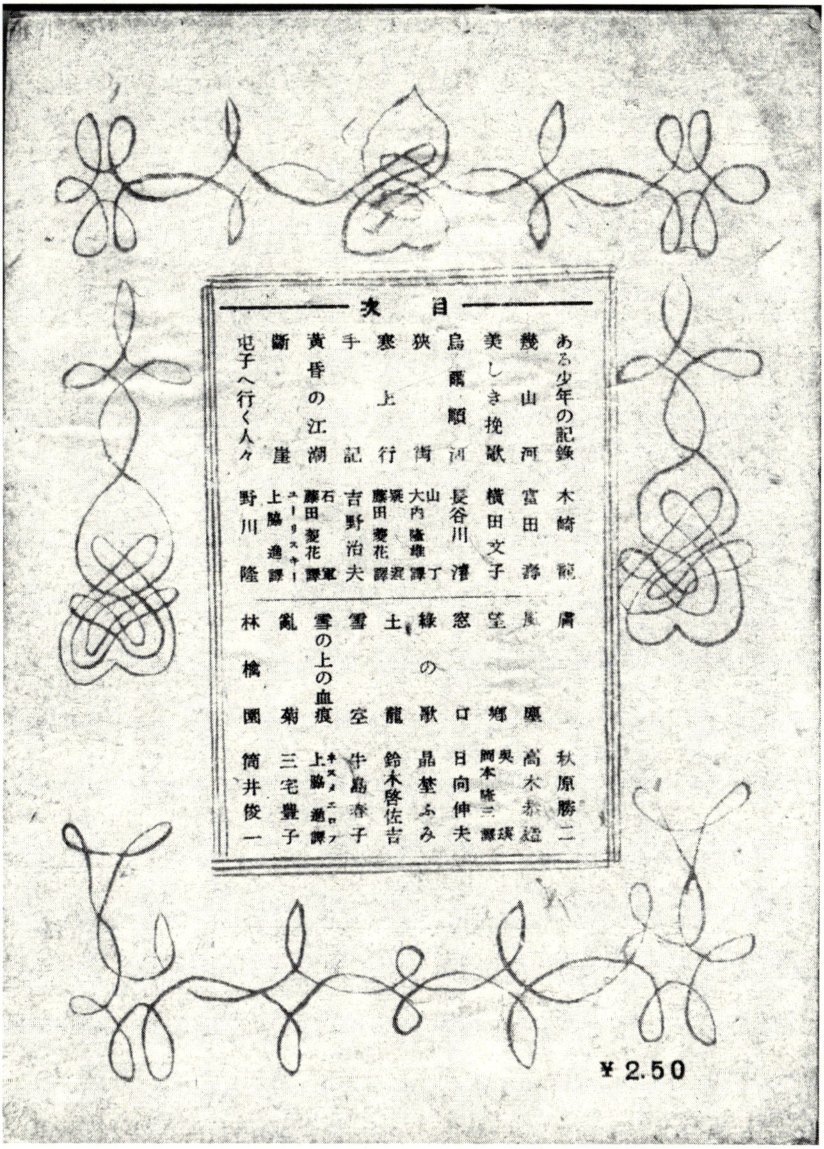

目次

ある少年の記録	木崎龍
幾山河	富田壽
美しき挽歌	横田文子
烏爾順河	長谷川濬
狹街	山丁 大内隆雄譯
寒上行	疑遲 藤田菱花譯
手記	吉野治夫
黄昏の江湖	石軍 藤田菱花譯
斷崖	ユーリスキー 上脇進譯
屯子へ行く人々	野川隆
廣	秋原勝二
風塵	高木恭造
望鄉	吳瑛 岡本隆三譯
窓口	日向伸夫
綠の歌	晶埜ふみ
土龍	鈴木啓佐吉
雪空	牛島春子
雪の上の血痕	キスメニロフ 上脇進譯
亂菊	三宅豊子
林檎園	筒井俊一

¥2.50

him. This highlights the regime's fear of Koreans, who were joining resistance movements in border areas.[64] Korean or Han Chinese "ethnic consciousness," or *minzoku isshiki,* also diverged from the state's goals in that it not only referred to the Korean independence movement but also implied unity with Republican China, which was at war with Japan. This was at odds with the regime's *minzoku kyôwa* principles and a danger to a unified Japanese

Empire. It is also why official media so insistently referred to Han Chinese as "Manchurians."

By 1944, Kawabata, though his name is still listed as chief editor of Volume 2, along with the others listed above, seems to have retreated from the Japan side of the project, releasing himself from having total responsibility for it.[65] In addition, Yamada's introduction appears first, with Kawabata's following it. The fewer Japanese authors represented, and the addition of more Chinese along with one Mongol, show a desire to achieve more "balance" in the representation of ethnic groups.[66] Other reasons for this may include the intensification of the war in Japan, with the frequent disruptions of Allied bombings and the consequent displacement of Kawabata and his other Japanese editors. These factors were compounded by the growth of anti-Japanese resistance movements among Han Chinese in Manchukuo, which also affected surveillance of the Japanese population. Yet, continued Chinese involvement in Kawabata's project from 1942 to 1944 was seen as crucial to the building of a new multi-ethnic literature and, therefore, culture in Manchukuo.

In his introduction to *Manshûkoku kaku minzoku sôsaku senshû 1*, Kawabata points out his role as a traveller and how this enabled him to get a glimpse of the creation of Manchukuo's new literature:

> In my role as tourist, I momentarily had two viewpoints concerning Manchukuo's literature. One of these was the issue of the lofty ideals of Manchurian literature. As said by the writers of this country, literature as new as the country perhaps creates a myth of national construction, or perhaps, guides a history of its creation. Moreover, five ethnicities/races are launching this type of literature together. On this virgin soil, both the significance of literature and its mission have appeared as extremely clear to me. Another one of my viewpoints concerned the issue of Manchurian literature's mundane reality. The exhortations of the nation and [its] general desires are still dawning, organizations to publish literature still have not been set up, and the market is constricted.[67]

While supporting ethnic cohesion in literary efforts in this "virgin" territory now under Japanese guidance, Kawabata advocates the creation of a publishing infrastructure to develop a market for new literary production while the nation converts its ideals into reality. Citing the Manchukuo Publicity and News Bureau's new post-*Prospectus* focus, he was particularly concerned about literature's role in creating a national narrative. In fact, he strongly believed that literature was directly tied to the successful communication of Manchukuo's national ideals.

Though most compositions, with regard to both topic and author, reflect Japanese cultural concerns during wartime, a few works achieved Kawabata's utopian dream of cultural and literary innovation in Manchukuo. However, yet again, one was by a Japanese author originally from the archipelago. Kawabata's 1942 edition included the short story "Tonsu ni iku hitobito" ("The People Going to Dunzi"),[68] by the former proletarian writer Nogawa Takashi, whose earlier work had been nominated for the Akutagawa Prize.[69] Finding his own rural utopia in Manchukuo, Nogawa portrayed Chinese peasants in a sympathetic light while viewing their communal society as consistent with his former Marxist ideals. Some themes echoed those of the proletarian literature movement of the 1920s and 1930s, while lacking its political import. Nogawa's short story fit Kawabata's criteria for describing Manchukuo's development in agricultural areas, with Japanese shown working harmoniously with other ethnic groups, such as the majority Han Chinese. The focus on the lower classes also paralleled Kawabata's earlier fascination with the poor and the marginalized, with Manchuria seemingly a space in which these inequalities could be resolved in the form of a communal society.

However, contrary to Kawabata's hopes, most of the texts in these two volumes were largely influenced by the Japanese effort to create a utopian fantasy of racial harmony and cooperation but, instead, merely represented the multifaceted propaganda of the central Manchukuo government in Shinkyô. This plan to create a thriving multi-ethnic literature under Japanese auspices had been voiced four years earlier in Yamaguchi's article entitled "Contemporary Literature in Manchuria," in which he notes: "It may be said that modern literature in the new State is now well on the road to development. The future appears promising, for through the harmonization of Japanese, Manchurian, Chinese and Occidental literature, a new literature of the highest standards will eventually be born."[70] This new literature, represented by the stories in multi-ethnic literary collections edited by Yamada in 1940 and by him and Kawabata in 1942 and 1944, provided scenes of local colour in an exotic, fertile space ripe for the growth of Manchukuo's ideals.[71] Kawabata's introduction notes that Manchurian literature was important in that it provided a template for Japan's "advance southward," with Han Chinese enjoying a leading role. The increasing percentage of Han Chinese authors and, to some extent, White Russians, with the corresponding omission of Korean authors in the 1944 edition, is a prime example of this. Thus, the texts had little to do with the positive portrayal of *Manshû* or the creation of a national narrative for Manchukuo for *each* ethnic group. Presumably, the Japanese authors of these works either lived in Manchukuo or spent a significant amount of time developing their literary careers there before returning to Japan. The bulk of the literary compositions were written by Japanese men in Japanese – the few exceptions were translated into Japanese. Despite Kawabata's best intentions, it is clear that his utopian desire to set up an *independent* literary culture in Manchukuo was soon lost in the cultural propaganda of Imperial Japan's war effort.

This is apparent in his introduction to *Manshûkoku kaku minzoku sôsaku senshû 1,* in which Kawabata stresses the Japanese Army's "advance" into the less-developed regions of Southeast Asia, while asserting that Manchukuo now served as a template for the building of culture in other nations in the Japanese-controlled Greater East Asia Co-Prosperity Sphere.[72] In the Manchukuo context, he viewed this as a joint effort between the Japanese and Han Chinese ethnic groups, and he believed that literature, in particular, had a role to play in the realization of the regime's ideals:

> Japan has now even progressed southward in its war, yet there is no other country but Manchukuo constructing [its] nation with other ethnicities and launching [its] culture. Because Pan-Asian ideals were first put into practice in Manchuria, if they are not attained here, then not only might it be assumed that they cannot be attained anywhere, but [this is] also [of importance] because we are implementing them together with the Han ethnicity (race) – these are Manchuria's [most] important *raisons d'être.*[73] It goes without saying that this is because there is no other superior race quite like the Han Chinese ethnic group. In looking at the cultural domain, it is obvious that this is so.[74]

Kawabata proposed that Manchukuo's cultural development, with the help of the Chinese, provided a shining example to be emulated by other Asian countries that had been "liberated" by Japan. In early 1942, Singapore was conquered by Japanese troops, and the domestic Japanese government sent Japanese intellectuals there to support the propaganda efforts of the renamed Japanese-led state of *Shônan* (Enlightened South). Kawabata refers to this in his introduction, but he expresses some doubt as to *when* these ideals might be achieved. This area also had populations of Chinese merchants and elites – a fact often not evident in Japanese publications.[75] However, in contrast to peoples of mostly Malay descent in newly Japanese-conquered territories in Southeast Asia,[76] Kawabata asserted that the Han Chinese were the only culturally superior ethnic group in Asia, similar to the modern and adaptable Japanese.[77] For this reason, he believed that they were worthy of Manchukuo's being established as an *independent* new nation under initial Japanese tutelage. This was why the project was of such importance.[78]

As noted by Richard H. Mitchell, Japanese sinologists often viewed China as symbolic of "their cultural roots, a foil for the problems of modernity, and the referent for their concepts of Asia."[79] This idea of China as an "other," and a convenient point of comparison with a more dynamic Japan, resembles Kawabata's complex attitude toward and anxieties about China, as expressed in his introduction to *Manshûkoku kaku minzoku sôsaku senshû 1.* Interestingly, he warns of the current Chinese threat while professing great admiration for China's traditional (and therefore unchanging) culture. His contemporary, Haruyama, also echoes this idea in his 1943 writings, which focus on Manchukuo's culture and Japan's role in supporting it.

On the way back to Japan after his spring 1941 visit to Manchukuo before the Tokyo round-table discussion on culture in June, Kawabata stopped in Beijing, where he met with various Chinese writers. Chinese authors in occupied Beijing and Manchuria parallelled to each other in their depictions of desolation, while "the negativity of local Chinese literature testifie[d] to the alienation most writers felt towards Japanese colonial rule."[80] Kawabata sensed the inner turmoil of his Chinese counterparts and departed with mixed feelings. While the famed Japanese author generated warm memories of his visit in the Japanese-occupied former Qing imperial capital, his hosts expressed a more cautionary view of Japan's wartime politics. This is evident in Kawabata's advocating literary creation as a positive, cooperative effort between Japanese and Han Chinese writers in Manchukuo, but he added a disconcerting caveat: "As I had traveled to Beijing myself, I knew that there were Han Chinese who stretched their hands out to Japanese literary figures who should put their strengths together to construct a new path of literature. Our greatest friend as well as our greatest enemy can be none other than the Han ethnic group."[81] Moreover, the cover of *Manshûkoku kaku minzoku sôsaku senshû 1* features a stylized watercolour by Japanese artist K'ai Mihachirô. It depicts a spiralling red and green opium poppy against an ominous, cloudy black background – a dark and unedifying image for a literary collection with lofty purposes.

On the one hand, Kawabata obviously assumed that the cultural views of Chinese in Japanese-occupied Beijing were no different from those in Manchukuo in terms of the joint Japanese-Chinese mission to create new literature in territories under Japanese occupation. However, most significantly, he lets slip his knowledge that Han Chinese writers cooperated with resistance movements against Japan. Wu Ying, whose work appears in both volumes of *Manshûkoku kaku minzoku sôsaku senshû,* supported anti-Japanese resistance – as, to varying degrees, did Gu Ding.[82] According to Norman Smith: "Colonial officials sponsored Chinese literary production in order to legitimate their rule, but they could not completely control writers who were influenced not only by censors and state directives but also by their own agendas and audiences."[83] Indeed, the bleakness of the Manchukuo depicted in Wu's works and those of her counterparts belied the bright vision for the new state proposed by Japanese propagandists like Mutô. Kawabata's passage further reinforces the great contrast between Manchukuo's utopian ideals and the violent reality of military aggression behind its takeover (as well as the lead-up to the Second Sino-Japanese War sparked by the Marco Polo Bridge Incident outside of Beijing).

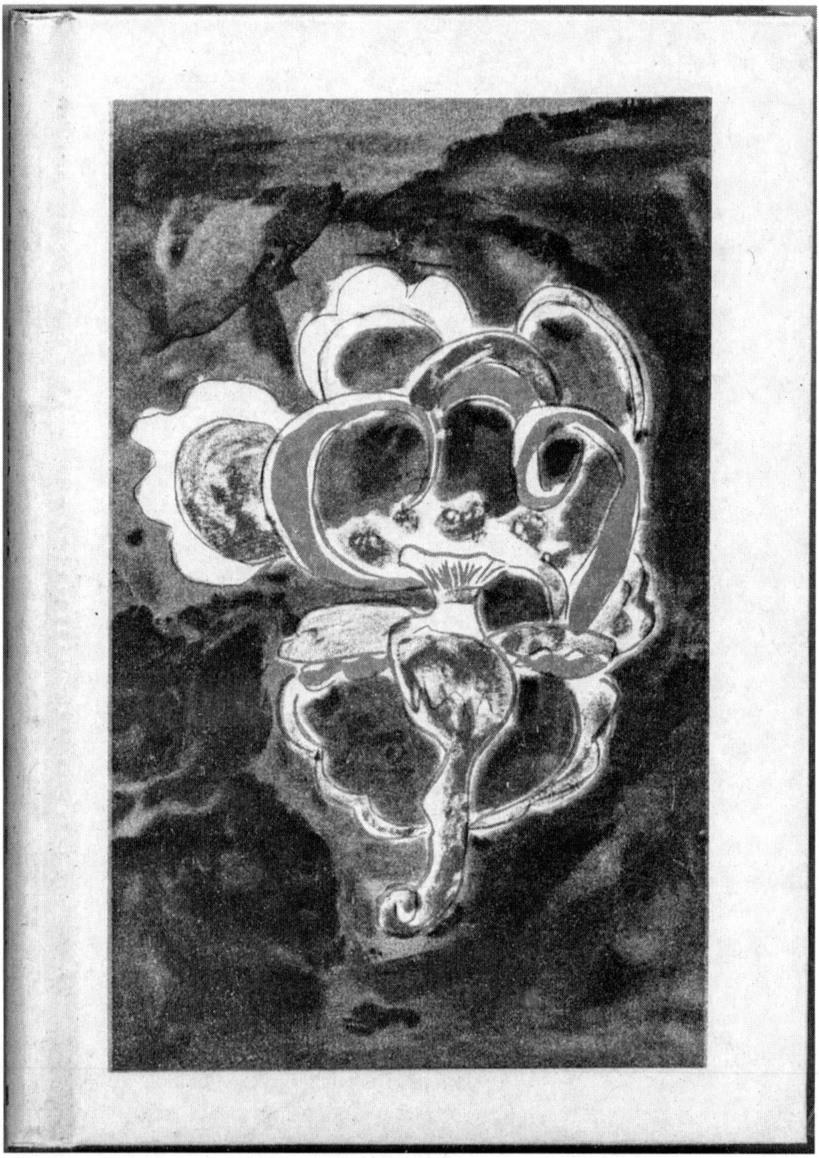

Figure 26 Front cover, *Manshûkoku kaku minzoku sôsaku senshû* (1) [Anthology of literary works by each ethnic group in Manchukuo (1)], 1942, author's personal collection.

Conclusion

As resistance by anti-Japanese movements increased among Han Chinese and ethnic Koreans, the diverse cultures of the five ethnic groups officially composing the Manchukuo state were no longer viewed as harmonious but, rather, as potential threats. The Japanese-led government feared that they might stimulate subversion through the raising of ethnic consciousness. In his introduction to a volume supposedly celebrating the literary compositions of Manchukuo's five ethnicities, Kawabata, as one of Japan's most prominent critics, warned about the possible dangers of Han Chinese nationalism to a state now oriented toward a predominantly Japanese culture.

Until the early 1940s, the Manchukuo regime, under Ishiwara's relatively liberal policies, allowed Japanese intellectuals to engage in mild criticism of its endeavours. However, with the US entry into the Second World War following Imperial Japan's December 1941 attack on Pearl Harbor, the political climate in Manchukuo drastically changed, and, from 1941 to 1942, the state launched an all-out attack on any political expression that diverged from national aims.[84] Mass arrests of suspected communists occurred in 1942 among a Japanese population already subject to self-discipline by organizations like the Concordia Association and the ever-present surveillance of the *Kempeitai*. After July 1937, the Manchurian region increasingly served as a military base for attacking China south of the Great Wall, and, after 1941, Manchukuo soon became the centre for operations in Southeast Asia. Writers in Japan and the colonies were drafted to depict the war effort in China proper and elsewhere as part of a *pen-butai* (pen brigade). Their wartime activities included cultural initiatives. Kawabata was initially attracted to a project that showcased Manchurian literature composed by the five ethnicities due to both its idealism and because of his being compelled to do so by the political climate.

It is evident that, with the advent of total war and Japan's deepening military engagement in China and Southeast Asia, Manchukuo's cultural activities, along with its political fate, were inseparable from domestic Japan. Much of what the media produced after visits by Japanese intellectuals reflected Manchukuo's political bond with Japan. In the early 1940s, as an important domestic Japanese literary figure, Kawabata served to bring legitimacy to Manchukuo's cultural endeavours. However, the war's intrusion into even the cultural domain ultimately made the realization of his ideals impossible. His retreat from the project in 1944 hints at his growing disillusionment with the growth of a multi-ethnic literary culture in Manchukuo. The collected stories Kawabata edited are important to historians in that they convey the sentiments of Imperial Japan's failed utopian experiment in nation building and stand as a precedent to its ruthless pan-Asianist policies in conquered areas of Southeast Asia from 1942 to 1945.

According to Sakuramoto Tomio, many Japanese intellectuals proceeded with a flurry of self-reflective writings in the immediate postwar period; however, after Japan was reconstructed and began enjoying the post-Korean War "economic miracle" after 1955, questions about war responsibility abruptly ceased, with Japanese intellectuals plunging into a deep silence that haunts scholars to the present day.[85] Not surprisingly, Kawabata's introduction to his first edition of multi-ethnic literature in Manchukuo did not appear in his *zenshû* (collected works) until over a decade after his death. This is typical for Japanese authors, since, in the prosperous postwar period infused by a Cold War climate, many of them covered up their involvement in having promoted an unwinnable war.

CONCLUSION

The Reflected Utopia Darkens: Manchukuo, Imperial Japan's Surrender, and Postwar Issues

After 1937, while serving as a base for Japanese military operations in China and Southeast Asia, Manchukuo increasingly became a site for anti-Japanese resistance activities. Previous chapters reveal how wartime exigencies first intensified cultural efforts but then slowly eroded Japanese enthusiasm for utopian cultural experimentation in Manchukuo. This echoed domestic Japan's post-1940 restrictions on and reorganization of cultural activities. Nevertheless, what was most damaging to the construction of a new (Japanese-led) culture in Manchukuo was the subordination of cultural efforts to the burgeoning needs of Imperial Japan's multi-front war. From 1944 onwards, fewer resources could be devoted toward the printing of any kind of materials related to cultural or propaganda initiatives. Art supplies and film also became increasingly scarce. This was due to the impending "decisive battle," or *kessen,* which would ultimately determine the fate of the archipelago and its imperial capital Tokyo, the seat of the Japanese emperor and, therefore, the nation's epicentre. This anxious climate deeply affected Manchukuo.

In early August 1945, the Japanese inhabitants of Manchukuo learned of a devastating new American weapon that had obliterated the city of Hiroshima in a three-kilometre radius over "ground zero." Soon afterwards, as was promised the Allies after Hitler's surrender, Stalin abrogated his neutrality agreement with Japan. Asada Sadao believes that the twin shock of the first atomic bomb's attack on Hiroshima on 6 August, coupled with the Soviet invasion of Manchukuo two days later, finally provided enough incentive for the Japanese government to surrender.[1] It was not known how many atomic bombs the United States had in its possession, but during a day of governmental wavering, another bomb was dropped on Nagasaki, with equally devastating results. In the meantime, Manchukuo's occupants waited with bated breath for the chaos that would arise from defeat and Soviet occupation.

After the Soviet Army crossed Manchukuo's borders, the Kantô Army fled with its dependants, leaving Japanese rural settlers defenceless against the marauding troops of Russian prisoners who had been released for military service. In coastal cities like Dairen, SMRC workers vied fiercely for scarce seats on trains and ships leaving for Japan. However, their working-class and rural counterparts, along with Japanese who lacked the proper connections, were much less fortunate. Women blackened their faces to protect them against rape, and men attempted to clothe themselves in Chinese garments. While fleeing toward coastal ports, Japanese mothers left their babies with sympathetic Chinese families, hoping that they could reclaim them once political conditions stabilized. Tragically, these children grew up without knowing their Japanese relatives and were often not reunited until the 1980s, when they were exposed to a culture and language with which they had no contact and from which they felt alienated.[2]

Suk-jung Han and Thomas DuBois argue that,[3] for about five years, Manchukuo had enjoyed a semi-sovereign status; however, the years from 1937 to 1945 were overshadowed by the state's military connections to Imperial Japan during the deepening China conflict. Therefore, after the Soviet invasion and the Japanese surrender, Japan's quick abandonment of the region it had controlled for almost fifteen years highlighted the fact that Manchukuo had very much served as a satellite state. The region was swiftly reabsorbed into China following a few years' occupation by Soviet forces, and it became one of the first to accept communism after the 1948 invasion of the People's Liberation Army. Postwar reconstruction after the founding of the People's Republic of China took precedence over historical reflection on Manchukuo's time under Japanese occupation. In the following decades, the Chinese built on Japan's industrial base in northeast China and began to subscribe to a largely negative discourse on the Japanese occupation, or *lunxian shidai,* which persists into the present.

Many of the Japanese memoirs of the Manchukuo period arose only after the Japanese government's recognition of the People's Republic of China in 1972.[4] A further period of popular reflection in the press and in other accounts occurred in the 1980s due to the media's obsession with the *zanryû kôji,* or "left-behind orphans." The 1990s showed a rapid growth in Japanese scholarly investigations of Manchuria- and Manchukuo-related topics. Since the mid-1990s, when Kawamura Minato and Yamamurô Shin'ichi pioneered scholarship on occupied Manchuria, many new works have appeared in both Japanese and English, centring on Manchuria, Manchukuo, and the Japanese individuals involved in constructing the political, economic, and cultural framework of the region both before and after the Manchukuo period. A veritable *Manshû buumu* (Manchuria boom) has arisen since then, with study groups like the *Manshûkoku bungaku kenkyûkai* (Manchurian Literature Study Group) and others cropping up in the first decade of the twenty-first century. In addition, much to the chagrin of domestic and foreign researchers in Japan, flea market finds and used bookstore materials related to culture in Manchuria and Manchukuo now fetch hefty prices after having sufferred bargain status in the 1980s and earlier.[5] In Tokyo, in the 1990s and early 2000s, Yumani shobô began the trend of publishing works centring on Manchukuo-themed scholarly research and reprints of texts. Recently, the Fuji Publishing Company has also been instrumental in publishing materials pertaining to the study of occupied Manchuria.[6] For example, in 2004, Okamura Keiji published a book listing the organizations collecting Manchukuo-related materials, which includes a discussion of where they are presently archived.[7] As of 2005, the Tokyo-based Colonial Culture Research Group has compiled an important compendium of historical materials on culture in Manchukuo.[8]

In the late 1990s and early 2000s, North American scholars also began examining these issues. More recent studies in Japan and North America (including this one) focus on Manchukuo's culture. This is a growing trend with great interdisciplinary potential. For example, international conferences like the "Confluence of Foreign Cultures in Harbin Symposium" held in July 2008 at the Tokyo University of Foreign Studies, and the July 2009 conference entitled "Early 20th-Century Northeast China and Harbin: Their Social, Cultural, and Political Encounters with the World," jointly organized by the Universität Heidelberg and Heilongjiang University in Harbin, emphasize exchanges between scholars from Asia, Europe, and North America. These efforts by Japanese presses, universities, and research groups point to a growing contemporary scholarly interest in the cultural aspects of this historical moment in Sino-Japanese history, when Japanese ideologues embarked on a utopian nation-building experiment.

Lingering Issues Surrounding Political Conversion

Most of the intellectuals featured in this book did engage in various forms of self-reflection after Japan's defeat, but their published works usually experienced a roughly ten-year time lag. This corresponds with poor publishing conditions, the slow recovery of Japan's art world, and the fact that it was only after the end of the US Occupation that Japanese intellectuals once again felt free to explore wartime topics that might have been subject to American censorship. Moreover, after 1955, a political system arose that emphasized consensus and economic reconstruction, thus helping to temper outward dissent. This allowed some to channel their concerns into an examination of their past. The Liberal Democratic Party, which emerged as the dominant party in postwar democratic Japan, focused largely on centre-right agendas. Moreover, due to American procurements and officers' requisitions, the Japanese economy received a large boost from the 1950-53 Korean War, and ordinary Japanese soon began to feel an improvement in their material conditions. The Korean conflict was even referred to as "a gift from the gods" by Liberal Democratic politicians such as Yoshida Shigeru (1878-1967), who served as prime minister from 1948 to 1954 in one of the longest-running terms in Japan's history. Thus, no longer so concerned with economic survival, Japanese intellectuals could once again devote more of their time to cultural production.

Chapter 6 reveals how a presumably unrepentant Mutô, a former champion of Manchukuo, published his self-reflections in 1951. This was followed by an investigation of his associate Amakasu in 1956 and, less apologetically, a 1988 revisionist account of his time in Manchukuo amidst a rising climate of Japanese exceptionalism.[9] Mutô was relatively quick to reflect on his wartime responsibility, no doubt because his high connections in the Japanese government allowed him a relatively comfortable material life during a time when most Japanese were suffering from severe shortages. It was also much to his advantage to write his initial piece in the early 1950s in order to rehabilitate himself as a self-proclaimed mouthpiece for Japan's Christians. The latter enjoyed good relations with the Americans and were a symbol of a newly democratic postwar Japan.

Intriguingly, it was not until 1957 that Honda Shûgo published his scholarly investigation of the *tenkô* literature phenomenon.[10] By this time, Japan had undergone the "reverse course" and was following a more conservative line of political development. Apparently, this rendered the self-reflections of the left less threatening because now their pronouncements were expressed on paper rather than in the strikes, demonstrations, and marches of the late 1940s and early 1950s. Not surprisingly, amidst a flurry of self-reflection on the part of formerly left-leaning writers, Yamada penned his own treatise on conversion, which appeared in 1958.[11]

Kawabata, on the other hand, due to the privilege his status afforded him, either deliberately hid his involvement with Manchukuo or simply avoided the topic altogether. As an establishment author, his considerable wealth and increasing postwar fame insulated him from some of the worst ravages of postwar reconstruction. Comfortably ensconced in his Kamakura estate, Kawabata shielded himself from Tokyo's distressing rubble and began to complete his masterwork *Yukiguni,* which would later garner him the Nobel Prize in Literature. More tellingly, his earlier *zenshû* did not contain the introduction to his co-edited 1942 collection of multi-ethnic literature in Manchukuo. It was not until the late 1980s, and almost two decades after his death, that it appeared.

Those engaged in artistic production also responded to the Manchukuo experiment in various ways. In the early 1960s, the photographer Fuchikami helped compile nostalgic collections of his work during the Manchukuo period, but they do not reveal the historical context of Japan's occupation of China's northeast; rather, they present images of the period in an evocative, sepia-toned glow. The artists who accompanied Fukuzawa on his trip to Manchukuo also neglected to write postwar accounts of their journey to the region, though both Suzuki and Shimizu had depicted the China conflict as war record artists. Certainly, not all of Japan's cultural producers (including those in some way involved in depicting the Manchukuo experiment) felt the need to reflect, and some, like Kawabata, looked for a way to put the dark memories of defeat behind them.

Others never returned to Japan. Ai Mitsu, for example, had been sent to the front and died for his efforts. As seen in Chapter 4, he perished of illness in a Shanghai hospital before he could reflect on his wartime responsibility, harbouring the psychological disposition of a man torn between two conflicting poles – lack of enthusiasm toward a war he reluctantly supported, while compelled to perform what he perceived as his patriotic duty towards his nation and fallen comrades. This internal struggle, as evidenced in his letters to his wife Kie, contributed to his further debilitation. In addition, the news of the wholesale destruction of Tokyo due to Allied firebombs, as well as the fact that his former hometown had been hit by an atomic bomb, no doubt weighed on him and whittled away any hope of recovery.

As one of the more famous cultural producers investigated in this book, Fukuzawa engaged in his own revisionism when he reinterpreted images from his most famous paintings. Many Japanese artists did this, implying that they had somehow "resisted," and new postwar readings of their work by Japanese curators and art historians also supported this discourse of resistance. As with Kawabata, Fukuzawa's wealth and fame as the artistic voice of Japan's prewar surrealist moment allowed him the luxury of a relatively quick return to his artistic endeavours. In 1948, he completed a painting, *Haisen gunzô (Group Portrait of the Defeated in War),* whose image of writhing humanity echoes a smaller image in his most famous Manchukuo-inspired piece *Ushi.*[12] He later said that these oxen reveal the paper-mâché-like nature of the hollow state, which, like these strong draft animals, only appears to be strong. The heap of bodies represents oppressed labourers. In Fukuzawa's 1948 painting, strong men seem crushed into the ground, oozing blood, while their bodies look like they are in various states of decay, though their muscles still appear well formed. Vast golden plains of sand and foothills on the horizon evoke the borders of southeastern Manchuria.

In sum, it appears that Japanese intellectuals dealt with their wartime responsibility in ways that were in line with their vocations. For example, Mutô, in his new guise as preacher and evangelist, appeared to have a new position that did not differ much from that of propagandist or judge. Kawabata became more comfortable among a literary set that had distanced itself from politics, and, with his rising fame, he decided not to reinvestigate his wartime past but, instead, concentrated on restarting his literary career. Yamada had been imprisoned by the Soviets, and he returned to an early

1950s Japan in which socialists and communists were embraced to showcase the new democracy as well as lauded as exemplars of resistance. No doubt indoctrinated during his imprisonment, Yamada performed a new *tenkô* to conform more to his earlier political ideals, although he now tempered his youthful radicalism of the late 1920s and early 1930s. Yet, the Manchukuo experience seemed to so haunt him that he wrote a novel (which would appear posthumously) exploring Japan's development of biological weapons. Thus, one cannot make one generalization about the formerly left-oriented or avant-garde Japanese cultural producers investigated in this study. Each bears close examination as an individual buffeted by historical forces.

Obviously, the issue of wartime responsibility is not a new one. Nevertheless, earlier Cold War concerns in East Asia waylaid a more nuanced investigation of Japan's wartime past and influenced the postwar creation of a narrative in which a small cabal of militarists led ordinary Japanese astray as "innocent" victims of the imperial state's fascist agenda. The "Economic Miracle" from the mid-1950s into the early 1990s enabled the dominance of the conservative Liberal Democratic Party, which also influenced the collusion of Japanese scholars in presenting an over-simplification of the nation's prewar and wartime past. Even in Japanese secondary literature since the 1980s, many authors still propose a paradigm of resistance versus collaboration. However, with the attenuation of Cold War tensions following the 1989 fall of the Berlin Wall and the early 1990s dissolution of the Soviet Union, scholars have begun to challenge this conceit.

English-language materials on Japan from the last two decades also reveal this growing trend. A few of these are worth highlighting for how they complicate the binary view of resistance/collaboration and complement the issues I raise in my own research. In 1994, Sheldon Garon showed how, in the interwar and wartime periods, a shared discourse of modernity and modernization motivated Japanese from both sides of the political spectrum to support various state reform initiatives.[13] Garon's argument also applies to my study of why intellectuals of both left-wing and right-wing orientations supported the Manchukuo project, emphasizing a trail-blazing model of East Asian modernity. Appearing in 2003, Curtis Anderson Gayle's investigation reveals that the desire of Japanese Marxist historians to create a "collective national consciousness," or *minzoku isshiki,* to further social revolution in the post-Occupation period actually homogenized views of the past by privileging a certain discourse. This was because many believed "the Japanese nation could best lay claim to a new domain of political resistance by demarcating cultural authenticity in terms of national history and an elaborate cultural past."[14] Intriguingly, here individuals from both the left and more conservative political orientations could concur, and even collaborate, in the postwar Japanese project of national reconstruction and the rebuilding of a "healthy" self-image. *Minzoku isshiki,* this precursor to the 1970s and 1980s discourse of *Nihonjinron,* or "theories of Japaneseness," also affected reflections on individual wartime responsibility, especially in relation to other Asian nations and Japan's Manchukuo experiment. Not surprisingly, the breakdown of *Nihonjinron* after the burst of the economic bubble and the challenge to Liberal Democratic dominance in 1993 also corresponded with the rise of the "Manchuria boom."

In 2005, Samuel Yamashita published an important study investigating the various ways ordinary Japanese subjects both supported the war effort and passively resisted it, especially by writing diaries, in what Samuel Hynes calls "small acts of resistance."[15] By using individual narratives composed during an anxiety-ridden time, Yamashita's text displays a complicated and, indeed, realistic view of the conflicted nature of support for Imperial Japan's wartime endeavours. These are merely a few of the growing numbers of studies that examine wartime responsibility among Japanese, revealing debates that, in this book, I hope to extend to research on Japanese intellectuals and Manchukuo.

Scholarly Contributions and Points of Departure

One of the key points that I highlight is the fact that these Japanese intellectuals were, for the most part, drawn to Manchukuo rather than pushed out of an increasingly politically inhospitable Japan. Many of the more liberal members of prewar Japan enthusiastically supported the Manchukuo political experiment, while others were attracted to the prospect of creating the new state's culture along lines that were not tenable in domestic Japan. Participating in the task of utopian image formation allowed them to project various dreams onto the Manchurian canvas – an idea first articulated by Louise Young in English-language scholarship. My own work shows how the multifaceted visions of East Asian modernity "discovered" by certain Japanese intellectuals in Manchukuo compelled them to produce works supportive of the new state regardless of their earlier anti-imperialist, left-wing views. Because they created these images as a "reflected utopia," their cultural production intersected with Imperial Japan's official propaganda efforts and revealed how the arts were used to glorify the Empire. This process intensified after 1938, when cultural representations with a Manchurian theme accelerated, especially in literature.

Here, I show that the Japanese framers of the Manchukuo project attracted formerly left-wing cultural producers to create positive accounts of the state's modernization program and, thereby, fought an ideological propaganda war that, through culture, was ultimately supportive of imperialist expansionism. Intriguingly, the "avant-garde" propaganda they produced in the form of essays, short stories, oil paintings, sketches, and photographs reflects a complicated picture of complicity with, and ambivalence toward, the colonialist project in Japanese-occupied northeast China. These contradictory images, and the subjects that were omitted, offer a reasonably accurate view of Japanese representations of the colonies in the interwar and wartime periods.

I hope that this book will prompt a flurry of scholarship on "unofficial" forms of Japanese Manchukuo-themed propaganda by North American, Japanese, Chinese, and Korean scholars specializing in cultural history and literary studies as well as art history. In various archives scattered throughout Japan and the United States, Manchukuo-related materials are so copious in both Japanese and English that the portion of sources partially covered in my work is just the tip of a very deep iceberg. Due to the materials I have chosen, this book is somewhat biased toward a Japanese point of view, and it should be read as an attempt to put these materials into their proper historical context rather than as an attempt at historical revisionism. Other than a series of short research trips to archives and historical sites in Dairen, Harbin, and Tieli, and interaction with a limited number of Chinese informants, most of my sources were procured in Japan and the United States, with my ideas being formed, in part, during discussions with Japanese scholars and their North American counterparts.[16]

It would be of much scholarly interest to determine contemporaneous Chinese reactions to the images in *Manshû gurafu,* the paintings produced by Fukuzawa and his associates, and the stories written by Yamada and Mutô. The latter two began their careers as figures who were essentially on opposite sides of the political spectrum, but they met as cultural collaborators in the Manchukuo context. Was their audience comprised exclusively of Japanese- and English-speaking Westerners? What impact might the distribution channels of various media, or the display of art, have had on how the Chinese received their works? How and what did the Chinese think of them? All of these questions are important points of departure, and I hope that this book will help to stimulate further research on these topics.

Notes

Introduction

1 I use the term "Manchukuo" to refer to this nominally independent nation established in 1932 because it is the term most commonly used in English-language scholarship. In Japanese, the term is *Manshûkoku,* and in Chinese, it is *Manzhouguo,* usually prefaced by *wei* (false). Prior to 1932, most sources in Japanese refer to this region in northeast China as *Manshû,* or "Manchuria" (its English translation). Prewar English-language sources use the Japanese convention, which implies a false distinction between Manchukuo and China. If they made any distinction between China and Manchukuo at all, republican-era Chinese sources and Chinese people referred to the latter as *Dongbei,* or "the Northeast." I use the pre-1932 term "Manchuria" because this is the term the intellectuals whom I investigate commonly used to refer to the geographical area of northeast China (not the post-1932 Japanese-run state) both before and after 1932. For more about the nomenclature of Manchukuo, see Prasenjit Duara, *Sovereignty and Authenticity: Manchukuo and the East Asian Modern* (Lanham, MD: Rowman and Littlefield, 2003); Gavan McCormack, "Manchukuo: Constructing the Past," *East Asian History* 2 (1991), 105-24; and Yamamurô Shin'ichi, *Kimera: Manshûkoku no shôzô* [Chimera: A portrait of Manchukuo] (Tokyo: Chûô kôronsha, 1993).

2 Kawamura Minato, "One View of the History of Japanese Proletarian Literature: On Nogawa Takashi," David Rosenfeld trans., essay delivered at the Proletarian Literatures of East Asia Symposium, University of Chicago, 2002, 1-4.

3 Donald Keene, *Dawn to the West: Japanese Literature of the Modern Era – Fiction* (New York: Holt, Rinehart, and Winston, 1984), 847. For more about *tenkô,* or political conversion, in the literary work or personal "confessions" of formerly left-wing Japanese writers and intellectuals, see Honda Shûgo, *Tenkô bungaku-ron* [Discourse on political conversion literature] (Tokyo: Mirai-sha, 1957). Keene cites this figure from Honda.

4 Louise Young, *Japan's Total Empire: Manchuria and the Culture of Wartime Imperialism* (Berkeley: University of California Press, 1998), 282-302. See also Yamamurô Shin'ichi's seminal analysis of occupied Manchuria (Yamamurô, *Kimera*), which concurs with Young's conclusion.

5 Sheldon Garon, "Rethinking Modernization and Modernity in Japanese History: A Focus on State-Society Relations," *Journal of Asian Studies* 53, 2 (1994): 346-56.

6 Joshua Fogel, trans., *Life along the South Manchurian Railway: The Memoirs of Itô Takeo* (New York: M.E. Sharpe, 1988), xv-xvi, 12.

7 When I use the term "cultural production," I am assuming Pierre Bourdieu's appropriation of Karl Marx's base and superstructure argument. The superstructure, of which intellectuals are a part, is informed by transformations in a socio-economic landscape, or base, converging with politics.

8 See Takeba Jô, *Ikyô no modanizumu: Fuchikami Hakuyô to Manshû shashin sakka kyokai* [Modernism on foreign soil: Fuchikami Hakuyô and the Manchuria Photographic Artists Association] (Nagoya: Nagoya City Museum of Art, 1994).

9 Alan Tansman, *The Aesthetics of Japanese Fascism* (Berkeley: University of California Press, 2009), 12.

10 Founded in 1932 to serve as an organ of mass mobilization, the Concordia Association disseminated official and unofficial propaganda directly to the Manchukuo public. Its members initially included government officials and educators, but soon extended to others with varying levels of political enthusiasm. After April 1937, all youth aged sixteen to nineteen were forced to join its Youth League.

11 Barak Kushner, *The Thought War: Japanese Imperial Propaganda* (Honolulu: University of Hawaii Press, 2006), 19 (emphasis mine).

12 Ibid.

13 Chapter 1 discusses what modernism and avant-garde meant in interwar Japan and how they were expressed in the Manchukuo context.

14 Peter O'Connor, "General Introduction: Japanese Propaganda Books in the Modern Period – Writing against the Tide," in *Japanese Propaganda: Selected Readings, Series 1 – Books 1872-1943,* ed. Peter O'Connor (Kent, UK: Global Oriental, 2004), 9.

15 Young, *Japan's Total Empire,* 68.

16 O'Connor, "General Introduction," 9.

17 Ibid.

18 Ibid., 17.

19 Young, *Japan's Total Empire,* 69.

20 Jacqueline Atkins, *Wearing Propaganda: Textiles on the Home Front in Japan, Britain, and the United States* (New Haven: Yale University Press, 2005). More recently, inspired by Atkins's pioneering work, Kushner wrote the introduction to an exhibition catalogue featuring the MHJ Collection for the "Dreams of Empire: Japanese Propaganda Textiles" exhibition at the San Francisco Arts of the Pacific Asia Show held in February 2011. See Barak Kushner, *Dreams of Empire: Japanese Propaganda Textiles* (Waregem, BE: Cassochrome, 2011). I thank Kushner for pointing out Atkins's catalogue, and for sending me the above catalogue.

21 See Kushner, "A Funny Thing Happened to Me on the Way to the Front," in Kusnher, *Thought War,* 85-116.

22 Ibid., 6.

23 For sources on Japanese wartime propaganda in Manchukuo written by Japanese scholars, see Kishi Toshihiko, "Fusion and Crack between Cultural Policy and Placation Policy in Manchukuo," Ten Thousand Shares Research *Journal of Manchurian Studies* October (2007): 93-129, available at http://www.earticle.net/. For information on Manchukuo's propaganda system before 1937, see Hirano Ken'ichirô, ed., *Nitchû sensôki no Chûgoku ni okeru shakai bunka henyô* [The Acculturation of Society and Culture in China during the Sino-Japanese Period] (Tokyo: Tôyô Bunko, 2007). See also Kobayashi Hideo, *Teikoku Nihon to sôryokusen taisei* [Imperial Japan and the total war system] (Tokyo: Yûshi-sha, 2004); Yamamoto Taketoshi, "The Japanese Army's Radio Strategy in Manchuria," the Institute of 20th-Century Media, Waseda University, at http://www.waseda.jp/; and Yamamurô, *Kimera.* For sources in Chinese, see Feng Weiqun, "'Wenyi zhidao gangyao' chulong yihou" [After the appearance of the summary of guidelines to art and literature] in *Weiman wenhua* [Manchukuo culture] volume 6 of the *Weiman shiliao congshu* [Series of Manchukuo historical materials], eds. Sun Bang and Yu Haiying, (Changchun: Jilin Renmin Chubanshe, 1993), 13-14; and Kazeta Eiki, "Wei Manzhouguo wenyi zhengce de zhankai" [The development of bogus Manchukuo's literary rules and regulations], in *Dongbei lunxian shiqi wenxue guoji xueshu yantaohui lunwenji* [Collection of papers from the International Symposium on Literature of the Enemy-Occupied Northeast], ed. Feng Weiqun, Wang Jianzhong, Li Chunyan, and Li Shuquan, 156-81 (Shenyang: Shenyang chubanshe, 1992).

24 See Kishi Toshihiko, *Manshûkoku no bijyuaru.medeia* [Manchukuo's visual media (subtitled in English as *Manchuria's Graphic Media Empire*)] (Tokyo: Yoshikawa kôbun-kan, 2010).

25 Unfortunately, this database no longer exists under the auspices of Kanagawa University in Yokohama, Japan.

26 Lincoln Cushing and Ann Thompkins, *Chinese Posters: Art from the Great Proletarian Cultural Revolution* (San Francisco: Chronicle Books, 2007), 10-11.

27 Of course, consumption or viewing of these various visual media does not necessarily mean agreement with the ideological aims of the regime.
28 See also Igor Golomstock, *Totalitarian Art in the Soviet Union, the Third Reich, Fascist Italy, and the People's Republic of China* (New York: Icon [Harpe], 1990 [Overlook Press, 2011]). Golomstock, during his tenure as a docent in the Pushkin Museum during the 1950s, observed that young Russian children often did not know the difference between depictions of Soviet heroes and images of Hitler. This led him to postulate that a kind of heroic realism animated much of totalitarian art, regardless of the regime's fascist or communist nature. This imagery became common and familiar to its viewers, thus serving as an important propaganda vehicle.
29 Kushner, *Thought War,* 9.
30 Alan Tansman, *The Aesthetics of Japanese Fascism* (Berkeley: University of California Press, 2009), 1.
31 Ibid.
32 For example, a substantial rise in Manchukuo-themed literary materials begins in 1939 (29) and reaches a peak in 1943 (59); despite dropping by over half in 1945 (21), they are still higher than they were in 1938 (14). Just these few statistics underline the importance of literary production to the Manchukuo regime and constitute a flood of informal propaganda on the part of Japanese writers. See *Shokuminchi bunka kenkyûkai* [Colonial Culture Research Group], ed., *"Manshûkoku" bunka saimoku* [An outline of culture in Manchukuo] (Tokyo: Fuji shuppan, 2005), 4. These years also correspond to Mutô Tomio's term as propaganda chief and evince his furthering of Japanese intellectuals and others involved in literary production in or about Manchukuo. I examine this issue in chapters 2, 6, and 7.
33 Chairman Mao believed that revolutionary culture "prepares the ground ideologically before the revolution comes and is an important, indeed essential, fighting front in the general revolutionary front during the revolution." Quoted in Cushing and Thompkins, *Chinese Posters,* 7. Originally from Beijing Foreign Languages Press, ed., *Quotations from Chairman Mao Tse-tung* (first English edition, Beijing: Beijing Foreign Languages Press, 1966), 199.
34 Kurehara Korehito, "Musankaikyû geijutsu undô no shin dankai" [A new stage in the proletarian arts], *Zen'ei: Musankaikyû geijutsu zasshi* [Avant-Garde: Proletarian arts magazine], January 1928, 17-24.
35 To my knowledge, a *comprehensive* English-language monograph of Japanese proletarian culture and the arts has not yet been published, with the exception of the special edition on "Proletarian Arts in East Asia: Quests for National, Gender, and Class Justice," compiled by Heather Bowen-Struyk, guest editor, *positions: east asia cultures critique* 14, 2 (2006). Ken Kawashima's study on Korean labour illuminates Korean working-class culture in Japan from a sociological and political standpoint but does not cover Japanese left-wing literature or the arts in a more general fashion. See Ken Kawashima, *The Proletarian Gamble: Korean Workers in Interwar Japan* (Durham, NC: Duke University Press, 2009). However, in Japan, many recent reprints of original proletarian texts have been issued by such left-oriented centres as the Ohara Institute of Social Research. Most reprints of Manchukuo materials are currently published by Fuji shuppan.
36 In the context of wartime Japan, Zeljko Cipris proposes that "such factors as jingoism, combative egos, power worship, or considerations of profit and prestige ensure that numerous academics, journalists, writers, and critics will pronounce eloquently in favor of the warring state and exhort their compatriots to back it without question." See Zeljko Cipris, "Responsibility of Intellectuals: Kobayashi Hideo on Japan at War," *Japan Focus,* available at http://old.japanfocus.org/.
37 Kushner defines "imperial propaganda" as the intersection of empire and propaganda (emphasis mine). Kushner, *Thought War,* 11.

Chapter 1: Laying the Groundwork for the Japanese Avant-Garde Propagandists

1 For further information on SMRC's founding, organizational structure, funding, and political planning, see Ramon H. Myers, "Japanese Imperialism in Manchuria: The South Manchurian Railway Company, 1906-1933," in *The Japanese Informal Empire in China, 1895-1937,* ed.

Peter Duus, Ramon H. Myers, and Mark R. Peattie, 101-32 (Princeton: Princeton University Press, 1989). See also South Manchuria Railway Company, *Fifth Report on Progress in Manchuria to 1936* (Dairen: South Manchuria Railway Company, 1936); and Nishizawa Yasuhiko, *Mantetsu: "Manshû" no kyôjin* [The South Manchurian Railway Company: Manchuria's giant] (Tokyo: Kawade shobô, 2000).

2 Myers, "Japanese Imperialism in Manchuria," 104.

3 Nishizawa, *Mantetsu,* 23.

4 Ibid.

5 Ibid.

6 Ibid.

7 In contemporary times, pollution has yellowed and corroded this once imposing limestone structure, which houses the records of SMRC and its associated research department as a historical archive maintained by the Chinese government.

8 Bruce A. Ellerman and Stephen Kotkin, eds. *Manchurian Railways and the Opening of China: An International History,* (Armonk, NY: M.E. Sharpe, 2010), 195.

9 South Manchuria Railway Company, *Manshû gurafu* [Manchuria graph] 3, 5 (1936): N.p.

10 Y. Tak Matsusaka, "Japan's South Manchuria Railway Company in Northeast China, 1906-34," in Ellerman and Kotkin, *Manchurian Railways,* 42.

11 In 1928, Kantô Army officers plotted the assassination of Zhang Zuolin (1875-1928), a powerful Manchurian warlord who governed northeast China, which was allied to Chiang's weak republic. After his train car passed over SMRC track near Shenyang, a bomb exploded in his compartment. Due to the delayed Japanese response to his medical care, Zhang later died from his injuries. The Kantô Army eliminated him because, in allying with Chiang and encouraging the construction of parallel rail lines by Chinese firms, he was perceived to be a threat to SMRC and, thus, to broader Japanese strategic interests in the region. His son, Zhang Xueliang (1898-2001), a womanizer who was addicted to heroin and living in self-imposed exile in Paris, was not viewed as a competent replacement for his father. The Japanese referred to him as "the Young Marshal," and the Kantô Army believed that, on his return after his father's assassination, he could be easily manipulated. This turned out to be a grave miscalculation since Emperor Hirohito (1901-89) ultimately condemned the manouevre as an act of insubordination, and no further military operations ensued. The fallout from this incident brought down the Tanaka cabinet.

12 Three years later, following the 1931 Manchurian Incident, when Kantô Army conspirators once again planted a bomb on SMRC tracks near Chinese barracks in Shenyang, the imperial throne did nothing to prevent the escalation of an event blamed on Chinese guerrillas.

13 Kobayashi Hideo, *Mantetsu: "Chi no shûdan" no tanjô to shi* [The South Manchuria Railway Company: The birth and death of the knowledgeable group] (Tokyo: Hirofumi-kan, 1996), 39-41. See also Joshua Fogel, trans., *Life along the South Manchurian Railway: The Memoirs of Itô Takeo* (New York: M.E. Sharpe, 1988), 13-15.

14 Myers, "Japanese Imperialism in Manchuria," 126.

15 See Joshua Fogel, *The Literature of Travel in the Japanese Rediscovery of China, 1862-1945* (Stanford: Stanford University Press, 1996).

16 Joshua A. Fogel, "Japanese Literary Travelers in Prewar China," *Harvard Journal of Asiatic Studies* 49, 2 (1989): 580.

17 *Manchuria: Semi-Monthly Publication of the Manchuria Daily News* (December 1936), back of cover page.

18 South Manchuria Railway Company, *Fifth Report,* 144.

19 Today, one can still visit or stay at the hotel, christened *Dalian binguan* (Dalian Guesthouse) after the region was incorporated into Communist China. From 1945 to 1954, the Soviets used it as their occupation headquarters, and the smell of cigars seems to linger deep into the night in suites laden with heavy maroon velvet furniture covered with delicate white crocheted doilies. After coming into contact with ghosts of the past while viewing the prewar photographs hanging on the walls, guests can now sit in the postcolonial dining room and eat a hearty Chinese-style breakfast.

20 For a reprint in Japanese, see Natsume Sôseki, *Man Kan tokoro dokoro* [Here and there in Manchuria and Korea] (Tokyo: Aozora bunko [Internet Archive], 1999), available at http://

www.archive.org/. An English translation of this travelogue can be found in Inger Brody, ed., *Rediscovering Natsume Sôseki: With the First English Translation of Travels in Manchuria and Korea,* trans. Inger Brody and Samuel T. Tsunematsu (London: Global Oriental, 2000).

21 On my first trip to Harbin by air in January 2000, I was greeted by the quaint English-language sign, "Harbin – A Civilized Airport." No doubt, much was lost in translation, but it shows how, in developing the northeast, even the current PRC government is concerned with communicating a discourse of modernity not unlike that communicated by the Japanese in prewar times.

22 Uchida Michio, "Natsume Sôseki in Manchuria and Korea," *Acta Asiatica: Bulletin of the Institute of Eastern Culture* 79 (2000): 2.

23 According to Uchida ("Natsume Sôseki," 16): "Sôseki's tour through Manchuria and Korea had its origins in an unreflecting dependence on state demands aiming at Western modernization and an advance into the Asian continent, and naturally, and also regrettably, *Man Kan tokoro dokoro* turned into a work marked throughout by the arrogance and insensitiveness toward the people of Asia to which many Japanese were prone."

24 Upper-class Chinese also expressed disdain for their country's lowest classes. However, if an observer was Japanese, his view already contained an element of imperialistic superiority, especially if he had been invited to the region specifically to observe Japanese development schemes.

25 See Lao She, *Rickshaw Boy* (New York: Reynal and Hitchcock, 1945). The author began the novel in 1936, after which it was serialized in the Chinese magazine Yuzhoufeng from January 1937.

26 See Pearl S. Buck, *The Good Earth* (New York: John Day Company, 1931).

27 For more on how Kitagawa and Anzai viewed colonial Manchuria, see Annika A. Culver, "Colonial Manchuria in the Surrealist Imagination: The Poetry and Prose of Kitagawa Fuyuhiko as Modernist History," *Proceedings of the Association for Japanese Literary Studies* 4 (2003): 264-77; and Annika A. Culver, "Two Japanese Avant-Garde Writers' Views of Gender Relations and Colonial Oppression in Manchuria, 1929-1931," *US-Japan Women's Journal* 37 (2009): 91-116.

28 Fogel, *Life along the South Manchurian Railway,* 31.

29 See Annika A. Culver, "The Making of a Japanese Avant-Garde in Dairen, 1924-1937," *History Compass* 2 (2007): 347-61.

30 "Colonial encounter" and "contact zone" are two phrases created by Mary Louise Pratt. See Mary Louise Pratt, "Introduction: Criticism in the Contact Zone," in *Imperial Eyes: Travel Writing and Transculturation* (New York: Routledge, 1992), 6.

31 This phrase appears in Seiji Lippit, *Topographies of Japanese Modernism* (New York: Columbia University Press, 2002), 75.

32 Oguma Eiji, *A Genealogy of Japanese Self-Images,* trans. David Askew (Melbourne, AU: Trans-Pacific Press, 2002), 64-81. See also the Japanese original, Oguma Eiji, *Tan'itsu minzoku shinwa no kigen: "Nihonjin" no jigazô no keifu* [The origins of the myth of the homogenous nation: A genealogy of Japanese self-images] (Tokyo: Shinyôsha, 1995), 101.

33 A fascination for the abject on the part of left-oriented Japanese can be viewed as an alternative to the shiny perfection of a capitalist-driven bourgeois modernity. Leftists like Hayashi Fumiko (1904-51) saw Dairen as a stepping-stone for a grand tour through the new Soviet Union, which she planned to take once conditions stabilized under Lenin's 1924 New Economic Plan.

34 Maruyama Masao, "The Ideology and Dynamics of Japanese Fascism," in *Thought and Behavior in Modern Japanese Politics,* ed. Ivan Morris (London: Oxford University Press, 1963), 82-83.

35 Ibid., 35.

36 Ibid., 36-38.

37 According to Maruyama (*Thought and Behavior,* 82): "One cannot overlook the significance of the conversion to fascism within the proletarian movement. As I have said before, this was performed by the Akamatsu and Kamei group in the Social Mass Party and groups like Asô's, which led the Labor-Peasant Party and its successors ... With the decline of party politics in Japan the social elements that had made up the lobbyist groups largely flowed

into the right-wing societies ... The leaders of Japanese fascism were not obliged to manipulate or counter any strong proletarian movement; and, in the absence of a *bourgeois* democratic background, they were able to effect a comparatively smooth consolidation."

38 In Chapter 2, I further discuss the rise of left-wing activism and the Japanese proletarian movements in the late 1920s.

39 Matsuoka Yôsuke (1880-1946), who would enjoy a term as SMRC president beginning in 1935, originally coined the *seimeisen* concept.

40 Yuma Totani, "20th Century Japanese History: From Meiji to Heisei," lecture delivered at the Asian Studies Development Program ("Infusing Asian Studies into the Curriculum"), East West Center, Honolulu, Hawaii, June 2009.

41 Nishizawa Yasuhiko believes that, without SMRC's power and aid, the Kantô Army could never have set up the Manchurian Incident, and the founding of Manchukuo would never have taken place. The Kantô Army had its origin in a small police force that was maintained to patrol SMRC-administered portions of track that Japan had garnered after the Russo-Japanese War. See Nishizawa, *Mantetsu,* 70.

42 Prasenjit Duara, *Sovereignty and Authenticity: Manchukuo and the East Asian Modern* (Lanham, MD: Rowman and Littlefield, 2003), 1.

43 See Akira Iriye, *After Imperialism: The Search for a New Order in the Far East, 1921-1931* (New York: Imprint Publications, 1990).

44 Herbert Bix, *Hirohito and the Making of Modern Japan* (New York: Harper Collins, 2000), 245.

45 Condemned by the League of Nations as a violation of international law, Manchukuo was only recognized as an independent nation by five of thirteen countries: Japan, fascist Italy, Nazi Germany, Ecuador, and the Vatican.

46 Though Manchukuo was technically framed as an independent nation, the Kantô Army operated under, and served as a symbol of, Japanese authority. In addition, every Chinese official in the Manchukuo government was subject to the command of a higher Japanese leader. As a border region touching China (south of the Great Wall), Mongolia, and the Soviet Union, Manchuria was portrayed by the Japanese imperial government as being plagued by bandits *(hizoku)* and threatened by communist guerrillas. Thus, the Japanese military and the *Kempeitai* constituted a visible presence whose purpose was to ensure political stability for Japanese colonists and wealthy Chinese who chose to collaborate with the regime to protect their assets.

47 Thomas David Dubois, "Inauthentic Sovereignty: Law and Legal Institutions in Manchukuo," *Journal of Asian Studies* 69, 3 (2010): 749. I thank Ron Suleski for pointing out this source.

48 Ibid.

49 Ibid.

50 Bix, *Hirohito,* 188

51 Ibid.

52 Tsukase Susumu, *Manshûkoku: "Minzoku kyôwa" no jitsuzô* [Manchukuo: A true portrait of ethnic/racial harmony] (Tokyo: Yoshikawa kôbun-kan, 1998), 19-21.

53 Gregory Kasza, *The State and the Mass Media in Japan, 1918-1945* (Berkeley: University of California, 1988), 48-51. For example, the centre left-oriented integrated magazine *Chûô kôron (Central Review)* initially criticized the Manchurian Incident, carrying articles by Inomata Tsunao and Yoshino Sakuzô; however, state censors later steered it in a more moderate direction. In his article, Yoshino notes that "behind the passivity of the press was also a dearth of dissension in civil society." See Yoshino Sakuzô, "Minzoku to kaikyû to sensô" [Nations, classes, and war], *Chûô kôron* [Central Review] (January 1932), 50. However, by 1932, most journals, magazines, and news organs either did not criticize the Manchurian Question or actively supported state recognition of Manchukuo.

54 See Louise Young, "War Fever," in *Japan's Total Empire: Manchuria and the Culture of Wartime Imperialism* (Berkeley: University of California Press, 1998), 55-114.

55 Sandra Wilson, "The Past in the Present: War in the Narratives of Modernity in the 1920s and 1930s," in *Being Modern in Japan: Culture and Society from the 1910s to the 1930s,* ed. Elise K. Tipton and John Clark (Honolulu: University of Hawaii Press, 2000), 179. In total, Japan lost around eighty thousand soldiers, with about 120,000 wounded. Total casualties reached up to 200,000 (in a conflict actually fought over control of Korea).

56 Tsukase, *Manshûkoku,* 18.

57 Kimura Ryôji, *Dairen monogatari* [A tale of Dairen] (Tokyo: Kenkôsha, 1974), 11 (my translation).

58 Wilson, "Past in the Present," 183.

59 See Faye Yuan Kleeman, "Inscribing Manchuria: Gender, Ideology, and Popular Imagination," *East Asian History* 30 (2005): 47-66.

60 Parts of this section are adapted from Annika A. Culver, "'Between Distant Realities': The Japanese Avant-Garde, Surrealism, and the Colonies, 1924-1943" (PhD diss., University of Chicago, 2007), 50-61.

61 See Ibid.; Culver, "Colonial Manchuria in the Surrealist Imagination; Culver, "Making of a Japanese Avant-Garde; Annika A. Culver, "Modernity in Conflict: Destabilizing Images of the Modern in the Poetry of Kitagawa Fuyuhiko" (MA thesis, University of Chicago, 2002).

62 See Omuka Toshiharu and Mizusawa Tsutomu, eds., *Modanizumu/nashonarizumu: 1930 nendai Nihon no geijutsu* [Modernism/nationalism: Japanese art of the 1930s] (Tokyo: Serika shobô, 2003).

63 Gennifer Weisenfeld, ed., "Guest Editor's Introduction," in "Visual Cultures of Japanese Imperialism," special issue, *positions: east asia cultures critique* 8, 3 (2000), 595: 591-603. This phrase, which belongs to Raymond Williams, is quoted in John Tomlinson, *Cultural Imperialism* (Baltimore: Johns Hopkins University Press, 1991), 5.

64 Raymond Williams, "Metropolitan Perceptions and the Emergence of Modernism," in *The Politics of Modernism: Against the New Conformists* (London: Verso Books, 1989), 44.

65 Ibid.

66 Mary Louise Pratt defines contact zones as "multidimensional spaces within which subjects on all sides are constituted in and by their relations with others." See Mary Louise Pratt, "Introduction: Criticism in the Contact Zone," in *Imperial Eyes: Travel Writing and Transculturation* (London: Routledge, 1992), 6.

67 Karen Thornber defines this term as "the physical and creative spaces where dancers, dramatists, musicians, painters, sculptors, writers, and other artists from cultures/nations in unequal power relationships grapple with and transculturate one another's creative output." See Karen Laura Thornber, *Empire of Texts in Motion: Chinese, Korean, and Taiwanese Transculturations of Japanese Literature* (Cambridge, MA: Harvard University Press, 2009), 2.

68 Williams, *Politics of Modernism,* 44. Williams's study is also relevant to my investigation of the cultural relationship between originally Tokyo-based Japanese intellectuals and Manchukuo, which is seen as part of the Japanese Empire. In various chapters, I examine the historical context and works of these formerly avant-garde cultural producers. I believe that Pratt's notion that the centre was informed by the periphery during the age of imperialism is especially relevant to Japanese cultural production as it relates to Manchukuo. Indeed, since the early part of the twentieth century, Japanese avant-garde authors and artists, in observing the Empire's periphery and engaging in travel writing or creating art depicting the "otherness" of the East Asian continent, have evinced this concept. In analyzing what "avant-garde" means in the Manchukuo context, I must address the distinction between modernism and avant-garde. This is why, in my title, I place "avant-garde" within quotation marks and identify the works of these Japanese writers, artists, and photographers as "modernist," thus emphasizing their collaborative, rather than their radical, political tendencies. For my discussion of "modernism" and "avant-garde," I rely on the works of Raymond Williams, Peter Bürger, and Andrew Hewitt.

69 Williams, *Politics of Modernism,* 33.

70 This phrase is part of Wesley Sasaki-Uemura's discussion of Pratt's phrase "contact zones" in the context of labour activist Tanigawa Gan's organization of miners' unions in early postwar Japan. His assessment would certainly also be relevant to the colonial space on the East Asian continent. See Wesley Sasaki-Uemura, "Tanigawa Gan's Politics of the Margins in Kyushu and Nagano," *positions: east asia cultures critique* 7, 1 (1999): 137-38.

71 "Distant realities" is a phrase used by Miryam Sas to describe the position of Japanese surrealist writers. She notes that "a vision of alterity, a foreign space located somewhere 'beyond,' plays a crucial role in formulations of avant-garde praxis for both the Japanese and French contexts." However, I believe that "distant realities" could also refer to the positions

of the colonies (or Manchuria/Manchukuo) and domestic Japan, modernity and "tradition," East and West, or the bourgeoisie and the proletariat. See Miryam Sas, *Fault Lines: Cultural Memory and Japanese Surrealism* (Stanford, CA: Stanford University Press, 1999), 6; and Culver, "Between Distant Realities," 1.

72 Williams, *Politics of Modernism,* 34.

73 Peter Bürger, *Theory of the Avant-Garde,* trans. Michael Shaw (Minneapolis: University of Minnesota Press, 1984), 22.

74 Ibid.

75 Ibid., 22-24.

76 Ibid., 49.

77 Ibid., 15-34. Art historian T.J. Clark even dates the naissance of modernism (and possibly a European avant-garde) to the French Revolution, with Jacques-Louis David's 1793 painting of an assassinated Marat in his bathtub. See T.J. Clark, *Farewell to an Idea: Episodes from a History of Modernism* (New Haven, CT: Yale University Press, 2001), 15.

78 One of the most obvious differences is that some writers and artists working in the mode of Surrealism had little concern as to whether or not their works were associated with the praxis of everyday life. These people were less politically radical, less interested in creating works for the masses, than the members of the constructivist group MAVO, but their activities still generally fit Bürger's definition of the avant-garde. However, artists like Koga Harue illustrated magazine and book covers, thus enabling a mass audience to appreciate their work. In the early 1930s, in the mass-circulated *Chûô kôron (Central Review),* the poet and short story writer Kitagawa published several stories intended to capture the realities of the colonial space. And, in the early 1920s, at the beginning of his career as a poet, he started the short poetry movement *(tanshi undô)* to reflect a poetic vision of reality that was more closely related to the real-life experience of the modern. See Culver, "Modernity in Conflict."

79 In 1921, Takahashi, naming himself *Dadaisuto* (Dadaist) Shinkichi, handed out informational pamphlets in Hibiya Park, a traditional locus of political protest in Tokyo, to illustrate his Dadaist philosophy, which included a manifesto. He also wrote *Dadaisuto Shinkichi no shi* [The poems of the Dadaist Shinkichi]. If we apply Bürger's definition of the avant-garde, Takahashi can be considered the "first" avant-garde poet in Japan, which is how he is referred to in the reputable *Kôji-en* Japanese dictionary. See Won Ko, *Buddhist Elements in Dada: A Comparison of Tristan Tzara, Takahashi Shinkichi, and Their Fellow Poets* (New York: New York University Press, 1977).

80 In 1909, Marinetti issued his "Manifesto of Futurism" in the Paris newspaper *Le Figaro,* but he later worked in support of Mussolini. See Andrew Hewitt, *Fascist Modernism: Aesthetics, Politics, and the Avant-Garde* (Stanford, CA: Stanford University Press, 1993), 98.

81 Ibid.

82 Ibid.

83 In this sense, Japan followed a trajectory of economic development similar to Europe's, though this was collapsed into the span of several decades rather than nearly two centuries.

84 Mizusawa Tsutomu, curator of the Kamakura Museum of Modern Art, personal interview, Hayama, September 2003; and Williams, *Politics of Modernism,* 67. See also Omuka Toshiharu, "Taishô-ki no shinkô bijutsu undô to 'Gekijô no Sanka'" [The progressive art movement in the Taishô period and the theatre of the Third Section], *Art Vivant* 33 (1989): 89.

85 See Wada Hirofumi, "Dairen no abuan gyarudo to Kitagawa Fuyuhiko" [Dairen's avant-garde and Kitagawa Fuyuhiko] in *Kan* [Area] 10 (2002): 208-17; and Wada Hirofumi, ed., *Nihon no abuan gyarudo* [Japan's avant-garde] (Tokyo: Seikai shisô-sha, 2005), 4-34.

86 See Sas, *Fault Lines;* William Gardner, *Advertising Tower: Japanese Modernism and Modernity in the 1920s* (Cambridge, MA: Harvard University Press, 2006).

87 Gennifer Weisenfeld, *MAVO: Japanese Artists and the Avant-Garde, 1905-1931* (Berkeley: University of California Press, 2002), 2.

88 Wada, *Nihon no abuan gyarudo,* 4-34.

89 Gardner, *Advertising Tower,* 34.

90 John Clark, "Artistic Subjectivity in the Taishô and Early Shôwa Avant-Garde," in *Japanese Art after 1945: Scream against the Sky,* ed. Alexandra Munroe (New York: Harry N. Abrams, 1994), 41.

91 Kanbara Tai writes: "We are youths who intend to proceed bravely, lively, freely, and steadily along the forefront of art with a clear vision and firm belief ... Needless to say we are not a group of old soldiers gathered under the same principle. In order to develop each of our arts, we shall each go the way we desire. If a reason for establishing this group and hereby holding the 1st Exhibition and lecture is required, it is nothing but the enthusiasm and joy of a group of young men who love and respect each other and *want voluntarily to be avant-garde for the era to come."* Quoted in Tanaka Atsushi and Matsumura Eri, eds., *Koga Harue: Sôsaku no purosesu* [Koga Harue: The creative process] (Tokyo: Tokyo National Museum of Modern Art, 1991), 129 (emphasis mine).

92 Munroe, *Japanese Art after 1945,* 22. See also Renato Poggioli, *The Theory of the Avant-Garde,* trans. Gerald Fitzgerald (Cambridge, MA: The Belknap Press of Harvard University Press, 1968), 9.

93 See also Poggioli, *Theory of the Avant-Garde,* 9.

94 Gardner, *Advertising Tower,* 34. See Gardner's discussion of the literary critics Hirabayashi Hatsunosuke and Senuma Shigeki, who were among the few in Japan who used these terms in the late 1920s and early 1930s (Gardner, *Advertising Tower,* 276n52).

95 See Tansman, *Aesthetics of Japanese Fascism.*

96 On 15 March 1928, the Japanese government strengthened the Peace Preservation Law, which made it a crime punishable by death to attack the imperial institution. The government proceeded to make mass arrests of individuals suspected of activities promoting the spread of communism and targeted leftists in Tokyo and other large Japanese cities.

97 See Lu Yuanming, Suzuki Sadami, and Liu Jianhua, eds., *Manshû Rôman* [Manchuria romance (reprint of quarterly review in Manchuria)], vols. 1-7 (Tokyo: Yumani shobô, 2002-3). As co-editor, Suzuki also wrote the critical notes.

Chapter 2: Literature in Service of the State

1 Prasenjit Duara, *Sovereignty and Authenticity: Manchukuo and the East Asian Modern* (Lanham, MD: Rowman and Littlefield, 2003), 17.

2 Louise Young, *Japan's Total Empire: Manchuria and the Culture of Wartime Imperialism* (Berkeley: University of California Press, 1998), 291.

3 Ibid.

4 Much of this section has been adapted from Annika A. Culver, "'Between Distant Realities': The Japanese Avant-Garde, Surrealism, and the Colonies, 1924-1943" (PhD diss., University of Chicago, 2007), 336-43.

5 For more about Japan in the 1920s, see Minami Hiroshi, "Owari ni: Taishô kara Shôwa he" [In conclusion: From Taishô to Shôwa] in Minami Hiroshi, *Taishô bunka* [Taishô culture] (Tokyo: Keisô shobô, 1965), 370-83.

6 The Japanese prime minister Wakatsuki Reijirô (1866-1949) headed this cabinet, which was in existence from 1926 to 1927. In 1931, he acceded to this position the second time with the Minseitô Party, but he resigned after the Manchurian Incident.

7 For an in-depth discussion of this topic, see H.D. Harootunian, *Overcome by Modernity: History, Culture, and Community in Interwar Japan* (Princeton: Princeton University Press, 2000).

8 See Culver, "Between Distant Realities," 45-147, for a lengthy discussion of literary surrealism and its socio-political context in Japan. Surrealism in Japan broke off from literary modernism around 1925, with its proponents viewing it as more radical and politically engaged than the latter. Around 1930, writers such as Kitagawa Fuyuhiko advocated surrealism as a means toward revolution, while castigating what they saw as the growing formalism of the writers associated with the influential poetry journal *Shi to shiron (Poetry and Poetics),* a venue for debates on this avant-garde movement.

9 Yamada had been active in promoting and writing in proletarian-themed publications since their earliest history, beginning in 1923 with the *Tanemaku hito (The Sower)* coterie.

10 See Yamada Seizaburô, *Nihon puroretaria bungei undo shi* [A history of the proletarian literature and arts movement] (Tokyo: Sôbunkaku, 1930).

11 See Yamada Seizaburô, *Nihon puroretaria bungei riron no haten* [The development of the theory of Japanese proletarian literature and arts] (Tokyo: Sôbunkaku, 1931). See also Hisamatsu Sen'ichi and Yoshida Sei'ichi, eds., *Kindai Nihon bungaku jiten* [Dictionary of modern Japanese literature] (Tokyo: Tokyo-dô, 1954), 731.

12 Heather Bowen-Struyk, "Proletarian Arts in East Asia," *Japan Focus,* available at http://www.japanfocus.org/. For an expanded version of this article, see Heather Bowen-Struyk, "Proletarian Arts in East Asia: Quests for National, Gender, and Class Justice," *positions: east asia cultures critique* 14, 2 (2006): 251-76.

13 See Akita Ujaku and Yamada Seizaburô, *Bunka undô-shi* [A history of cultural movements] (Tokyo: Iwanami shôten, 1932).

14 Hisamatsu and Yoshida, *Kindai Nihon bungaku jiten,* 731.

15 Gregory Kasza, *The State and the Mass Media in Japan, 1918-1945* (Berkeley: University of California Press, 1988), 44.

16 Ibid.

17 Selected writings by Kitagawa and his views of labour and colonial Manchuria are discussed in Annika A. Culver, "Colonial Manchuria in the Surrealist Imagination: The Poetry and Prose of Kitagawa Fuyuhiko as Modernist History," *Proceedings of the Association for Japanese Literary Studies* 4 (2003): 264-77.

18 *Tenkô ronsô* [Debates on tenkô (political conversion)] in *Kindai bungaku ronsô jiten* [Dictionary of debates on modern (Japanese) literature], ed. Hasegawa Izumi (Tokyo: Shibun-dô, 1962), 237-38.

19 Ibid., 238. For more about the three general types of *tenkô,* and the postwar debates surrounding this phenomenon, see ibid., 237-40.

20 Donald Keene, *Dawn to the West: Japanese Literature of the Modern Era – Fiction* (New York: Holt, Rinehart, and Winston, 1984), 847. For more about *tenkô,* or political conversion, in the literary works or personal "confessions" of formerly left-wing Japanese writers and intellectuals, see Honda Shûgo, *Tenkô bungaku-ron* [Discourse on political conversion literature] (Tokyo: Mirai-sha, 1957).

21 George Beckman and Genji Okubô, *The Japanese Communist Party, 1922-1945* (Stanford: Standord University Press, 1969), 244.

22 See Yamada Seizaburô, *Jigo zange* [Personal confessions] (Tokyo: Rikugei-sha, 1938).

23 This section developed out of discussions with Kobayashi Hideo of Waseda University in spring 2005. I thank Kobayashi for bringing Ishiwara's cultural initiatives to my attention. Another intriguing place to which Japanese activists on both sides of the political spectrum fled was Shanghai, where the International Settlement also provided a safe haven for their activities. See Joshua A. Fogel, "The Other Japanese Community: Leftwing Japanese Activities in Wartime Shanghai," in *Wartime Shanghai,* ed. Wen-hsin Yeh, 39-56 (Florence, KY: Routledge, 1998).

24 Kobayashi Hideo, *"Manshû" no rekishi* [The history of Manchuria] (Tokyo: Kodansha gendai shinso, 1966, 2004), 231-43.

25 Kawamura mentioned this in his November 2002 speech at a symposium at the University of Chicago. See Kawamura Minato, "One View of the History of Japanese Proletarian Literature: On Nogawa Takashi," trans. David Rosenfeld, paper delivered at the Proletarian Literatures of East Asia Symposium, University of Chicago, 2002.

26 For more on Yamada's postwar reflections on his political conversion, see Yamada Seizaburô, *Tenkô-ki* [Chronicle of a political conversion] (Tokyo: Riron-sha, 1957-58).

27 See Yamada Seizaburô, *Manshûkoku bunka kensetsuron* [Discourse on the construction of culture in Manchukuo] (Shinkyô: Geibun shobô, 1943).

28 See Lu Yuanming, Suzuki Sadami, and Liu Jianhua, eds., *Manshû Rôman* [Manchuria romance (reprint of quarterly review in Manchuria)], vols. 1-7 (Tokyo: Yumani shobô, 2002-3).

29 This will be discussed further in Chapter 7.

30 Elise Tipton, *Modern Japan: A Social and Political History* (London: Routledge, 2002), 115.

31 Ibid., 116.
32 Personal discussion with Kobayashi Hideo at Waseda University, spring 2005.
33 Faye Yuan Kleeman, *Under an Imperial Sun: Japanese Colonial Literature of Taiwan and the South* (Honolulu: University of Hawaii Press, 2003), 65-66.
34 Duara, *Sovereignty and Authenticity,* 62.
35 Young, *Japan's Total Empire,* 267.
36 Duara, *Sovereignty and Authenticity,* 2.
37 See Nishizawa, *Mantetsu,* 70.
38 See Rana Mitter, *The Manchurian Myth: Nationalism, Resistance, and Collaboration in Modern China* (Berkeley: University of California Press, 2000).
39 Young, *Japan's Total Empire,* 69.
40 *Asahi Shimbun, Manchukuo: A Pictorial Record* (Tokyo: Asahi Shimbun Publishing Company, 1934), 1 (emphasis mine).
41 Ibid., 72.
42 Ibid., 16 (emphasis mine).
43 Japanese news media companies like the *Asahi Shimbun* were deeply invested in Japan's imperial thrust into Manchuria and its subsequent control of Manchukuo because they stood to profit from it. Stories of the success of Japan's empire sold copy and stimulated patriotic feelings in ordinary Japanese back in the home islands. See the recent Japanese investigations of this issue, brought out by the Asahi news organization itself. See *Asahi Shimbun "Kenshô. Shôwa hôdô" shuzaiban* [Asahi news "Censorship and Showa period reportage" news coverage team], *Shimbun to Shôwa: Asahi Shimbun "Kenshô. Shôwa hôdô"* [Newspapers and the Shôwa period: Asahi news "censorship and Showa period reportage"] (Tokyo: Asahi Bunko, 2010); and *Asahi Shimbun "Shimbun to sensô" shuzaiban* [Asahi news "newspapers and war news" coverage team]. *Shimbun to sensô (jô)* [Newspapers and war (Vol. 1)] (Tokyo: Asahi Bunko, 2011).
44 See Homi Bhabha, ed., *Nation and Narration* (London: Routledge, 1990).
45 Mary Louise Pratt, *Imperial Eyes: Travel Writing and Transculturation* (London: Routledge, 1992), 6.
46 The Regenstein Library's treasure trove of Japanese materials on Manchukuo, which is mostly geared toward an English-language audience, dates from the mid-1930s. This was when the Japanese government made an effort to legitimize the new state to an international audience that included prominent research universities like the University of Chicago and Harvard University, which boasts a similar cache now stored in the Harvard-Yenching Library.
47 Mark Peattie, *Ishiwara Kanji and Japan's Confrontation with the West* (Princeton, NJ: Princeton University Press, 1975), 253-54.
48 The head of the Manchukuo Publicity and News Bureau would eventually review an individual's résumé and would then consult with General Affairs Board officials and the Kantô Army's Fourth Section. See Mutô Tomio, *Watakushi to Manshûkoku* [Me and Manchukuo] (Tokyo: Bungei shunjû, 1988), 340.
49 Before 1932, it was primarily SMRC that extended invitations to tour Manchuria; after the establishment of Manchukuo, the Kantô Army shared this role. Since SMRC's Dairen inception, these two organizations were intricately linked with regard to propaganda endeavours, with the Kantô Army ensuring the region's defence. Prompted by Ishiwara's seeming welcome in the early 1930s, the SMRC served as a reservoir for Japan's disgraced leftists, while the Kantô Army absorbed extreme rightists who had been kicked out of the archipelago.
50 Yamamoto Taketoshi, "The Japanese Army's Radio Strategy in Manchuria," the Institute of 20th Century Media, available at http://www.waseda.jp/.
51 Yamada Seizaburô, ed., *Man Rô zai Man sakka tanpen senshû* [Anthology of short stories by Manchurian and Russian authors in Manchuria] (Tokyo: Shun'yôdô shoten, 1940), 1.
52 See "Concordia and Culture," special edition, *Manchuria,* 20 July 1938. This edition is discussed in further detail in Chapter 5.
53 Ibid., 1.
54 Ibid.

55 Yamada never uses the term "fascist culture," but, with historical hindsight, I believe it is appropriate, especially considering the fact that the Concordia Association was clearly a fascist organization.

56 Yamada Seizaburô, ed., Introduction, *Nichi Man Rô zai Man sakka tanpen senshû* [Anthology of Short Works by Japanese, Manchurian, and Russian Authors in Manchuria] (Tokyo: Shunyôdô, 1940), 2.

57 Ibid.

58 Tansman's concept of the "fascist moment" evolved from Christopher Bollas's "fascist state of mind," or "an inclination to thoughts, feelings, and acts of binding that purge the mind of the messy diversity of contradictory views and fills the gap left by that purging with 'material icons.'" See Alan Tansman, *The Aesthetics of Japanese Fascism* (Berkeley: University of California Press, 2009), 18-21.

59 Ibid., 18.

60 This appears to be a reference to a Taoist monastery in Cao Xueqin's early Qing-dynasty novel *Hong Lou Meng* [Dream of a red chamber] (1791).

61 Young, *Japan's Total Empire*, 291.

62 *Mutô kôhôsho-chô ni kiku zadankai: Senmon-ka wo tsukuru "bungei shidô yokô" wo megutte* [Round table discussion 1: Inquiring of publicity and news bureau chief Mutô concerning the "prospectus for the guidance of the arts and culture and the creation of specialists"] in *Manshû nichi nichi shimbun* [Manchukuo daily news], 4 July 1941.

63 Norman Smith, *Resisting Manchukuo: Chinese Women Writers under the Japanese Occupation* (Vancouver: UBC Press, 2007), 51.

64 However, this fame would return to haunt them after 1949. Their connections to the Japanese, and suspicions of collaboration, was the death knell of their post-Liberation careers and negatively affected their fate during the Cultural Revolution (1966-76).

65 It was, therefore, not incongruous for Yamada to continue his mission by serving as a co-editor with Kawabata and other famous Japanese or "Manchurian" writers in two collections of multi-ethnic literature (published in 1942 and 1944, respectively) during the intensification of the Japanese military's "advance southward" into Southeast Asia's multi-ethnic territories. In both editions, Gu Ding, a proponent of the *Yiwenzhipai* (Chronicle of the Arts Faction), appeared right after Kishida Kunio (1890-1954) and the former proletarian writer Shimaki, as part of the group of six editors representing multi-ethnic literary endeavours in Manchukuo. This is discussed in Chapter 7.

66 Shimaki Kensaku, *Manshû kikô* [Manchurian travelogue] (Tokyo: 1940), 3-4, Quoted in Donald Keene, *Dawn to the West: Japanese Literature of the Modern Era [Fiction]* (New York: Columbia University Press, 1998), 858.

67 Donald Keene, *So Lovely a Country Will Never Perish* (New York: Columbia University Press, 2010), 130-31.

68 Yamada Seizaburô, "Kaitaku zuihitsu: Hoshi to niji to" [Essay on development: With stars and rainbows] in South Manchuria Railway Company, *Manshû gurafu* [Manchuria graph] 8, 12 (1940): 118 (Yumani shobô reprint, 2008). Tieli is located in northeastern Manchukuo, to the northeast of Harbin, and it was a major site for the state's rural development initiatives in northern Manchuria. Naturally, self-defence against Stalinist Russia to the north played a role in the establishment of this settlement.

69 Yamada Seizaburô, *Kita Man no hito-yo* [A night in northern Manchuria] (Tokyo: Banrikaku, 1941).

70 Yamada Seizaburô, *Hito tsubu no come wo ai-suru kokoro* [A spirit that loves a grain of rice] (Osaka: Osaka-ya gô shoten, 1941).

71 Yamada Seizaburô, *Watakushi no kaitakuchi shuki* [My memoirs of the frontier](Tokyo: Shunyôdô shoten, 1942).

72 Yamada Seizaburô, *Manshûkoku bunka kensetsuron* [Discourse on the construction of culture in Manchukuo] (Shinkyô: Geibun shobô, 1943).

73 Shokuminchi bunka kenkyûkai [Colonial culture research group], ed., *"Manshûkoku" bunka saimoku* [An outline of culture in Manchukuo] (Tokyo: Fuji shuppan, 2005), 694.

74 Indeed, in Japanese, the *kanji* (character) *ken* appears in such words as *kenkoku* (national construction), *kensetsu* (construction of buildings, or ideas), and even *kenkô* (health).

75 After a Manchukuo tour, the former avant-garde author Haruyama Yukio (1902-94) echoed Yamada's concepts in his 1943 *Manshû no bunka* [Manchuria's culture], which also linked cultural construction to versions of Pan-Asianism like those described above. Arguably, in 1942, the establishment author Kawabata first articulated a version of Haruyama's ideas, and Yamada might also have been inspired by Kawabata when he collaborated with him to edit the first compiled volume of multi-ethnic literature (also in 1942). Chapter 7 further discusses these issues.

76 Yamada Seizaburô, *Kenkoku retsuden* [A biography of the construction of the country] (Shinkyô: Manshû shimbun-sha, May 1943); *Kenkoku retsuden* (Shinkyô: Manshû shimbun-sha, October 1943); *Kenkoku retsuden* (Shinkyô: Manshû nippô Shinkyô – sha shuppan-bu, July 1944); *Kenkoku retsuden* (Shinkyô: Manshû nippô-sha, March 1945).

77 Yamada Seizaburô, *Shinsei Chûgoku yûki* [Travelogue in the new China] (Shinkyô: Manshû kôron-sha, 1944).

78 Quoted in *"Manshûkoku" bunka saimoku* [An outline of culture in Manchukuo] (Tokyo: Fuji shuppan, 2005), 701.

79 Yamada Seizaburô, ed., *Zai Man sakka shôsetsu-shû: Rô Sû* [Collection of novels by authors in Manchuria: Lao Song]. (Shinkyô: Tô A bunka tôsho kabushiki gaisha, January 1944).

80 Hisamatsu and Yoshida, *Kindai Nihon bungaku jiten,* 731.

81 Yamada Seizaburô, *Tenkô-ki: Hyôsetsu no jidai* [Record of a political conversion: Period of ice and snow (purification)] (Tokyo: Rironsha, 1958).

82 See Yamada Seizaburô, *Saikinsen gunji saiban: Kiroku shôsetsu* [Military tribunal on biological warfare: A documentary novel] (Tokyo: Tôhô shuppansha, 1974).

83 See Frederick Dickinson, "Biohazard: Unit 731 in Postwar Japanese Politics of National 'Forgetfulness,'" *Japan Focus,* available at http://japanfocus.org.

Chapter 3: Surrealism in Service of the State

1 Correspondence with Otani Shôgo, August, 2012. See also Haruwara Shinobu, "Shimizu Toshi nikki no kenkyû: 15 nen sensôki wo chûshin ni" [Research on Shimizu Toshi's diary: centring on the 15-years war] in *Kajima bijutsu kenkyû* [Kajima art research] *nenpyô dai 23 gô bessetsu* [annual edition, volume 23, special edition] (Tokyo: Kajima Foundation for the Arts, 2006), 341-42.

2 In the late Taishô period, Tanizaki Jun'ichirô (1886-1965) details this nostalgia for a "lost Japan" in many of his works, as indicated in his many writings about China in his *zenshû* [collected works]. See Atsuko Sakaki, "Japanese Perceptions of China: The Sinophilic Fiction of Tanizaki Junichirô," *Harvard Journal of Asiatic Studies* 59, 1 (1999): 195; Atsuko Sakaki, *Obsessions with the Sino-Japanese Polarity in Japanese Literature* (Honolulu: University of Hawaii Press, 2005). For other Japanese authors' nostalgic impressions, spurred on by an encounter with China, of what Japan had lost, see Kawamoto Saburô, *Taishô gen'ei* [Taishô illusions] (Tokyo: Shinchôsha, 1990). To see how the same can be said about Japanese avant-garde artists in late Taishô and early Shôwa, see Annika A. Culver, "Migishi Kôtarô's Shanghai: Sino-Japanese Cultural Exchange and an Artist's Romancing of an Aesthetic Ideal in Turbulent Times, 1926-1930," *Stanford Journal of East Asian Affairs* 8, 1 (2008): 68-86.

3 Chapter 5 discusses this topic in further detail. See Onizuka Hiroshi and Iida City History Research Institute, eds., *Manshû imin: Iida Shimo Ina kara no messeiji* [Manchurian immigrants: A message from Iida City and the Ina Valley] (Tokyo: Gendai-shi ryo shuppan, 2007); Mariko Tamanoi, *Memory Maps: The State and Manchuria in Postwar Japan* (Honolulu: University of Hawaii Press, 2009); and Sandra Wilson, "The 'New Paradise': Japanese Emigration to Manchuria in the 1930s and 1940s." *International History Review* 17, 2 (1995): 249-86.

4 For more on Tachibana Shiraki's plans for Japanese rural settlement of Manchuria, see Lincoln Li, *The China Factor in Modern Japanese Thought: The Case of Tachibana Shiraki, 1881-1945* (Albany: State University Press of New York, 1996).

5 For more on Tachibana Kôzaburô's thought, see William Theodore de Bary, Carol Gluck, and Arthur E. Tiedemann, eds., *Sources of Japanese Tradition, 1600-2000,* 2nd ed. (New York: Columbia University Press, 2006), 2:269.

6 For more on this topic, see H.D. Harootunian, *Overcome by Modernity: History, Culture, and Community in Interwar Japan* (Princeton: Princeton University Press, 2000).

7 For example, since the early part of the twentieth century, Harbin boasted indoor plumbing in most of its Western structures. This was also true of Dairen. For more on this topic, see Soren Clausen and Stig Thogerson, *The Making of a Chinese City: History and Historiography in Harbin* (New York: Sharpe, 1996). Also, Kimura Ryôji mentions that airplanes fascinated early twentieth-century Japanese colonists in Dairen. The city's airfield was located in the area near Higashi kôen chô (East Garden Village) and Minamiyama rei (Southern Mountain Range), where an air show was held on 25 July 1914. See Kimura Ryôji, *Dairen monogatari* [A tale of Dairen] (Tokyo: Kenkôsha, 1974), 36, my translation. By 1936, there were seventeen air routes in Manchukuo. See South Manchuria Railway Company, *Fifth Report on Progress in Manchuria to 1936* (Tokyo: Herald Press, 1936), 74-75.

8 This characteristic, in part, aided in the Kantô Army's military takeover and pacification of the region between 1931 and 1933. Since individual landlords controlled large areas of land with local mercenary armies, negotiation with Chinese elites often helped avoid further skirmishes. Wealthy Chinese protected their interests by collaborating in this way with the Japanese.

9 Kimura, *Dairen monogatari,* 194 (my translation).

10 Ibid., (my translation and emphasis).

11 *Harubin to fûzoku: Genchi shashin shû* [Harbin and its customs: Photo collections of the colonies] (Shinkyô: Nisshin yôko, possibly late 1930s to 1942), n.p.

12 Yamada's 1940 edited volume of Chinese and Russian authors also features a sketch of a rustic doorway festooned with Chinese ornaments and copies of *Spring Festival Couplet* (see Chapter 2). See Yamada Seizaburô, ed., *Man Rô zai Man sakka tanpen senshû* [Anthology of short works by Japanese, Manchurian, and Russian authors in Manchuria](Tokyo: Shunyôdô shoten, 1940).

13 This image, as well as the following photographs of Harbin's *chûreitô* (war memorial) and *kenkoku kinenbi* (monument commemorating Manchukuo's founding), inserts the publication firmly into Japan's post-1937 wartime agenda, in which Manchuria served as a base for military operations in China proper.

14 These layers of settlement, first by Han Chinese and then by Russians, point to the successive colonial policies of both Imperial China and Imperial Russia. Japan is merely the latest player in the imperially sponsored colonization of the region.

15 *Manchuria: Semi-Monthly Publication of the Manchuria Daily News* (July 1938), inside cover preceding an essay on the Manchukuo *Kyôwa-kai* [Concordia Association].

16 Norman Smith, *Resisting Manchukuo: Chinese Women Writers under the Japanese Occupation* (Vancouver: UBC Press, 2007), 105 and 113-14.

17 Victor Zatsepine, of the University of Hong Kong, is currently investigating how Russian architecture, science, education, and religion continued to thrive in the 1930s but adjusted to a new vision of Manchukuo, whereby Russians, with some ambivalence, responded to, celebrated, or rearticulated the kinds of utopian messages emanating from the Japanese rulers. His study, to be published by UBC Press, is forthcoming.

18 Tsuruta Gorô, *Banseiki no sobyô* [A Half Century of Sketches] (Tokyo: Chûô kôron bijutsu shuppan, 1975), 128.

19 Personal discussion with Otani Shôgo, curator, the National Museum of Modern Art in Tokyo, 12 April 2005.

20 Fujiyama Kazuo, "Fine Art of Manchuria," in *Manchuria* (July 1938), 37. Chapter 4 discusses in further detail Fujiyama's activities as a Manchukuo bureaucrat fashioning the new state's culture through what Prasenjit Duara calls "a vision consistent with the marginalization of the Chinese." See Prasenjit Duara, *Sovereignty and Authenticity: Manchukuo and the East Asian Modern* (Lanham, MD: Rowman and Littlefield, 2003), 174.

21 Fujiyama makes these comments about "Manchurian" (Han Chinese) artists: "There are some artists that follow the well-established traditions of Japanese art, well trained and voiced in the Japanese style, but there are others who follow the set patterns without incorporating any new creative departures, while still others are exercising much ingenuity to revolutionize their paintings." See Fujiyama, "Fine Art of Manchuria," 36.

22 Ibid., 35.

23 Ibid. (emphasis mine). The chief executive of Manchukuo was the former Qing emperor, Henry Aisin Gioro PuYi (1908-67). In 1934, the Japanese promoted him to the position of

"His Imperial Majesty the Emperor of Manchukuo" to more fully differentiate him and his puppet nation from Chiang Kai-Shek's nationalist China. This also served to connect Pu Yi more closely to the Japanese Empire's influence and, by somewhat restoring his imperial role, ensured his loyalty.

24 Mary Louise Pratt, *Imperial Eyes: Travel Writing and Transculturation* (New York: Routledge, 1992), 6.

25 Thornber defines an "artistic nebulae" as "the physical and creative spaces where dancers, dramatists, musicians, painters, sculptors, writers, and other artists from cultures/nations in unequal power relationships grapple with and transculturate one another's creative output." See Karen Laura Thornber, *Empire of Texts in Motion: Chinese, Korean, and Taiwanese Transculturations of Japanese Literature* (Cambridge, MA: Harvard University Press, 2009), 2.

26 Haruyama, *Shimizu Toshi nikki no kenkyû: 15-nen sensôki wo chûshin ni,* 341.

27 For a scholarly investigation of tourism in the Japanese Empire, which expanded after 1940 to places like Manchukuo, see Kenneth Ruoff, *Imperial Japan at Its Zenith: The Wartime Celebration of the Empire's 2,600th Anniversary* (Ithaca, NY: Cornell University Press, 2010). In 1940, at select Manchukuo sites, the Japan Tourist Bureau hoped to promote four themes to Japanese (and foreign) visitors: (1) Japanese battle sacrifices in the Russo-Japanese War, which justified Japan's special interests there; (2) Japan's efforts to "bring modernity to a backward area"; (3) the "primitive nature" of its non-Japanese residents; and (4) the Empire's efforts to be "the caretaker of Asian civilization" (129-30).

28 A 1939 Japan Tourist Bureau-endorsed article entitled "Travel in Manchoukuo" touts: "Dairen, Mukden, Hsinking, Harbin – these are familiar names but each has its own characteristics which must be appreciated. Dairen is a western city but with Japanese daintiness; Mukden, especially the old town, is a true Manchou center; *Hsinking, the new capital, reflects the image of the new, growing, vigorous State;* Harbin retains its glamorous pre-war Russian atmosphere. Besides these there are Kirin, where the Manchou dynasty was cradled and which today is a quiet resort; Chengte or Jehol which was made famous by the lamaseries and imperial retreat loved by Emperor Chien Lung; various spas such as Tangkangtzu, Wulunpei, and Halun Arshan, the last named in the Hsingan Mountains; *Chiamussu, which is known to all Japanese as one of the first places of Japanese immigrant settlement.* For those inclined to view industrial Manchoukuo, there are Fushun and Anshan, the coal and iron centers which today boast of many companion plants. *In fact a visit to almost any place is interesting and informative, or even surprising, considering the fact that Manchoukuo is still a babe among nations" (Manchuria Daily Times, Manchuria* (15 August 1939), 1371 [emphasis mine]).

29 Louise Young, *Japan's Total Empire: Manchuria and the Culture of Wartime Imperialism* (Berkeley: University of California Press, 1998), 69.

30 Alan Tansman, *The Aesthetics of Japanese Fascism* (Berkeley: University of California Press, 2009), 27.

31 This is a version of Young's term, which designates as "unofficial propagandists" those who produced any kind of media on Manchuria that supported the aims of the Japanese government. See Young, *Japan's Total Empire,* 68-78.

32 Tansman, *Aesthetics of Japanese Fascism,* 12.

33 Ibid., 27.

34 Chapter 4 discuss this issue in more depth.

35 Ogawa Bijutsukan [Ogawa Art Museum], ed. *Jihitsu no nikki to suisai. Dessin de saguru: Shimizu Toshi, taiÔ soshite kikokugo no kiseki* [Personal diary and watercolors. Investigating the tracks of Shimizu Toshi during his sojourn in Europe and return to Japan through his sketches. (Tokyo: Ogawa Bijutsukan, 1999), 18.]

36 For more about the *Dokuritsu bijutsu-kai,* see Annika A. Culver, "'Between Distant Realities': The Japanese Avant-Garde, Surrealism, and the Colonies, 1924-1943" (PhD diss., University of Chicago, 2007), chap. 1.

37 It is not clear whether the "Fuki" mentioned in Andre Thirion's study of the surrealists at the Rue du Chateau was Fukuzawa, though he most likely knew of their milieu. There are no extant Japanese sources that indicate Fukuzawa met Breton.

38 Otani Shôgo, ed., *Chiheisen no yume: Shôwa 10 nendai no gensô kaiga* [Dreams of the horizon: Fantastic paintings in Japan, 1935-1945] (Tokyo: Tokyo National Museum of Modern Art, 2003), 138.

39 Iino Masahito, *"Manshû bijutsu" nenpyô* [Chronology of art in Manchuria] (Kôfu City: Yoneya, 1998), 31.
40 Iino, *"Manshû bijutsu" nenpyô,* 32.
41 Ibid. (my translation and emphasis). I suspect that the critic mixed up the names of Suzuki (who focuses on development) and Shimizu (who specializes in horses).
42 Not all Japanese artists were enthralled by Manchuria or the Manchukuo experiment, nor did they all depict such themes in their work. Exuding an ominous darkness and loneliness, Ai Mitsu's few remaining works from his 1935 Manchukuo trip contest this vision. I further discuss this issue in Chapter 4.
43 See Annika A. Culver, "The Making of a Japanese Avant-Garde in Dairen, 1924-1937," *History Compass* 2 (2007): 347-61.
44 Thornber, *Empire of Texts in Motion,* 2.
45 This name may be a classical Chinese literary reference.
46 Egawa Yoshihide, *Dairen no shururearisumu "Gokakai" o megutte* [About the surrealist Five Fruits Group in Dairen] in *Nihon bijutsu sôkô: Sasaki Kôzô Sensei koki kinen ronbunshû* [Japanese art manuscripts: Collected essays commemorating Professor Sasaki Kôzô's seventieth birthday, (Tokyo: Meitoku shuppansha, 1998), 663.
47 Along with Anzai, Takiguchi Takeshi was one of the organizers of *A* and a frequent contributor to *Shi to shiron.* They also had close connections with Kitagawa Fuyuhiko, who translated Breton's *Second Manifesto of Surrealism* into Japanese.
48 After 1941, Takiguchi Shuzô and Fukuzawa both endured police persecution due to their correspondence with Breton, whom, at the time, Japanese authorities still thought to be a communist. Subsequently, other writers and painters subscribing to surrealism also became targets of police surveillance and were under pressure to reform their thought.
49 After 1941, the Japanese government believed that surrealism was linked to communism, and, as part of its anti-communist operations, systematically repressed organizations in both domestic Japan and in the colonies that professed an interest in promoting this literary and aesthetic philosophy.
50 Egawa, *Dairen no shururearisumu "Gokakai" o megutte,* 663.
51 Ibid.
52 Ozaki Shinjin, "Japanese Surrealism in the Late 1930s: The 'Space of Formless Matter' and the 'Space of Macroscopic Creatures.'" In *Japanese Modern Art: Painting from 1910-1970,* ed. Irmtraud Schaarschmidt-Richter (Zurich: Stemmle Publishers, 2000), 61.
53 The first two copies of the magazine include the names of these Dairen-based surrealist artists.
54 Fukuzawa's painting *Ushi* can usually be found on display at the Tokyo National Museum of Modern Art, where it is rotated with the rest of the permanent collection.
55 Personal conversation, Otani Shôgo, October 2003. See also Otani, *Chiheisen no yume,* 22.
56 Ibid. 138.
57 Otani Shôgo, personal conversation during a private viewing of the work in the Tokyo National Museum of Modern Art, October 2003.
58 Otani, *Chiheisen no yume,* 14-15. In correspondence in August 2012, Otani noted that the original image of the golden glass came from *Cahiers d'art* 5-6 (1933), according to Hayamizu Yutaka of the Hyôgô Prefectural Museum of Art.
59 Otani Shôgo, personal conversation during a private viewing of the work in the Tokyo National Museum of Modern Art, October 2003.
60 Fukuzawa Ichiro, *Manshû, Mizue* [Watercolor] 368 (1935): 298.
61 Suzuki's painting *Yokotawareru Manshû dojin* can be found on display at the Setagaya Art Museum in Tokyo.
62 Suzuki Yasunori, "Manshû domin to dôbutsu" [Manchurian natives and animals], *Atorie* [Atelier] 12, 8 (1935): 26-28.
63 See Kawabata Yasunari, *Chôjû* [Of birds and beasts], in *Kaizô* [Reconstruction] (1933).
64 My translation. Original in Kitagawa Fuyuhiko, *Sensô* [War] (Tokyo: Yumani shobô, 1995), 16 (my translation), (original published in Tokyo by Kôseigaku shoten, 1929)
65 See Hisamatsu Sen'ichi and Yoshida Sei'ichi, eds., *Kindai Nihon bungaku jiten* [Dictionary of modern Japanese literature] (Tokyo: Tokyo-dô, 1954); Oda Setsushin and Nihon kindai

bijutsu-kan (Museum of Modern Japanese Literature), eds., *Nihon kindai bungaku dai jiten – dai nikkan* [Great dictionary of modern Japanese literature – 2] (Tokyo: Kôdansha, 1977); and Donald Keene, *Dawn to the West: Japanese Literature of the Modern Era (Poetry, Drama, Criticism)* (New York: Holt, Rinehart, and Winston, 1984), 337.

66 Suzuki's 1936 painting *Kokutô kensetsu* may be viewed at the Tomioka City Museum in the Fukuzawa Ichirô Memorial Gallery.

67 South Manchuria Railway Company, *Fifth Report on Progress in Manchuria to 1936* (Dairen: South Manchuria Railway Company, 1936), 74-75.

68 Ibid., 75.

69 Smith, *Resisting Manchukuo,* 127.

70 Ibid., 125.

71 Shimizu's painting *Môko fûkei (kôgen. onna. uma.)* may be viewed at the Tochigi Prefecture Museum of Fine Arts.

72 See Culver, "Between Distant Realities," 265-332.

73 This can also be seen in the photography of Fuchikami and the Manchuria Photographic Artists Association, discussed in Chapter 5.

Chapter 4: The Lure of Artistic Vision and the Commercial Prerogative

1 Ai Mitsu is most well known for his haunting 1938 surrealist painting *Fûkei (Me no aru fûkei) [Scene (Scene with an Eye)],* which depicts a dream-like crouching lion and an eye rendered in deep earth colours, including browns, reds, and ochre. This work is currently displayed in the National Museum of Modern Art in Tokyo. This masterpiece, containing layers of revisions and earlier scenes that the artist "erased" under further coats of paint, received a prize in the eighth *Dokuritsu-ten* (Independent Arts Exhibition) in the late 1930s, during the deepening of the China conflict.

2 Biographical information on Ai Mitsu in this chapter was collected from Egawa Yoshihide, "Ai Mitsu nidai" [A second topic on Ai Mitsu], in *Ai Mitsu to kôyû no gakatachi* [Ai Mitsu and his artist friends], ed. Hiroshima Prefectural Art Museum and Iwate Prefectural Art Museum, 174-79 (Hiroshima: Hiroshima Prefectural Art Museum, 2001), 174-79; and Otani Shôgo, Matsumoto Tôru, Arikawa Ikuo, Wada Koichi, Fujisaki Aya, and Kakuda Arata, eds., *Seitan hyaku-nen Ai Mitsu ten* [Exhibition honouring Ai Mitsu one hundred years after his birth] (Tokyo: Mainichi Newspapers, 2007).

3 Otani et al., *Seitan hyaku-nen Ai Mitsu ten,* 177.

4 See Usami Shô, *Ikebukuro Monparunasu* [Ikebukuro Montparnasse] (Tokyo: Shûei-sha, 1990).

5 Formed following the 1923 Great Kantô Earthquake, this avant-garde artists' group comprised Murayama and four other artists at its core who performed in plays and dances or created art and sculptures. Their works challenged art institutions and gender roles and took on some elements of German Constructivism and Expressionism, which had influenced Murayama during his sojourn in Berlin.

6 Ibid., 90.

7 Annika A. Culver, "Migishi Kôtarô's Shanghai: Sino-Japanese Cultural Exchange and an Artist's Romancing of an Aesthetic Ideal in Turbulent Times," *Stanford Journal of East Asian Affairs* 8, 1 (2008): 74. To read the poem in its original, see Migishi Kôtarô, "Shanhai no ehon," *Serekuto* [Select] 1, 8 (1930): 1, 6-7. For an English translation, see Annika A. Culver, "'Between Distant Realities': The Japanese Avant-Garde, Surrealism, and the Colonies, 1924-1943" (PhD diss., University of Chicago, 2007), app. A, 445-52. For a discussion of the poem and its symbolism, see Hokkaidô Migishi Kôtarô Art Museum, *"Shanhai no ehon": Chûgoku modan toshi no shi* ["Shanghai picture book": A poem about China's modern city] (Sapporo: Hokkaidô Migishi Kôtarô Art Museum, 1990), 8-14.

8 Otani et al., *Seitan hyaku-nen Ai Mitsu ten,* 199.

9 Ibid., 199.

10 Fujisaki Aya, "Ai Mitsu and Hiroshima," in Otani et al., *Seitan hyaku-nen Ai Mitsu ten,* 185.

11 Otani et al., *Seitan hyaku-nen Ai Mitsu ten,* 186.

12 Japanese agents who manufactured an attack on Nichiren monks in the city provoked this skirmish in which Chinese soldiers valiantly fought against Japanese troops stationed in Shanghai.

13 Otani et al., *Seitan hyaku-nen Ai Mitsu ten,* 185.
14 John Clark, "Artistic Subjectivity in the Taishô and Early Shôwa Avant-Garde," in *Japanese Art after 1945: Scream Against the Sky,* ed. Alexandra Munroe (New York: Harry N. Abrams, 1994), 53.
15 Chiba Yoshi, *Fuan to gensô: Kanten ni okeru "Manshû" hyôshô no seiji-teki imi* [Disquiet and illusion: The political meaning of images of Manchuria in official art exhibitions], in *Hyôshô/teikoku/gendâ: Seisen kara reisen he* [Representation, empire and gender: From the sacred war to the Cold War], Ikeda Shinobu, ed. (Research Project Report, Graduate School of Humanities and Social Sciences, Chiba University, 2008), 38.
16 Fujiyama Kazuo, "Fine Art of Manchuria," in "Manchuria: Concordia and Culture in Manchukuo," special edition of *Manchuria Daily Times,* 20 July 1938, 35.
17 Ibid.
18 Ibid.
19 Ibid., 36.
20 Chiba, *Fuan to gensô,* 52-53.
21 Ibid., 52.
22 Ibid., 53.
23 Ibid.
24 Fujiyama, "Fine Art of Manchuria," 37.
25 Ibid. 36.
26 For an explanation of why anti-establishment art did not always mean "avant-garde," see John Szostak's study of "traditional" Japanese art painted in ink and watercolours, or *Nihonga,* and how various artists attempted to "modernize" it. See John Donald Szostak, "The *Kokuga Sôsaku Kyôkai* and Kyoto *Nihonga* Reform in the Meiji, Taishô, and Early Shôwa Years, 1900-1928" (PhD diss., University of Washington, 2005).
27 Joshua Fogel, trans., *Life along the South Manchurian Railway: The Memoirs of Itô Takeo* (New York: M.E. Sharpe, 1988), 27.
28 Hiroshima Prefectural Art Museum and Iwate Prefectural Art Museum, eds. *Ai Mitsu to kôyû no gakatachi* [Ai Mitsu and his artist friends] (Hiroshima: Hiroshima Prefectural Art Museum, 2001), 45.
29 Ibid.; Tsuruta Gorô, *Banseiki no sobyô* [A Half Century of Sketches] (Tokyo: Chûô kôron bijutsu shuppan, 1975), 128.
30 Personal discussion with curator Otani Shôgo, 12 April 2005.
31 John Clark, "Surrealism in Japan," Monash Asia Institute, Japanese Studies Centre, occasional paper 28, (1997), 48 (1-80). This is a compilation of original papers re-published in a re-arranged form: John Clark, "Surrealism in Japan" in M. Lloyd, T. Gott, and C. Chapman, *Surrealism: Revolution by Night* (Canberra: National Gallery of Australia, 1993), 204-13; and "The Japanese Avant-Garde before 1945" in Alexandra Munroe, ed., *Japanese Art after 1945: Scream Against the Sky* (New York: Harry Abrams, 1994), 40-53.
32 Otani et al., *Seitan hyaku-nen Ai Mitsu ten,* 181. A contemporary US example is the widely recognized "Support our troops" initiative following the 2001 Afghanistan invasion and the second Iraq War in 2003. Even the most vehement anti-war protestors still hoped to boost the morale of American troops, despite what they felt were the misguided decisions of the US government under the George W. Bush administration. Even now, many liberal Americans who disagree with the invasion's rationale actively contribute to "care package" drives for US troops in these two hotspots. They believe that the troops deployed are only performing their duty and personally had no control over the government's flawed decision-making process. This differs little from the *imon bukurô* (comfort bags) that Japanese civilians of all political stripes prepared for the Imperial Army. However, after 1932, the Japanese government and its bureaucracy were increasingly staffed by members of the military who could not be voted out of office.
33 Ibid., 200.
34 Barak Kushner, *The Thought War: Japanese Imperial Propaganda* (Honolulu: University of Hawaii Press, 2006), 38.
35 John Clark, "Surrealism in Japan," Monash Asia Institute, Japanese Studies Centre, occasional paper 28, (1997), 48.

36 Otani et al., *Seitan hyaku-nen Ai Mitsu ten,* 195.
37 Clark, "Surrealism in Japan," 11, 44.
38 Hiroshima Prefectural Art Museum and Iwate Prefectural Art Museum, *Ai Mitsu to kôyû no gakatachi,* 10.
39 Otani et al., *Seitan hyaku-nen Ai Mitsu ten,* 95.
40 Ibid.
41 Ishimura Kie, *Ishimura no koto* [About Ishimura], in *Ai Mitsu,* ed. Kikuchi Yoshi'ichirô, rev. ed. (Tokyo: Toki no bijutsusha, 1965), 137.
42 Kitawaki's prescient 1937 wartime work *Kûkô* [Airport] features two maple seeds, evoking aircraft, amidst an oppressive black sky, and near a menacing-looking inverted dried sunflower head. See Yamada Satoshi, *"SF kûsô kagaku" kaiga: "Kûkô"* [Science fiction fantasy science painting: Airport] in *Nihon no kindai bijutsu 10: Fuan to sensô no jidai* [Japanese Modern Art 10: Era of Anxiety and War], ed. Mizusawa Tsutomu, 65-75 (Tokyo: Otsuki shoten, 1992).
43 Egawa Yoshihide, *Ai-Mitsu: Yure ugoku jidai no konseki* [Ai Mitsu: Traces of an uncertain age] (Tokyo: Tokushima Modern Art Museum, 1994), 59. A reproduced photo of the wörk may be found in Otani et al. *Seitan hyaku-nen Ai Mitsu ten,* plate 100.
44 Ibid., 181.
45 Ibid., 140.
46 Ibid., 182.
47 Takiguchi Shûzô, "Bijutsu bunka kyôkai ten ni tsuite" [Concerning the society for art and culture exhibition], *Mizue* [Watercolour] 435 (1941): 120.
48 Ibid., 120.
49 *Mizue* [Watercolour] 434 (1941): 126.
50 Akiyama Kunio, Suzuki Kurazô, Kuroda Senkichirô, and Araki Sueo, "Kokubô kokka to bijutsu: Gaka wa nani wo subeki ka" [The national defence state and art: What should artists do?] *Mizue* [Watercolor] 434 (1941): 129-39.
51 Ibid., 129.
52 In Japanese, *kindaiteki dentô.*
53 Takiguchi Shûzô, "Kindai bijutsu no ba'ai" [The circumstances of modern art], *Mizue* [Watercolour] 435 (1941): 150-51.
54 Araki Sueo, "Bijutsu bunka seisaku no kihon rinen: Ashita he no seishin sôzô to sono hôsaku" [The fundamental ideology of art and culture policies: The creation of a tomorrow-oriented spirit and its measures], *Mizue* [Watercolour] 437 (1941): 382.
55 Ibid.
56 Matsumoto Shunsuke, "Ikiteru gakka" [Living artists], *Mizue* [Watercolour] 437 (1941): 477-80.
57 See Tan'ô Yasunari and Kawade Akihisa, eds., *Imeiji no naka no sensô: Ni Sei. Nichi Rô kara Reisen made* [War in images: From the Sino-Japanese and Russo-Japanese wars until the Cold War] (Tokyo: Iwanami shoten, 1996). See also Harisei Ichirô, Sawaragi Noi, Kuraya Mika, Kawada Akihisa, Hirase Reita, and Otani Shôgo, eds., *Sensô to bijutsu, 1937-1945* [Art in wartime Japan, 1937-1945] (Tokyo: Kokushokan kôkai, 2007).
58 Ibid., 37.
59 See Chapter 5's discussion of the artist Asai Kan'emon's (1901-83) 1943 painting *Hôshû (Homare no kazoku)* [Good harvest (family of distinction)] (Figure 25), which features a Madonna-like Japanese mother with her red-kimono attired toddler son amidst the northern Manchurian plains.
60 Yamamurô Shin'ichi, *Kimera: Manshûkoku no shôzô* [Chimera: A portrait of Manchukuo] (Tokyo: Chûô kôronsha, 1993), 226-27.
61 Chinese scholars have remarked that this made "the Chinese people into Japanese imperial subjects." Quoted in Prasenjit Duara, *Sovereignty and Authenticity: Manchukuo and the East Asian Modern* (Lanham, MD: Rowman and Littlefield, 2003), 66.
62 Yamamurô, *Kimera,* 226-27.
63 Ôbama Shigeru, "Dialogue on the Culture of Manchoukuo," *Manchuria,* 25 December 1939, 1613.
64 Iino Masahito, *"Manshû bijutsu" nenpyô* [Chronology of Manchurian art] (Kôfu City: Yamanashi Prefecture Museum of Art, 1998), 3.

65 Ibid.
66 It was also around this time that photographic images of the Manchukuo and Shôwa emperors became permanent features of occupied Manchuria's classrooms.
67 Kimura Ryôji, *Dairen monogatari* [A tale of Dairen] (Tokyo: Kenkôsha, 1974), 31.
68 From a letter of Ai Mitsu to his wife, Kie. See Otani et al., *Seitan hyaku-nen Ai Mitsu ten,* 175.
69 Ibid., 154 (my translation).
70 Ibid., 182.
71 Peter O'Connor, ed., *Japanese Propaganda: Selected Readings, Series 1 – Books 1872-1943* (Kent, UK: Global Oriental, 2004), 9.
72 Louise Young, *Japan's Total Empire: Manchuria and the Culture of Wartime Imperialism* (Berkeley: University of California Press, 1998), 68.
73 O'Connor, *Japanese Propaganda,* 17.

Chapter 5: Reflections of Labour and the Construction of the New State

1 Mariko Tamanoi, *Memory Maps: The State and Manchuria in Postwar Japan* (Honolulu: University of Hawaii Press, 2009), 1-3. In the text, Tamanoi calls Terashima by the first name "Banji" rather than "Manji," the name used by Japanese curators.
2 South Manchuria Railway Company, *Manshû gurafu* [Manchuria graph] 1 (January 1939), n.p.; and Takeba Jô, ed., *Ikyô no modanizumu: Fuchikami Hakuyô to Manshû shashin sakka kyôkai* [Modernism on foreign soil: Fuchikami Hakuyô and the Manchuria Photographic Artists Association] (Nagoya: Nagoya City Museum of Art, 1994), 71.
3 Tamanoi, *Memory Maps,* 2.
4 See Annika Culver, "Two Japanese Avant-Garde Writers' Views of Gender Relations and Colonial Oppression in Manchuria, 1929-1931," *US-Japan Women's Journal* 37 (2009): 91-116; and Annika A. Culver, "Colonial Manchuria in the Surrealist Imagination: The Poetry and Prose of Kitagawa Fuyuhiko as Modernist History," *Proceedings of the Association for Japanese Literary Studies* 4 (2003): 264-77.
5 Yumani shobô reprint, *Manshû gurafu* [Manchuria graph] *dai gokan dai roku gô (dai 35 gô)* [Volume 5, number 6 (number 35)] (Tokyo: Yumani shobô, 2008), 158.
6 The previous year's June 1936 edition was also dedicated to art photography and also had a cover that displayed a young Chinese woman knitting next to a stove.
7 Yumani shobô, *Manshû gurafu,* 5, 6 (no. 35), 147.
8 Ibid., 154.
9 Ibid., 155.
10 In Fuchikami Hakuyô, *Manshû shashin nenkan* [Manchuria photography annual] May 1930. See also Iizawa Kôtarô, ed., *Nihon no shashin-ka 6: Fuchikami Hakuyô to Manshû shashin sakka kyôkai* [Fuchikami Hakuyô and the Manchuria Photographic Artists Association] (Tokyo: Iwanami shoten, 1998), image 12.
11 The caption is translated into English as "The Evening Sun." See Yumani shobô reprint, *Manshû gurafu* 7, 1 (1939): 25.
12 Norman Smith, *Resisting Manchukuo: Chinese Women Writers under the Japanese Occupation* (Vancouver: UBC Press, 2007), 111.
13 Ibid.
14 H.D. Harootunian, *Overcome by Modernity: History, Culture, and Community in Interwar Japan* (Princeton: Princeton University Press, 2000), xxi.
15 Alan Tansman, *The Aesthetics of Japanese Fascism* (Berkeley: University of California Press, 2009), 19.
16 Ibid.
17 Ibid.
18 Background information on Fuchikami comes from Iizawa Kôtarô, *Shashin no yûtopia: Fuchikami Hakuyô to Manshû shashin sakka kyôkai* [Utopia in photographs: Fuchikami Hakuyô and the Manchuria Photographic Artists Association] in *Kan* [Area] 10 (2002): 232-39; Iizawa Kôtarô and Takeba Jô, eds., *Nihon no shashin-ka 6: Fuchikami Hakuyô to Manshû shashin sakka kyôkai* [Japanese photographers, volume 6: Fuchikami Hakuyô and the Manchuria Photographic Artists Association] (Tokyo: Iwanami shoten, 1998); and Anne Tucker, Kôtarô

Iizawa, and Naoyuki Kinoshita, *The History of Japanese Photography* (New Haven: Yale University Press, 2003).

19 Iizawa, *Shashin no yûtopia,* 232.

20 See Fuchikami's photograph *Mâboisuto no shôzô* [Image of a MAVOist] in Iizawa and Takeba, *Nihon no shashin-ka 6,* image 2.

21 SMRC's Presidential Information Division was established in April 1927. Iizawa and Takeba, *Nihon no shashin-ka 6* 67.

22 Iizawa and Takeba, *Nihon no shashin-ka 6,* 67; and Iizawa, *Shashin no yûtopia,* 234.

23 Iizawa and Takeba, *Nihon no shashin-ka 6,* 67.

24 Iizawa, *Shashin no yûtopia,* 234.

25 This is the same artist who later illustrates the cover box for the two multi-ethnic Manchurian literature collections coedited by Kawabata Yasunari and Yamada Seizaburô with four other prominent Japanese and Manchurian writers in 1942 and 1944, respectively.

26 Tucker et al., *History of Japanese Photography,* 320.

27 Iizawa, *Shashin no yûtopia,* 232.

28 Tucker et al., *History of Japanese Photography,* 320.

29 Ibid., 321.

30 Kobayashi Hideo, *Mantetsu: "Chi no shûdan" no tanjô to shi* [The South Manchuria Railway Company: The birth and death of the knowledgeable group] (Tokyo: Hirofumi-kan, 1996), 170.

31 Iizawa and Takeba, *Nihon no shashin-ka 6,* 67; and Tucker et al., *History of Japanese Photography,* 320.

32 Tucker et al., *History of Japanese Photography,* 372, 374.

33 Iizawa and Takeba, *Nihon no shashin-ka 6,* 67.

34 Ibid.

35 Collected by the Tokyo Metropolitan Museum of Photography in 1995, reproductions of works by Fuchikami, Baba, Saotome, Yoneki, Doi, Aoyama, Mizuma, Okada, and Date can be found in one of the most comprehensive catalogues available in Japan, with more than 240 reproductions by over seventy photographers. It also includes an English translation of an essay on the brief history of Japanese modernist photography from 1920 to 1945. See Tokyo Metropolitan Museum of Photography, ed., *Nihon kindai shashin no seiritsu to tenkai* [The founding and development of modern photography in Japan] (Tokyo: Tokyo Metropolitan Culture Foundation, Tokyo Metropolitan Museum of Photography, 1995).

36 See Kamakura Museum of Modern Art, ed., *Nihon no shashin 1930 ten* [Japanese photography in the 1930s] (Kamakura: Kamakura Museum of Modern Art, 1988).

37 Tucker et al., *History of Japanese Photography,* 321.

38 Ibid.

39 Ibid.; and Iizawa and Takeba, *Nihon no shashin-ka 6,* 67.

40 Iizawa, *Shashin no yûtopia,* 232.

41 See Takeba, *Ikyô no modanizumu.*

42 Takeba Jô, "The Age of Modernism: From Visualization to Socialization," in Tucker et al., *History of Japanese Photography,* 155.

43 Ibid., 156.

44 See Culver, "Two Japanese Avant-Garde Writers," 91-116.

45 For more on migration, see Thomas Gottshang and Diana Lary, *Swallows and Settlers: The Great Migration from North China to Manchuria* (Ann Arbor: Center for Chinese Studies, 2000).

46 Yi Xianshi, *Nihon no tairiku seisaku to Chûgoku tôhoku* [Japan's policy on the continent and China's northeast] (Tokyo: Rokkô shuppan, 1989), 269-70.

47 South Manchuria Railway Company, *Manshû gurafu* [Manchuria graph] 4, 5 (May 1936): n.p. Yumani shobô reprint, *Manshû gurafu* [Manchuria graph] *dai yokkan dai go gô (dai 35 gô)* [Volume 4, number 5 (number 22)] (Tokyo: Yumani shobô, 2008).

48 In Japan, cherry blossoms are usually in bloom around the first week of April. Even in colder Manchuria, the buds would be in bloom toward the end of that month. Yumani shôbô reprint, *Manshû gurafu* [Manchuria graph] *dai yokkan dai go gô (dai 35 gô)* [Volume 4, number 5 (number 22)] (Tokyo: Yumani shobô, 2008), 83.

49 See Yumani shobô, *Manshû gurafu,* 6, 8 (number 49), 185.
50 The Japanese captions are more detailed (and convey more nuance) than do the English translations. This is also the case with the descriptions of the photographs, which often run as bilingual versions. See Yumani shobô, *Manshû gurafu,* 6, 8 (number 49), 185.
51 Ibid.
52 Chinese names are written using the prewar Wade-Giles Romanization system, but sometimes, Japanese periodicals misspell them. Ibid., 185.
53 Ibid., 185.
54 South Manchuria Railway Company, *Manshû gurafu* [Manchuria graph] 3, 5 (May 1936): n.p.; Yumani shobô reprint, *Manshû gurafu* [Manchuria graph] *dai yokkan dai go gô (dai 35 gô)* [Volume 4, number 5 (number 22)] (Tokyo: Yumani shobô, 2008), 90.
55 Ibid., n.p.; Yumani shobô, 4, 5, 91.
56 Ibid., n.p.; Yumani shobô, 4, 5, 89.
57 The word *chôjin,* or "superman," was in fact used to describe them.
58 *Manshû rôdô nenkan* [Manchuria labour yearbook] (Xinjing, Manchukuo: Ganshodô shôten, 1940), 26, 40.
59 Fang Jun and Wang Shengli, eds., *Zhiminzhe de jiayuan* [The homes of colonists] (Dalian: Liaoning People's Press, 1998), 296.
60 Ibid., 297.
61 Ibid., 331.
62 In Chinese, *Fuchang huagong geshi huishe.* (*Kabushiki gaisha* is substituted for Japanese.)
63 Fang and Wang, *Zhiminzhe de jiayuan,* 331.
64 Ibid., 330-31.
65 In addition, the substandard nature of these dwellings led many to engage in the insalubrious habits of opium smoking and prostitution, ostensibly for a respite from these harsh conditions (despite the fact that they contributed to further illness). These immigrants from Shandong and Hebei endured inhumanly long hours and poor living conditions in order to save money to support their families back in their rural hometowns, to which they briefly returned each year during the Chinese New Year holiday.
66 Fang and Wang, *Zhiminzhe de jiayuan,* 326.
67 Ibid., 330-31.
68 This group included small numbers of Japan-educated upper-class Koreans who had taken Japanese names in order to assimilate as Japanese subjects.
69 Yumani shobô reprint, *Manshû gurafu,* 4, 6 (number 23), 116 (my translation).
70 From 1936 to 1939, there were three issues featuring the art photography of Fuchikami and the MPAA.
71 South Manchurian Railway Company, *Manshû gurafu* [Manchuria graph] 5, 6 (June 1937): n.p.; Yumani shobô reprint, *Manshû gurafu* [Manchuria graph], 5, 6 (number 35), 158.
72 Tansman, *Aesthetics of Japanese Fascism,* 19.
73 Iizawa, *Shashin no yûtopia,* 236.
74 See Takeba, *Ikyô no modanizumu.*
75 Chinese nationalists under Chiang Kai-Shek and the Japanese named the Tangu Truce after a location near Shanhaiguan where the Great Wall of China meets the sea. It was to provide a buffer zone between China and Manchukuo and to limit the hostilities of the Kantô Army from penetrating further into China proper by sacrificing the Northeast.
76 From Tatsuo Kawai, *The Goal of Japanese Expansion,* 1938 reprint (Westport: Greenwood Press, 1973), 67. Quoted in Zeljko Cipris, "The Responsibility of Intellectuals: Kobayashi Hideo on Japan at War," *Japan Focus,* available at http://old.japanfocus.org/.
77 See Louise Young, *Japan's Total Empire: Manchuria and the Culture of Wartime Imperialism* (Berkeley: University of California Press, 1998), 69-78.
78 *Sôgô shuppan nenkan* [General publishing yearbook] (Tokyo: Tosho kenkyûkai, 1932), 963. Quoted in Young, *Japan's Total Empire,* 70.
79 South Manchurian Railway Company, *Manshû gurafu* [Manchuria graph] 1, 2 (November 1933): n.p.; Yumani shobô reprint, *Manshû gurafu* [Manchuria graph] 1, 2 (number 2) (Tokyo: Yumani shobô), 21.

80 Kari Shepherdson-Scott argues in her dissertation that these wide-open, vast spaces represent the "continental sublime." She believes that this concept is what makes the images so politically supportive of Japan's utopian project in Manchukuo. See Kari Shepherdson-Scott, "Romancing the Frontier: Fuchikami Hakuyô, Art Photography, and the Promotion of a Cultural Connoisseur" (PhD diss., Duke University, 2011).

81 Ibid., n.p. See also Yumani shobô reprint, *Manshû gurafu* 1, 1, 22-23.

82 South Manchuria Railway Company, *Fifth Report on Progress in Manchuria to 1936* (Dairen: South Manchuria Railway Company, 1936), 132.

83 Ibid.

84 Ibid.

85 Ibid. The publication is referring to Binjiang Province, located in the area near Harbin in what is now Heilongjiang Province in the People's Republic of China.

86 Yumani shobô reprint, *Manshû gurafu* [Manchuria graph] 4, 12 (number 29) (Tokyo: Yumani shobô, 2008), 226.

87 This was corroborated in my conversations with Liu Yong, whose grandfather Liu Shan-Zheng was the son of a landlord family in Qing'an (Qingcheng, or Keijô, prior to the 1949 liberation) near the Tieli Japanese development area in northern Manchuria. In Japanese maps from 1938, the Liu family estate, or Liu Yuan-zi, can be found equidistant between Tieli (Tetsuryô) and Qing'an (Qingcheng, or Keijô).

88 Yumani shobô reprint, *Manshû gurafu* [Manchuria graph], 6, 11 (number 52) (Tokyo: Yumani shobô, 2008), 244; *Manshû gurafu* (Dairen, November 1938), n.p.

89 Ibid.

90 For more on the villages from which these rural Japanese settlers came, with the majority coming from the Nakano area, see Iida-shi rekishi kenkyûsho-hen [Historical Research Institute of Iida City], ed., *Manshû imin: Iida Shimo Ina kara no messeji* [Manchurian immigrants: A message from Iida City in the Ina Valley] (Tokyo: Gendai shiryô shuppan, 2007).

91 Other than the ever-present tofu also consumed by Han Chinese, Japanese settlers would have had to accustom themselves to the heavy meat of local main dishes (a high-protein diet's being necessary to overcome the cold). Impoverished Chinese made do with a diet of millet porridge, wilted cabbage, pickled vegetables, and frozen tofu.

92 Preceding these immigrant families were the volunteer Youth Corps, consisting of young teenage boys who began to cultivate the land in camps that were ruled by harsh military discipline. For more on the Youth Corps, see Ronald Suleski, "Reconstructing Life in the Youth Corps Camps of Manchuria, 1938-1945: Resistance to Conformity," *East Asian History* 30 (2005): 67-90.

93 Yumani shobô reprint(2008) 4, 12 (number 29), 226; *Manshû gurafu* (December 1936), n.p.

94 Ibid., 235.

95 Michael Baskett, *The Attractive Empire: Transnational Film Culture in Imperial Japan* (Honolulu: University of Hawaii Press, 2008), 127-28. Cesar Franck headed the German side of the production, while Amakasu Masahiko (1891-1945) of *Man'ei* [Manchurian Film Association] directed the shooting in Manchukuo.

96 Yumani shobô reprint (2008) 6, 11 (number 52), 244; *Manshû gurafu* (Dairen, November 1938), n.p.

97 At the same time, in Nazi Germany Adolph Hitler clamoured for more *Lebensraum* (living space) for the ethnic German population, using this as an excuse to expand into neighbouring regions/countries harbouring large German-speaking populations, like the Sudetenland and Austria. This edition came out a few months following the 1938 Munich Conference, at which the League of Nations countries appeased Hitler in the hopes that he would be satisfied with the territory he had so far acquired.

98 Yumani shobô reprint (2008) 6, 11 (number 52), 244; *Manshû gurafu* (Dairen, November 1938), n.p.

99 Ibid.

100 Yumani shobô reprint (2008) 7, 1 (number 54), 12. *Manshû gurafu* (Dairen, January 1939), n.p.

101 Yumani shobô reprint (2008) 6, 11 (number 52), 244; *Manshû gurafu* (Dairen, November 1938), n.p.

102 Tokunaga Sunao, *Sengentai* [The pioneers] (Tokyo: Kaizô-sha, 1939).
103 The images of the sheep even resemble Terashima's pictorialist photos. See http://www.youtube.com/.
104 Otani Shôgo, ed., *Chiheisen no yume: Shôwa 10 nendai no gensô kaiga* [Dreams of the horizon: Fantastic paintings in Japan, 1935-1945] (Tokyo: Tokyo National Museum of Modern Art, 2003), 92.
105 In Japan, even today, parents bring children attired in their best clothing to the local shine on their third, fifth, and seventh birthdays for a blessing.
106 See Daqing Yang, *Technology of Empire: Telecommunications and Japanese Imperialism, 1930-1945,* Harvard East Asian Monographs, 219 (Cambridge, MA: Harvard University Asia Center Press, 2003).
107 Tucker et al., *History of Japanese Photography,* 323.

Chapter 6: The Manchukuo Publicity and News Bureau's War of Words and Images

1 See Mutô Tomio, "Invention and Free Love: A Play in One Act," in "Concordia and Culture in Manchukuo," special edition of *Manchuria Daily News,* 20 July 1938.
2 Mutô Tomio, *Manshû sanka* [Song in praise of Manchuria] (Hôten [Fengtian]: Hakukaze shobô, 1941).
3 Due to the many recent fine studies on Amakasu Masahiko and film in Manchukuo, I concentrate on art and literature in this study. Chapter 7 discusses literature after the 1941 issuing of the *Geibun shidô yôkô (Prospectus for the Guidance of the Arts and Culture).* (Also, film lies outside the realm of my expertise as a cultural historian.) See, for example, Michael Baskett, *The Attractive Empire: Transnational Film Culture in Imperial Japan* (Honolulu: University of Hawaii Press, 2008); Peter B. High, *The Imperial Screen: Japanese Film Culture in the Fifteen Years'* War (Madison: University of Wisconsin Press, 2003); Sanô Shin'ichi, *Amakasu Masahiko: Ranshin no kôya* [Amakasu Masahiko: Vast plains of a ravaged soul] (Tokyo: Shinchô-sha, 2008); and Yamaguchi Takeshi, *Maboroshii no kinema Man'ei: Amakasu Masahiko to katsudôya gunzô* [The Manchurian film association and the cinematics of illusion: Amakasu Masahiko and his group of activists] (Tokyo: Heibonsha, 1989). For a more comprehensive list of Japanese, Chinese, and English sources, see Jim Cheng, *An Annotated Bibliography for Chinese Film Studies* (Hong Kong: Hong Kong University Press, 2004), 50-1.
4 Early autobiographical information on Mutô is from Mutô Tomio, *Manshûkoku no danmen* [A cross-section of Manchukuo] (Tokyo: Kindai-sha, 1956), 254-55.
5 Mark R. Mullins, "Christianity as a Transnational Social Movement: Kagawa Toyohiko and the Friends of Jesus," *Japanese Religions* 32, 1/2, p. 77, available at Japanese-religions.jp/.
6 Ibid. 82-83.
7 George B. Bickle, Jr., "Thy Kingdom Come on Earth: Some Reflections on the Social Gospel Movement in Japan," *Contemporary Religions in Japan* 9, 3 (1968): 194.
8 See George B. Bickle, Jr., "Utopianism and Social Planning in the Thought of Kagawa Toyohiko," *Monumenta Nipponica* 25, 3/4 (1970): 447-53.
9 Mutô Tomio, *Watakushi to Manshûkoku* [Manchukuo and me] (Tokyo: Bungei shunjû), 12. A lingering memory of Kagawa's 1960 urging prompted Mutô to finally write the above book in a 1980s climate of historical revisionism, evoking apologetics and nostalgia for the Manchukuo experiment.
10 Stephen C. Mercado, *The Shadow Warriors of Nakano: A History of the Imperial Japanese Army's Elite Intelligence School* (Dulles, VA: Brasseys, 2002), 189.
11 Mutô, *Watakushi to Manshûkoku,* 12.
12 Ibid., 12. According to Mutô, Hoshino hoped to have his funeral performed at the same church in which his father had been pastor and that in death, he would be an honest Christian.
13 Mutô, *Manshûkoku no danmen,* 254.
14 In a general amnesty, Amakasu was let out of prison by the Japanese emperor.
15 For a scathing indictment of Amakasu and his connections to the opiate trade that financed Kantô Army operations, see Mark Driscoll, *Absolute Erotic, Absolute Grotesque: The Living, Dead, and Undead in Japan's Imperialism, 1895-1945* (Durham, NC: Duke University Press, 2010), 233, 252-60, 266, 291, and 295.

16 Kishi Toshihiko, "Fusion and Crack between Cultural Policy and Placation Policy in Manchukuo," *Ten Thousand Shares Research* [Journal of Manchurian studies] October (2007): 94, available at http://www.earticle.net/.
17 Mutô, *Manshûkoku no danmen,* 254.
18 Mutô, *Watakushi to Manshûkoku,* 211.
19 Ibid., 229.
20 Mutô, *Manshûkoku no danmen,* 86-90.
21 In terms of the historical significance of Manchukuo's establishment of diplomatic relations with the two fascist countries in Europe, the trip was successful. However, the delegation felt snubbed by Hitler and Nazi Germany since his meeting with only one Japanese delegation member made them feel like an afterthought, and they only received two German guides while Mussolini offered them five. Hitler did not want any distractions during this historic conference, his attention being focused on other issues.
22 Mutô, *Watakushi to Manshûkoku,* 244-46.
23 Ibid, 244-46. For reactions to Amakasu's appointment, see also High, *Imperial Screen,* 275-6.
24 Baskett, *Attractive Empire,* 39.
25 Kishi, "Fusion and Crack," 101. In fact, Japanese-language films and radio of any kind were much appreciated by Japanese settlers in border regions as they offered a nostalgic taste of the homeland they had so recently left.
26 Ibid., 101.
27 Driscoll, *Absolute Erotic,* 295.
28 Mutô, *Watakushi to Manshûkoku,* 249-61.
29 See Mutô Tomio, "The Spirit of Hsieh-ho: A New Philosophy" in "Concordia and Culture in Manchoukuo," special edition, *Manchuria,* 20 July 1938.
30 Mutô, "Invention and Free Love," 72-82.
31 Ibid.
32 Ibid., 82.
33 Ibid., 79.
34 Ibid., 82.
35 Mutô, *Manshûkoku no danmen,* 250, even notes that Amakasu hoped to whole-heartedly sacrifice his life for his country and thus delayed marriage until thirty-three, when his higher-ranking officers convinced him of the benefits of having an heir and family.
36 High, *Japanese Film Culture,* 276.
37 Mutô, *Manshûkoku no danmen,* 109-12.
38 Mark Peattie, *Ishiwara Kanji and Japan's Confrontation with the West* (Princeton, NJ: Princeton University Press, 1975), 253-54.
39 Mutô, *Watakushi to Manshûkoku,* 190.
40 Gavan McCormack, "Manchukuo: Constructing the Past," *East Asian History* 2 (1991), 115.
41 Slavoj Žižek, *Tarrying with the Negative: Kant, Hegel, and the Critique of Ideology* (Durham, NC: Duke University Press, 1993), 210.
42 Cohen was one of the first postwar compilers of a political theory collection on forms of governance. See Carl Cohen, *Communism, Fascism, and Democracy: The Theoretical Foundations* (New York: Random House, 1962), 332.
43 William Miles Fletcher also applies this example to Japan, while Manchukuo would, of course, be an even more fitting case. See William Miles Fletcher, *The Search for a New Order: Intellectuals and Fascism in Prewar Japan* (London: Oxford University Press, 1982).
44 Alan E. Steinweis, *Art, Ideology, and Economics in Nazi Germany: The Reich Chambers of Music, Theater, and the Visual Arts* (Chapel Hill: University of North Carolina Press, 1993), 17.
45 Mutô, *Watakushi to Manshûkoku,* 194.
46 Ibid.
47 Ibid.
48 Ibid.
49 Ibid., 217.
50 Ibid.
51 Prasenjit Duara, *Sovereignty and Authenticity: Manchukuo and the East Asian Modern* (Lanham, MD: Rowman and Littlefield, 2003), 75.

52 It is not my aim to list all these sources, but a number of them can be found by looking under those published by the Manchukuo Publicity and News Bureau, the larger, umbrella organization that headed the Concordia Association.
53 Some Japanese scholars, such as Yamamoto Taketoshi of Waseda University, call this the "Information Bureau" since it was usually termed "Bureau of Information" in English-language materials.
54 Mutô Tomio, "The Spirit of Hsieh-Ho: A New Philosophy," and "An Outline of the Manchoutikuo Hsieh-ho-hui" in "Concordia and Culture in Manchoukuo," special edition of *Manchuria,* 20 July 1938.
55 Mutô, "Spirit of Hsieh-Ho," 1-2.
56 Mutô, "Outline of the Manchoutikuo Hsieh-ho-hui," 13.
57 Bureau of Information and Publicity, Department of Foreign Affairs, *Manchoukuo: Handbook of Information* (Hsinking: Manchoukuo Government, 1933), 19.
58 Ibid., 16.
59 Tessa Morris-Suzuki, "A Descent into the Past: The Frontier in the Construction of Japanese Identity." In *Multicultural Japan: Paleolithic to Postmodern,* ed. Donald Denoon, Mark Hudson, Gavan McCormack, and Tessa Morris-Suzuki (Cambridge: Cambridge University Press), 89.
60 Ibid., 88.
61 Mutô, "Spirit of Hsieh-Ho," 1.
62 Ibid., 8.
63 Ibid., 9.
64 Peter Duus, *The Japanese Discovery of America: A Brief History with Documents* (New York: Bedford Books, 1997), 27-28.
65 Mutô, "Outline of the Manchoutikuo Hsieh-ho-hui," 23. Here, we can sense echoes of Mutô's Christian socialist mentor Kagawa Toyohiko's "Kingdom of God Movement," terminated in Japan in 1934.
66 Mutô, "Outline of the Manchoutikuo Hsieh-ho-hui," 22.
67 Ibid., 21.
68 The author's grandfather-in-law Liu Shanzheng, personal interview at his son's home in Tieli, PRC, January 2000. Liu, retired head of the Tieli Education Department, came from a landlord family, which owned much of the territory between Qing'an (Qingcheng or Keijô in the Manchukuo period) and Tieli (Tetsuryô in the Manchukuo period) as well as a soybean oil factory. Due to his good Japanese language skills, which he learned in school, he served as the family's comprador for its business.
69 Ibid.
70 Mutô, "Outline of the Manchoutikuo Hsieh-ho-hui," 13.
71 Ibid., 21.
72 Ibid., 22.
73 Alan Tansman, *The Aesthetics of Japanese Fascism* (Berkeley: University of California Press, 2009), 18. However, this merging with a greater whole can also be indicative of Mutô's earlier utopian Christian beliefs and sense of mission as inspired by the teachings of his mentor Kagawa.
74 Marilyn Ivy, "Forward: Fascism, Yet?" in *The Culture of Japanese Fascism,* ed. Alan Tansman (Durham, NC: Duke University Press, 2009), xi.
75 Personal interview, Tang Xiang, history research group preceptor, Third Municipal Junior High School, Harbin, China, 31 January 2000. Incidentally, the building in which he teaches once served as a Japanese military police training facility in Harbin. It is close to the train station and, therefore, optimally situated for spying on the comings and goings of travellers who might be carrying information or planning subversion. Harbin was a centre of Chinese resistance activities in the 1930s and 1940s, and it was also one of the first areas to come under the communist umbrella in 1948 during the civil war.
76 Literally *Shufu Zhongguoren fankang yizhi de zuoyong*. Personal interview, Tang Xiang, history research group preceptor, Third Municipal Junior High School, Harbin, China, 31 January 2000.
77 Ibid., 23.

78 Barak Kushner, *The Thought War: Japanese Imperial Propaganda* (Honolulu: University of Hawaii Press, 2006), 6.
79 Ibid.
80 Taketoshi Yamamoto, "The Japanese Army's Radio Strategy in Manchuria," the Institute of 20th-Century Media, Waseda University, available at http://www.waseda.jp/.
81 For example, in 1929, the Tokyo Imperial University-educated activist Iwasaki Akira wrote an article on left-wing propaganda in the USSR. It is entitled "Senden sendô" (Propaganda and Agitation [Agit-Prop]), and it focuses on Soviet constructivism and Eisenstein's films. In 1931, Lu Xun translated it, and it appeared in the Shanghai-based publication *Mengya (Germination),* which also had a strong impact on the left-wing Chinese film world. Interestingly, after Iwasaki was arrested in the mid-1930s and spent time in jail as a result of his activism, he was offered a job with the Manchurian Film Association – another example of an intellectual who was able to translate his political ideals into right-wing proletarianism in support of Manchukuo.
82 Tôzawa Tetsuhiko, "Senden no igi" [The meaning of propaganda], in *Senbu geppô* [Pacification monthly] 3, 3 (1938): 18-25; and Yamamoto Taketoshi, ed., *Jûgonen sensô gyokumitsu shiryô-shû* [Collection of top-secret materials from the Fifteen Years' War], *Hokan 25* [Supplementary edition 25] of *Senbu geppô* [Pacification monthly] (Tokyo: Fuji shuppan, 2005), 96-98.
83 Ibid., 25.
84 See John Mullen, "Propaganda and Dissent in British Popular Song during the Great War," (no publisher, 2011), 1-15, halshs.archives-ouvertes.fr/docs/00/68.../6T_C2011_13JMullen.pdf.
85 Tamura Toshio, "Zentaishugi kokka no okeru senden hôshin" [Propaganda policies in totalitarian countries], *Senbu geppo* [Pacification monthly] 3, 9 (1938): 2-15. See also Yamamoto, 65-69.
86 Tamura, *Zentaishugi kokka no okeru senden hôshin,* 15; Yamamoto, *Jûgonen sensô gyokumitsu shiryô-shû,* 68.
87 Tamura, *Zentaishugi kokka no okeru senden hôshin,* 2-15; Yamamoto, *Jûgonen sensô gyokumitsu shiryô-shû,* 65-69.
88 Tamura Toshio, "Senden-sen ni okeru: Bunkajin no batteki" [The selection of cultural figures for the propaganda war] in Tamura, *Zentaishugi kokka ni okeru senden hôshin,* 15.
89 On propaganda before 1937, see Hirano Ken'ichirô, ed., *Nitchû sensôki no Chûgoku ni okeru shakai bunka henyô* [The Acculturation of Society and Culture in China during the Sino-Japanese Period] (Tokyo: Tôyô Bunko, 2007).
90 Kishi, "Fusion and Crack," 95.
91 *Manshû jijô annai-sho* [Manchurian Affairs Information Bureau], *Manshû kankei shiryô shûsei* [Collection of materials related to Manchuria] (Hôten [Fengtian]: Osaka-ya gô shoten, 1939), 779.
92 Kishi, "Fusion and Crack," 95.
93 Taketoshi Yamamoto, "The Japanese Army's Radio Strategy in Manchuria.
94 Ôbama Shigeru, "Dialogue on the Culture of Manchoukuo," *Manchuria,* 25 December 1939, 1613.
95 "Governmental Structure of Manchukuo," *Manchuria,* April 1940, 131.
96 Duara, *Sovereignty and Authenticity,* 224.
97 Manshûkoku tsûshin-sha [Manchukuo News Agency], ed., *Manshûkoku gensei kôtoku 5-nen ban* [The current situation of Manchukuo in the fifth year of Kangde (facsimile edition)] (Tokyo: Kress Publication, 2000), 55-56.
98 In my seminar entitled "American Perspectives of Modern Japanese History," during a one-month visiting appointment at Beijing University in April 2007, a Japanese graduate student and former journalist mentioned an extraordinary memory of his late father. According to this Kantô Army doctor, preparations were made prior to the 7 July "Incident" to move troops into the area around Beijing. Originally, "Suzuki" hoped to receive a master's degree in Sino-Japanese history at Beijing University, but he decided instead to focus on rural cooperatives because he feared right-wing Japanese activists if, on his return to Japan, he dared bring this manoeuvre up in public scholarship.

99 Kobayashi Hideo, *Ryûjôkô jiken o megutte: Ryûjôkô jiken rokujusûnen ni yosete* [On the Marco Polo Bridge incident: Some sixty years after the Marco Polo Bridge incident], *Rekishigaku kenkyû* [History research] 699 (July 1997): 30-35.
100 Kishi, "Fusion and Crack," 96.
101 Ibid., 97. This paragraph is heavily indebted to Kishi's careful study of the hierarchy of the *Kôhôsho's* penetration into localities from the Shinkyô central office.
102 See Rana Mitter, *The Manchurian Myth: Nationalism, Resistance, and Collaboration in Modern China* (Berkeley: University of California Press, 2000).
103 Not all Japanese-German co-projects were successful. This has to do with the fact that Germans, despite their alliance with Japan, harboured racist attitudes toward the non-white Japanese. For example, Michael Baskett argues that the film *Atarashiki tsuchi* could be viewed as a failure of the fascist cultural alliance. See Baskett, *Attractive Empire.*
104 Kushner, *Thought War,* 9-10.
105 Gregory Kasza, *The State and the Mass Media in Japan, 1918-1945* (Berkeley: University of California, 1988), 170-71.
106 "Cultural History of Manchoukuo: Sadly Hampered at Time of Warlord Regime Present Government Plans to Institute System to Give Best Possible Kind of Knowledge," *Manchuria,* 1 August 1937, 491.
107 Takahashi Motoichi, "Kôhô gyôsei-ron: Manshûkoku kôhô gyôsei wo chûshin ni" [Discourse on the administration of publicity and news: Focusing on the administration of publicity and news in Manchukuo], *Senbu geppo* [Pacification monthly] 3, 9 (1938): 16-29. See also Yamamoto, *Jûgonen sensô gyokumitsu shiryô-shû,* 69-72.
108 Takahashi, *Kôhô gyôsei-ron,* 19.
109 Aside from my analysis, the information in this paragraph comes from Kawamura Kiyoshi, ed., *Manshû kankei shiryô shûsei* [Collection of materials related to Manchuria], (Shinkyô: Manchurian Affairs Information Bureau, 1938), 779.
110 This is what it is called in English translation in Ôbama, "Dialogue on the Culture of Manchoukuo," 1613.
111 Ibid.
112 Kishi, "Fusion and Crack," 98-99.
113 A discussion of what Mutô means by culture, and how he defines it in the 1941 context of the *Geibun shidô yokô,* may be found in the next section.
114 Ôbama, "Dialogue on the Culture of Manchoukuo," 1613.
115 Ibid.
116 Tamura Toshio, Director of the Education Bureau, Manchukuo, "On Cultural Administration," *Manchuria,* 1 April 1940, 99.
117 Hiroshi Takama, Department of People's Welfare, "New Culture in Manchoukuo," *Manchuria,* 1 April 1940, 138.
118 Duara, *Sovereignty and Authenticity,* 224.
119 On 16 July 1940, Prime Minister Konoe appointed Matsuoka Yôsuke, a former president of SMRC, as foreign minister to Greater East Asia. Konoe hoped that Matsuoka, who was popular with the public, could control the Japanese military. The New Order was based on the Japan-Manchukuo-China allegiance and was to include Indochina and the East Indies.
120 Manshûkoku tsûshin-sha [Manchukuo News Agency], *Manshûkoku gensei kôtoku 5-nen ban,* 484, 503.
121 Mutô, *Watakushi to Manshûkoku,* 340.
122 Because of the nuances of translating Japanese into English, I prefer to translate *Geibun shidô yôkô* as "Prospectus for the Guidance of the Arts and Culture" rather than as Duara's "Summary of Guidelines to Art and Literature" (Duara, *Sovereignty and Authenticity,* 224); Kishi's "Guidelines on Art and Culture" (Kishi, "Fusion and Crack," 105); or Smith's "Artistic Guidelines" (Norman Smith, *Resisting Manchukuo: Chinese Women Writers under the Japanese Occupation* [Vancouver: UBC Press, 2007], 51). Both Duara and Smith work primarily with Chinese materials, and they translate the term according to Chinese understandings. Indeed, *Gangyao,* in Chinese, means "outline" (See the II entry for *yao* 要 [fourth tone] in *The Concise English-Chinese Chinese-English Dictionary* [Hong Kong: Oxford University Press, 1986], 510),

but this is not the same as *yôkô,* which is listed in Japanese-language propaganda materials (and which, in Chinese, is read as *yaogang,* which is not a word). In Japanese, *yôkô*'s nuance is not the same as it is in Chinese, and it could mean either "outline, summary, (or) prospectus" (*Genius Japanese-English Dictionary,* electronic version). "Prospectus" has a future-oriented connotation, indicating a manual, guide, or handbook, so this is how I translate it.

123 Kishi, "Fusion and Crack," 106.

124 Duara, *Sovereignty and Authenticity,* 224.

125 Kishi, "Fusion and Crack," 107.

126 Ibid., 107.

127 Manshûkoku tsûshin-sha, *Manshûkoku gensei kôtoku 5-nen ban,* 592.

128 Kishi, "Fusion and Crack," 94-95.

129 Ibid., 107-8.

130 Iino Masahito, *"Manshû bijutsu" nenpyô* [Chronology of art in Manchuria] (Kôfu City: Yoneya, 1998), 4.

131 Quoted in Duara, *Sovereignty and Authenticity,* 224; and Feng Weiqun, "'Wenyi zhidao gangyao' chulong yihou" [After the appearance of the Summary of Guidelines to Art and Literature], in *Weiman wenhua* [Manchukuo culture], *Weiman shiliao congshu* [Series of Manchukuo historical materials] volume 6, ed. Sun Bang and Yu Haiying (Changchun: Jilin Renmin Chubanshe, 1993), 13-14.

132 Duara, *Sovereignty and Authenticity,* 224.

133 English translation in Kishi, "Fusion and Crack," 108. See also Mutô, *Manshûkoku no bunka seisaku,* 1-2.

134 Quoted in Ibid., 108.

135 Mutô Tomio, "Manshûkoku no bunka seisaku: Geibun shidô yôkô ni tsuite" [Cultural policies in Manchukuo: Concerning the prospectus for the guidance of the arts and culture)], in *Dokushojin* [Reader], *Manshûkoku bunka no dôkô to bunken: Kenkoku jûnen keishuku tokushû* [Cultural trends and literary works in Manchukuo: Special edition celebrating the tenth anniversary of the nation's founding] (September 1942), 1.

136 Ibid., 1.

137 The Prospectus itself comprises the first and second pages of the article. See Ibid., 1-2.

138 Steinweis, *Art, Ideology, and Economics,* 33.

139 Ibid., 1.

140 Iino, *Manshû bijutsu nenpyô,* 70.

141 These four included the Manchurian Dramatists Association *(Manshû gekidan kyôkai),* the Manchurian Musicians Association *(Manshû gakudan kyôkai),* the Manchurian Artists Association, and the Manchurian Writers and Artists Association. See Iino, *Manshû bijutsu nenpyô,* 76.

142 Ibid., 73.

143 Ibid., 76.

144 Steinweis, *Art, Ideology, and Economics in Nazi Germany,* 1.

145 Ibid., 17.

146 Ibid., 41-42.

147 Ibid., 21.

148 Yamamoto, "Japanese Army's Radio Strategy," 20.

149 Steinweis, *Art, Ideology, and Economics in Nazi Germany,* 1.

150 Yamamoto, "Japanese Army's Radio Strategy," 8.

151 For example, the literary giant Kawabata was invited specifically by the newspaper as an authoritative cultural figure from domestic Japan and, thus, as an appropriate spokesman for this notable, well-publicized debate on culture and the arts in the Manchukuo context. The next chapter explores the writer's impressions of Manchukuo and its culture as well as issues surrounding Kawabata's role in stimulating literary endeavours in Manchukuo.

152 Quoted in Iino, *Manshû bijutsu nenpyô,* 72 (my translation).

153 Ibid., 72.

154 See Chapter 2 for a discussion of Mutô's fostering of the leadership of writers like Yamada under this new system.

155 Mutô, *Watakushi to Manshûkoku,* 340.

156 Iino, *Manshû bijutsu nenpyô,* 49.
157 On 12 July 1941, in the evening edition of the *Manshû nichi nichi shimbun,* it was stated that Ishii Hakutei would be serving as one of the judges for the fourth national art exhibition in Manchukuo. See ibid., 72.
158 Chiba Yoshi, *Fuan to gensô: Kanten ni okeru "Manshû" hyôshô no seiji-teki imi* [Disquiet and illusion: The political meaning of images of Manchuria in official art exhibitions], in *Hyôshô/teikoku/gendâ: Seisen kara reisen he* [Representation, empire and gender: From the sacred war to the Cold War], ed. Ikeda Shinobu (Research Project Report, Graduate School of Humanities and Social Sciences, Chiba University, 2008), 53.
159 As explained previously, this usually means the Han Chinese population, both because they numbered about 90 percent of the total population in the area and because, aside from the Japanese population, they had the greatest access to cultural, economic, and political capital.
160 Last stanza (number 12) in Mutô Tomio, *Manshû sanka* [Song of praise for Manchuria] (Hôten [Fengtian]: Hakukaze shobô, 1941), 14-15 (my translation).
161 Notably, Amakasu was one of the bureaucrats who did not abscond after 15 August 1945. Instead, with the 8 August invasion of Manchukuo and the southward advance of his fiercely hated enemy, the communist Soviets, he took his life by swallowing potassium cyanide capsules. In *Manshûkoku no danmen,* Mutô praises Amakasu for this "sacrificial act," whereby he remained with the Manchurian people. However, this was also a cowardly act that enabled him to avoid responsibility as he may well have feared reprisals from the Russians, who would have tried him for war crimes.
162 Anne Tucker, Kôtarô Iizawa, and Naoyuki Kinoshita, *The History of Japanese Photography* (New Haven: Yale University Press, 2003), 323.
163 Mutô, *Manshûkoku no bunka seisaku,* 1-8.
164 Smith, *Resisting Manchukuo,* 55.
165 Quoted in ibid., 55. See also Xu Naixiang and Huang Wanhua, *Zhongguo kangzhan shiqi lunxianqu wenxue shi* [History of the literature of the enemy-occupied territories during the war against Japan] (Fuzhou: Fujian jiaoyu chubanshe, 1995), 264.
166 The following chapter contains a fuller discussion of why this is so.
167 Mutô, *Manshûkoku no danmen,* 254.
168 Driscoll, *Absolute Erotic,* 295.
169 Kishi, "Fusion and Crack," 122.
170 Ibid.
171 Ibid. And see Amakasu Masahiko, "Geibunjin ni nozomu: Kessen geibuntaikai ni okeru aisatsu" [My hopes for artists and writers: Introductory remarks at the Arts Congress at a time of decisive war], *Geibun* [The arts], January 1945, 35-6.
172 Kishi, "Fusion and Crack," 125.
173 Ibid., 123.
174 Mutô, *Manshûkoku no danmen,* 254.
175 Ray A. Moore and Donald L. Robinson, *Partners for Democracy: Crafting the New Japanese State under MacArthur* (New York: Oxford University Press 2004), 39.
176 Ibid.
177 Ibid.
178 Mutô Tomio, *Zaigunbi wo ikidôru tsuihôsha no kokuhaku* [Confessions of an exile indignant against remilitarization] (Tokyo: Bunrin-dô, 1951). I thank Mark Driscoll for recommending this earlier source, which he believes contains more candid information, with Mutô reflecting on his war responsibility (personal conversation, July 2008, Tokyo). By the 1980s, rising currents of nationalism and feelings of *Nihonjinron* (Japanese exceptionalism) sustained Mutô's later account. His 1988 memoirs, *Watakushi to Manshûkoku,* are much less contrite and were written at the height of Japan's postwar economic strength, when *Nihonjinron* proponents and Japan's right-wing adherents began to criticize a "self-chastizing" view of history.
179 Mutô, *Manshûkoku no danmen,* 254; and "Religion: Evangelism Is War," no author listed *Time Magazine,* 65, issue 6, 7 February 1955, 59, 1 p. available at http://www.time.com/.

180 "Religion: Nyuzu for Japan" no author listed, *Time Magazine,* 60, issue 23, 57, 1 p., 8 December 1952, available at http://www.time.com/.
181 "Religion," no author listed.
182 See Mutô, *Manshûkoku no danmen.* Here, Mutô provides a cursory discussion of his war responsibility. However, the text is mostly a homage to his deceased friend Amakasu. This memoir began with a picture taken in 1938, when Mutô solidified his friendship with Amakasu during their goodwill tour of Europe. There is also a photograph of Amakasu's body at his funeral, and his last testament is reproduced in the book.
183 "Religion," no author listed.
184 Ibid.
185 As of 2007, Japan's population numbered 128 million, and, according to a 2005 report by the Agency for Cultural Affairs, 3 million Japanese self-identified as "Christian." However, of this number, many identified with more than one religion, including Buddhism, Shintoism, and several of the "New Religions." See US Department of State, "International Religious Freedom Report 2007 (Japan): Bureau of Democracy, Human Rights, and Labor," available at http://www.state.gov/.
186 After his mentor H.W. Meyers joined the faculty at Kobe Theological Seminary, Kagawa transferred from Meiji Gakuin and joined him to finish his studies in Kobe. See Mullins, "Christianity as a Transnational Social Movement," 72.
187 See Mutô Tomio, *Kagawa Toyohiko zenshû daijesuto* [Digest of Kagawa Toyohiko's collected works] (Tokyo: Kirisuto shimbun-sha, 1966).

Chapter 7: The Legitimization of a Multi-Ethnic Literary Culture in Manchukuo

1 An Association for Asian Studies Northeast Asian Committee summer research grant in Tokyo during July 2008 funded part of the research for this chapter. Prior research was also conducted in Tokyo at Waseda University under a 2004-5 Fulbright USIIE Graduate Research Fellowship. I also thank Tan'o Yasunori of Waseda University for finding an original 1942 copy of the volume *Manshûkoku kaku minzoku sôsaku senshû (1)* for me to purchase through a bookseller he knew. This chapter was initially presented at the November 2007 Association for Japanese Literary Studies at Princeton University, and a much-revised version was presented at the March 2009 Annual Meeting for the Association of Asian Studies in Chicago in a panel entitled "Re-Examining Kawabata Yasunari: Cultural Nationalism and the War." I thank panel organizer Miho Matsugu, discussant Eiji Sekine, and fellow panelists Charles Cabell and Hiromi Dollase, along with all those who gave comments. A prior, much-abridged version of this chapter was published in "Manchukuo and the Creation of a New Multi-Ethnic Literature: Kawabata Yasunari's Promotion of 'Manchurian' Culture, 1941-1942," in Richard King, Cody Poulton, and Katsuhiko Endo, eds., *Sino-Japanese Transculturation: From the Late Nineteenth Century to the End of the Pacific War* (Lanham, MA: Lexington Books, 2012), 189-208.
2 See Aaron Gerow, *A Page of Madness: Cinema and Modernity in 1920s Japan* (Ann Arbor, MI: Center for Japanese Studies, University of Michigan, 2008).
3 See Kawabata Yasunari, *The Scarlet Gang of Asakusa,* trans. Alisa Freedman (Berkeley: University of California Press, 2005). Kawabata's novel was first serialized in the *Tokyo Asahi Shimbun* [Tokyo Morning News] from 20 December 1929 until 16 February 1930, and was completed currently in *Kaizô* [Reconstruction] vol. 12, 9 (1930), and in *Shinchô* [New Currents] 27, 9 (1930).
4 See Kawabata Yasunari, *Yukiguni* [Snow country] (Tokyo: Iwanami shoten, 1952, rev. 2003); and Kawabata Yasunari, *Snow Country,* trans. Edward G. Seidensticker (New York: Vintage Books, 1996).
5 Sandra Wilson, "The Past in the Present: War in the Narratives of Modernity in the 1920s and 1930s," in *Being Modern in Japan: Culture and Society from the 1910s to the 1930s,* ed. Elise K. Tipton and John Clark (Honolulu: University of Hawaii Press, 2000), 183 (emphasis in original).
6 Barak Kushner, *The Thought War: Japanese Imperial Propaganda* (Honolulu: University of Hawaii Press, 2006), 10-11.

7 Zeljko Cipris, "Responsibility of Intellectuals: Kobayashi Hideo on Japan at War," *Japan Focus,* available at http://old.japanfocus.org/.
8 Fukuda Kugao, "Bungei jûgô undô," special issue, *Kokubungaku kaishaku to kanshô* [Understanding and appreciating national literature studies] May (1982): 561-62.
9 Alan E. Steinweis, *Art, Ideology, and Economics in Nazi Germany: The Reich Chambers of Music, Theater, and the Visual Arts* (Chapel Hill: University of North Carolina Press, 1993), 3.
10 Ibid., 35 (emphasis mine).
11 Prasenjit Duara, *Sovereignty and Authenticity: Manchukuo and the East Asian Modern* (Lanham, MD: Rowman and Littlefield, 2003), 17.
12 For more on "ethnicity" and "race" in Manchuria and Manchukuo, see Mariko Asano Tamanoi, "Knowledge, Power, and Racial Classifications: The 'Japanese' in 'Manchuria,'" *Journal of Asian Studies* 59, 2 (2000): 248-76.
13 See Kawamura Minato, *Bungaku kara miru "Manshû gozoku kyôwa" no yume to genjitsu* [Envisioning the dream and reality of Manchuria's harmony of the five races through literature] (Tokyo: Yoshikawa Hirofumi bunkan, 1998); Kawamura Minato, *Umi wo watatta Nihongo: Shokuminchi no "Kokugo" no jikan* [The Japanese language overseas: The time of national language in the colonial territories] (Tokyo: Seichi-sha, 1994); and Komagome Takeshi, *Shokuminchi teikoku Nihon no bunga tôgô* [The cultural integration of Imperial Japan with the colonies] (Tokyo: Iwanami shoten, 1996).
14 Perhaps this is because, by this time (1932), Korea had been under direct Japanese imperial control for over two decades. It had been taken over as a protectorate in 1905, following the Russo-Japanese War, and then annexed by Japan in 1910. Koreans provided the most active resistance both to the Kantô Army during its takeover of Manchuria and then to the Manchukuo regime itself. Though the Korean language was allowed to persist on an informal level, and Koreans ran local Korean-language papers, the use of Japanese was strictly enforced in the Japanese-headed educational system, which was tied to that of the imperial centre. In Korea, it was not until the *Nai Sen-ittai* (Domestic Japan and Korea as One Body) campaign in 1938 that the strictness of Japanese rule slightly relaxed, and efforts were made to allow a small measure of *cultural* specificity in Korea through the nominal revival of Korean culture and the promotion of more Koreans to higher political positions. However, the *Nai Sen-ittai* initiative had come too late, and many Koreans harboured great resentment against Japan for the initial brutality of colonial rule and the subsequent Japanese attempt at the selective destruction of much of Korean culture.
15 For more about the total war system in Imperial Japan and its colonies, see Kobayashi Hideo, *Teikoku Nihon to sôryokusen taisei* [Imperial Japan and the total war system] (Tokyo: Yûshi-sha, 2004).
16 Hasegawa Magohei, *Kyokujitsu no hatameku tokoro* [The places where the flag of the rising sun flutters in the wind] (Tokyo: Banseisha, 1937).
17 Ibid., Introduction.
18 This is the same as the Manchukuo Publicity and News Bureau, or the *Kôhôsho,* in charge of Manchukuo's propaganda and media activities.
19 By "Manchurian," Yamaguchi means "Mandarin Chinese." This term is used to separate the Chinese language from its associations with China proper south of the Great Wall. See Yamaguchi Shinichi, "Contemporary Literature in Manchuria," in "Concordia and Culture in Manchukuo" special edition of *Manchuria,* published by *Manchuria Daily News,* 20 July 1938, 27.
20 Ibid.
21 This centralization referred to by Obama pertains to matters falling under a more general "culture" category, like that defined by Mutô in 1941: "The Department of People's Welfare also handles all affairs relating to education, religion, public health, sanitation and art. Cultural activities related to communications and radio broadcasting are in the hands of the Department of Communications." See Obama Shigeru, "Dialogue on the Culture of Manchoukuo," in *Manchuria,* published by *Manchuria Daily News,* 25 December 1939, 1613.
22 According to Norman Smith, these included "rebellious tendencies toward the current political situation; criticism of the national polity without sincerity, or of a non-constructive nature; agitation of citizens to antagonistic emotions; exclusive use of darkness to depict

life before and after the establishment of the nation; use of decadent thought as the main point; concerning love lust, to describe that moment with; recreational love that denigrates chastity, lust, abnormal sexual desire or acting wrongly out of personal considerations, incest or adultery; description of commission of a crime, written very cruelly or seriously; use of matchmakers and domestics as the main topic, and especially exaggerated descriptions of the customs and human relationships of the entertainment districts." Norman Smith, *Resisting Manchukuo: Chinese Women Writers under the Japanese Occupation* (Vancouver: UBC Press, 2007), 50. See also Yu Lei, *Ziliao* [Data], in Feng Weiqun, Wang Jianzhong, Li Chunyan, Li Shuquan, eds., *Dongbei lunxian shiqi wenxue guoji xueshu yantaohui lunwenji* [Collection of papers from the International Symposium on Literature of the Enemy-Occupied Northeast] (Shenyang: Shenyang chubanshe, 1992), 181.

23 *Mutô kôhôsho-chô ni kiku – zadankai: Junbungaku wo kibô, saikin de wa "Shunren" ga kessaku* [Inquiring of Publicity and News Bureau chief Mutô – round-table discussion: Envisioning a pure literature, recently "Spring Festival Couplet" is a masterpiece], *Manshû nichi nichi shimbun* [Manchuria daily news], 5 July 1941, 1.

24 In traditional China, during the Spring Festival held in late January or early February, two couplets of poetry were brushed on red paper in black ink and then pasted upside-down for luck on the two sides of the main entranceway to the family home.

25 Kimura Ryôji, *Dairen monogatari* [A tale of Dairen] (Tokyo: Kenkôsha, 1974), 197.

26 See Culver, "Transnationalism, Surrealism, and the Avant-Garde in the Japanese Empire, 1924-1941," in Culver, "'Between Distant Realities,'" 45-147.

27 "Mutô kôhôsho-chô ni kiku – zadankai: Senmonka wo tsukuru, 'geibun shidô yôkô' wo megutte" [Inquiring of Publicity and News Bureau chief Mutô – round-table discussion: The creation of specialists, concerning the prospectus for the guidance of the arts and culture], *Manshû nichi nichi shimbun* [Manchuria daily news], 4 July 1941. See also Iino Masahito, *'Manshû bijutsu' nenpyô* [Chronology of 'Manchurian art'] (Kôfu: Yamanashi Prefecture Museum of Art, 1998), 4. For a contemporary Japanese description of the consolidation process under the *Prospectus* and its effects on culture in Manchukuo, see Haruyama Yukio, *Manshû no bunka* [Manchurian culture] (Hôten [Fengtian, Manchukuo]: Osakaya gô shoten, 1943), 356.

28 *Senmonka wo tsukuru,* 1; Iino, *'Manshû bijutsu' nenpyô,* 70.

29 Smith, *Resisting Manchukuo,* 51. The regulations are listed in Yu, *Ziliao,* 174-8.

30 Smith, *Resisting Manchukuo,* 51.

31 *Senmonka wo tsukuru,* 1.

32 Ibid.

33 Smith, *Resisting Manchukuo,* 51.

34 I thank Norman Smith for giving me the dates for these authors. See Smith, *Resisting Manchuko,* 51.

35 Gu Ding, "Xianhua wentan" [Gossip about literary circles], in *Gu Ding zuopin xuan* [Selected works of Gu Ding], ed. Li Chunyan (Shenyang, PRC: Chunfeng wenyi, 1995), 9.

36 Rana Mitter, *The Manchurian Myth: Nationalism, Resistance, and Collaboration in Modern China* (Berkeley: University of California Press, 2000).

37 Iino, *"Manshû bijutsu" nenpyô,* 72.

38 Strangely, the microfilm copies of the 7 July edition of the *Manchuria Daily News* were missing from Waseda University's microfilm media collection. The date 7 July 1941 marks the fourth anniversary of the beginning of the Second Sino-Japanese War.

39 Not long after participating in this round-table discussion, both Miki and Ozaki would be brought into police custody for their Marxist convictions and alleged communist connections. After his arrest in the early 1940s, Miki died in prison in September 1945. During the infamous 1941 *Mantetsu jiken* (SMRC Incident) Ozaki was implicated in the Sorge Affair, where he was accused of spying for the Soviet Union due to his connections with Richard Sorge and Agnes Smedley. He was tried and executed.

40 Gennifer Weisenfeld, ed., "Guest Editor's Introduction," in "Visual Cultures of Japanese Imperialism," special issue, *positions: east asia cultures critique* 8, 3 (2000): 592.

41 Haruyama's impressions from his first visit to Manchukuo appeared in his first book. See Haruyama Yukio, *Manshû fûbutsushi* [Manchurian scenery] (Tokyo: Seikatsusha, 1941).

42 This publication often featured the writings of Takiguchi Shûzô, Kitagawa Fuyuhiko, and others who promoted literary surrealism in Japan. In 1930, Kitagawa condemned it as not politically radical enough and formed his own journal entitled *Shi. Genjitsu (Poetry. Reality).*
43 Haruyama, *Manshû no bunka,* 334-36.
44 Ibid., 329-30.
45 Ibid., 331.
46 Ibid., 330-31.
47 Donald Keene, *Dawn to the West: Japanese Literature of the Modern Era – Fiction* (New York: Holt, Rinehart, and Winston, 1984), 820.
48 Ibid., 821.
49 Gavan McCormack, "Manchukuo: Constructing the Past," *East Asian History* 2 (1991): 109.
50 In the story appearing in *Kaizô,* Kawabata's character Chikako goes to Manchukuo after her failure as a dancer in Japan. This move seemingly transformed her, with the "wildness" of the region distorting her feminine character and sexuality, while calling her Japaneseness into question. See Charles Cabell, "Eugenic Thought in Kawabata Yasunari's 'Of Birds and Beasts,'" paper presented at the Annual Meeting of the Association for Asian Studies, Chicago, March 2009.
51 Discussed by Hiromi Dollase, "Kawabata's Wartime Message in *Utsukushii tabi* [Beautiful Voyage]," paper delivered at Annual Meeting of the Association for Asian Studies, Chicago, March 2009.
52 I thank Kawabata scholar and translator Martin Holman of the University of Missouri for pointing this out after my presentation of parts of this text at the 2009 Association for Asian Studies meeting in Chicago. He noted that, as scholars, we are all in part complicit in the agendas of our state and federal governments in so far as our institutions and research receive funding. Kawabata's attraction to the Manchukuo endeavour, *gozoku-kyôwa* ideals, and Pan-Asianist rhetoric supported by a fascist wartime Japan has parallels with our own current focus on globalization initiatives and diversity education in state-run academic institutions. The growth of Asian studies programs also proceeds with these broader governmental initiatives in mind.
53 Robert R. Tomes, *Apocalypse Then: American Intellectuals and the Vietnam War, 1954-1975* (New York: New York University Press, 1998), 37.
54 Peter O'Connor, "General Introduction: Japanese Propaganda Books in the Modern Period – Writing against the Tide," in *Japanese Propaganda: Selected Readings, Series 1 – Books 1872-1943,* ed. Peter O'Connor (Kent, UK: Global Oriental, 2004), 9.
55 For an expansion of the topics discussed in this section, see Annika A. Culver, "'Between Distant Realities': The Japanese Avant-Garde, Surrealism, and the Colonies, 1924-1943" (PhD diss., University of Chicago, 2007), chap. 5. I also thank Charles Cabell of Tokyo University for sharing with me key chapters of his dissertation, including Chapter 3, "The Empire Dressed in Nationalist Drag: Kawabata's Essays on Manshûkoku," in Charles Cabell, "Maiden Dreams: Kawabata Yasunari's Beautiful Japanese Empire, 1930-1945" (PhD diss., Harvard University, 1999). Cabell also provided astute comments on my translated passages from Kawabata's introduction, illuminating grammatically complex passages.
56 See Kawabata Yasunari, *Manshûkoku kaku minzoku sôsaku senshû* 1 [Anthology of literary works by each ethnic group in Manchukuo 1] (Tokyo: Sôgansha, 1942); and *Manshûkoku kaku minzoku sôsaku senshû* 2 [Anthology of literary works by each ethnic group in Manchukuo 2] (Tokyo: Sôgansha, 1944). A copy of the first volume was donated by Kawabata to the *Nihon kindai bungakukan* (Museum of Modern Japanese Literature) in Tokyo. I thank the librarians at this institution for locating and copying rare sources for me in 2004-5 and in July 2008. This chapter evolved out of the fortuitous discovery of the two original volumes of literature edited in part by Kawabata in 1942 and 1944. They have recently been reprinted by Yumani shobô in the *Nippon shokuminchi bungaku-sei senshû* (Collection of the Essence of Japanese Colonial Literature) series (2000). I also wish to express my gratitude to Iino Masahito, curator at the Yamanashi Prefectural Museum of Art, for sending me invaluable materials, including the privately published *"Manshû bijutsu" nenpyô (Chronology of "Manchurian Art")* and a chronology of the wartime activities of artists, entitled *Sensô ni itta gakkatachi (Artists at War).*

57 See the original copyright page in Kawabata, *Manshûkoku kaku minzoku kaku minzoku sôsaku senshû,* 1.

58 Kawabata is indicated as first among the list of editors in the 2000 reprints of the two editions. See *Manshûkoku kaku minzoku sôsaku senshû 1, 2* (Tokyo: Yumani shobô, 2000). In fact, in the two originals, from 1942 and 1944, respectively, he is listed as first on the *second* line of editors, after Gu Ding.

59 For more on Wu Ying and the complex role of other Chinese women writers in the state, see Smith, *Resisting Manchukuo.* Information on Shi Jun and others can be found in Xu Naixiang and Huang Wanhua, eds., *Zhongguo kangzhan shiqi lunxianqu wnexue shi* (History of the literature of the enemy-occupied territories during China's war of resistance] (Fuzhou: Fujian jiaoyu chubanshe, 1995).

60 *Shokuminchi bunka kenkyûkai* [Colonial culture research group], ed., *"Manshûkoku" bunka saimoku* [An outline of culture in Manchukuo] (Tokyo: Fuji shuppan, 2005), 199-200.

61 Ibid.

62 Ibid., 201-2.

63 I thank Kim Jaeyong, professor of Korean literature at Wonkwang University, South Korea, for indicating this to me after his lecture entitled "The Representation of Manchuria in Korean Literature in the Late Colonial Period," delivered at the meeting of the *Manshûkoku bungaku kenkyû-kai* (Manchukuo Literature Research Group) in Tokyo on 7 July 2008. Kim clarified my questions on Yom's dates and edited work via email on 21 April 2009.

64 Kim Jaeyong, comments, Tokyo, 7 July 2008.

65 *Shokuminchi bunka kenkyûkai, Manshûkoku bunka saimoku,* 202.

66 Ibid.

67 Kawabata, *Manshûkoku kaku minzoku sôsaku senshû* 1, 6.

68 Ibid., 250-77.

69 Nogawa's novel *Gobô (Burdock Root)* was nominated for the Akutagawa prize. See Kawamura, "One View of the History of Japanese Proletarian Literature," 4.

70 Kawamura Minato, "One View of the History of Japanese Proletarian Literature: On Nogawa Takashi," David Rosenfeld trans., paper delivered at the Proletarian Literatures of East Asia Symposium, University of Chicago, 2002, 1-4.

71 This may be a facile assessment at best of the thirty-seven works in the two collections, which, as historical documents indicative of the climate of the era, beg to be translated by future scholars. Individual stories, like those by Nogawa and Gu Ding, evince the influence of proletarian literature. My own work on Kitagawa and Anzai Fuyue shows that proletarian themes can be intertwined with more complex agendas and political sympathies on the part of the author. See Annika A. Culver, "Colonial Manchuria in the Surrealist Imagination: The Poetry and Prose of Kitagawa Fuyuhiko as Modernist History," *Proceedings of the Association for Japanese Literary Studies* 4 (2003): 264-77; and Annika Culver, "Two Japanese Avant-Garde Writers' Views of Gender Relations and Colonial Oppression in Manchuria, 1929-1931," *US-Japan Women's Journal* 37 (2009): 91-116.

72 Kawabata, *Manshûkoku kaku minzoku sôsaku senshû* 1, 5.

73 I thank Charles Cabell for answering my questions about this phrase and offering feedback on my translation.

74 Kawabata, *Manshûkoku kaku minzoku sôsaku senshû* 1, 5.

75 Many of these Chinese are actually Hakka, from Fujian and Guandong provinces, and are ethnically distinct from the Han Chinese of Manchuria, who originally came from the northern Chinese provinces of Shandong and Hebei. Due to their diet and genetic differences, northern Han Chinese tend to be taller than people in the southernmost regions of China and Southeast Asia.

76 For more on this topic, see Faye Yuan Kleeman, *Under an Imperial Sun: Japanese Colonial Literature of Taiwan and the South* (Honolulu: University of Hawaii Press, 2003).

77 Kitagawa, who was a surrealist poet active in the proletarian literature movement in the 1930s and who was sent to Singapore in February 1942 with a troop of writers, wrote disparagingly of the shorter, darker-skinned inhabitants. See the conclusion of Annika A. Culver, "Modernity in Conflict: Destabilizing Visions of the Modern in the Poetry of Kitagawa Fuyuhiko" (MA thesis, University of Chicago, 2002).

78 Kawabata, *Manshûkoku kaku minzoku sôsaku senshû 1,* 5.
79 Richard H. Mitchell, "Japan's Peace Preservation Law of 1925: Its Origins and Its Significance," *Monumenta Nipponica* 28, 3 (1973): 269.
80 Smith, *Resisting Manchukuo,* 10.
81 Kawabata, *Manshûkoku kaku minzoku sôsaku senshû* 1, 6.
82 See Smith, *Resisting Manchukuo.*
83 Ibid., 11.
84 For a more detailed description of the Manchukuo regime's organized targeting of a supposed communist conspiracy through the persecution of intellectuals and other alleged sympathizers, see Louise Young, *Japan's Total Empire: Manchuria and the Culture of Wartime Imperialism* (Berkeley: University of California Press, 1998), 301-2.
85 See Sakuramoto Tomio, *Kûhaku to sekinin: Senjikan no shijin-tachi* [Blank and responsibility: Poets during wartime] (Tokyo: Mirai-sha, 1983).

Conclusion: The Reflected Utopia Darkens

1 Asada Sadao, *Culture Shock and Japan-American Relations: Historical Essays* (St. Louis: University of Missouri Press, 2007), 174.
2 For a recent study of historical memories of the *hikiagesha,* or "repatriates," see Mariko Tamanoi, *Memory Maps: The State and Manchuria in Postwar Japan* (Honolulu: University of Hawaii Press, 2009).
3 See Suk-jung Han, "The Problem of Sovereignty: Manchukuo, 1932-1937," *positions: east asia cultures critique* 12, 2 (2004): 457-78.
4 See, for example, Kimura Ryôji, *Dairen monogatari* [A tale of Dairen] (Tokyo: Kenkôsha, 1974).
5 For example, in July 2008, I purchased an original copy of Kawabata Yasunari, Yamada Seizaburô, Kitamura Kenjirô, Gu Ding, Kishida Kunio, and Shimaki Kensake, eds., *Manshûkoku kaku minzoku bungaku sen 1* [Anthology of Literary Works by Each Ethnic Group in Manchukuo, 1] (Tokyo: Sôgansha, 1942) for 10,600 yen, or nearly US$100, from a used bookseller in Nagano. Otani Shôgo notes that these works, whose historical value is now being recognized, were sold very cheaply in the postwar period until the 1990s.
6 In furthering the combined interests of scholarship with advertising the wares of the press, representatives from Fuji Publishing Company, like Hosoda Satoshi, helpfully came to a July 2008 meeting of the Manchukuo Literature Research Group in the Shibuya ward of Tokyo. They displayed some of their latest publications and also encouraged suggestions for reprints while giving us advertising flyers featuring recent texts. Needless to say, most of us bought books at the meeting or headed out to Junkudô in Ikebukuro later in the week. Even this small example shows how the study of Manchukuo has become an increasingly popular (and lucrative) field in contemporary Japan.
7 Okamura Keiji, *"Manshûkoku" shiryô shûseki kikan gaikan* [Survey of organizations collecting Manchukuo materials] (Tokyo: Fuji shuppan, 2004).
8 See Shokuminchi bunka kenkyûkai [Colonial culture research group], *"Manshûkoku" bunka saimoku* [An outline of culture in Manchukuo] (Tokyo: Fuji shuppan, 2005). In 1994, Ronald Suleski compiled the first edition of Manchukuo-related materials in North American scholarship. See Ronald Suleski, *The Modernization of Manchuria: An Annotated Bibliography* (Hong Kong: The Chinese University Press, 1994).
9 See Mutô Tomio, *Manshûkoku no danmen* [A cross-section of Manchukuo] (Tokyo: Kindai-sha, 1956); *Watakushi to Manshû* [Manchukuo and Me] (Tokyo: Bungei shunjû, 1988); and Mutô Tomio, *Zaigunbi wo ikidôru tsuihôsha no kokuhaku* [Confessions of an exile indignant against remilitarization].
10 See Honda Shûgo, *Tenkô bungaku-ron* [Discourse on political conversion literature] (Tokyo: Mirai-sha, 1957).
11 See Yamada Seizaburô, *Tenkô-ki: Hyôsetsu no jidai* [Record of a political conversion: Period of ice and snow (purification)] (Tokyo: Rironsha, 1958).
12 This image can be seen at the Gunma Prefectural Museum of Art. A reproduction can be found in Kawakita Michiaki, Toyama Hideo, Takashina Shûji, Ooka Makoto, and Donald

Keene, eds., *Shôwa no yoga hyaku-sen ten* [Our all-time favourites: Western-style art masterworks of the Showa period] (Tokyo: Asahi Shimbun, 1989), 60.

13 Sheldon Garon, "Rethinking Modernization and Modernity in Japanese History: A Focus on State-Society Relations," *Journal of Asian Studies* 53, 2 (1994): 346-56. Garon's text also discusses general themes in Japanese studies from the immediate postwar period until the early 1990s, stressing the importance of modernization theory for the 1970s and 1980s and its recent (for 1994) criticisms.

14 Curtis Anderson Gayle, *Marxist History and Postwar Japanese Nationalism* (London: Routledge, 2003), 1.

15 Samuel Yamashita, *Leaves from an Autumn of Emergencies: Selections from the Wartime Diaries of Ordinary Japanese* (Honolulu: University of Hawaii Press, 2005), 27.

16 At the University of Guelph, Norman Smith plans to organize a multinational conference entitled "Cultural Construction in Manchukuo," for which we hope to compile an edition of expanded versions of the papers presented, which represent the viewpoints of scholars from China, Japan, Korea, and North America.

Bibliography

Primary Sources (Japanese)

Akita Ujaku, and Yamada Seizaburô. *Bunka undô-shi* [A history of cultural movements]. Tokyo: Iwanami shoten, 1932.

Amakasu Masahiko. "Geibunjin ni nozomu: kessen geibuntaikai ni okeru aisatsu" [My hopes for artists and writers: Introductory remarks at the arts congress at a time of decisive war]. *Geibun* [The arts] (January 1945): 35-36.

Asahi gurafu [Asahi graph].

Asahi Shimbun [Asahi news]. 1931-44.

Atorie [Atelier]. Tokyo: Yûshûdô, 1931-44.

Chûô bijutsu [Central arts]. Tokyo: Yûshûdô, 1931-44.

Fuchikami Hakuyô. *Manshû no kaisô: Fuchikami Hakuyô hencho* [Memories of Manchuria: Edited by Fuchikami Hakuyô]. Tokyo: Keigadô shuppan, 1966.

Fukuzawa Ichirô. "Manshû" [Manchuria]. *Mizue* [Watercolour] 368 (1935): 298.

Haruyama Yukio. *Manshû no bunka* [Manchurian culture]. Tokyo: Osaka-ya go shôten, 1943.

Hasegawa Magohei. *Kyokujitsu no hatameku tokoro* [The places where the flag of the rising sun flutters in the wind]. Tokyo: Banseisha, 1937.

Hatoyama Ichirô. "Kenkoku no shisô ni tsuite" [On the philosophy of the construction of the nation (radio broadcast)]. *Fujo shimbun* [Support news], 14 February 1932.

Hôtei Toshihiro. *Kyû "Manshû" bungaku kankei shiryô shû 1, 2.* [Collection of literature-related materials of former Manchuria, vols. 1 and 2]. Tokyo: Roku-un shobô, 2000.

Kawabata Yasunari, Yamada Seizaburô, Kitamura Kenjirô, Gu Ding, Kishida Kunio, and Shimaki Kensaku, eds. *Manshûkoku kaku minzoku bungaku senshû 1, 2.* [Anthology of literary works by each ethnic group in Manchukuo, vols. 1 and 2]. Tokyo: Sôgansha, 1942 and 1944.

Kawamura Kiyoshi, ed. *Manshû kankei shiryô-shûsei* [Collection of materials related to Manchuria]. Shinkyô: Manshû jijô annai-sho [Manchurian Affairs Information Bureau], 1938.

Kimura Ryôji. *Dairen monogatari* [A tale of Dairen]. Tokyo: Kenkôsha, 1974.

Kitagawa Fuyuhiko. *Sensô* [War]. Tokyo: Yumani shobô, 1995.

–. *Sensô* [War]. Tokyo: Kôseigaku shoten, 1929 (original).

Kurehara Korehito. "Musankaikyû geijutsu undô no shin dankai" [A new stage in the proletarian arts]. *Zen'ei: Musankaikyû geijutsu zasshi* [Avant-Garde: Proletarian arts magazine], January 1928, 17-24.

Lu Yuanming, Suzuki Sadami, and Liu Jianhua, eds. *Manshû Rôman* [Manchuria Romance (reprint of quarterly review in Manchuria)], vols. 1-7. Tokyo: Yumani shobô, 2002-3.

Manshû rôdô nenkan [Manchuria labour yearbook]. Xinjing, Manchukuo: Ganshodô shoten, 1940.

Manshûkoku tsûshin-sha [Manchukuo News Agency], ed. *Manshûkoku gensei kôtoku 5-nen ban* [The current situation of Manchukuo in the Fifth Year of Kangde (facsimile edition)]. Tokyo: Kress Publication, 2000.
Migishi Kôtarô. "Shanhai no ehon." *Serekuto* [Select] 1, 8 (1930): 1, 6-7.
Mutô Tomio. *Kagawa Toyohiko zenshû daijesuto* [Digest of Kagawa Toyohiko's collected works]. Tokyo: Kirisuto shimbun-sha, 1966.
–. *Manshû sanka* [Song in praise of Manchuria]. Hôten [Fengtian]: Hakukaze shobô, 1941.
–. *Manshûkoku no danmen* [A cross-section of Manchukuo]. Tokyo: Kindai-sha, 1956.
–. *Watakushi to Manshû.* [Manchuria and me]. Tokyo: Bungei shunjû, 1988.
–. *Zaigunbi wo ikidôru tsuihôsha no kokuhaku* [Confessions of an exile indignant against remilitarization]. Tokyo: Bunrin-dô, 1951.
Natsume, Sôseki. *Man Kan tokoro dokoro* [Here and there in Manchuria and Korea]. Tokyo: Aozora bunko [Internet archive], 1999, available at http://www.archive.org/.
South Manchurian Railways Company (SMRC). *Manshû gurafu* [Manchuria graph]. Dairen: South Manchuria Railway Company, 1933-44.
–. *Manshû gurafu* [Manchuria graph] 1, 2 (1933): n.p.
–. *Manshû gurafu* [Manchuria graph] 3, 5 (1936): n.p.
–. *Manshû gurafu* [Manchuria graph] 5, 6 (1937): n.p.
–. *Manshû gurafu* [Manchuria graph] 1, 2 (number 2), Tokyo: Yumani shobô, 2008 (reprint).
–. *Manshû gurafu* [Manchuria graph] *dai yokkan dai go gô (dai 35 gô)* [Volume 4, number 5 (number 22)] Tokyo: Yumani shobô, 2008 (reprint).
–. *Manshû gurafu* [Manchuria graph] 4, 12 (number 29) Tokyo: Yumani shobô, 2008 (reprint).
–. *Manshû gurafu* [Manchuria graph] *dai gokan dai roku gô (dai 35 gô)* [Volume 5, number 6 (number 35)] Tokyo: Yumani shobô, 2008 (reprint).
–. *Manshû gurafu* [Manchuria graph], 6, 11 (number 52). Tokyo: Yumani shobô, 2008 (reprint).
–. *Manshû gurafu* [Manchuria graph], 7, 1 (number 54). Tokyo: Yumani shobô, 2008 (reprint).
–. *Manshû to Mantetsu* [Manchuria and the South Manchuria Railway]. Dairen: South Manchuria Railway Company, 1937.
Sôgô shuppan nenkan [General publishing yearbook]. Tokyo: Tosho kenkyûkai, 1932.
Tokunaga Sunao. *Sengentai* [The pioneers]. Tokyo: Kaizôsha, 1939.
Tsuruta Gorô. *Banseiki no sobyô* [A Half Century of Sketches]. Tokyo: Chûô kôron bijutsu shuppan, 1975.
Yamada Seizaburô. *Manshûkoku bunka kensetsuron* [Discourse on the construction of culture in Manchukuo]. Shinkyô (Changchun): Geibun shobô, 1943.
–. *Jigo zange* [Personal confessions]. Tokyo: Rikugei-sha, 1938.
–, ed. *NichiManRô zai Man sakka tanpen senshû* [Anthology of short works by Japanese, Manchurian, and Russian Authors in Manchuria]. Tokyo: Shunyôdô, 1940.
Yamamoto Taketoshi, ed. *Jûgonen sensô gyokumitsu shiryô-shû* [Collection of top secret materials from the Fifteen Years War]. Hokan 25 [supplementary edition 25] of *Senbu geppô* [Pacification Monthly]. Tokyo: Fuji shuppan, 2005 (reprint).
–. *Senbu geppô* [Pacification Monthly] volume 2, 1937.12-1938.7 edition. Tokyo: Fuji shuppan, 2005 (reprint).
Yoshino Sakuzô. "Minzoku to kaikyû to sensô" [Nations, classes, and war]. Chûô kôron [Central Review]. January 1932: 50.
Zen'ei geijutsuka dômei [Avant-garde artists league]. *Zen'ei antaû-gardo: Musan kaikyû geijutsu zasshi* [Vanguard avant-garde: Proletarian art magazine]. Tokyo: Senki fukkoku-ban kankôkai, 1980 (July 1927-April 1928 reprints).

Primary Sources (English)

Brody, Inger, ed. *Rediscovering Natsume Sôseki: With the First English Translation of Travels in Manchuria and Korea.* Trans. I. Brody and S.T. Tsunematsu. London: Global Oriental, 2000.

Bureau of Information and Publicity, Department of Foreign Affairs, Manchoukuo Government. *The Voice of the People of Manchukuo.* Hsinking, Manchukuo: Bureau of Information and Publicity, December, 1932.

–. *Manchukuo: Handbook of Information.* Hsinking, Manchukuo: Manshû Nippon-sha, 1933.

Enjôji, S., ed. *Pictorial Manchuria.* Hsinking, Manchukuo: Kyodo Printing Company, 1940.

Japanese Delegation to the League of Nations. *The Manchurian Question: Japan's Case in the Sino-Japanese Dispute as Presented before the League of Nations.* Geneva: Japanese Delegation to the League of Nations, 1933.

Manchuria Daily News. Manchuria: Semi-Monthly Publication of the Manchuria Daily News. Hsinking, Manchukuo: *Manchuria Daily News,* 1936-40.

O'Connor, Peter. "General Introduction – Japanese Propaganda Books in the Modern Period: Writing against the Tide," in *Japanese Propaganda: Selected Readings (Series 1: Books 1872-1943, a Collection in Ten Volumes),* ed. Peter O'Connor, 1-36. Kent, UK: Global Oriental, 2004.

South Manchuria Railway Company. *Fifth Report on Progress in Manchuria to 1936.* Dairen: South Manchuria Railway Company, 1936.

–. "Tourism." *Milestones of Progress* (monthly supplement of *Contemporary Manchuria*) 1, 1 (1939): 17-18.

Secondary Sources (Japanese)

Asahi Shimbun "Kenshô. Shôwa hôdô" shuzaiban [Asahi news censorship and Showa period reportage news coverage team]. *Shimbun to Shôwa: Asahi Shimbun "Kenshô. Shôwa hôdô"* [Newspapers and the Shôwa period: Asahi news censorship and Showa period reportage]. Tokyo: Asahi Bunko, 2010.

Asahi Shimbun "Shimbun to sensô" shuzaiban [Asahi news newspapers and war news coverage team]. *Shimbun to sensô (jô)* [Newspapers and war (vol. 1)]. Tokyo: Asahi Bunko, 2011.

Chiba Yoshi. "Fuan to gensô: Kanten ni okeru 'Manshû' hyôshô no seiji-teki imi" [Disquiet and illusion: The political meaning of images of Manchuria in official art exhibitions]. In *Hyôshô/teikoku/genda: Seisen kara reisen he* [Representation, empire, and gender: From the Sacred War to the Cold War], ed. Ikeda Shinobu, 18-53 (Chiba: Research Project Report, Graduate School of Humanities and Social Sciences, Chiba University, 2008).

Egawa Yoshihide. "Dairen no shururearisumu 'Gokakai' o megutte" [About the surrealist Five Fruits Group in Dairen]. In *Nihon bijutsu sôkô: Sasaki Kôzô Sensei koki kinen ronbunshû* [Japanese art manuscripts: Collected essays commemorating Professor Sasaki Kôzô's seventieth birthday]. Tokyo: Meitoku shuppansha, 1998.

Fukuda Kugao. "Bungei jûgô undô." in *Kokubungaku kaishaku to kanshô bessetsu* [Understanding and appreciating national literature studies, special issue]. Tokyo: Shibundô, 1982: 561-62.

Harisei Ichirô; Sawaragi, Noi; Kuraya, Mika; Kawada, Akihisa; Hirase, Reita; Otani Shôgo, eds. *Sensô to bijutsu, 1937-1945* [Art in wartime Japan, 1937-1945]. Tokyo: Kokushokan kôkai, 2007.

Haruwara Shinobu. *Shimizu Toshi nikki no kenkyû–15-nen sensôki wo chûshin ni–* [Research on Shimizu Toshi's Diary – Centring on the 15-Years War]. In *Kajima bijutsu kenkyû* [Kajima Art Research] nenpyô dai 23 gô bessetsu (annual edition, volume 23, special edition). Tokyo: Kajima bijutsu zaidan [Kajima Foundation for the Arts], 2006.

Hasegawa Izumi, ed. *Kindai bungaku ronsô jiten* [Dictionary of debates on modern (Japanese) literature]. Tokyo: Shibun-dô, 1962.

Hirano Ken'ichirô, ed. *Nitchû sensôki no Chûgoku ni okeru shakai bunka henyô* [The Acculturation of Society and Culture in China during the Sino-Japanese Period]. Tokyo: Tôyô Bunko, 2007.

Hiroshima Prefecture Museum. *Ai Mitsu to kôyû no gakka-tachi.* [Ai Mitsu and his artist colleagues]. Hiroshima: Hiroshima Prefecture Museum, 2001.

Hisamatsu Sen'ichi, and Yoshida Sei'ichi, eds. *Kindai Nihon bungaku jiten* [Dictionary of modern Japanese literature]. Tokyo: Tokyo-dô, 1954.

Hokkaidô Migishi Kôtarô Art Museum. *"Shanhai no ehon": Chûgoku modan toshi no shi* [Shanghai picture book: A poem about China's modern city]. Sapporo: Hokkaidô Migishi Kôtarô Art Museum, 1990.

Honda Shûgo. *Tenkô bungaku-ron* [Discourse on political conversion in literature]. Tokyo: Mirai-sha, 1957.

Iino Masahito. *"Manshû bijutsu" nenpyô* [Chronology of Manchurian art]. Kôfu City: Yamanashi Prefecture Museum of Art, 1998.

Iizawa Kôtarô. "Shashin no yûtopia (Fuchikami Hakuyô to Manshû shashin sakka kyôkai)" [Utopia in photographs (Fuchikami Hakuyô and the Manchuria Photographic Artists Association)], *Kan* [Area] 10 (2002): 232-39.

Kamakura Museum of Modern Art, ed. *Nihon no shashin 1930 ten [Japanese photography in the 1930s].* Kamakura: Kamakura Museum of Modern Art, 1988.

Kawakita Michiaki, Toyama Hideo, Takashina Shûji, Ooka Makoto, and Donald Keene, eds. *Shôwa no yôga hyaku-sen ten* [Our all-time favourites: Western-style art masterworks of the Showa period]. Tokyo: Asahi Shimbun, 1989.

Kawamoto Saburô. *Taishô gen'ei* [Taishô illusions]. Tokyo: Shinchôsha, 1990.

Kawamura Minato. *Bungaku kara miru "Manshû gozoku kyôwa" no yume to genjitsu* [Envisioning the dream and reality of Manchuria's harmony of the five races through literature]. Tokyo: Yoshikawa Hirofumi bunkan, 1998.

–. *Manshû hôkai: "Dai Tô A bungaku" to sakka-tachi.* [The collapse of Manchuria: Greater East Asian literature and its writers]. Tokyo: Bungei shunjû, 1997.

Kikuchi Yoshi'ichirô, ed. *Ai Mitsu,* rev. ed. Tokyo: Toki no bijutsusha, 1965.

Kishi Toshihiko. *Manshûkoku no bijyuaru.medeia* [Manchukuo's visual media]. Tokyo: Yoshikawa kôbun-kan, 2010.

Kobayashi Hideo. *"Manshû" no rekishi* [The history of Manchuria]. Tokyo: Kodansha gendai shinso, 2004 [1966].

–. *Mantetsu: "Chi no shûdan" no tanjô to shi* [The South Manchuria Railway Company: The birth and death of the knowledgable group]. Tokyo: Yoshikawa Hirofumi-kan, 1996.

–. "Ryûjôkô jiken o meggute: Ryûjôkô jiken rokujusûnen ni yosete" [On the Marco Polo Bridge Incident: Some sixty years after the Marco Polo Bridge Incident]. *Rekishigaku kenkyû* [History research] 699 (1997): 30-35.

–. *Teikoku Nihon to sôryokusen taisei* [Imperial Japan and the total war system]. Tokyo: Yûshi-sha, 2004.

Komagome Takeshi. *Shokuminchi teikoku Nihon no bunka tôgô* [The cultural integration of Imperial Japan and the colonies]. Tokyo: Iwanami shoten, 1996.

Minami Hiroshi. *Owari ni: Taishô kara Shôwa he* [In conclusion: From Taishô to Shôwa]. In *Taishô bunka* [Taishô culture], ed. Hiroshi Minami, 370-83. Tokyo: Keisô shobô, 1965.

Mizusawa Tsutomu, ed. *Nihon no kindai bijutsu 10: Fuan to sensô no jidai* [Japanese modern art 10: Era of anxiety and war]. Tokyo: Otsuki shoten, 1992.

Nishizawa Yasuhiko. *Mantetsu: "Manshû" no kyôjin* [The South Manchurian Railway Company: Manchuria's giant]. Tokyo: Kawade shobô, 2000.

Oda Setsushin, and Nihon kindai bijutsu-kan [The museum of modern Japanese literature], eds., *Nihon kindai bungaku dai jiten: Dai nikkan* [Great dictionary of Modern Japanese literature: 2]. Tokyo: Kôdansha, 1977.

Ogawa Bijutsukan, ed. [Ogawa Art Museum]. *Jihitsu no nikki to suisai. Dessin de saguru: Shimizu Toshi, taiÔ soshite kikokugo no kiseki* [Personal diary and watercolors. Investigating the tracks of Shimizu Toshi during his sojourn in Europe and return to Japan through his sketches.] Tokyo: Ogawa Bijutsukan, 1999.

Okamura Keiji. *"Manshûkoku" shiryô shûseki kikan gaikan* [Survey of organizations collecting Manchukuo materials]. Tokyo: Fuji shuppan, 2004.

Omuka Toshiharu, and Mizusawa Tsutomu, eds., *Modanizumu/nashonarizumu: 1930 nendai Nihon no geijutsu* [Modernism/nationalism: Japanese art of the 1930s]. Tokyo: Serika shobô, 2003.

–. "Taishô-ki no shinkô bijutsu undô to 'Gekijô no Sanka'" [The progressive art movement in the Taishô period and the theatre of the Third Section]. *Art Vivant* 33 (1989): 89 (42-93).

Otani Shôgo. *Chiheisen no yume: Shôwa 10 nendai no gensô kaiga* [Dreams of the horizon: Fantastic paintings in Japan, 1935-45]. Tokyo: Tokyo National Museum of Modern Art, 2003.

Otani Shôgo, Matsumoto Tôru, Arikawa Ikuo, Wada Koichi, Fujisaki Aya, Kakuda Arata, eds. *Seitan hyaku-nen Ai Mitsu ten* [Exhibition honouring Ai Mitsu one hundred years after his birth]. Tokyo: Mainichi Newspapers, 2007.
Sakuramoto Tomio. *Kûhaku to sekinin: Senjikan no shijin-tachi* [Blank and responsibility: Poets during wartime]. Tokyo: Mirai-sha, 1983.
Sanô Shin'ichi. *Amakasu Masahiko ranshin no kôya* [Amakasu Masahiko: Vast plains of a ravaged soul]. Tokyo: Shinchô-sha, 2008.
Shokuminchi bunka kenkyûkai [Colonial culture research group]. *"Manshûkoku" bunka saimoku* [An outline of culture in Manchukuo]. Tokyo: Fuji shuppan, 2005.
Takeba Jô. *Ikyô no modanizumu: Fuchikami Hakuyô to Manshû shashin sakka kyôkai.* [Modernism on foreign soil: Fuchikami Hakuyô and the Manchuria Photographic Artists Association]. Nagoya: Nagoya City Museum of Art, 1994.
–, ed. *Nihon no shashin-ka 6: Fuchikami Hakuyô to Manshû shashin sakka kyôkai* [Japan's photographers 6: Fuchikami Hakuyô and the Manchuria Photographic Artists Association]. Tokyo: Iwanami shoten, 1998.
Tokyo Metropolitan Museum of Photography, ed. *Nihon kindai shashin no seiritsu to tenkai* [The founding and development of modern photography in Japan]. Tokyo: Tokyo Metropolitan Culture Foundation, Tokyo Metropolitan Museum of Photography, 1995.
Tsukase Susumu. *Manshûkoku: "Minzoku kyôwa" no jitsuzô* [Manchukuo: A true portrait of ethnic/racial harmony]. Tokyo: Yoshikawa kôbun-kan, 1998.
Usami Shô. *Ikebukurô Monparunasu* [Ikebukuro Montparnasse]. Tokyo: Shûei-sha, 1990.
Yamada Seizaburô. *Saikinsen gunji saiban: Kiroku shôsetsu* [Military tribunal on biological warfare: A documentary novel]. Tokyo: Tôhô shuppansha, 1974.
–. *Tenkô-ki: Hyôsetsu no jidai* [Record of a political conversion: Period of ice and snow (purification)]. Tokyo: Rironsha, 1958.
Yamaguchi Takeshi. *Maboroshii no kinema Man'ei: Amakasu Masahiko to katsudôya gunzô* [The Manchurian Film Association and the cinematics of illusion: Amakasu Masahiko and his group of activists]. Tokyo: Heibonsha, 1989.
Yamamurô Shin'ichi. *Kimera: Manshûkoku no shôzô* [Chimera: A portrait of Manchukuo]. Tokyo: Chûô kôron shin-sha, 1993.
Yi Xianshi. *Nihon no tairiku seisaku to Chûgoku tôhoku* [Japan's policy on the continent and China's northeast]. Tokyo: Rokkô shuppan, 1989.
Yoshimi Yoshiaki. *Kusa no ne no fashizumu: Nihon minshû no sensô taiken* [Grassroots fascism: The war experience of the Japanese public]. Tokyo: Tokyo Daigaku shuppankai, 1987.
Wada Hirofumi. "Dairen no abuan gyarudo to Kitagawa Fuyuhiko" [Dairen's avant-garde and Kitagawa Fuyuhiko]. *Kan* [Area] 10 (2002): 208-17.
–. ed., *Nihon no abuan gyarudo* [Japan's avant-garde]. Tokyo: Seikai shisô-sha, 2005.
Wakakuwa Midori. *Sensô ga tsukuru joseizô: Dainiji Sekai Taisenka no Nihon josei dôin no shikakuteki puropaganda* [Images of women fashioned by war: The Visual Propaganda of Mobilized Japanese Women During Wartime]. Tokyo: Chikuma shobô, 1995.

Secondary Sources (Chinese)

Fang Jun, and Wang Shengli, eds. *Dalian jin bainian fengyun tulu (diguozhuyi qinlue Dalian shi zongshu)* [Collected records of recent events in Dalian in the past one hundred years (Collection of books on the history of imperialist invasion in Dalian)]. Dalian: Liaoning People's Press, 1998.
–. *Zhiminzhe de jiayuan* [The homes of colonists]. Dalian: Liaoning People's Press, 1998.
Feng Weiqun. "Wenyi zhidao gangyao' chulong yihou" [After the appearance of the summary of guidelines to art and literature]. In *Weiman wenhua* [Manchukuo culture], *Weiman shiliao congshu* [Series of Manchukuo Historical Materials volume 6], ed. Sun Bang and Yu Haiying. Changchun: Jilin Renmin Chubanshe, 1993, 13-14.
Feng Weiqun, Wang Jianzhong, Li Chunyan, and Li Shuquan. *Dongbei lunxian shiqi wenxue guoji xueshu yantaohui lunwenji* [Collection of papers from the International Symposium on Literature of the Enemy-Occupied Northeast] Shenyang: Shenyang chubanshe, 1992.
Gu Ding. "Xianhua wentan" [Gossip about literary circles]. In *Gu Ding zoupin xhuan* [Selected works of Gu Ding], ed. Li Chuyan, 9. Shenyang: Chunfeng wenyi, 1995.

Ji, F., ed. *Dalian lao jianying* [Old scenes of Dalian]. Beijing: People's Fine Arts Press, 1997.
Kazeta Eiki. "Wei Manzhouguo wenyi zhengce de zhankai" [The development of bogus Manchukuo's literary rules and regulations]. In *Dongbei lunxian shiqi wenxue guoji xueshu yantaohui lunwenji* [Collection of papers from the International Symposium on Literature of the Enemy-Occupied Northeast], ed. Feng Weiquin, Wang Jianzhong, Li Chunyan, Li Shuquan, 156-81. Shenyang: Shenyang chubanshe, 1992.
Song Zengbin, ed. *Dalian lao jianzhu* [Old buildings in Dalian]. Dalian: Xinhua Publishing House, 2003.
Wang Xizhi, and Kang Xingfang, eds. *Dalian jin bainian shi* [The history of the past one hundred years of Dalian]. Dalian: Liaoning People's Press, 1999.
Xu Naixiang, and Huang Wanhua, eds. *Zhongguo kangzhan shiqi lunxianqu wenxue shi* [History of the literature of the enemy-occupied territories during China's war of resistance]. Fuzhou: Fujian jiaoyu chubanshe, 1995.

Secondary Sources (English)

Asada, Sadao. *Culture Shock and Japan-American Relations: Historical Essays*. Columbus, MO: University of Missouri Press, 2007.
Atkins, Jacqueline. *Wearing Propaganda: Textiles on the Home Front in Japan, Britain, and the United States*. New Haven: Yale University Press, 2005.
Baskett, Michael. *The Attractive Empire: Transnational Film Culture in Imperial Japan*. Honolulu: University of Hawaii Press, 2008.
Beckman, George, and Okubô Genji. *The Japanese Communist Party, 1922-1945*. Stanford: Stanford University Press, 1969.
Bhabha, Homi, ed. *Nation and Narration*. London: Routledge, 1990.
Bickle, George B., Jr. "Thy Kingdom Come on Earth: Some Reflections on the Social Gospel Movement in Japan." *Contemporary Religions in Japan* 9, 3 (1968): 194-201.
–. "Utopianism and Social Planning in the Thought of Kagawa Toyohiko." *Monumenta Nipponica* 25, 3/4 (1970): 447-53.
Bix, Herbert. *Hirohito and the Making of Modern Japan*. New York: Harper Collins, 2000.
Bowen-Struyk, Heather. "Proletarian Arts in East Asia," *Japan Focus*. Available at http://www.japanfocus.org/.
–. "Proletarian Arts in East Asia: Quests for National, Gender, and Class Justice." *positions: east asia cultures critique* 14, 2 (2006): 251-78.
Buck, Pearl S. *The Good Earth*. New York: John Day Company, 1931.
Bürger, Peter. *Theory of the Avant-Garde*. Minneapolis: University of Minnesota Press, 1984.
Cheng, Jim. *An Annotated Bibliography for Chinese Film Studies*. Hong Kong: Hong Kong University Press, 2004.
Clark, John. "Artistic Subjectivity in the Taishô and Early Shôwa Avant-Garde." In *Japanese Art after 1945: Scream Against the Sky*, ed. Alexandra Munroe, 41-53. New York: Harry N. Abrams, 1994.
–. "Surrealism in Japan," Monash Asia Institute, Japanese Studies Centre, occasional paper 28, (1997), 48 (1-80).
–. "Surrealism in Japan." In *Surrealism: Revolution by Night*, ed. M. Lloyd, T. Gott, and C. Chapman, 204-13 (Canberra: National Gallery of Australia, 1993).
Clark, T.J. *Farewell to an Idea: Episodes from a History of Modernism*. New Haven, CT: Yale University Press, 2001.
Clausen, S., and S. Thogerson, eds. *The Making of a Chinese City: History and Historiography in Harbin*. New York: M.E. Sharpe, 1996.
Cohen, Carl, ed. *Communism, Fascism, and Democracy: The Theoretical Foundations*. New York: Random House, 1962.
Culver, Annika A. "'Between Distant Realities': The Japanese Avant-Garde, Surrealism, and the Colonies, 1924-1943." PhD diss., University of Chicago, 2007.
–. "Colonial Manchuria in the Surrealist Imagination: The Poetry and Prose of Kitagawa Fuyuhiko as Modernist History." *Proceedings of the Association for Japanese Literary Studies* 4 (2003): 264-77.

–. "Manchukuo and the Creation of a New Multi-Ethnic Literature: Kawabata Yasunari's Promotion of 'Manchurian' Culture, 1941-1942." In *China, Japan, and the Dynamics of Transculturation: From the Late Nineteenth Century to the End of the Pacific War*, ed. Richard King, Cody Poulton, and Katsuhiko Endô, 189-208. Lanham, MD: Lexington Books, 2011.

–. "The Making of a Japanese Avant-Garde in Dairen, 1924-1937." *History Compass* 5/2 (2007): 347-61.

–. "Migishi Kôtarô's Shanghai: Sino-Japanese Cultural Exchange and an Artist's Romancing of an Aesthetic Ideal in Turbulent Times." *Stanford Journal of East Asian Affairs* 8, 1 (2008): 68-86.

–. "Two Japanese Avant-Garde Writers' Views of Gender Relations and Colonial Oppression in Manchuria, 1929-1931" *US-Japan Women's Journal* 37 (2009): 91-116.

Cushing, Lincoln, and Ann Thompkins. *Chinese Posters: Art from the Great Proletarian Cultural Revolution*. New York: Chronicle Books, 2007.

De Bary, William Theodore, Carol Gluck, and Arthur Tiedemann, eds., *Sources of Japanese Tradition, 1600-2000*. 2nd ed. New York: Columbia University Press, 2006.

Dickinson, Frederick. "Biohazard: Unit 731 in Postwar Japanese Politics of National 'Forgetfulness.'" *Japan Focus*. Available at http://japanfocus.org.

Driscoll, Mark. *Absolute Erotic, Absolute Grotesque: The Living, Dead, and Undead in Japan's Imperialism, 1895-1945*. Durham, NC: Duke University Press, 2010.

Duara, Prasenjit. *Sovereignty and Authenticity: Manchukuo and the East Asian Modern*. Lanham, MD: Rowman and Littlefield, 2003.

DuBois, Thomas David. "Inauthentic Sovereignty: Law and Legal Institutions in Manchukuo." *Journal of Asian Studies* 69, 3 (2010): 749-70.

Duus, Peter. *The Japanese Discovery of America: A Brief History with Documents*. New York: Bedford Books, 1997.

Duus, Peter, Ramon H. Myers, and Mark. R. Peattie, eds. *The Japanese Informal Empire in China, 1895-1937*. Princeton: Princeton University Press, 1989.

Eagleton, Terry, Frederic Jameson, and Edward Said. *Nationalism, Colonialism, and Literature*. Minneapolis: University of Minnesota Press, 1990.

Earhart, David. *Certain Victory: Images of World War II in the Japanese Media*. Armonk, NY: M.E. Sharpe, 2008.

Ellerman, Bruce A., and Stephen Kotkin, eds. *Manchurian Railways and the Opening of China: An International History*. Armonk, NY: M.E. Sharpe, 2010.

"Evangelism Is War." *Time*, 7 February 1955. Available at http://www.time.com/.

Fletcher, William Miles. *The Search for a New Order: Intellectuals and Fascism in Prewar Japan*. London: Oxford University Press, 1982.

Fogel, Joshua A., trans. *Life along the South Manchurian Railway: The Making of Itô Takeo*. Armonk, NY: M.E. Sharpe, 1988.

–. *The Literature of Travel in the Japanese Rediscovery of China, 1862-1945*. Stanford: Stanford University Press, 1996.

–. "The Other Japanese Community: Leftwing Japanese Activities in Wartime Shanghai." In *Wartime Shanghai*, ed. Yeh Wen-hsin, 39-56. Florence, KY: Routledge, 1998.

Garon, Sheldon. "Rethinking Modernity and Modernization in Japanese History: A Focus on State-Society Relations." *Journal of Asian Studies* 53, 2 (1994): 346-56.

Gayle, Curtis Anderson. *Marxist History and Postwar Japanese Nationalism*. London: Routledge, 2003.

Gerow, Aaron. *A Page of Madness: Cinema and Modernity in 1920s Japan*. Ann Arbor: Center for Japanese Studies, University of Michigan, 2008.

Golomstock, Igor. *Totalitarian Art in the Soviet Union, the Third Reich, Fascist Italy, and the People's Republic of China*. New York: Overlook Press, 2011.

Gottshang, Thomas, and Diana Lary. *Swallows and Settlers: The Great Migration from North China to Manchuria*. Ann Arbor, MI: Center for Chinese Studies, 2000.

Han, Suk-jung. "The Problem of Sovereignty: Manchukuo, 1932-1937." *positions: east asia cultures critique* 12, 2 (2004): 457-78.

Harootunian, H. *Overcoming Modernity: History, Culture, and Community in Interwar Japan*. Princeton: Princeton University Press, 2000.

Hewitt, Andrew. *Fascist Modernism: Aesthetics, Politics, and the Avant-Garde.* Stanford: Stanford University Press, 1993.

Iriye, Akira. *After Imperialism: The Search for a New Order in the Far East, 1921-1931.* New York: Imprint Publications, 1990.

–, ed. *The Chinese and the Japanese: Essays in Political and Cultural Interactions.* Princeton, NJ: Princeton University Press, 1980.

–. *Cultural Interactions of the Chinese and the Japanese in the Interwar Period.* Cambridge, MA: Harvard University Press, 1997.

Kasza, Gregory J. *The State and the Mass Media in Japan, 1918-1945.* Berkeley: University of California Press, 1988.

Kawabata Yasunari. *The Scarlet Gang of Asakusa.* Trans. Alisa Freedman. Berkeley: University of California Press, 2005.

Kawamura Minato. "One View of the History of Japanese Proletarian Literature: On Nogawa Takashi." Trans. David Rosenfeld. Paper delivered at the Proletarian Literatures of East Asia Symposium, University of Chicago, 2002.

Kawashima, Ken. *The Proletarian Gamble: Korean Workers in Interwar Japan.* Durham, NC: Duke University Press, 2009.

Keene, Donald. *Dawn to the West: Japanese Literature of the Modern Era (Fiction).* New York: Columbia University Press, 1998.

–. *So Lovely a Country Will Never Perish.* New York: Columbia University Press, 2010.

Kishi, Toshihiko. "Fusion and Crack between Cultural Policy and Placation Policy in Manchukuo." *Journal of Manchurian Studies* October (2007): 93-129. Available at http://www.earticle.net/.

Kleeman, Faye Yuan. "Inscribing Manchuria: Gender, Ideology, and Popular Imagination." *East Asian History* 30 (2005): 47-66.

–. *Under an Imperial Sun: Japanese Colonial Literature of Taiwan and the South.* Honolulu: University of Hawaii Press, 2003.

Ko, Won. *Buddhist Elements in Dada: A Comparison of Tristan Tzara, Takahashi Shinkichi, and Their Fellow Poets.* New York: New York University Press, 1977.

Kushner, Barak. *Dreams of Empire: Japanese Propaganda Textiles.* Waregem, BE: Cassochrome (MHJ Collection), 2011.

–. *The Thought War: Japanese Imperial Propaganda.* Honolulu: University of Hawaii Press, 2006.

Lao She. *Rickshaw Boy.* New York: Reynal and Hitchcock, 1945.

Laqueur, Walter. *Fascism: Past, Present, Future.* London: Oxford University Press, 1996.

Li, Lincoln. *The China Factor in Modern Japanese Thought: The Case of Tachibana Shiraki, 1881-1945.* Albany: State University Press of New York, 1996.

Lippit, Seiji M. *Topographies of Japanese Modernism.* New York: Columbia University Press, 2002.

McCormack, Gavan. "Manchukuo: Constructing the Past." *East Asian History* 2 (1991): 105-24.

Maruyama, Masao. "Fascism – Some Problems: A Consideration of Its Political Dynamics." In *Thought and Behavior in Modern Japanese Politics,* ed. Ivan Morris, 157-76. London: Oxford University Press, 1969.

–. "The Ideology and Dynamics of Japanese Fascism." In *Thought and Behavior in Modern Japanese Politics,* ed. Ivan Morris, 25-83. London: Oxford University Press, 1969.

Mercado, Stephen C. *The Shadow Warriors of Nakano: A History of the Imperial Japanese Army's Elite Intelligence School.* Dulles, VA: Brasseys, 2002.

Mitter, Rana. *The Manchurian Myth: Nationalism, Resistance, and Collaboration in Modern China.* Berkeley: University of California Press, 2000.

Moore, Ray A., and Donald L. Robinson. *Partners for Democracy: Crafting the New Japanese State under MacArthur.* New York: Oxford University Press, 2004.

Morris-Suzuki, Tessa. "A Descent into the Past: The Frontier in the Construction of Japanese Identity." In *Multicultural Japan: Paleolithic to Postmodern,* ed. Donald Denoon, Mark Hudson, Gavan McCormack, and Tessa Morris-Suzuki, 81-94. Cambridge: Cambridge University Press, 1996.

Mullins, Mark R. "Christianity as a Transnational Social Movement: Kagawa Toyohiko and the Friends of Jesus." *Japanese Religions* 32, 1 and 2 (2007): 69-87.

Munroe, Alexandra, ed. *Japanese Art after 1945: Scream Against the Sky.* New York: Harry N. Abrams, 1994.

Li Narangoa, and Robert Cribb, eds. *Imperial Japan and National Identities in Asia, 1895-1945.* London: Routledge, 2005.

"Nyuzu for Japan," *Time,* 8 December 1952. Available at http://www.time.com/.

Oguma Eiji. *A Genealogy of "Japanese" Self-Images.* Trans. David Askew. Melbourne, Australia: Trans Pacific Press, 2002.

Ozaki, Shinjin. "Japanese Surrealism in the Late 1930s: The 'Space of Formless Matter' and the 'Space of Macroscopic Creatures.'" In *Japanese Modern Art: Painting from 1910-1970,* ed. Irmtraud Schaarschmidt-Richter, 61. Zurich: Stemmle Publishers, 2000.

Peattie, Mark. *Ishiwara Kanji and Japan's Confrontation with the West.* Princeton, NJ: Princeton University Press, 1975.

Poggioli, Renato. *The Theory of the Avant-Garde.* Trans. Gerald Fitzgerald. Cambridge, MA: Belknap Press of Harvard University Press, 1968.

Pratt, Mary Louise. *Imperial Eyes: Travel Writing and Transculturation.* London: Routledge, 1992.

Ruoff, Kenneth. *Imperial Japan at Its Zenith: The Wartime Celebration of the Empire's 2600th Anniversary.* Ithaca, NY: Cornell University Press, 2010.

Sakaki, Atsuko. "Japanese Perceptions of China: The Sinophilic Fiction of Tanizaki Junichirô." *Harvard Journal of Asiatic Studies* 59, 1 (1999): 187-218

–. *Obsessions with the Sino-Japanese Polarity in Japanese Literature.* Honolulu: University of Hawaii Press, 2005.

Sas, Miryam. *Fault Lines: Cultural Memory and Japanese Surrealism.* Stanford: Stanford University Press, 1999.

Sasaki-Uemura, Wesley. "Tanigawa Gan's Politics of the Margins in Kyushi and Nagano." *positions: east asia cultures critique* 7, 1 (1999): 137-38.

Shao, Dan, and Ronald Suleski, eds. "Manchuria as a Borderland." Special issue, *East Asian History* 30 (2005).

Shepherdson-Scott, Kari. "Romancing the Frontier: Fuchikami Hakuyô, Art Photography, and the Promotion of a Cultural Connoisseur." PhD diss., Duke University, 2011.

Smith, Norman. *Resisting Manchukuo: Chinese Women Writers under the Japanese Occupation.* Vancouver: UBC Press, 2007.

Steinweis, Alan E. *Art, Ideology, and Economics in Nazi Germany: The Reich Chambers of Music, Theater, and the Visual Arts.* Chapel Hill: University of North Carolina Press, 1993.

Suleski, Ronald. *The Modernization of Manchuria: An Annotated Bibliography.* Hong Kong: Chinese University Press, 1994.

–. "Reconstructing Life in the Youth Corps Camps of Manchuria, 1938-1945: Resistance to Conformity." *East Asian History* 30 (2005): 67-90.

Szostak, John Donald. "The Kokuga Sôsaku Kyôkai and Kyoto Nihonga Reform in the Meiji, Taishô, and Early Shôwa Years, 1900-1928." PhD diss., University of Washington, 2005.

Tamanoi, Mariko. *Memory Maps: The State and Manchuria in Postwar Japan.* Honolulu: University of Hawaii Press, 2009.

Tansman, Alan. *The Aesthetics of Japanese Fascism.* Berkeley: University of California Press, 2009

–, ed. *The Culture of Japanese Fascism.* Durham, NC: Duke University Press, 2009.

Thornber, Karen Laura. *Empire of Texts in Motion: Chinese, Korean, and Taiwanese Transculturations of Japanese Literature.* Cambridge, MA: Harvard University Press, 2009.

Totani, Yuma. "20th-Century Japanese History: From Meiji to Heisei." Lecture delivered at the Asian Studies Development Program "Infusing Asian Studies into the Curriculum," East West Center, Honolulu, Hawaii, June 2009.

Tucker, Anne, Iizawa Kôtarô, and Kinoshita Naoyuki. *The History of Japanese Photography.* New Haven: Yale University Press, 2003.

Uchida, Michio. "Natsume Sôseki in Manchuria and Korea." *Acta Asiatica* 79 (2000): 2-20.

US Department of State. *International Religious Freedom Report 2007 (Japan): Bureau of Democracy, Human Rights, and Labor.* Available at http://www.state.gov/.

Yamamoto, Taketoshi. "The Japanese Army's Radio Strategy in Manchuria." Institute of 20th Century Media, Waseda University, available at http://www.waseda.jp/.

Yamashita, Samuel Hideo. *Leaves in an Autumn of Emergencies: Selections from the Wartime Diaries of Ordinary Japanese*. Honolulu: University of Hawaii Press, 2005.

Yang, Daqing. *Technology of Empire: Telecommunications and Japanese Imperialism, 1930-1945*. Harvard East Asian Monographs, 219. Cambridge, MA: Harvard University Asia Center, 2003.

Young, Louise. *Japan's Total Empire: Manchuria and the Culture of Wartime Imperialism*. Berkeley: University of California Press, 1998.

Weisenfeld, Gennifer, ed., "Guest Editor's Introduction," in "Visual Cultures of Japanese Imperialism," special issue, *positions: east asia cultures critique* 8, 3 (2000): 591-603.

Williams, Raymond. *The Politics of Modernism: Against the New Conformists*. London: Verso Books, 1989.

Wilson, Sandra. "The Past in the Present: War in the Narratives of Modernity in the 1920s and 1930s." In *Being Modern in Japan: Culture and Society from the 1910s to the 1930s*, ed. Elise Tipton and John Clark, 170-84. Honolulu: University of Hawaii Press, 2000.

–. "The 'New Paradise': Japanese Emigration to Manchuria in the 1930s and 1940s." *International History Review* 17, 2 (1995): 249-86.

Zeljko, Cipris. "Responsibility of Intellectuals: Kobayashi Hideo on Japan at War." *Japan Focus*. Available at http://old.japanfocus.org/.

Žižek, Slavoj. *Tarrying with the Negative: Kant, Hegel, and the Critique of Ideology*. Durham, NC: Duke University Press, 1993.

Personal Interviews (Chinese, Japanese, and English)

Kobayashi Hideo, professor of history, Waseda University, Tokyo, Japan. November-December 2004. February 2005.

Liu Shanzheng, former head of the Tieli Education Department, Japanese interpreter and comprador for the Liu family soybean oil factory in Qing'cheng during the Manchukuo period, Tieli, Heilongjiang Province, China. January-February 2000, September 2001, and February 2005.

Mizusawa Tsutomu, head curator, Kamakura Museum of Modern Art, Hayama, Japan. September-October 2003.

Otani Shôgo, curator, Tokyo National Museum of Modern Art, Tokyo, Japan. Fall 2003. November 2004-Spring 2005.

Tang Xiang, history research group preceptor, Third Municipal Junior High School, Harbin, China. January 2000.

Index

Note: "(f)" after a number indicates a figure.